For over a quarter of a century, Gary R. Habermas has focused his research on the resurrection of Jesus of Nazareth. And for some time now, Gary has been recognized by myself and others as the top expert on the topic. A former student of Gary's, Mike Licona is also a leading "resurrection scholar" today. From these two come a tool that is broad in its scope, thorough and detailed in its depth, providing the fruit of considerable intellect and vigorous labor on this topic. Combined with a very creative style that is user friendly to the learner, I know of no other source quite like it. It may be the most thorough defense of the historicity of the resurrection.

J. P. MORELAND
Distinguished Professor of Philosophy, Talbot School of Theology
Biola University

Having known Gary Habermas's detailed and long-standing work on the resurrection and the history of its interpretation, it is a pleasure to see not only this compilation of many years of study, but also research on the subject by Mike Licona. When one couples this volume with the recent work of N. T. Wright on resurrection, one has to say that there is now a formidable intellectual gauntlet that has been thrown down, supported by meticulous research and powerful arguments, that challenges any view of the Easter events that does not include the bodily resurrection of Jesus. I highly recommend this rigorous and vigorous treatment of this subject which in so many ways is the most crucial one for Christian faith and praxis.

BEN WITHERINGTON III
Professor of New Testament, Asbury Theological Seminary

These pages examine Jesus' resurrection from every conceivable viewpoint: the powerful evidence that it did occur, the strident objections that it did not, and the tools of logic necessary in deciding which is true. Habermas and Licona marshal the testimony of the primary sources in admirable fashion. To my knowledge, the chapters addressing naturalistic theories are the most comprehensive treatment of the subject anywhere. This *Summa* offers compelling proof that the central event in human history *did* occur.

PAUL L. MAIER
Russell H. Seibert Professor of Ancient History
Western Michigan University

This compelling book is the most comprehensive defense of Jesus' resurrection anywhere. You won't find a more thorough treatment of naturalistic theories. Its extensive endnotes by themselves are worth the price of the book! And you'll enjoy using the innovative CD to help you master the material. If you're interested in knowing the evidence for the resurrection and sharing it with others, then you must read this book!

LEE STROBEL
Author, *The Case for Christ*

The historical resurrection of Jesus is truly the foundation of the Christian faith. Mike and Gary have created a phenomenal resource, that is both user-friendly and up-to-date, to equip believers to defend this crucial issue and to apply it to their personal lives. I highly recommend this resource to both the scholar and layperson.

JOSH MCDOWELL
Author, *The New Evidence That Demands a Verdict*

There is nothing like this on the market. It is interesting, engaging, and crucial material.

NORMAN L. GEISLER
President, Southern Evangelical Seminary

The resurrection of Jesus Christ from the dead is the cornerstone of Christianity. Gary Habermas and his protégé Mike Licona have distinguished themselves as leading experts on the evidence for this all-important event.

D. JAMES KENNEDY
Senior Minister, Coral Ridge Presbyterian Church

Undoubtedly, the resurrection of Jesus is the primary testimony of the early church, but it is missing in many contemporary evangelistic programs. This book with its innovative software will not only entertain, but it will help us reeducate the church about the central message of the church. This is one set of materials that I can highly recommend.

L. RUSS BUSH
Senior Professor of Philosophy of Religion
Southeastern Baptist Theological Seminary

The world has gone computer-mad and there is nothing as addictive as interactive CDs. My wife is appalled at the time I myself spend at the console (both Mac and PC) engaged in just such activity. Defenders of historic Christian faith need to capture this area for Jesus Christ, and that is exactly the function of Habermas and Licona's *The Case for the Resurrection of Jesus*. It provides an ideal opportunity for computer novices and computer experts, whatever their age, to interact with the solid case for the resurrection of Jesus Christ—and thus to face the necessity of making a personal decision concerning the truth of the entire Christian message. The CD's combination of the serious and the entertaining is a solid accomplishment.

JOHN WARWICK MONTGOMERY
Professor of Apologetics and Law, Trinity College and Theological Seminary

By far *the best* teaching tool on the topic.

RON TACELLI
Boston College

The
CASE
for the
Resurrection
of JESUS

The
CASE
for the
Resurrection
of JESUS

Gary R. Habermas
Michael R. Licona

Kregel
Publications

ISBN 978-0-8254-2788-6

Printed in the United States of America

11 12 / 17

To Jennifer, Richard, James, and Austin.
—Gary

To Debbie, my bride and the love of my life.
—Mike

Be wise in the way you act toward outsiders;
make the most of every opportunity.
—Colossians 4:5 NIV

Contents

Preface

At some point in their Christian walk, many believers ask some difficult questions: Is Christianity really true? Are there any good reasons to know which religion is true? Could it be that God does not really exist? These are important questions, and we have an intense interest in their answers. After all, if atheism is true, then why should we subject ourselves to the teachings of Jesus? Why should we insist on views that alienate others, especially the claim that Jesus is the only way to heaven? If the Christian view of reality is wrong, we may be missing out on something. At least we are needlessly straining relationships with others. More important, if Christianity is false, let's find the truth about God and live accordingly. Even if it would disappoint others, why should we keep faith in a system that fails to provide what we want—eternal life? Not many Christians ask such questions. Some never question their faith, perhaps because they are afraid of the answers they might receive. If life is comfortable, let's not shake it to the point that radical change is required. Besides, how can anyone really find definite answers to these ultimate questions?

The authors of this volume did ask these questions as young men. We determined to find some answers. We cannot tell you that we looked at the evidence without presuppositions or biases. Facing issues of this magnitude, it's unreasonable to think that anyone comes to the investigation with no personal hopes or preexisting beliefs. However, intellectual integrity requires that we set aside biases to the point that we can recognize them for what they are. Then we can ask tough questions and conduct responsible research. As we wrestled with faith questions over the years, we received patient help from others. Ultimately we became impressed with the evidence in favor of Christianity. In our opinion, the quality and quantity of evidence that Christianity is true far surpasses the evidence in favor of any other religion or worldview. After several years, we arrived at a strong conclusion: *The evidence suggests that God exists and has actually revealed himself to us in Jesus Christ. The evidence attests that Christians have the most accurate view of reality.*

As their faith becomes more energized and confident, many Christians increasingly want to share their faith with others. However, they may quickly discover that it is one thing to learn the data and an entirely other matter to share it in meaningful ways. Some approaches "work," and others don't. Hardly anyone will listen patiently as we spout off a ten-minute argument for Jesus' resurrection from the dead. If effective dialogue is to take place, we must learn how to summarize arguments in less than thirty seconds. We must then be able to field follow-up questions and carry on dialogue on related issues with concise comments.

Many Christians have asked the same tough questions we posed. Some of them who asked too openly were rebuked for entering forbidden areas. Perhaps the area was forbidden because the "more mature" Christians had not the slightest idea how to answer such questions. Maybe the pastor who rebuked the seeker had buried questions and doubts inside his own heart. Nonbelievers also ask tough questions of believers. Addressing those questions is a challenge. Satisfying answers to hard questions require reflective thought and research. We must provide reasonable answers to our nonbelieving friends.

This volume and its accompanying interactive software are tools to encourage Christians in their faith and to help them share with others the evidence for Jesus' resurrection. Depending on the type of reading to which you are accustomed, this book and software may be easy or challenging. It is our goal to present the data in an easily read manner, while maintaining intellectual integrity. Our motto is: *Everything should be as simple as possible, but no simpler.* This book is written for laypeople, so we are not exhaustive in providing evidence or refuting every objection that can be raised. Although we have attempted to include data that will be informative for the scholar, we have elected to write for the person who doesn't have a background of advanced study of matters related to Jesus' resurrection. Many more details have been supplied in the endnotes, and we have listed sources there for those who want to go further. Not all evidences or refutations are provided here. We were selective in an effort to be succinct. Readers may use some of these arguments in situations we do not discuss. Whether you are new to the evidence for Jesus' resurrection or are a seasoned veteran in defending the Christian faith, we pray you will find this tool helpful.

Gary R. Habermas and Michael R. Licona

Acknowledgments

Our sincere gratitude goes to Donald Patterson and Allen Morell of D. P. Associates, Inc., for producing the software and creating the charts used throughout the text. Their desire was to take part in creating an effective tool for the body of Christ. The technical team at D. P. Associates, including Bill Kleindienst, Walter Osborn, Steve Pierce, and Carla Kieckhefer, was very professional and a joy to work with. I would like to thank Nathan Quade, who originally provided the idea for the interactive software.

I (Mike) offer many thanks to my bride, Debbie, for enduring countless requests out of the blue to review sections of chapters to see if they made sense. She was patient with me while I was "in the zone," intensely focused on this work. I also thank my two kids, Alex and Zach, who sacrificed time with their daddy, sometimes willingly and sometimes not.

As always, I (Gary) thank my wife, Eileen, for countless kindnesses that freed me to share in this project in an unhindered manner. She has always expressed her love by giving herself. No more could be asked. I am grateful beyond words.

Our gratitude goes to the following individuals for their significant editorial input to this project, without which the presentation of this material would have suffered greatly: Doris Baker, Dr. David Beck, Ginny Bellamy, Marjorie Bottorff, Bill Cage, Dr. Chris Clayton, Bruce Colkitt, Teddi Colkitt, Mark Davis, Suzanne Hayes, Jennifer Hayes, Kathy Laser, Dr. Cherral Mason, Dr. Gordon

McAlister, Bob Payne, Cynthia Peters, Amy Ponce, Kate Rockey, Jacki Schottler, and Marty West. We would also like to thank attorney Craig Mytelka of Virginia Beach for reviewing the *Resurrection Challenge* software.

I (Mike) would like to thank all of the Ministry Partners of *RisenJesus* for their continual prayers and financial support. These made it possible for me to work on this project in a timely manner. I am blessed to have them as team members and friends.

This entire project was a team effort and could not have been completed alone. Without D. P. Associates, Inc., the graphics throughout the text and the interactive software would not exist. Without those who read the manuscript and provided countless editorial comments, the quality and readability of this contribution would have been far inferior. Without the Ministry Partners of *RisenJesus*, completion of this project would have been significantly delayed. Most important, without Jesus, there would be no Resurrection to write about.

How to Use This Book and Software

This book and the accompanying CD are designed as a self-study course on the evidence for Jesus' resurrection and how to use this evidence to share your faith. Read and familiarize yourself with the information, one section at a time. For example, read chapters 3–4 in part 2 and become well acquainted with the summary charts in those chapters. For your convenience, the appendix contains a detailed outline for quick reference. Once you have completed part 2, install the software and take Quiz 1. After you have successfully completed it, you are ready to move on to part 3. Repeat the process for part 3, then take Quiz 2 before reading the final chapters. Relax. No one will be looking over your shoulder as you take the quizzes. They are designed to be fun and are simply a means to help you master the information.

Once you have successfully completed this course, congratulations. You should then be ready to share your faith using the evidence for Jesus' resurrection, and feel comfortable handling the questions on the subject that are asked by the overwhelming majority of people you meet. You will be able to converse on the evidence better than most pastors and even better than many scholars.

Practice by asking a close friend to role-play with you. Have them play the skeptic. Ask them to be tough. Then begin to engage skeptics in a conversation about Jesus' resurrection. Perhaps you know a few from work, your neighborhood, or within your family.

Look for opportunities to teach at your church. Senior high, college and career, singles, and other adult-education classes can provide a great forum to share the information and solidify your knowledge. It is often said that the best way to learn something is to teach it.

You may check Mike Licona's Web site at www.risenjesus.com for additional teaching resources on sharing your faith using the evidence for the resurrection of Jesus.

A Life to Die For
Sharing Your Faith

Introduction to Part 1
Let the Discussion Begin

In July 2000, ABC network television news anchor Peter Jennings produced a program titled *The Search for Jesus*. Of the seven New Testament scholars interviewed, four belonged to the Jesus Seminar, a group that denies most historic Christian teachings about Jesus Christ. These radical theologians have received a lot of exposure through the mass media. News organizations have found that their controversial ideas seem novel to the public.[1] The irony is that, while this group provides "expert" commentary for the popular press, most genuine scholars of all viewpoints reject their conclusions. Regarding the Jesus Seminar, Emory University's Luke Timothy Johnson comments that the group is "self-selected," not on grounds of quality scholarship, but on its members' prior commitment to a radical liberal viewpoint.[2] Craig Blomberg of Denver Seminary writes, "The Jesus Seminar and its friends do not reflect any consensus of scholars except for those on the 'radical fringe' of the field. Its methodology is seriously flawed and its conclusions unnecessarily skeptical."[3]

In the Jennings documentary, Jesus Seminar co-founder John Dominic Crossan was awarded over one-quarter of the air time allotted to the New Testament scholars,[4] fostering the appearance that Jesus Seminar views, and particularly those of Crossan, represent the majority view of scholarship. Yet, Crossan himself has publicly admitted that his views do not represent most scholars.[5] Such imbalance might be compared to producing a program on the American

23

spirit at the beginning of the twenty-first century, in which four of the seven citizens interviewed belong to the Communist Party U.S.A., with the most time given to the organization's president. Unfortunately, in the case of *The Search for Jesus*, the average television viewer is not equipped to recognize how misleading this interesting production is. Such unbalanced treatment of this sort must be answered, and individual believers are in the best position to do this through their own networks of friends.[6]

"Americans generally have an abysmal level of knowledge of the Bible," Johnson observes. "In this world of mass ignorance, to have headlines proclaim that this or that fact about [Jesus] has been declared untrue by supposedly scientific inquiry has the effect of gospel. There is no basis on which most people can counter these authoritative-sounding statements."[7] This is where the Christian's role in sharing his or her faith requires some knowledge of the facts about Jesus and his resurrection. Blomberg comments, "The problem is that other worldviews and religions make the same claims as we do. To defend your view in the marketplace of religious ideas, you have to be able to give reasons for why you believe the Bible's claims about itself."[8] The apostle Peter told us to "sanctify Christ as Lord in your hearts, always being ready to make a defense[9] to everyone who asks you to give an account for the hope that is in you, yet with gentleness and reverence" (1 Peter 3:15).

It is the objective of this book and software to equip you to do just that.

Chapter 1

Unwrapping the Gift
Evangelism and the Resurrection of Jesus

O ne Sunday morning there was a salesman who was sitting in the back of a
church having trouble staying awake. Toward the end of the sermon the
preacher said something that caused the salesman to wake up, sit up straight,
and begin listening intently. When the preacher gave the invitation, the salesman was the first to go up front. The counselor who met him asked what the
preacher had said that caused him to come forward. The salesman answered,
"He mentioned 'the great commission'!"

In Jesus' last words to his disciples, he said, "Go therefore and make disciples
of all the nations, baptizing them in the name of the Father and the Son and the
Holy Spirit, teaching them to observe all that I commanded you . . ." (Matt.
28:19–20). This statement has become known among Christians as "the Great
Commission."[1] Sharing your faith with others can be very fulfilling when you
realize that you are bringing the greatest news a person could ever hear to someone who needs to hear it. *Through Jesus one can have sins forgiven and receive
eternal life.* This good news or "gospel" is the primary message that Christians
should want to share. Its importance transcends all the politically sensitive topics into which we can get drawn with nonbelievers, from abortion to homo-
sexuality. What is the "gospel"? *Gospel* is defined by a minimum of three essential
facts in the book of Acts[2] and Paul's letters[3]: (1) the deity of Jesus; (2) the death
of Jesus in our place; and (3) the resurrection of Jesus. Other facts are involved,

but these three are always present or implied. The good news to the world is that the sovereign Lord of the universe has overthrown the powers of darkness by conquering death.

The apostle Paul wrote that this message "'is near you; it is in your mouth and in your heart'—that is, the word of faith we are proclaiming: That if you confess with your mouth 'Jesus is Lord,' and believe in your heart that God raised him from the dead, you will be saved."[4] The message was that, in order to have eternal life, one must acknowledge and be committed to Jesus as the Son of God, the Sovereign over all things, and the Savior who died for us and was raised from the dead by God. This message stands in contrast to the impassioned message of many of today's religious leaders, who believe that what one believes about God does not matter.

Proclaiming that message now can be difficult in a culture that is constantly bombarded with a potpourri of worldviews and religions to consider. Christianity is no longer the default religion of Western culture, so someone who is seeking the truth about God and religion hardly knows where to go. Islam has a certain appeal because of its unswerving dogmatism. Buddhism appeals to those intrigued with mysticism or who desire to escape material reality. Judaism has an ancient, cultural appeal. Christianity has the virtue of being better known than other faiths to people in the West. But, as we have seen, it is also the most misrepresented by the media.

Jesus' resurrection is a crucial issue

For the writers of the New Testament, Jesus' resurrection was the focal point of their teachings. Peter wrote that we have an indestructible inheritance awaiting us in heaven, made available "through the resurrection of Jesus Christ from the dead."[5] Paul wrote that belief in Jesus' resurrection from the dead is required for eternal life.[6] In fact, Paul was so adamant about the importance of Jesus' resurrection that he wrote, "And if Christ has not been raised, your faith is worthless; you are still under condemnation for your sins. In that case, all who have died believing in Christ have perished!"[7] For Paul, if Jesus did not rise from the dead, Christianity is false, we will be judged for our sins by the true God, and Christians who have died are lost. In addition, Paul writes a few verses later, "If the dead are not raised, 'let us eat and drink, for tomorrow we die.'"[8] In other words, if Jesus' resurrection did not occur, we may as well live it up, because this life is all there is.

Anyone can claim anything. Jesus asserted that he was speaking truth from

God. When someone makes such a lofty claim, critics rightly ask for the evidence. Jesus' critics asked him for a sign, and he said he would give them one—his resurrection.[9] It is the test by which we could know that he was telling the truth.[10]

Such a historical test of truth is unique to Christianity. If Jesus *did not* rise from the dead, he was a false prophet and a charlatan whom no rational person should follow. Conversely, if he *did* rise from the dead, this event confirmed his radical claim.

Let's consider this interesting test. Notice that he did not offer some simplistic proof that has questionable importance. This is the case with some other religions. Muslims tell us to follow Islam because only God could have written the Qurʾan: "And if ye are in doubt as to what We have revealed from time to time to Our servant [Muhammad], then produce a Sura like thereunto; and call your witnesses or helpers (If there are any) besides Allah, if your (doubts) are true."[11] In other words, the Qurʾan is such a wonderful text that it must be from God. Mormons make a similar claim about the *Book of Mormon*: "And when ye shall receive these things, I would exhort you that ye ask God, the Eternal Father, in the name of Christ, if these things are not true; and if ye shall ask with a sincere heart, with real intent, having faith in Christ, he will manifest the truth of it unto you, by the power of the Holy Ghost. And by the power of the Holy Ghost ye may know the truth of all things."[12] According to Mormons, if you read the *Book of Mormon* with an open mind and ask God to show you if it is true, he will confirm it. While we can be impressed by the impact of these literary works on millions of lives, skepticism regarding these tests is warranted. All that is demanded is a subjective judgment. If one were to compare the first sura in the Qurʾan with Psalm 19, many a reader would conclude that Psalm 19 is superior in almost every respect, although both perhaps contain much the same message.[13] What about those who have read the *Book of Mormon* with a sincere heart, a real intent to know the truth, and belief that Christ will provide wisdom, yet are persuaded that this volume is *not* true or divinely given? In Mormonism, the data from archaeology and huge problems relating to the *Book of Abraham* pose serious challenges to the validity of the Mormon faith that may very well be insurmountable.[14] Yet the well-intentioned Mormon interprets his subjective feelings of confidence in the validity of Mormonism on the testimony of the Holy Spirit.

Another problem with these tests is that Islam and Mormonism are mutually exclusive. In other words, they possess conflicting truth claims to be the only true way to God. Both provide different ways to God. Yet *both* cannot be the *only* true way to God. This leaves us with the conclusion that the exclusivity claims of one or both of these religions are incorrect, as are their truth tests.

Jesus' test is different in that it leaves no room for ambiguity. Either Jesus rose from the dead confirming his claims to divinity or he was a fraud. This external test does not negate the inward assurance that Christians believe comes from God, rather it substantiates it. The Christian is not wrong to advise the seeker of religious truth to pray that God will speak through Scripture and to approach God's Word with sincere openness. Romans 8:16 informs us that assurance from God's Spirit comes to the Christian. What Jesus' resurrection does is to confirm that the assurance we experience is really from God's Spirit. *The external evidence of Jesus' resurrection confirms the truth we have received via God's written revelation.*

So what is one to do when a follower of a modern alternative spirituality movement and a Christian both claim assurance that God's Spirit is affirming their understanding of truth? We have the external test that, if Jesus actually rose from the dead, it appears the truth of Christianity is confirmed and all adherents to conflicting beliefs must reassess whether their assurance came from a spirit other than God's or was the result of self-delusion.

Of course, the test of Jesus' resurrection is not very useful, if we cannot determine whether it actually occurred. Is there enough evidence for a rational person to be justified in concluding that Jesus' resurrection was a real event in history? Christians should be delighted to find that the evidence for Jesus' resurrection is extremely compelling, even when using only a small collection of strongly attested historical facts to support the event.

The resurrection is also an excellent starting point for confirming the trustworthiness of the Bible. Considering Jesus' claims to being divine, if he rose from the dead, he may indeed be divine and have some profound things to tell us. We might anticipate that the disciples of such a man would devote themselves to spreading his teachings. Their writings and willingness to suffer and die would be a natural, expected reaction to a reality of immense importance. Where are such writings if not in the New Testament? Not only is the New Testament what we might expect it to be, but most of it comes from those who were in a position to be reliable witnesses of what Jesus said and did.

The ramifications of Jesus' resurrection go beyond the realm of the theological into the practical. When God seems silent and far away, Jesus' resurrection encourages us. Although we may not understand why God is being silent for the moment, we can have the assurance given in his Word that he loves us and knows our situation. We can know that our sufferings are temporary, since we have an indestructible inheritance in heaven. We can know this because if Jesus rose from the dead, Christianity is not just a nice story like Santa Claus; Christianity is true.

Thus, Jesus' resurrection is at the spotlight of major Christian doctrine and practice. Belief in it is a requirement for salvation. By it we can be assured of God's love, our inheritance in heaven, and the truthfulness of Christianity. And it is the foundation for an argument for the trustworthiness of the New Testament.[15]

Did Jesus Predict His Resurrection?

Contrary to New Testament teachings, some scholars doubt that Jesus actually predicted his resurrection. However, there are at least four reasons for holding that the claims are authentic:

1. Jesus' predictions concerning his resurrection are usually denied because the resurrection itself is denied as a historical event. However, if the resurrection event is historical, then the reason for rejecting Jesus' predictions concerning it is ineffective.

2. When Jesus predicted his resurrection from the dead, we are told that the disciples did not seem to have a clue what he was talking about or simply did not believe (Mark 8:31–33; 9:31–32; 14:27–31; Luke 24:13–24). Even when his empty tomb was discovered, it is reported that the first conclusion was that someone had stolen the body (John 20:2, 13–15). When the women reported that they had seen him risen, the disciples thought they were telling an idle tale (Luke 24:10–12). Upon viewing the empty tomb, they still did not know what to think (John 20:9). Thomas simply refused to believe (John 20:24–25). Now it seems quite unlikely that the disciples or early Christians who highly respected them would invent sayings of Jesus that would place them in such a bad light. This is what is referred to as the "principle of embarrassment," which will be discussed later, and argues strongly in favor of the authenticity of the predictions of Jesus concerning his resurrection.

3. Jesus' use of the title "Son of Man" in reference to his resurrection predictions (Mark 8:31; 9:31; 10:33–34) weighs in favor of authenticity. As argued in chapter 10 ("Who Did Jesus Think He Was?"), one reason for thinking that Jesus claimed this title is that it is recorded by multiple sources. Further, the New Testament epistles never refer to Jesus in this manner. But neither did the Jews think of the Son of Man in the sense of a suffering Messiah (see Dan. 7:13–14). So the principle of dissimilarity points to authenticity here. This criterion "focuses on words or deeds of Jesus that cannot be derived either from Judaism at the time of Jesus or from the early Church after him" (John P. Meier, *A Marginal Jew*, vol. 1 [New York: Doubleday, 1991], 171). For these reasons, Jesus' predictions concerning his resurrection, especially when connected to the "Son of Man," look quite authentic.

4. Jesus' predictions concerning his resurrection are multiply attested: Matthew 12:38–40; 16:1–4, 21; 17:23; 20:19; Mark 8:31–32; 9:31; 10:33; Luke 9:22; John 2:18–21. Cf. Mark 14:58; Luke 11:29–30.

Proof does not aim at "absolute historical certainty"

Can Jesus' resurrection from the dead be proven? The answer may vary depending on one's definition of what constitutes proof. When it comes to any event that occurred in antiquity, the historian attempts to decide the matter with some degree of historical certainty. He has no videotapes or photographs available to him. Rather, he employs certain criteria using the known data in order to reach conclusions. Some data are more certain than others and, therefore, carry more weight.

Plenty of events occurred in the distant or even recent past for which we have little or no data. Lack of attestation does not mean that the event did not occur, only that we have difficulty verifying it from an objective historical perspective.[16] There may be, however, other reasons to hold that an event actually occurred, even though it is not strongly attested historically. Suppose that Bob claims that he was state champion in high school wrestling competition. We did not know Bob in high school and are not in a position to verify this claim, nor do we know any of Bob's old schoolmates. His high school burned down a few years ago, destroying trophies and official records of the event. Any yearbook or newspaper account from the period could be inaccurate. Should we believe Bob? If our experience with Bob has revealed that he is a trustworthy person who has never lied to us before, then we may have reason to believe him, especially if there is no evidence to the contrary.

Likewise, we might argue that we can have assurance that many of the events described in the Bible occurred, even though historical inquiry has not yet produced confirming evidence through the spade of the archaeologist or the pen of the secular historian. In the past, the Bible has demonstrated that its accounts are trustworthy as far as they have been verified.[17] Moreover, the Bible has never been controverted by solid historical data. Therefore, the benefit of the doubt should go to the Bible in places where it cannot be verified, when there is no evidence to the contrary, and when it seems clear that the author intended for us to understand the event as historical.

When it comes to history, we can only speak of probability, not 100 percent certainty. However, do not be discouraged that in historical terms Jesus' resurrection cannot be established with absolute certainty. For one, all worldviews share the same challenge. Neither atheism nor any of the world's religions can be demonstrated with absolute certainty. Can we know with *100 percent* certainty that all of us were not created just five minutes ago, complete with our memories and the food in our stomachs? Of course not. Second, even outside of worldviews, virtually nothing can be established with 100 percent certainty. Can we know with 100 percent certainty that George Washington was the first President of the United States of America rather than a mythical figure? Perhaps documents were forged and stories invented in a conspiracy to encourage the citizens of a new country. We can know that this was not the case with a high degree of certainty. In historical inquiry, professional historians talk in terms of the strength of probability that an event occurred. In fact, we can think in terms of a line graph with a full spectrum of historical certainties.

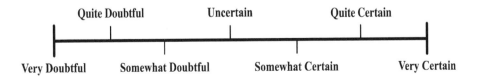

In reference to Jesus' resurrection, we are inquiring to see what we can *know* with reasonable historical certainty when historical inquiry is applied. Where does "reasonable historical certainty" start on our graph? This is a somewhat subjective question. We would place it somewhere to the right of "somewhat certain" and continue on to the "very certain" point of the spectrum.[18]

In historical inquiry, the historian combs through the data, considers all the possibilities, and seeks to determine which scenario best explains the data. Unlike an attorney, the historian often has no living witnesses available to cross-examine. Moreover, few historical witnesses may leave a record. Looking at the writings that are available, the historian may be able to examine and compare other writings by the same author and perhaps his or her contemporaries to determine what the author probably meant by a certain statement. Background information and principles have helped historians uncover what happened with reasonable certainty.[19]

Historians are also concerned with *plausibility*, a principle the legal community likewise employs. Annette Gordon-Reed, a law professor at New York Law School explains:

> Demanding that individual items of evidence amount to proof sets a standard that can only be met in the rarest of circumstances, either in history or in the law. . . . The evidence must be considered as a whole before a realistic and fair assessment of the possible truth of this story can be made. . . . To deal with the concern that accusations are easily made (whether in a legal or nonlegal context), the burden of proof is normally allocated to the accuser. The accuser can meet the burden by offering a certain quantum of evidence, which varies depending upon the nature of the accusation, for example—in the context of legal disputes—proof beyond a reasonable doubt for criminal charges or, for civil charges, *proof that makes the truth of an accusation more probable than not.*[20]

The standards of evidence do not require that the case for something is irrefutable. Such 100 percent certainty is only possible in the rarest of circumstances. Rather, the standard requires proof beyond a reasonable doubt in criminal cases and proof that makes the truth of an accusation more probable than not in civil cases. If this is not understood, our criteria for proof may be unrealistic. Applying this to the facts about Jesus, scholar Graham Twelftree observes that "A position is demonstrated, when the reasons for accepting it 'significantly' outweigh the reasons for not accepting it. . . . This leaves a large gray area where positions are held to be 'likely' or 'probable.' . . . A finding of historicity is essentially a default position, meaning that we have no other reasonable way to account for the presence of a story in the text."[21]

Twelftree sets the standard for belief that something was really said or truly happened at the point when the reasons for accepting it significantly outweigh the reasons for rejecting it. If there are no reasonable opposing theories, a finding of historicity is the default position.

Therefore, when it comes to proving any historical event, we must remember that we are looking for whether we can ascertain with a reasonable amount of certainty that the event occurred. Surprisingly, Jesus' resurrection has quite a bit going for it in terms of the data, which makes it an interesting topic for historical investigation. The fact that the evidence for it is quite good, is striking.[22]

We would like to point out that, for the Christian, there is a difference between knowing that Jesus rose from the dead with reasonable historical certainty and living on the personal assurance that Christianity is true. Paul wrote in Romans 8:16 that "the Spirit Himself testifies with our spirit that we are children of God." The Christian has the Holy Spirit who testifies to her that Christianity is true and that she belongs to God. The historical certainty we have of Jesus' resurrection only reinforces that God's Spirit has indeed spoken to us.

Evidence is part of sharing the gospel

People seldom immediately accept Jesus as Lord or believe he rose from the dead just because the Bible says so. If they genuinely seek to know the truth, they ask tough questions. Good preparation and practice will always help you answer them. Remember Peter's words: "Sanctify Christ as Lord in your hearts, always being ready to make a defense to everyone who asks you to give an account for the hope that is in you, yet with gentleness and reverence."[23] Many of those with whom you talk will want evidence. Relax—this book will help you present a solid case and answer even difficult questions.

That does not mean that by answering the questions you can "reason" someone into becoming a Christian. Nothing could be further from the truth. The New Testament teaches that God alone draws people to himself for salvation. If God is not involved in the process, conversion will not take place

(John 6:44; Rom. 3:11). So why be concerned with the evidence? The answer is not so much theological as it is methodological. The Great Commission of Matthew 28:19–20 explains that God has chosen us to be his messengers of salvation. While it is up to God to draw others, he has decided to involve the human element in the process and he uses our differences in personality for his glory. For example, one of the authors enjoys watching a football game on television, while his wife would prefer to immerse herself in a "chick flick." On a long car ride his wife would rather listen to music than cassette tapes of debates on the existence of God between atheist and Christian philosophers. Some of us like to read novels, whereas others enjoy the intellectual challenge of a philosophy book or a stimulating historical documentary on television. What about the non-Christians you meet? Some readily identify with the experiential evidence of what the gospel has done in changing a person's life. Others think, "Bah, humbug on your experiences. Adherents of other religions claim religious experiences too. Give me evidence!" For some, evidence will not matter. For others, it is all they want. The Holy Spirit can use both sorts of conversations to speak salvation to different human hearts.

The apostle Paul adjusted his preaching to match his audience. When speaking to Jews, he appealed to the Jewish Scriptures, what we call the Old Testament (Acts 17:2). He shared this common ground with his Jewish countrymen. However, when standing before a non-Jewish audience, like the intellectuals of Athens in Acts 17, he did not appeal to the Scriptures (Acts 17:16–31). Instead he cited secular writers and poets known to his audience.[24] The *message* of the gospel never changed. The *method* Paul used to present it did.[25] You must determine how to relate to the person with whom you share your faith, for it is up to you to do the work of sharing. But it is up to God to do the heart work and we should rely on him to produce the fruit.

Some well-meaning believers become angry that we want to give evidence to nonbelievers. They object, "Providing evidence takes away the faith factor. You should only present the gospel. We simply give them the gospel and share a testimony of how the Lord has changed our lives." While their intent is noble, we believe they are naïve. Why is their personal testimony in addition to the gospel an "inspired" method or any different than sharing evidences when presenting the gospel? If it is wrong to present *the gospel plus apologetics*, then why is it right to give *the gospel plus testimony?* The apostles did not limit themselves to a simple statement of the gospel. They were prepared to answer the tough questions and we should too.

But no matter how good the evidence, a saving belief still requires faith. The story has been told of a high wire expert who walked over Niagara Falls. To the amazement of all, he walked a wheelbarrow filled with 150 pounds of potatoes over the rope to the other side. His 120-pound assistant removed the bags of potatoes and placed her foot in the wheelbarrow and he asked, "How many of you believe that I can place a human in the wheelbarrow and walk that person safely to the other side?" Everyone yelled, "We believe!" He then said, "Who will volunteer to get in the wheelbarrow?" Believing the facts is one thing. Acting upon them is faith.

People offer all sorts of reasons for not accepting Christ. Many times they reject Christianity just because they don't like it for some emotional reason. They may be offended by Jesus' claim to be the only way to heaven or the Bible's prohibition of homosexual behavior. Others excuse themselves with intellectual objections, such as the impossibility of Jesus' resurrection or the problem of evil. Whatever the superficial objection, it may only be a smoke screen for a deeper reason that the person simply does not want to believe. For someone with a hidden agenda, neither a personal testimony nor any evidence will make a difference. However, there are those God is calling and they have a genuine interest and openness, even though they may seem outwardly hostile. For these, an appropriate testimony or evidence will show them that they are safe to trust Christ.

The Holy Spirit's work is essential in order for a person to come to Christ. Who you are and your personal testimony are also very important. Evidence is a tool in your pocket. If you are sharing your faith actively, you will find yourself reaching for it frequently.

Chapter 2

History 101

Before we approach the evidence for Jesus' resurrection, let's become familiar with some of the principles historians employ to determine whether a
particular account of history is credible.[1] This brief overview will assist us when
we assess the evidence for Jesus' resurrection. These principles are important because historical data, such as archaeological finds, documents, and eyewitnesses,
are all we have to tell us of events that occurred and people who lived in antiquity.

The principles we are about to look at are not hard rules of evidential proof.
Rather they guide the historian in assessing accounts of the past. A historian
who is able to apply one or more of the following principles to a text can conclude with much greater confidence whether a certain event occurred. We will
not cover all of the principles for evaluating facts that sometimes prove useful,
but have only included those that normally come into play when evaluating
evidence regarding the Resurrection. These are the principles that will be used
throughout this book.[2]

Five historical principles speak to Resurrection

The importance of careful evaluation of sources is well known to police in-
vestigators. A detective is assigned to reopen the case of an automobile accident
that occurred five years ago. She learns that the accident involved the collision

of a blue car and a red car in an intersection. A group of five people waiting for a bus witnessed the accident. Three left when their bus arrived. However, one of the three told two others who came up to the bus stop after the accident that "the red car ran a red light." When the police came, both drivers as well as those at the bus stop were questioned.

1. Multiple, independent sources support historical claims.

When an event or saying is attested by more than one independent source, there is a strong indication of historicity. It is important to determine whether the source is really independent. Suppose a friend told you of a crime he had witnessed. You told someone else, who in turn told a third person. There would not be three independent sources for the accident, but one. However, if your friend and his brother both witnessed the crime and both told you about it, you would have two independent sources.

In our car accident illustration, one driver is hurt and is taken to the hospital. The other driver claims that the light was green for him and that the driver who has now been taken from the scene went through a red light. Those at the bus stop claim that the red car was going through a red light when it hit the blue car. If only the driver of the blue car makes this claim, it may be difficult to ascertain who is telling the truth, since there would be conflicting accounts. The existence of several independent sources at the bus stop who claim that they saw the red car go through the red light increases the likelihood that the driver of the blue car is telling the truth.

Let's add a twist to our story. The people at the bus stop give conflicting accounts of which car ran the red light. Although the conflicting testimonies confuse the situation, the detective has no reason to question whether the accident occurred. There is other data, such as the two damaged cars. Witnesses agree that the accident did occur. The uncertainty concerns who ran the red light. Also, the fact that the witnesses disagree indicates that they had not consulted one another in order to bring about agreement. Their independent testimonies provide multiple attestation to the fact of the accident.

2. Attestation by an enemy supports historical claims.

If testimony affirming an event or saying is given by a source who does not sympathize with the person, message, or cause that profits from the account, we have an indication of authenticity. An enemy generally is not considered to be biased in favor of a certain person, message, or cause. Suppose one of the witnesses to the accident was a friend of the one driving the red car. This witness admitted that his friend was the one who ran the red light. The new detective weighs this testimony as somewhat stronger than the testimonies of the other eyewitnesses. A witness who would be considered somewhat unfriendly to the driver of the blue car attested to his innocence.

John Adams, the second president of the United States, was known for his high standards of integrity, although this did not prevent his political enemies from attacking him. Alexander Hamilton was one such enemy. In a scathing fifty-four-page pamphlet published to hurt Adams in a forthcoming election, Hamilton accused him of having "great intrinsic defects of character," "disgusting egotism," "eccentric tendencies," "bitter animosity," and an "ungovernable temper." Yet Hamilton made no charges of corruption, and he acknowledged Adams's patriotism and integrity.[3] If Adams's mother or wife had spoken of his integrity, we might have reason to believe them, yet with reservation. When even his enemies acknowledged his integrity, the matter is pretty well established.[4]

3. Embarrassing admissions support historical claims.

An indicator that an event or saying is authentic occurs when the source would not be expected to create the story, because it embarrasses his cause and "weakened its position in arguments with opponents."[5] The police officer asks both drivers if they have previously disobeyed a traffic signal. The driver of the red car says "no." The driver of the blue car admits that he caused an accident ten years ago because he ran a red light. The detective may tend to believe the entire testimony of the driver of the blue car over that of the red car driver because he willingly shared information although it would tend to embarrass or hurt him. He appears to be attempting to tell the truth.

Law professor Annette Gordon-Reed wrote articles arguing that Thomas Jefferson, the third president of the United States, fathered children by his slave Sally Hemings. Before DNA results proved her correct, one of the arguments she employed in support of her position related to the Principle of Embarrassment. A declaration from a close Jefferson relative recorded the observation that it was obvious that Jefferson's "blood ran in [the] veins" of Sally Hemings's children and that one child could be mistaken for Jefferson. She argued that this testimony must be regarded as strong evidence indeed. "Declarations against interest are regarded as having a high degree of credibility because of the presumption that people do not make up lies in order to hurt themselves; they lie to help themselves," she wrote.[6]

In other words, this statement by Jefferson's relative damaged the reputation of Jefferson and his family, given the social prejudices of the time when it was made. A relative would not likely have invented a statement that would hurt himself. Therefore, this statement weighs in favor of the argument that Sally Hemings bore children for Jefferson.

4. Eyewitness testimony supports historical claims.

Eyewitness testimony is usually stronger than a secondhand account. Two eyewitnesses remained at the bus stop when police arrived. Their report would carry more weight than that of the three who only heard a secondhand account after they arrived on the scene. If all of the eyewitnesses at the bus stop had left before police arrived, the secondhand reporters would provide support for the story that the red car went through the red light. They had been told this by eyewitnesses. Their testimony might be inelligible hearsay in a court of law, but a police investigator could take it into account. Historians must consider testimony of secondhand witnesses as they attempt to arrive at a conclusion regarding what happened.

5. Early testimony supports historical claims.

The closer the time between the event and testimony about it, the more reliable the witness, since there is less time for exaggeration, and even legend, to creep into the account. Within two years of the accident, battles between insurance companies push the matter to court. At the trial, several eyewitnesses to the accident testify to what they saw. This is eyewitness testimony, and it is also early. Now suppose that thirty years after the accident some fact surfaces to suggest that the driver of the red car had deliberately staged the automobile accident in an attempt to kill the driver of the blue car. The detective on the case obtains statements from living eyewitnesses. He has eyewitness testimony, but it is not early. Obviously, the ideal is to have firsthand accounts that were recorded soon after the events being studied.

Since the historian does not have a certified video record of what occurred in antiquity, these principles are commonsense guides for evaluating the written record of something that is alleged to have happened. A balance scale of judgment is mentally installed into the brain of the historian who combs through the evidence. When she sees something in favor of the authenticity of the event, the principles run through her mind. Do any apply? If so, a weight goes into the dish on one side of the balance. The bar tips to that side. But another piece of evidence weighs against the event. A weight goes into the other dish.

With some events in antiquity, the scale may be pretty evenly balanced. In that case, no decision can be made. In determining the truth of another alleged event, the scale tips very definitely, one way or the other. When the scale tips significantly in favor of an event there is reason to believe it is "historical," that is "it really happened." In the real life of historical study, there is no magical truth-sensing scale, and one historian's evaluation often differs from another's. Still, a process of evaluation does take place. We will be sifting the data for and against Jesus' resurrection being an actual event of history.

Some Testimony Is Stronger Than Others

Historians employ a number of common-sense principles in assessing the strength of a testimony. Here are five of those principles:

1. Testimony attested to by multiple independent witnesses is usually considered stronger than the testimony of one witness.
2. Affirmation by a neutral or hostile source is usually considered stronger than affirmation from a friendly source, since bias in favor of the person or position is absent.
3. People usually don't make up details regarding a story that would tend to weaken their position.
4. Eyewitness testimony is usually considered stronger than testimony heard from a second- or thirdhand source.
5. An early testimony from very close to the event in question is usually considered more reliable than one received years after the event.

"Just the Facts, Ma'am"

Introduction to Part 2

The Minimal Facts Approach

Comedian Emo Philips describes a discussion between two men on a bridge. One is ready to jump and the other is trying to talk him out of it.

I said, "Are you a Christian or a Jew or a Hindu or what?"

He said, "A Christian."

I said, "Small world! Me too. Protestant or Catholic or Greek Orthodox?"

He said, "Protestant."

I said, "Me too! What franchise?"

He said, "Baptist."

I said, "Me too! Northern Baptist or Southern Baptist?"

He said, "Northern Baptist."

I said, "Me too! Northern Conservative Baptist or Northern Liberal Baptist?"

He said, "Northern Conservative Baptist."

I said, "Me too! Northern Conservative Fundamentalist Baptist, Great Lakes Region, or Northern Conservative Fundamentalist Baptist, Eastern Region?"

He said, "Northern Conservative Fundamentalist Baptist, Great Lakes Region."

I said, "Me too! Northern Conservative Fundamentalist Baptist, Great Lakes Region Council of 1879, or Northern Conservative Fundamentalist Baptist, Great Lakes Region Council of 1912?"

He said, "Northern Conservative Fundamentalist Baptist, Great Lakes Region Council of 1912."

I screamed, "Die, heretic!" and pushed him over.[1]

The minimal facts approach seeks evidence with a high degree of certainty

On the one hand, are we presenting too large a package of doctrines and practices for nonbelievers to accept in order to become a Christian? Are we sharing the gospel *and* . . . how they must be baptized by immersion? . . . how they must speak in tongues? . . . how they must read only a certain version of the Bible? . . . how they must look for the pre-Tribulation return of Christ? . . . how they must believe that the earth is only six thousand years old? . . . how they must accept the five points of Calvinism? . . . how they must pay a tithe to the local church?

On the other hand, isn't the gospel a crucial subject? In our conclusion to this volume, we will discuss the shape of the gospel in some detail. For now, we will define it as the good news of the deity, death, and resurrection of Jesus—Jesus is God; Jesus died for me; and Jesus is alive.

When presenting the evidence for the Resurrection, let's stick to the topic of Jesus' resurrection. This means that we do not digress into a side discussion on the reliability of the Bible. While we hold that the Bible is trustworthy and inspired, we cannot expect the skeptical nonbeliever with whom we are dialoguing to embrace this view. So, in order to avoid a discussion that may divert us off of our most important topic, we would like to suggest that we adopt a "minimal facts approach." This approach *considers only those data that are so strongly attested historically that they are granted by nearly every scholar who studies the subject, even the rather skeptical ones.* This definition of *minimal facts* will play a large part in the method used in the chapters that follow. Most facts we use meet two criteria: *They are well evidenced and nearly every scholar accepts them.* We present our case using the "lowest common denominator" of agreed-upon facts. This keeps attention on the central issue, instead of sidetracking into matters that are irrelevant. This way we can present a strong argument that is both supportable and compelling.[2]

One of the strengths of this approach is that it avoids debate over the inspiration of the Bible.[3] Too often the objection raised frequently against the Resurrection is, "Well, the Bible has errors, so we can't believe Jesus rose." We can quickly push this point to the side: "I am not arguing at this time for the inspiration of the Bible or even its general trustworthiness. Believer and skeptic alike accept the facts I'm using because they are so strongly supported. These facts must be addressed."

Once, while I (Licona) was speaking on the evidence for Jesus' resurrection to a group of medical students at the University of Virginia, an atheist stood up to say that he couldn't believe Jesus rose from the dead because the Bible contains contradictions. He then proceeded to read from a book written by another atheist that cited one such alleged contradiction. I answered that volumes of books have been written to answer such charges about the Bible. However, even if this man read those books, and rejected the answers they gave, that would not matter at all in proving that Jesus did not rise from the dead. I had presented historical facts that were strongly attested by the majority of scholars, including skeptics. Historians recognize that most writings of antiquity contain factual errors and propaganda. They still can identify kernels of historical truth in those sources. If they eliminated a source completely because of bias or error, they would know next to nothing about the past. Thus, if this student continued to reject the inspiration of the Bible, there was still the collection of historical facts that remained to be answered.

In that discussion, I could have changed the subject to a defense of the Bible. I could have attempted to answer the specific contradiction alleged in the book that had been quoted. Something might have been accomplished in such an exchange, for the trustworthiness of the Bible is important. However, students at the meeting would not have had to face the more central topic—the fact of Jesus' resurrection. The side issues about alleged contradictions could have gone on endlessly. But we are not told in the Bible that one must believe in its inspiration or inerrancy in order to have eternal life. We are told that belief in Jesus' resurrection is essential in order to have eternal life.[4]

When we talk to unbelievers, therefore, we should keep to the subject that matters most. In the words of consultant Steven Covey, "The main thing is to keep the main thing the main thing."[5]

Since we can establish that Jesus rose from the dead without appealing to the reliability or inspiration of the Bible, we will keep these topics as separate issues. The point is not that we must avoid using the New Testament when considering Jesus' resurrection. Rather, we simply must approach the New Testament as we would any other book in antiquity. For example, Tacitus is considered the greatest Roman historian. Scholars recognize that Tacitus sometimes writes with a heavy bias, but they are still able to benefit greatly from his work.

They weed through the bias and use historical study techniques to yield much that can be known with a great deal of historical certainty.[6]

The New Testament is a compilation of writings from various authors that the early church considered authoritative. Scholars debate the dating and authorship of several books. However, this will not concern us in discussing the Resurrection. In our "minimal facts approach," we only consider content that is strongly evidenced and considered historical by virtually all who study the subject. Although critical scholars frequently question the authorship and date of the Gospels and Acts, most of them accept that these writings contain a fair amount of teachings that can be traced to the disciples and Jesus.

This is not to imply that we accept what the skeptical scholars say, it just means that we will leave debates about the Bible's authority to others. We will instead take advantage of the fact that most scholars, even skeptical ones, grant that some things are true in the Bible. When they do agree, the point they accept must be pretty well established by available historical data. Further, if most skeptics are willing to reject a natural theory, even though that theory supports their opposition to Jesus' resurrection, it must be that the theory cannot be supported by evidence.

No fact or theory finds total agreement or disagreement. Skeptical scholars are notorious for disagreeing with one another. Extreme, radical positions can always be found, though these remain in the minority. Some skeptics of Jesus' resurrection persist in arguing for a far-fetched opposing theory, although there may be little or no support for it. If we look hard enough, we will find people who deny that *we* exist. Thus, our minimal facts include what *nearly all* scholars hold, including skeptical ones. Seldom can we speak about what *all* agree on, for seldom do they all agree.

In a "minimal facts approach," we also should focus our efforts on presenting evidence *for* Jesus' resurrection, rather than on the inadequacies of opposing theories. This communicates that there is too much good evidence to consider and address for us to waste time picking on opponents. It avoids giving the appearance that one must run to the defensive. After focusing on the evidence for a while, it may be time to address various opposing theories if an unbeliever raises them.

Minimal Facts Approach

The "minimal facts approach" considers only data that meet two criteria:

1. The data are strongly evidenced.
2. The data are granted by virtually all scholars on the subject, even the skeptical ones.

A skeptic ought not be allowed to merely cite apparent contradictions in the Bible and say that the Resurrection has been disproved. The "minimal facts approach" builds a case using facts with a high degree of certainty, facts that any skeptic probably accepts. These facts need to be addressed. If a skeptic takes a position that even the majority of skeptical scholars reject, we can argue individually for the minimal facts that we are using. So if a skeptic prefers to take another position, that's okay. In doing so, the believer now has an opportunity to present much more data in support of the argument for Jesus' resurrection. The skeptic will need to respond.

Chapter 3

A Quintet of Facts (4 + 1)
The First Two

As we approach the positive evidence for Jesus' resurrection, keep in mind the "minimal facts approach" explained in the introduction to part 2. In particular, remember that we will consider data that are so strongly evidenced historically that nearly every scholar regards them as reliable facts. Elsewhere, Habermas lists twelve historical facts.[1] For our purposes here, though, we will focus on just a few of them.[2] Our objective will be to build a strong yet simple case for Jesus' resurrection on just a few facts. All four meet our "minimal facts approach" criteria. They are backed by so much evidence that nearly every scholar who studies the subject, even the rather skeptical ones, accepts them. A fifth fact will be added that enjoys acceptance by an impressive majority of scholars, though not by nearly all. That's why we refer to these as the "4 + 1." In this chapter we will discuss the first two of these five facts.

Throughout chapters 3–8, the major points are illustrated graphically using charts. Some may find these illustrations to be a helpful way to remember ideas.

The first fact: Jesus died by crucifixion

Crucifixion was a common form of execution employed by the Romans to punish members of the lower class, slaves, soldiers, the violently rebellious, and those accused of treason.[3] The first-century Jewish historian Josephus reports that during the fall of Jerusalem in A.D. 70, the Roman soldiers felt such hatred toward the Jews that they crucified a multitude of them in various postures.[4] Crucifixion was a very torturous death. In the first century B.C., Cicero calls it the most horrendous torture.[5] So hideous was the act of crucifixion upon a man that he also writes that "the very word 'cross' should be far removed not only from the person of a Roman citizen but from his thoughts, his eyes and his ears."[6] Tacitus in the second century refers to it as "the extreme penalty."[7]

That Jesus was executed by crucifixion is recorded in all four gospels. However, a number of non-Christian sources of the period report the event as well. Josephus writes, "When Pilate, upon hearing him accused by men of the highest standing amongst us, had condemned him to be crucified . . . ."[8] Tacitus reports, "Nero fastened the guilt [of the burning of Rome] and inflicted the most exquisite tortures on a class hated for their abominations, called Christians by the populace. Christus, from whom the name had its origin, suffered the extreme penalty during the reign of Tiberius at the hands of one of our procurators, Pontius Pilatus."[9]

Lucian of Samosata, the Greek satirist, writes, "The Christians, you know, worship a man to this day—the distinguished personage who introduced their novel rites, and was crucified on that account."[10] Mara Bar-Serapion, writing to his son from prison comments, "Or [what advantage came to] the Jews by the murder of their Wise King, seeing that from that very time their kingdom was driven away from them?"[11] Although Mara does not mention crucifixion as the mode of Jesus' execution, he does say that he was killed. The Talmud reports that "on the eve of the Passover Yeshu was hanged."[12] *Yeshu* is *Joshua* in Hebrew. The equivalent in Greek is Iēsous[13] or *Jesus*. Being hung on a tree was used to describe crucifixion in antiquity.[14] Clearly, Jesus' death by crucifixion is a historical fact supported by considerable evidence.

The highly critical scholar of the Jesus Seminar, John Dominic Crossan, writes, "That he was crucified is as sure as anything historical can ever be."[15] (We will save the crucial medical evidences favoring Jesus' crucifixion for chapter 5.)

The second fact: Jesus' disciples believed that he rose and appeared to them

There is a virtual consensus among scholars who study Jesus' resurrection that, subsequent to Jesus' death by crucifixion, his disciples really believed that he appeared to them risen from the dead. This conclusion has been reached by

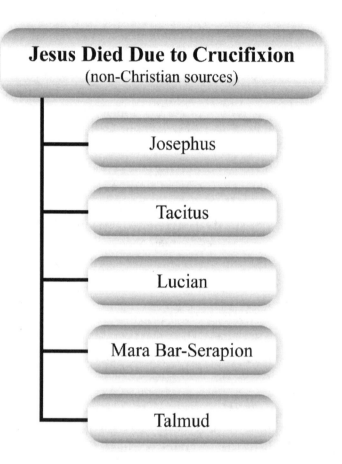

Jesus Died Due to Crucifixion
(non-Christian sources)

- Josephus
- Tacitus
- Lucian
- Mara Bar-Serapion
- Talmud

data that suggest that (1) the disciples themselves claimed that the risen Jesus had appeared to them, and (2) subsequent to Jesus' death by crucifixion, his disciples were radically transformed from fearful, cowering individuals who denied and abandoned him at his arrest and execution into bold proclaimers of the gospel of the risen Lord. They remained steadfast in the face of imprisonment, torture, and martyrdom. It is very clear that they sincerely believed that Jesus rose from the dead.

There is almost unanimous consensus among scholars to this belief on the part of the disciples. Suppose a skeptic said, "I don't believe that the Bible is inspired by God, and I'm not so certain the four gospels were written by the four alleged authors. So how do you trace these claims back to the lips of the disciples themselves? Furthermore, even if you could trace them to the disciples, just because they claimed something doesn't mean they believed it. They could have been lying." These are fair questions. Using our minimal facts approach, there is no need to defend the position that Matthew, Mark, Luke, and John wrote the four gospels while discussing Jesus' resurrection. Instead, we are going to look at a number of ancient sources that will lead us to our conclusion regarding the beliefs of the disciples.

They claimed it.

First, Jesus' disciples claimed he rose from the dead and appeared to them. This conclusion can be reached from nine early and independent sources that fall into three categories: (1) the testimony of Paul about the disciples; (2) the oral tradition that passed through the early church; and (3) the written works of the early church.

Paul provides very strong evidence for establishing the Resurrection claims of the original disciples.[16] He claimed that his own authority in the church was equal to that of the other apostles.[17] That authority was acknowledged by a number of the apostolic fathers soon after the completion of the New Testament. Two of those early writers may have been disciples of the apostles.[18] Paul reported that he knew at least some of the other disciples, even the big three, Peter, James, and John.[19] Acts reports that the disciples and Paul knew and fellowshipped with one another.[20] Other early Christian writers within one hundred years of Jesus also seemed to hold that the disciples and Paul were colleagues, since they included Paul in the group called "apostles."[21] Therefore, what he has to say concerning the other apostles is important.

After writing on the resurrection of Jesus in 1 Corinthians 15:3–8, Paul said he worked harder than all of the other apostles (15:10), but that whether "it was I or they, this [i.e., Jesus' resurrection appearances] is what we preach" (15:11 NIV).[22] Thus, Paul knew the apostles personally and reports that they claimed that Jesus rose from the dead.

The skeptic may respond, "But this is from the Bible, and I don't believe the Bible," as though you are using the Bible to prove the Bible. This blanket rejection will not do. We are not assuming inspiration or even the general reliability of the New Testament in our case for Jesus' resurrection. In our minimal facts approach, we are only regarding the New Testament as an ancient volume of literature containing twenty-seven separate books and letters. Then we are entertaining only those data that are well evidenced and accepted by nearly every scholar who studies the subject, even the rather skeptical ones. Paul is a source independent of the original disciples. We must remember that, although all of the writings of the New Testament were composed during the first century, it was not until later that they were compiled into a single volume that we now call the New Testament.

The ancients did not have our tools for recording and passing along information. Tape recorders were nonexistent and the individual copies that could be made by hand could not reach many, for few people knew how to read. So they relied on oral tradition to teach others. Scholars identify several instances in which oral traditions have been copied into the writings that comprise the New Testament. These include carefully constructed creeds, hymns, story summaries, and poetry. These are significant, since the *oral tradition had to exist prior to the New Testament writings in order for the New Testament authors to include them.* This takes us back to some of the earliest teachings of the Christian church, teachings that predate the writing of the New Testament. Let's look at two types of oral tradition found in the New Testament that will support our point that the original disciples claimed that Jesus rose from the dead and appeared to them.

Creeds were a popular means to pass along important information in a format friendly to memorization and retention. They served for learning and stating faith and doctrine. A good example is the "Apostles Creed" which many of us have recited at one time or another: "I believe in God the Father Almighty; Maker of Heaven and Earth; and in Jesus Christ his only Son our Lord; who was conceived by the Holy Ghost, born of the Virgin Mary; suffered under Pontius Pilate, was crucified, dead, and buried. . . ." This creed lays out several doctrines in a format easily memorized. We should not be surprised to find quite a few creeds that the early church formed, which are quoted by several of the New Testament authors.

One of the earliest and most important is quoted in Paul's first letter to the Corinthian church (c. A.D. 55). He wrote in 15:3–5, "For I delivered to you as of first importance what I also received, that Christ died for our sins according to the Scriptures, and that He was buried, and that He was raised on the third day according to the Scriptures, and that He appeared to Cephas, then to the twelve."[23] Several factors mark this as an ancient creed that was part of the earliest traditions of the Christian church and that predate the writings of Paul.[24] In fact, many critical scholars hold that Paul received it from the disciples Peter and James while visiting them in Jerusalem three years after his conversion. If so, Paul learned it within five years of Jesus' crucifixion and from the disciples themselves.[25] At minimum, we have source material that dates within two decades of the alleged event of Jesus' resurrection and comes from a source that Paul thought was reliable.[26] Dean John Rodgers of Trinity Episcopal School for Ministry comments, "This is the sort of data that historians of antiquity drool over."[27]

Since tape recorders were unavailable in the first century, recorded dialogues, such as the sermons of Jesus and his apostles, had to have been summaries prepared after the fact by those who had heard them. Most sermons last longer than five minutes. Yet most of the sermons in the New Testament can be read in that amount of time or less.[28] For these reasons and others, most scholars agree that many of the sermons in Acts contain oral summaries included in the text that can be traced to the earliest teachings of the church and *possibly* to the disciples themselves.[29] We say "possibly to the disciples" because we are considering only what we can argue from in our "minimal facts approach," not because we doubt the testimony of Luke. At minimum, these appear to have been standard sermons preached during the earliest times of the church, contemporaneous to the apostles, attributed to the apostles, and in agreement with Paul's eyewitness testimony that this is what they were preaching. Admittedly, this does not prove that these sermons proclaiming Jesus' resurrection and appearances were coming off the lips of the apostles. But if we are not there, we are very close.

Sources that cannot be ignored are the Gospels themselves. No matter how skeptical the critic might be concerning the Gospels, it is well-accepted that all four gospels (i.e., Matthew, Mark, Luke/Acts, John) were written during the first century. Each gospel attests to the resurrection of Jesus,[30] and Acts is the sequel to the third gospel, Luke. This means that four accounts were written within seventy years of Jesus at the latest, reporting the disciples' claims that Jesus rose from the dead.[31]

The apostolic fathers are the church leaders who succeeded the apostles. It is probable that some of these men had fellowshipped with the apostles or were instructed and appointed by them, or they were close to others who had known the apostles.[32] Therefore, there is a strong likelihood that their teachings can be traced back to the apostles themselves. The following apostolic fathers taught that the apostles were dramatically impacted by Jesus' resurrection.

Clement, bishop of Rome (c. 30–100), may have been the Clement to whom Paul refers in Philippians 4:3, although this cannot be confirmed. We do have a letter that we know Clement wrote to the church in Corinth around the year

95. Around 185, the early church father, Irenaeus gives some behind-the-scenes information about that letter. "Clement was allotted the bishopric. This man, as he had seen the blessed apostles, and had been conversant with them, might be said to have the preaching of the apostles still echoing, and their traditions before his eyes. Nor was he alone, for there were many still remaining who had received instructions from the apostles. In the time of this Clement, no small dissension having occurred among the brothers at Corinth, the Church in Rome dispatched a most powerful letter to the Corinthians."[33] Around 200, the African church father, Tertullian wrote, "For this is the manner in which the apostolic churches transmit their registers: as the church of Smyrna, which records that Polycarp was placed therein by John; as also the church of Rome, which makes Clement to have been ordained in like manner by Peter."[34]

If Irenaeus and Tertullian are correct, Clement had seen the apostles and had fellowshipped with them, particularly Peter. This would render great historical value to Clement's writings concerning the apostles and their teachings.

Does Clement mention the resurrection of Jesus? In his letter to the Corinthian church, Clement writes, "Therefore, having received orders and complete certainty caused by the resurrection of our Lord Jesus Christ and believing in the Word of God, they went with the Holy Spirit's certainty, preaching the good news that the kingdom of God is about to come."[35] Clement writes that Jesus' apostles were fully assured by Jesus' resurrection. If he knew the apostles, Clement would be in a good position to report whether they had been teaching Jesus' resurrection, especially since he notes that it is the church's central teaching.

Irenaeus also reported information regarding Polycarp (c. 69–c. 155): "But Polycarp also was not only instructed by apostles, and conversed with many who had seen Christ, but was also, by apostles in Asia, appointed bishop of the Church in Smyrna, whom I also saw in my early youth, for he tarried [on earth] a very long time, and, when a very old man, gloriously and most nobly suffering martyrdom, departed this life, having always taught the things which he had learned from the apostles."[36] Irenaeus states that Polycarp was taught by the apostles, taught others what he had learned from them, appointed by the apostles as bishop of the church in Smyrna, and had talked with many who had seen Jesus.

Irenaeus also makes mention of Polycarp in a letter to Florinus which is now lost but fortunately preserved by the early church historian Eusebius of Caesarea (c. 263–c. 339) as saying, "When I was still a boy I saw you in Lower Asia with Polycarp, when you had high status at the imperial court and wanted to gain his favor. I remember events from those days more clearly than those that happened recently . . . so that I can even picture the place where the blessed Polycarp sat and conversed, his comings and goings, his character, his personal appearance, his discourses to the crowds, and how he reported his discussions with John and others who had seen the Lord. He recalled their very words, what they reported about the Lord and his miracles and his teaching—things that Polycarp had heard directly from eyewitnesses of the Word of life and reported in full harmony with Scripture."[37] Furthermore, Tertullian wrote that the apostle John appointed Polycarp.[38]

Polycarp was martyred in Smyrna (modern Izmir, Turkey) around the year 160 at the age of eighty-six.[39] Around 110, he wrote a letter to the Philippian church, speaking of the righteousness and endurance witnessed in the lives of several including "Paul himself and the other apostles." Of them he says, "For they did not love the present age, but him who died for our benefit and for our sake was raised by God."[40] In fact, Polycarp mentions the resurrection of Jesus five times in his letter to the church in Philippi.[41]

As with Clement, if Irenaeus and Tertullian are correct that Polycarp had been taught and appointed by the apostles, his statements concerning Jesus' resurrection can be linked to these apostles, since, as their central teaching, it makes the most sense that they would have wanted to preserve it above all other doctrines.

The nine sources in the three categories above point to multiple, very early, and eyewitness testimonies to the disciples' claims of witnessing the risen Jesus.[42] The late New Testament critic at the University of Chicago, Norman Perrin, who rejected Jesus' resurrection wrote, "The more we study the tradition with regard to the appearances, the firmer the rock begins to appear upon which they are based."[43] Now, of course, the mere fact that the disciples claimed that they saw the risen Jesus does not alone merit the conclusion that Jesus rose from the dead, since anyone can make a claim. However, as we will see in a moment, the data reach beyond the mere claim they made.

To help remember this wealth of data when sharing with someone, use the acronym *POW!* (*"Paul, Oral* Tradition, *Written* Tradition"). When presenting our evidence, we can start off using *POW!* and unpack it if and when needed. For example, if someone challenges you to establish that the original disciples really made the claim that the risen Jesus had appeared to them, you might respond with the following: "That's a great question. Let me give you three categories of evidence. First, we have *Paul* who claims to have known and fellowshipped with the disciples firsthand. He says that they said it. Second, we know of some very early *oral tradition* that was circulating within the church before the New Testament was even written and points to the disciples saying it. Third, we have *written tradition* that portrays or assumes the disciples saying that Jesus had appeared to them after he rose from the dead. In all, we have nine independent sources. So you can see why there is a virtually unanimous consensus among scholars today who hold that Jesus' original disciples said that he appeared to them risen from the dead."

This answer will be more than sufficient for the average person. However, some may ask you to explain one or more of your three categories a little further: "Wait a minute. What do you mean by 'oral tradition'?" Now you can unpack it a little by defining creeds and providing an example. You might say, "Creeds originated because of the need to pass along important information in a format that could be easily memorized. Take the creed in 1 Corinthians 15, for example. Most scholars would place the origin of this creed within five years of Jesus' crucifixion. This may be the earliest Christian tradition available, and it lists numerous appearances of the risen Jesus to his disciples and others." The idea is that you do not need to overload your friend's mind by immediately citing and explaining nine sources. Rather, present *POW!* and unpack it as needed. This also facilitates productive dialogue rather than an overwhelming lecture. The statement of *POW!* is quick, simple, and invites interaction.

They believed it.

After Jesus' death, the lives of the disciples were transformed to the point that they endured persecution and even martyrdom. Such strength of conviction indicates that they were not just claiming that Jesus rose from the dead and appeared to them in order to receive some personal benefit. They really believed it. Compare this courage to their character at Jesus' arrest and execution. They denied and abandoned him, then they hid in fear. Afterward, they willingly endangered themselves by publicly proclaiming the risen Christ.[44] These facts are validated by multiple accounts, both from early sources in the New Testament as well as outside of it.

One need only read through the book of Acts to find reports that the disciples were willing to suffer for their belief that the risen Jesus had appeared to them.[45] Clement of Rome, mentioned earlier, reports the sufferings and probably the martyrdoms of Peter and Paul:

Because of envy and jealousy, the greatest and most righteous pillars have been persecuted and contended unto death. Let us set the good apostles before our eyes. Peter, who because of unrighteous envy endured, not one or two, but many afflictions, and having borne witness went to the due glorious place. Because of envy and rivalries, steadfast Paul pointed to the prize. Seven times chained, exiled, stoned, having become a preacher both in the East and in the West, he received honor fitting of his faith, having taught righteousness to the whole world, unto the boundary on which the sun sets; having testified in the presence of the leaders. Thus he was freed from the world and went to the holy place. He became a great example of steadfastness.[46]

Polycarp, in the above-cited letter to the church in Philippi, mentioned the "unlimited endurance" the church had seen in Ignatius, Zosimus, Rufus, the apostle Paul, and the rest of the apostles, among others. He added, "They are in the place due them with the Lord, in association with him also they suffered together. For they did not love the present age. . . ."[47] Through Polycarp, we know that Paul, other apostles, and other believers suffered for their faith. Polycarp himself would follow their example of strength and conviction in the face of martyrdom.

Ignatius was bishop of the church in Antioch in Syria. While en route to his martyrdom in Rome, about 110, he wrote seven letters, six to churches and one to his friend and colleague, Polycarp. Since the apostles trained Polycarp, Ignatius is certain to have been well acquainted with apostolic teachings. Ignatius recorded the willingness of the disciples to suffer for their beliefs. In his letter to the church in Smyrna where Polycarp was bishop he wrote, "And when [Jesus] came to those with Peter, he said to them: 'Take, handle me and see that I am not a bodiless demon.' And immediately they handled him and believed, having known his flesh and blood. Because of this they also despised death; but beyond death they were found."[48] Ignatius said that, having seen the risen Jesus, the disciples were so encouraged that "they also despised death" as had their Master.[49] The Greek word for "despised" is better translated "cared nothing for" or "disregarded."[50] Not only did they act in a manner that they thought little of dying, but Ignatius adds that "beyond death they were found," most likely referring to their attitude toward death being proved or demonstrated by their own boldness when the moment of execution actually came. Even if Ignatius's comment doesn't refer to their moments of death, he at least means that the disciples were so strengthened by seeing the risen Jesus that they preached without a thought for their earthly fates because they knew that immortality awaited them. Think of an employee who suffers under an unreasonable boss, then suddenly inherits enough money to become independently wealthy. With the money deposited safely in a personal account, the employee can go to work on the last day and smile at whatever abuse the supervisor dishes out.

Tertullian was an early church father who wrote just prior to 200. He reports the martyrdoms of Peter and Paul:

> That Paul is beheaded has been written in their own blood. And if a heretic wishes his confidence to rest upon a public record, the archives of the empire will speak, as would the stones of Jerusalem. We read the lives of the Caesars: At Rome Nero was the first who stained with blood the rising faith. Then is Peter girt by another, when he is made fast to the cross. Then does Paul obtain a birth suited to Roman citizenship, when in Rome he springs to life again ennobled by martyrdom.[51]

According to Tertullian, if one did not want to believe the Christian records concerning the martyrdoms of some of the apostles, he could find the information in the public records, namely "the lives of the Caesars."[52] Tertullian says that Peter was crucified and Paul was beheaded under Nero, who was the first emperor to execute Christians. Since Nero was emperor between A.D. 54 and 68, we know that Peter and Paul must have been martyred within that period. It is even more probable that their martyrdoms occurred in 64. In that year, Rome was burned. According to the early second-century Roman historian Tacitus, when the people blamed Nero for the fire, Nero turned the blame on Christians and began a horrible persecution, killing them brutally.[53]

Origen (c. 185–c. 254) is a church father. Many of his works are still available to us but some have been lost. In *Contra Celsum*, he relates how the disciples' devotion to the teachings of Jesus "was attended with danger to human life . . . [and that they] themselves were the first to manifest their disregard for its [i.e., death's] terrors."[54] A few chapters later, Origen writes, "Jesus, who has both once risen Himself, and led His disciples to believe in His resurrection, and so thoroughly persuaded them of its truth, that they show to all men by their sufferings how they are able to laugh at all the troubles of life, beholding the life eternal and the resurrection clearly demonstrated to them both in word and deed."[55] Another of Origen's writings relates that Peter had been crucified upside down and that Paul had been martyred in Rome under Nero.[56]

Eusebius (c. 263–c. 339) is called the first church historian. Having just come out of a severe persecution against Christians, he wrote *Ecclesiastical History*, in which he compiles a history of the Christian church up until his time of writing, about 325. Eusebius had at his disposal a wealth of resources, many which have since been lost. For the martyrdoms of Peter and Paul, he cites Dionysius of Corinth (writing about 170), Tertullian (writing about 200), and Origen (writing about 230–250).[57] He cites Josephus (writing about 95), Hegesippus (writing about 165–175), and Clement of Alexandria (writing about 200), on the martyrdom of James the brother of Jesus.[58]

All of these sources, biblical and non-biblical alike, affirm the disciples' willingness to suffer and die for their faith.[59] Of course the conviction of the disciples that Jesus rose from the dead and had appeared to them does not necessarily mean they were right. The skeptic might object, "Followers of other religions and causes have willingly suffered and died for their beliefs. Even atheists have willingly died for the cause of communism. This does not mean that their beliefs were true or worthy." Agreed, but this misses the point: The disciples' willingness to suffer and die for their beliefs *indicates that they certainly regarded those beliefs as true*. The case is strong that they did not willfully lie about the appearances of the risen Jesus. Liars make poor martyrs.

No one questions the sincerity of the Muslim terrorist who blows himself up in a public place or the Buddhist monk who burns himself alive as a political protest. Extreme acts do not validate the truth of their beliefs, but willingness to die indicates that they regarded their beliefs as true. Moreover, there is an important difference between the apostle martyrs and those who die for their beliefs today. Modern martyrs act solely out of their trust in beliefs that others have taught them. The apostles died for holding to their own testimony that they had *personally* seen the risen Jesus. Contemporary martyrs die for what they *believe* to be true. The disciples of Jesus died for what they *knew* to be either true or false.

A skeptic may reply, "How do you know that they *willingly* died for their beliefs? What if they were arrested and executed against their will and perhaps even recanted under torture before they died?" This is a fair question. From the early martyrdoms of Stephen[60] and James the brother of John[61] as well as the imprisonments and sufferings of Peter, Paul, and others,[62] the disciples became well aware that publicly proclaiming Jesus as risen Lord in certain times and places made suffering and, perhaps, martyrdom inevitable. Therefore, to continue on this path, fully aware of the probable outcome, was to demonstrate a *willingness* to endure suffering and martyrdom, regardless of whether these were actually experienced. Furthermore, the primary purpose of getting someone to recant under torture is to gain evidence by which to discourage others publicly. Recantation under torture would not necessarily indicate a change in the victim's mind. Nevertheless, there is no evidence of a recantation being announced. Instead, all the reports testify to steadfast courage during suffering.[63] If the news spread that several of the original disciples had recanted, we would expect that Christianity would have been dealt a severe blow. If those in management of a publicly traded company are bailing out, the workers are not going to dump their life savings into company stock. And yet we find early Christians willingly suffering and dying for their beliefs.[64]

In all, at least seven early sources testify that the original disciples willingly suffered in defense of their beliefs.[65] If we include the sufferings and martyrdoms of Paul and James the brother of Jesus, we have eleven sources.[66] Even the highly critical New Testament scholar Rudolf Bultmann agreed that historical criticism can establish "the fact that the first disciples came to believe in the resurrection" and that they thought they had seen the risen Jesus.[67] Atheistic New Testament scholar Gerd Lüdemann concludes, "It may be taken as historically certain that Peter and the disciples had experiences after Jesus' death in which Jesus appeared to them as the risen Christ."[68] Paula Fredriksen of Boston University comments, "I know in their own terms what they saw was the raised Jesus. That's what they say and then all the historic evidence we have afterwards attest to their conviction that that's what they saw. I'm not saying that they really did see the raised Jesus. I wasn't there. I don't know what they saw. But I do know that as a historian that they must have seen something."[69]

On the state of Resurrection studies today, I (Habermas) recently completed an overview of more than 1,400 sources on the resurrection of Jesus published since 1975. I studied and catalogued about 650 of these texts in English, German, and French. Some of the results of this study are certainly intriguing. For example, perhaps no fact is more widely recognized than that early Christian believers had real experiences that they thought were appearances of the risen Jesus. A critic may claim that what they saw were hallucinations or visions, but he does not deny that they actually experienced something.[70]

Notice what happens when we consider the fact of the disciples' claims and beliefs that they had actually seen the risen Jesus. Since the original disciples were making the claim that Jesus rose from the dead, his resurrection was not the result of myth making. His life story was not embellished over time if the

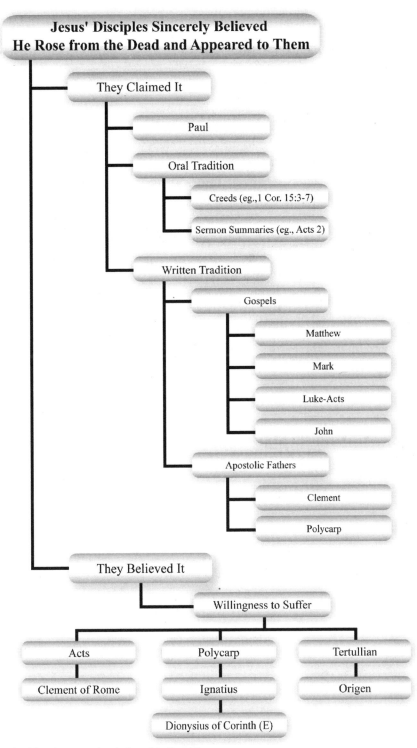

Jesus' Disciples Sincerely Believed He Rose from the Dead and Appeared to Them

- They Claimed It
  - Paul
  - Oral Tradition
    - Creeds (eg.,1 Cor. 15:3-7)
    - Sermon Summaries (eg., Acts 2)
  - Written Tradition
    - Gospels
      - Matthew
      - Mark
      - Luke-Acts
      - John
    - Apostolic Fathers
      - Clement
      - Polycarp
- They Believed It
  - Willingness to Suffer
    - Acts
    - Clement of Rome
    - Polycarp
    - Ignatius
    - Dionysius of Corinth (E)
    - Tertullian
    - Origen

(E) signifies the quotation is found in Eusebius

facts can be traced to the original witnesses. Moreover, if the direct witnesses *really believed* that he rose from the dead, we can dismiss contentions that they stole the body and made up the story. In fact, virtually all scholars agree on that point, whatever their own theological positions.

The disciples' belief that they had seen the risen Jesus is one powerful historical fact in the case for the Resurrection. Next we will examine three other facts surrounding the Resurrection that are strongly attested historically. These will serve as a collection of facts that support the view that what the disciples actually witnessed was indeed the risen Jesus.

The chart above contains quite a lot of details. So we have also included a condensed version below. This chart should help you see the information at a glance and assist you in remembering how to present the evidence in more of a snapshot version. Remember, you can present the three categories of evidence *(POW!)* and unpack them if and when the skeptic requests more information. However, since the information discussed in this chapter is perhaps more important than any other information in this book, we strongly encourage you to master the more detailed chart.

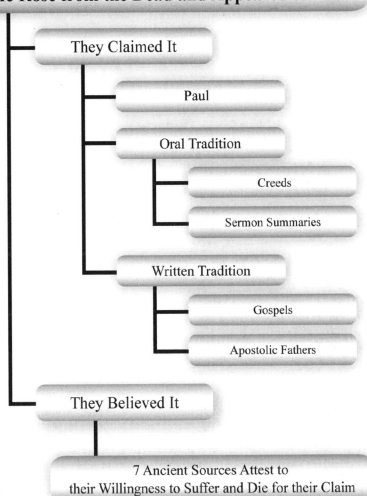

Jesus' Disciples Sincerely Believed He Rose from the Dead and Appeared to Them

- They Claimed It
  - Paul
  - Oral Tradition
    - Creeds
    - Sermon Summaries
  - Written Tradition
    - Gospels
    - Apostolic Fathers
- They Believed It
  - 7 Ancient Sources Attest to their Willingness to Suffer and Die for their Claim

Chapter 4

A Quintet of Facts (4 + 1)
The Last Three

We have established that Jesus' disciples claimed that they had seen him after he had risen from the dead. We also observed that we could go a step further and establish that they really believed what they were claiming. However, establishing that the disciples believed that Jesus rose from the dead falls short of confirming that he actually did rise, since people oftentimes embrace false beliefs and are incorrect concerning the things they think they have experienced. Are there any data that will lead us to believe that the disciples' claims to have seen the risen Jesus were true? We now turn our attention to three supporting facts.

The third fact: The church persecutor Paul was suddenly changed

Saul of Tarsus, better known by history as the apostle Paul, changed from being a skeptic who believed that it was God's will to persecute the church to becoming one of its most influential messengers. In his letters to the churches in Corinth,[1] Galatia,[2] and Philippi,[3] Paul himself writes of his conversion from being a persecutor of the church to one who strongly promoted the Christian message.[4] However, his pre-Christian actions against the church and his conversion are also recorded in Acts.[5] The story of Paul's conversion from persecutor to promoter of the church also appears to have been going around Judea within three years of his conversion. Paul hints at this in an interesting statement to the Galatians. He tells them that three years after his conversion he was not known by sight to the believers in Galatia. Rather these believers were told, "He who once persecuted us is now preaching the faith he once tried to destroy," verifying that others either knew or had heard of his pre-Christian actions against the church.[6] Thus, Paul's notorious pre-Christian activities and conversion are multiply attested. We have Paul's own testimony, Luke's record in Acts, and a story that was circulating among Christians in Judea.[7]

We must now ask the question: What caused this change in Paul? Why did one who persecuted Christians suddenly become one? Both Paul himself and Luke report that it was because he believed firmly that he had experienced an encounter with the risen Jesus.[8] Paul's conversion is so interesting because he was an enemy of the church when he claimed to have seen the risen Jesus.[9] Thus, Jesus' resurrection is testified to by friends and also by a foe.[10] His belief that he had witnessed the risen Christ was so strong that he, like the original disciples, was willing to suffer continuously for the sake of the gospel, even to the point of martyrdom.[11] This point is well documented, reported by Paul himself, as well as Luke, Clement of Rome, Polycarp, Tertullian, Dionysius of Corinth, and Origen.[12] Therefore, we have early, multiple, and firsthand testimony that Paul converted from being a staunch opponent of Christianity to one of its greatest proponents.

Certainly a skeptic may comment that Paul's conversion is no big deal, since many people have converted from one set of beliefs to another. However, the cause of Paul's conversion makes his different. People usually convert to a particular religion because they have heard the message of that religion from a secondary source and believed the message.[13] Paul's conversion was based on what he perceived to be a personal appearance of the risen Jesus. Today we might believe that Jesus rose from the dead based on secondary evidence, trusting Paul and the disciples who saw the risen Jesus. But for Paul, his experience came from primary evidence: the risen Jesus appeared directly to him. He did not merely believe based on the testimony of someone else.

Therefore, the difference is primary versus secondary sources. For most, belief is based on secondary sources. And even when religious belief is based on primary grounds, no other founder of a major religion is believed to have been raised from the dead, let alone have provided any evidence for such an event.[14] The disciples, Paul, and James—who we will look at in a moment—believed based on primary evidence.

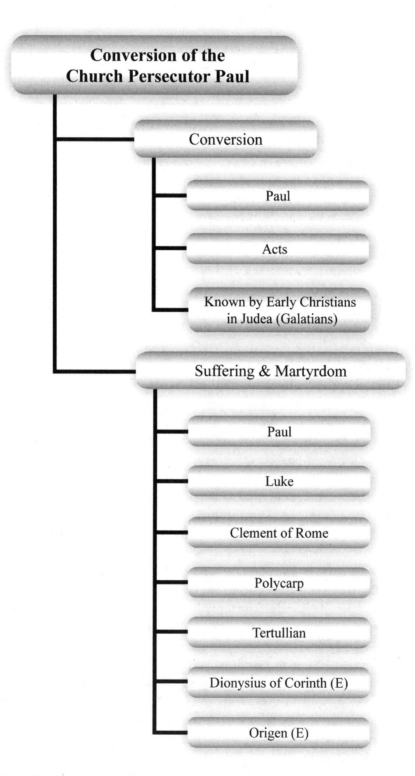

Conversion of the Church Persecutor Paul

- Conversion
  - Paul
  - Acts
  - Known by Early Christians in Judea (Galatians)
- Suffering & Martyrdom
  - Paul
  - Luke
  - Clement of Rome
  - Polycarp
  - Tertullian
  - Dionysius of Corinth (E)
  - Origen (E)

(E) signifies the quotation is found in Eusebius

The fourth fact: The skeptic James, brother of Jesus, was suddenly changed

In 2002, what was thought to be a significant archaeological discovery was made. An ancient ossuary or bone box dating to the first century was found with the inscription "James, son of Joseph, brother of Jesus." While controversy continues regarding the authenticity of the inscription, the fact that such a find enthralled the religious world shows the historical importance attached to James, the brother of Jesus.[15]

The Gospels report that Jesus had at least four brothers, James, Joseph, Judas, and Simon, plus unnamed sisters.[16] Josephus, the Jewish historian from the first century mentions "the brother of Jesus who was called the Christ, whose name was James."[17]

James appears to have been a pious Jewish believer. Paul's letter to the Galatians condemns legalistic men claiming affiliation with James who were teaching the churches in Galatia that Christians had to keep the Jewish law in addition to putting their faith in Jesus.[18] To resolve this issue, Peter, Paul, and Barnabas spoke before a church council in Jerusalem. James, apparently the leader of the council at the time, made the following pronouncement: "Therefore it is my judgment that we do not trouble those who are turning to God from among the Gentiles, but that we write to them that they abstain from things contaminated by idols and from fornication and from what is strangled and from blood."[19]

In the second century, Hegesippus reported that James was a pious Jew who strictly followed the Jewish law:

> James, the brother of the Lord, succeeded to the government of the Church in conjunction with the apostles. He has been called the Just by all from the time of our Savior to the present day; for there were many that bore the name of James. He was holy from his mother's womb; and he drank no wine nor strong drink, nor did he eat flesh. No razor came upon his head; he did not anoint himself with oil, and he did not use the [public] bath. He alone was permitted to enter into the holy place; for he wore not woolen but linen garments. And he was in the habit of entering alone into the temple, and was frequently found upon his knees begging forgiveness for the people, so that his knees became hard like those of a camel, in consequence of his constantly

bending them in his worship of God, and asking forgiveness for the people. Because of his exceeding great justice he was called the Just, and Oblias, which signifies in Greek, 'Bulwark of the people' and 'Justice,' in accordance with what the prophets declare concerning him.[20]

We do not have the same wealth of historical information on the life of James that we have for Paul. However, we have enough information to conclude that after the alleged event of Jesus' resurrection, James, the brother of Jesus, became a convert to Christianity because he believed the risen Jesus appeared to him. This conclusion is arrived at because

1. The Gospels report that Jesus' brothers, including James, were unbelievers during his ministry (Mark 3:21, 31; 6:3–4; John 7:5[21]).[22]
2. The ancient creedal material in 1 Corinthians 15:3–7 that we discussed earlier lists an appearance of the risen Jesus to James: "then He appeared to James."[23]
3. Subsequent to the alleged event of Jesus' resurrection, James is identified as a leader of the Jerusalem church (Acts 15:12-21; Gal. 1:19).[24]
4. Not only did James convert to Christianity, his beliefs in Jesus and his resurrection were so strong that he died as a martyr because of them. James's martyrdom is attested by Josephus, Hegesippus, and Clement of Alexandria. We no longer have any of the works of Hegesippus or the writings of Clement where the event is mentioned. However, sections have been preserved by Eusebius.[25] Therefore, his martyrdom is attested by both Christian and non-Christian sources.

We add that in appealing to the above biblical references, we are not appealing to the inspiration of the New Testament. Rather these references show that there are multiple as well as early testimonies to James's conversion. Although the personal appearance of Jesus to his brother James is reported only once in the New Testament (1 Cor. 15:7), it has the force of being part of the church's earliest tradition, as reported by Paul. Further, critical scholar Reginald Fuller explains that this is sufficient. Even without it, "we should have to invent" such an appearance in order to account for two things: James's conversion from skepticism and his elevation to the pastorate of the church in Jerusalem, the center of ancient Christianity.[26]

With James, we have another case of a skeptic converting to Christianity based on what he perceived was a personal appearance by the risen Jesus. As with Paul, we must ask the question: What happened to cause James to have such a conviction?

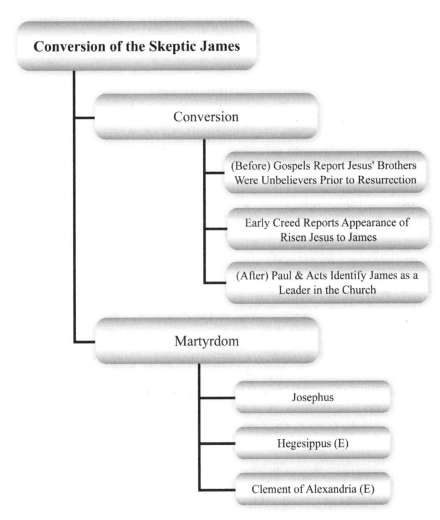

Conversion of the Skeptic James

Conversion

(Before) Gospels Report Jesus' Brothers Were Unbelievers Prior to Resurrection

Early Creed Reports Appearance of Risen Jesus to James

(After) Paul & Acts Identify James as a Leader in the Church

Martyrdom

Josephus

Hegesippus (E)

Clement of Alexandria (E)

(E) signifies the quotation is found in Eusebius

The fifth fact: The tomb was empty

The empty tomb of Jesus does not meet our two criteria of being a "minimal fact" because it is not accepted by nearly every scholar who studies the subject. Nevertheless, there is strong evidence for it, and it is accepted as a fact of history by an impressive majority of critical scholars.[27] Gary Habermas discovered that roughly *75 percent* of scholars on the subject accept the empty tomb as a historical fact. Let's look now at just three arguments for the empty tomb.[28]

The Jerusalem factor

Jesus was publicly executed in Jerusalem. His post-mortem appearances and empty tomb were first proclaimed publicly there.[29] It would have been impossible for Christianity to get off the ground in Jerusalem if the body had still been in the tomb. His enemies in the Jewish leadership and Roman government would only have had to exhume the corpse and publicly display it for the hoax to be shattered. Not only are Jewish, Roman, and all other writings absent of such an account, but there is a total silence from Christianity's critics who would have jumped at evidence of this sort. As we will see momentarily, this is not an argument from silence.

A rather recent attempt at explaining why Jesus' critics did not expose his corpse is that by the time they would have done it, the body would have been unrecognizable. If Acts is correct, the disciples began to proclaim the risen Jesus approximately fifty days after Jesus' crucifixion.[30] Accordingly, although the Jewish and Roman authorities would desire to produce the corpse, they understood that it would be unrecognizable due to decomposition. Knowing that the affect they desired to achieve could not be realized, they aborted the idea. This attempts to explain the absence of a record of exhumation and to eliminate the power behind the Jerusalem factor.[31]

There are at least two problems with this view: First, in the arid climate of Jerusalem, a corpse's hair, stature, and distinctive wounds would have been identifiable, even after fifty days.[32] Second, regardless of the condition of his body, the enemies of Jesus would still have found benefit in producing the corpse. Even a barely recognizable corpse could have dissuaded some believers, possibly weakening and ultimately toppling the entire movement. Since that was the goal, Jesus' enemies had every reason to produce his body, regardless of its condition. It is true that, upon viewing the corpse, many Christians would have claimed that it was a hoax. Nevertheless, there still would have been a huge exodus of believers who would have lost confidence in Christianity upon seeing an occupied tomb and a decaying corpse. This exodus would presumably have required the attention of the Christian apologists of the second and third centuries, such as Justin, Tertullian, and Origen.

We certainly would expect to have heard from Celsus, the second-century critic of Christianity, if Jesus' corpse had been produced. When he wrote against Jesus' resurrection, it would have been to his advantage to include this damaging information, had it been available. In short, if a body of *any* sort was discovered in the tomb, the Christian message of an empty sepulcher would have been falsified. Anything but an *empty* tomb would have been devastating to the Resurrection account.

Enemy attestation

If your mother says that you are an honest person, we may have reason to believe her, yet with reservation, since she loves you and is somewhat biased. However, if someone who hates you admits that you are an honest person, we have a stronger reason to believe what is being asserted, since potential bias does not exist. The empty tomb is attested not only by Christian sources. Jesus' enemies admitted it as well, albeit indirectly. Hence, we are not employing an argument from silence. Rather than point to an occupied tomb, early critics accused Jesus' disciples of stealing the body (Matt. 28:12–13; Justin Martyr, *Trypho* 108; Tertullian, *De Spectaculis* 30). There would have been no need for an attempt to account for a missing body, if the body had still been in the tomb. When the boy tells his teacher that the dog ate his homework, this is an indirect admission that his homework is unavailable for assessment. Likewise, the earliest Jewish claim reported regarding Jesus' resurrection was to accuse the disciples of stealing the body, an indirect admission that the body was unavailable for public display. This is the only early opposing theory we know of that was offered by Jesus' enemies.[33]

The testimony of women

If someone concocted a story in an attempt to deceive others, we presume that they would not knowingly invent data that could hurt the credibility of their story. For example, we have heard of those who, in attempting to promote themselves, have made up stories about their heroism in the military or of having an education they really did not possess. However, is it normal to invent and spread a story about oneself as a thief or habitual liar?

When we come to the account of the empty tomb, women are listed as the primary witnesses. They are not only the first witnesses mentioned. They are also mentioned in all four gospels, whereas male witnesses appear only later and in two gospels.[34] This would be an odd invention, since in both Jewish and Roman cultures, woman were lowly esteemed and their testimony was regarded as questionable, certainly not as credible as a man's. Consider the following Jewish writings:

> Sooner let the words of the Law be burnt than delivered to women. (Talmud, Sotah 19a)

> The world cannot exist without males and without females—happy is he whose children are males, and woe to him whose children are females. (Talmud, Kiddushin 82b)[35]

> But let not the testimony of women be admitted, on account of the levity and boldness of their sex, nor let servants be admitted to give testimony on account of the ignobility of their soul; since it is probable that they may not speak truth, either out of hope of gain, or fear of punishment. (Josephus, *Antiquities* 4.8.15)[36]

> Any evidence which a woman [gives] is not valid (to offer), also they are not valid to offer. This is equivalent to saying that one who is Rabbinically accounted a robber is qualified to give the same evidence as a woman. (Talmud, Rosh Hashannah 1.8)

According to the statement in Rosh Hashannah, a woman's testimony was given the same regard as that of a robber. Keeping in mind that the disciples were Jews, this provides an interesting context for Luke 24:11: "But these words appeared to them [the disciples] as nonsense, and they would not believe them [the women]." The Greek word employed in this text for "nonsense" means "idle talk, nonsense, humbug."[37] The Jewish view of women in that period was not unique. Some Romans shared a similarly low view of females. The Roman historian Suetonius (c. A.D. 115) writes of Caesar Augustus who was emperor at the time of Jesus' birth through A.D. 14:

Whereas men and women had hitherto always sat together, Augustus confined women to the back rows even at gladiatorial shows: the only ones exempt from this rule being the Vestal Virgins, for whom separate accommodation was provided, facing the praetor's tribunal. No women at all were allowed to witness the athletic contests; indeed, when the audience clamoured at the Games for a special boxing match to celebrate his appointment as Chief Priest, Augustus postponed this until early the next morning, and issued a proclamation to the effect that it was the Chief Priest's desire that women should not attend the Theatre before ten o'clock.[38]

Given the low first-century view of women that was frequently shared by Jew and Gentile, it seems highly unlikely that the Gospel authors would either invent or adjust such testimonies. That would mean placing words in the mouths of those who would not be believed by many, making them the primary witnesses to the empty tomb.[39] If the Gospel writers had originated the story of the empty tomb, it seems far more likely that they would have depicted men discovering its vacancy and being the first to see the risen Jesus.[40] Why would they not list the male disciples Joseph of Arimathea and Nicodemus and avoid the female issue altogether?[41] If the account of the empty tomb had been invented, it would most likely *not* have listed the women as the primary witnesses, since in that day a woman's testimony was not nearly as credible as a man's. Thus, the empty tomb appears to be historically credible in light of the principle of embarrassment.

The empty tomb is, therefore, well evidenced for historical certainty. Former Oxford University church historian William Wand writes, "All the strictly historical evidence we have is in favor of [the empty tomb], and those scholars who reject it ought to recognize that they do so on some other ground than that of scientific history."[42]

It should be noted that the empty tomb, by itself, proves little. If there were no credible accounts of appearances, it could be explained away by suggesting that someone stole the body. However, the empty tomb does not stand alone. It is consistent with the beliefs of the disciples, Paul, and James that Jesus rose from the dead, and belongs in a collection of historical data on the subject.[43]

Never has nothing meant so much as when we come to the empty tomb of Jesus. As was said of the television sitcom *Seinfeld*, it is "a story about nothing." And yet at the same time, it is a story about everything. If the tomb was empty because Jesus rose from the dead, then God exists and eternal life is both possible and available.

We may find the acronym J-E-T helpful in remembering our arguments for the empty tomb: the *J*erusalem Factor; *E*nemy Attested; and *T*estimony of Women.

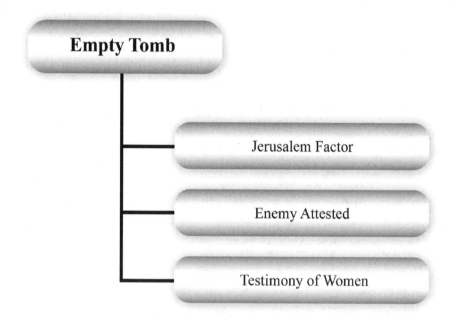

As mentioned earlier, Habermas surveyed almost thirty years of German, French, and English critical scholarship relating to Jesus' resurrection. Perhaps no fact is more widely recognized than that early Christian believers had real experiences that they thought were appearances of the risen Jesus. In particular, virtually all scholars recognize Paul's testimony that he had an experience that he believed was an appearance of the risen Jesus. Equally well recognized is that James, the brother of Jesus, was an unbeliever before he thought that he, too, met the risen Jesus. Seldom is the historical authenticity of any of these testimonies or the genuine belief behind them challenged by respected critical scholars, no matter how skeptical. Lastly, although the empty tomb lacks the nearly universal acceptance by critical scholars that these other events enjoy, the majority of scholars still clearly seem to think that it is probably also a historical fact.

Conclusion

We have presented evidence for Jesus' resurrection using a "minimal facts" approach, which considers only those data that are so strongly attested historically that even the majority of nonbelieving scholars accept them as facts. We have not appealed to or even suggested the inspiration or inerrancy of the Bible in order to support our case. Therefore, one cannot object to Jesus' resurrection simply because he or she rejects that the Bible is divinely inspired.

Using our "minimal facts" approach, we considered four facts that meet these stringent criteria and one additional fact that enjoys acceptance by an impressive majority of scholars, though not nearly every scholar. Let's look at what we now have. Shortly after Jesus' death, his disciples believed that they saw him risen from the dead. They claimed that he had appeared to individuals among them, as well as to several groups. Two of those who once viewed Jesus as a false prophet later

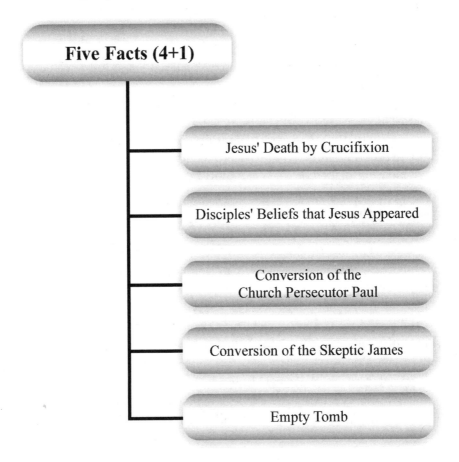

believed that he appeared to them risen: Paul, the church persecutor; and James, the skeptic and Jesus' brother. Both of them became Christians as a result. Therefore, not only do we have the testimony of friends; we have also heard from one enemy of Christianity and one skeptic. Finally, we have the empty tomb.

These facts point very strongly to Jesus' resurrection from the dead, which accounts for all five facts very nicely.

Is it true that God really loves us? Could it be that a relationship with God is truly available to us? Can we really have eternal life? If Jesus really rose from the dead, the answer is yes to all three questions. However, as any good historian and scientist knows, a good theory must be able to answer objections and competing theories. That is what we will look at next. Any opposing theory to Jesus' resurrection, however, is going to have to account for all of these facts as well as others.

For example, one might speculate that the disciples experienced grief hallucinations. But grief hallucinations cannot account for the empty tomb or the conversion of the church persecutor Paul, who had viewed Jesus as a false prophet and would not have grieved over his death.

One cannot argue that the disciples were lying about appearances and stole Jesus' body from the tomb, since we can establish that they truly believed that the risen Jesus had appeared to them. This would not have been the case if they had been lying.

We can also rule out the theory that the Resurrection story was a legend that developed over time and was not actually taught by the original disciples, since we can establish that those original disciples sincerely believed that the risen Jesus had appeared to them and taught it within a very short period of time after his crucifixion.

There are many other refutations of these opposing theories. These are some of the topics we will examine in the four chapters that follow.

These five facts that we have covered accomplish two things: (1) They provide compelling evidence for Jesus' resurrection and (2) they stand as data that must be accounted for by any opposing theory.

In the next four chapters we will let the skeptics take their best shot at coming up with other theories. We will see that opposing theories to date simply cannot account for our collection of facts, thereby leaving Jesus' resurrection as the best explanation of the known facts.

Before we move on though, it is time to reinforce what you have learned and have some fun! Study the information and especially the charts in part 2. Then install the software that came with this book on your computer. Read the directions for playing the game and select the "Quiz 1" option. This quiz includes true-or-false, multiple-choice, and fill-in-the-blank questions. Keep taking the quiz until you can score 80 or better. Once you have passed it, move on to part 3.

"Yes, But . . ."

Encountering Opposing Theories

Introduction to Part 3

Is Jesus' Resurrection the Only Explanation?

S ince the first reports of Jesus' resurrection, critics have formulated opposing theories to account for the known data. These are commonly referred
to as *naturalistic explanations*, because they appeal to a natural cause for the
event rather than a supernatural one. Interestingly, liberal scholars of the nine-
teenth century both rejected Jesus' resurrection and provided refutations of
most of these theories.[1] Neoorthodox scholar Karl Barth was perhaps the most
influential theologian of the twentieth century.[2] Barth pointed out how each
opposing theory to Jesus' resurrection suffers from many inconsistencies and
concluded, "today we rightly turn up our nose at this."[3] Raymond Brown, a
moderate New Testament scholar respected by liberals and conservatives alike,
echoed Barth, writing that twentieth-century critical scholars had rejected ex-
isting theories that oppose the Resurrection. He added that contemporary thinkers both ignore these theories and even treat them as unrespectable.[4]

Of course, this does not prohibit our unbelieving friends and colleagues from
bringing up these alternative theories. Most are unaware that these opposing
theories were refuted and dismissed years ago by other critical scholars. Even
some modern critics occasionally attempt to put a different spin on an old theory
and present it as a new possibility.[5] Inevitably, each attempt falls prey to the
same refutations that caused the demise of their predecessors.

Today, the prevalent view among sophisticated critics is that the disciples seem to have experienced something. But what it was may not be known, and the general bias is against resurrections. As Charles Hartshorne articulated in his comments pertaining to a public debate on Jesus' resurrection between Gary Habermas and prominent atheist philosopher Antony Flew, "I can neither explain away the evidences to which Habermas appeals, nor can I simply agree with Flew's or Hume's positions. . . . My metaphysical bias is against resurrections."[6]

In chapter eight, we will see that this type of response is inadequate as well.

It is fair to raise questions regarding an opposing theory to Jesus' resurrection. Aside from the faith factor, when it comes to reports of miracles, the historian must seek a natural explanation before considering a supernatural one.[7] Christians do this continually in examining reports of miracles in other religions. Our own faith is not exempt from similar investigation. When no plausible natural explanation is available—as is the case with Jesus' resurrection—and a historical context with obvious religious implications exists where a resurrection is at home—for example if Jesus performed miracles and claimed divinity[8]—there then are no reasons why a supernatural cause cannot be considered.

It is important to note that the existence of several opposing theories to Jesus' resurrection should not be seen as a threat to our Christian faith. If all of the theories fail to account for the known data, they cease to be anything more than unsuccessful attempts to explain what occurred in natural terms. A collection of unsuccessful attempts does not add up to one good one. Not only do these alternative theories have their own problems, but some are mutually incompatible with others. For example, the "apparent death theory" is incompatible with the "fraud 2 theory."

In your conversations with skeptics, you will find that sometimes their skepticism goes far beyond what is merited. At times, the skeptic demands that an explanation be so strong that no questions can be raised against it. If something cannot be proved with *100 percent* certainty, they will not accept it as true. Others would reject the data under any circumstances. Their position is rarely stated so bluntly, but the extent of their prejudice becomes clear in practice. If historians took this approach we could know very little about history.

It is also worthwhile to note that, just as the Christian can be expected to provide facts to support her claim that Jesus rose from the dead, the critic must do likewise for his opposing explanations. It is not good enough merely to state, for example, that Jesus' disciples hallucinated what they thought were actual appearances of the risen Jesus. The critic must provide good reason why the theory that the disciples hallucinated offers a better explanation for the facts than does Jesus' actual bodily resurrection.[9]

Let's look at the major opposing theories to Jesus' resurrection: Was Jesus' resurrection merely a legend or a lie? Could the disciples have experienced grief hallucinations or delusion, as do many in various cults? Is it possible that Jesus never actually died, and that his disciples mistook him as risen when he had merely come out of an unconscious state? Has science proven that a resurrection is impossible and, therefore, not a credible belief?

We will examine these major theories and others in chapters 5–8 and see why they fail to account adequately for the known facts. Since we have already seen that excellent evidence exists for Jesus' resurrection, if it can be demonstrated that all opposing theories fail to account for the known facts, Jesus' resurrection will be the only plausible explanation. Our objective is to arrive at the most plausible explanation of the data.

As you read through the various opposing theories and their refutations, you may be inclined to feel overwhelmed by the thought of having to know so much.[10] Relax. In a discussion with a skeptic, you will probably only need to know one or two refutations to answer your rather skeptical colleague. In many instances, simply remembering the five facts we have discussed in the two previous chapters is often enough, with the understanding that any theory must account for all five of them. This will be an invaluable and simple manner of refuting most theories. Although a theory may account for one or two of the five facts, the unexplained data will reveal the weaknesses of the theory. Charts have been included throughout in order to help you better understand and remember the data.

Chapter 5

Always Looking for a Way Out
Of Legends, Lies, and Lapses

S ome critics have suggested that Jesus' resurrection originated as a legend. There are at least three types of legend theory: (1) embellishments, (2) a nonhistorical literary style, and (3) myths in other religions.

Legend theories assume the story grew

Embellishment theories state that Jesus' disciples never claimed that he rose from the dead. Rather, as the story of Jesus and his teachings spread, they were embellished with supernatural details. This is much like the game "telephone," where a person in the front of a room whispers something to the person next to him who does the same until it reaches the last person in the back of the room. By then, the original message has changed substantially. If that much change can happen in one room over five minutes, what can happen over two thousand years stretching across the globe? Even in our own times when people tell stories of their childhood, details change. One example most will recognize is how far their grandfather walked to school and how deep the snow was in which he walked. Other stories contain gaps that were initially filled with "It probably happened like this," but were changed in subsequent conversations to "This is what happened." Changes and embellishments of this sort are common. And they seem to be even more so when they are said to involve incredible or miraculous stories. The more amazing something is, the faster its facts take on even grander proportions.

One example of legendary embellishments is the Buddhist scriptures. Siddhartha Gautama (c. 563–483 B.C.) founded Buddhism, but he left only oral traditions of his teaching. Buddhist scriptures of today arose from two traditions differentiated by the languages in which they are written, the older Pali and later Sanskrit. The Pali manuscripts are dated to the first century B.C. The later Sanskrit appeared at the beginning of the Christian era. This leaves plenty of time for legend to creep into the oral tradition, since the earliest writings didn't appear until approximately four hundred years after the founder's death. It is also notable that stories of miracles by Gautama almost all appear in the later Sanskrit texts. The Buddhist scriptures are highly suspect in that embellishments crept into the tradition over time.[1]

According to skeptic Robert Price, a long period of time is not always required in order for legend to develop. Price cites instances when legend spread even before the principal person of the legend had died.[2] Further, the phenomenon of Internet communication in our own time has shown how quickly legends can grow and spread, given the opportunity. For many of us, e-mails are a major part of life at home and at work. Numerous e-mails make the rounds, describing words and actions of prominent people and organizations that are just not true. Web sites have been created simply to set the record straight about these "urban legends."

Are embellishments responsible for the accounts of Jesus' resurrection that we see in the New Testament? The textual purity of the New Testament is rarely questioned in scholarship. It is well established and agreed among almost all who have seriously studied the ancient texts that the text is virtually the same as what was originally written.[3] Even critical scholars question very few words in the New Testament, and those words in question do not affect doctrinal issues.

The question in scholarship today is, "Did legend creep into Christian traditions *before* they were put in writing?" This is where we must show that legend is unlikely.

Several problems beset the embellishment view of Jesus' resurrection.[4]

First, the Resurrection story itself can be traced to the real experiences of the original apostles.[5] If embellishments added details over time so that the ending of the story became the resurrection of Jesus, then the original story told by the disciples most likely would not have included Jesus' resurrection. In short, the evidence from the disciples contradicts the embellishment explanation.

Second, Paul came to Christ through an experience in which he thought he encountered the risen Jesus. This account also dates very early. We need reasons for his conversion from unbelief, since his conversion was based on a personal appearance of Jesus and counts very heavily against embellishment.

Third, the same applies to James.

Fourth, the mere mentioning of an assertion is not evidence that it is true. While embellishments may be introduced into a text or oral tradition causing legend to accumulate over time, this certainly has not occurred with all ancient accounts. The key question is whether such legend is sufficient to account for the reports of Jesus' resurrection.[6] Each case must be considered separately.

Nonhistorical genre theories assume it was just a story

A genre is a type or class. There are different genres of music (e.g., classical, pop, jazz, rock, swing) and different genres of literature (e.g., romantic, fable, historical, scientific, philosophical). To claim that the disciples wrote in a non-historical genre is to claim that the disciples did not literally mean that Jesus rose from the dead but rather invented a fable about his rising and assigned him divine attributes in order to honor him and communicate a message.[7] An example of nonhistorical genre is found in Aesop's fables, in which the author never intended for us to believe that animals in ancient Greece really talked. Rather, he used this literary style in order to communicate points about various character traits in a creative manner.

Here is an example of what a skeptic might say when using this objection:

> Accounts of dying and rising gods are prevalent throughout the Greco-Roman world. The authors of that time never intended for their readers to believe that someone really rose from the dead but were simply honoring the heroes of their stories by ascribing traits of divinity to them. Therefore, when we read the New Testament accounts of Jesus' resurrection, we must recognize that the disciples never intended for their readers to believe that Jesus actually rose from the dead, either. Rather they were attempting to communicate a deeper message. This seems even more obvious when one considers the parabolic rhetoric frequently employed by Jesus. Most, if not all, of his parables include a fictitious story. If we focused on whether the story in the parable was an actual historical event, we would miss the message Jesus was trying

to tell us. Jesus' resurrection is, likewise, a fictitious account that was never intended to be regarded as historical. To focus on whether it was a real event is to miss the message that the disciples were attempting to communicate; that Jesus was a great man who changed the world and that his teachings will live on forever.[8]

Although the nonhistorical genre theory can seem quite reasonable at first glance, it is plagued with serious problems. First, it cannot account for the empty tomb, especially since this can be established by multiple arguments, even from texts outside the New Testament accounts.[9] In order to account for the empty tomb, an additional theory must be employed; for example, someone stole the body. However, as we will observe later, this theory is exceptionally weak. Also, *combination theories* inevitably produce a weak argument.[10]

Second, a fable or nice story would not have convinced Paul that Jesus had risen from the dead. Indeed, in light of his hostile attitude and actions toward Christians, as well as his own Jewish studies, he most likely would have perceived the gospel to be a poor Christian attempt to imitate Jewish fables that later came to be known as Midrash. An educated man, Paul was surely familiar with nonhistorical genre. It would not have lured him to follow the man he considered to be a false messiah who was cursed by God.[11] He would have feared such apostasy from true faith, for it would jeopardize his soul.

Third, the same applies to James. We have seen that he remained pious toward the Jewish law even after becoming a Christian.[12] It is extremely unlikely that he would change his worldview to follow the brother he believed to be a false prophet and jeopardize his soul, simply because he was moved by a story that Jesus' disciples had made up.

Fourth, if educated people knew about a nonhistorical genre of literature in the first century, they also were familiar with the *historical genre*. The mere existence of nonhistorical literature at the time of the Gospels is not evidence that these authors were using that genre. That would be the same as dismissing a modern history book as fictitious, based on the fact that some of the historical writer's contemporaries write fictional novels. Those who claim that Jesus' resurrection was presented in a nonhistorical genre must provide evidence to prove their assertion.

Fifth, if we look at the New Testament material on Jesus' resurrection, there are indicators that the accounts were meant to be understood as historical rather than mythical. Consider the two sermon summaries of Peter and Paul, recorded

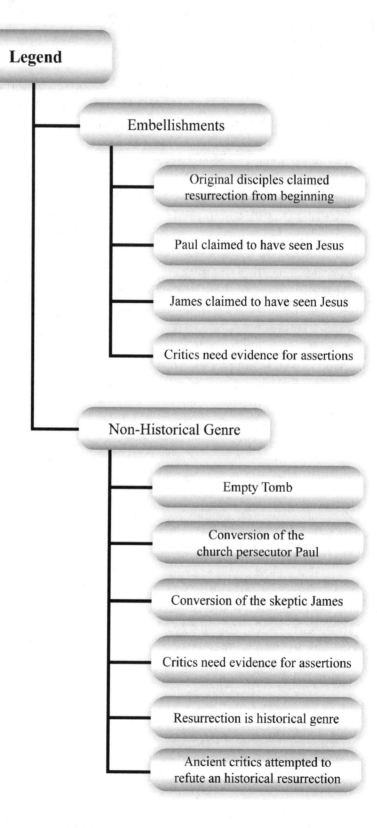

in Acts, that contrast King David's buried body with Jesus' resurrected body.[13] They claimed that Jesus' body did not decay in the grave as David's did, but rather was raised up by God. It is difficult to imagine how Peter and Paul could have been any clearer if they meant to communicate a literal, physical resurrection. If a mythical genre was being employed, Peter and Paul could have easily said, "David died, was buried, his body decayed, but his spirit has ascended to be with God. Jesus likewise died, was buried, and his body now decays. But as with David, his spirit has ascended to be with God where he is now seated at the right hand of power." This would more closely resemble mythical or vision language. The language the apostles employed, however, seems to have been historical.[14]

Sixth, the responses of early critics imply that the early church understood the resurrection of Jesus to be historical. The Jewish leaders accused the disciples of stealing Jesus' body. Although later, the second century critic Celsus (c. A.D. 170) responded to claims of Jesus' resurrection by suggesting he and/or his disciples performed magic or deception.[15] These arguments indicate that these critics thought they needed to respond to a claim of a literal and bodily resurrection.

We have looked at six reasons why the *nonhistorical genre theory* fails to explain all of the facts: (1) the empty tomb; (2) the conversion of Paul; (3) the conversion of James; (4) the need for evidence that the genre is nonhistorical; (5) the assumptions made in Scripture about the resurrection of Jesus being a literal, physical event in history; and (6) the fact that Christ's enemies regarded the story as meaning a literal event. Indeed, each of the first, second, third, and fifth points are sufficient to render the nonhistorical genre position as highly improbable. Collectively, the six arguments render the position virtually impossible.

The Resurrection story is a variation of myths in other religions

Reported miracles abound in other religions, including stories of risen saviors. Skeptics frequently cite Osiris, Tammuz, Adonis, Attis, and Marduk as examples of dying and rising gods. Did Christians copy or get inspiration from these pagan accounts? Why should one believe the Christian account of Jesus' resurrection while rejecting similar accounts in other religions? What makes the account of Jesus' resurrection more credible than these others?

Although it is true that other religions contain resurrection accounts, there are excellent reasons for accepting the story of Jesus' resurrection while rejecting the others.

First, the accounts of rising gods in other religions tend to be unclear. Justin Martyr, writing in about A.D. 150, considered several parallels of rising gods in other religions.[16] However, since the details of the stories are vague and unlike Jesus' resurrection, today's scholars would not regard the stories as parallels. Justin mentions the deaths and risings of the sons of Jupiter: Aesculapius was struck by lightning and ascended to heaven; after dying violent deaths, Baccus, Hercules, and a few other sons rose to heaven on the horse Pegasus. Justin then mentions Ariadne and others like her, though unnamed, who "have been declared to be set among the stars." Finally, he mentions the account of the cremation of the Roman emperor Augustus, during which someone swore that he saw Augustus's spirit in the flames ascend toward heaven.[17]

Justin's reason for mentioning these alleged parallels is noteworthy. At a time when Christians were brutally persecuted, Justin attempted to convince the Roman emperor that Christian teachings and claims were not all that different from the beliefs of other philosophies and religions that enjoyed Rome's favor. Therefore, there was no reason to persecute Christians.[18]

These stories look little like Jesus' resurrection. If we were to consider these as parallels to Jesus' resurrection, we would also have to consider every ghost story. The question is this: Do accounts such as those mentioned by Justin merit the conclusion that Christians copied, or were influenced by, them? The majority of critical scholars today say no. Moreover, while some skeptics like to celebrate these vague similarities, they fail to recognize what great differences exist in these accounts.

Let us look at some alleged parallel accounts that are more frequently appealed to. The first account of a dying and rising god that somewhat parallels the story of Jesus' resurrection appeared at least 100 years after the reports of Jesus' resurrection.[19] The earliest versions of the death and resurrection of the Greek mythological figure Adonis appeared after A.D. 150.[20] There are no accounts of a resurrection of Attis, the Phrygian god of vegetation who was responsible for the death and rebirth of plant life, until early in the third century A.D. or later.[21] Therefore, one cannot claim that the disciples were writing according to a contemporary literary style of dying and rising gods, since there is no literature contemporary to the disciples indicating that this was a genre of that period.[22]

That a resurrection was reported in the earlier accounts of these pagan deities is questionable. For example, there is not a clear death or resurrection of Marduk.[23] In the earliest versions of the story of Adonis, no death or resurrection is reported, and Adonis is the first clear parallel of a dying and rising god.

As noted above, a resurrection of Adonis is not reported until after A.D. 150.[24] There are conflicting accounts regarding Osiris's fate. Some accounts say he is assigned to the underworld, while others refer to him as the "sun." But there is no account that claims Osiris rose from the dead.[25]

However, we can note that the ancient Egyptian cult of Osiris is the only account of a god who survived death that predates Christianity. According to one version of the story, and there are several, Osiris was killed by his brother, chopped up into fourteen pieces and scattered throughout Egypt. The goddess Isis collected and reassembled his parts and brought him back to life. Unfortunately, she was only able to find thirteen pieces. Moreover, it is questionable whether Osiris was brought back to life on earth or seen by others as Jesus was.[26] He was given status as god of the gloomy underworld. So the picture we get of Osiris is that of a guy who does not have all of his parts and who maintains a shadowy existence as god of the mummies. As a friend, Chris Clayton, put it, Osiris's return to life was not a resurrection, but a zombification. Further, the hero of the account is not even Osiris, but Isis or even Horus, their son. This is far different than Jesus' resurrection account where he was the gloriously risen Prince of life who was seen by others on earth before his ascension into heaven.[27]

Second, accounts of miracles and rising gods in other religions lack evidence and can easily be accounted for by opposing theories. For example, the first miracle accounts of Muhammad do not appear until approximately seventy-five years after his death and are found in sources that many Islamic scholars regard as untrustworthy. Therefore, it is likely that they were influenced by developing legends.[28] Moreover, miracle reports from other religions are usually not multiply attested, and the first manuscript that reports the miraculous event is usually far removed in time from when the event allegedly took place.[29] Again, this makes legend-making influences a plausible explanation. The *Life of Apollonius* by Philostratus not only postdates Jesus by nearly 200 years, but it is also thought by some to be "the product of a conscious reaction against Christianity."[30] Thus, the large majority of parallels speak of an event that allegedly took place in the distant past. These stories were not written and circulated at a time when eye-witnesses were alive to discern the truth in the claims.

Third, claims of resurrections in other religions do not explain the evidence that exists for Jesus' resurrection. At best, these critical arguments suggest that the earliest Christians were writing according to a mythical genre of the day. However, we have already observed that such a theory is plagued with serious problems.[31]

On the one hand, the lack of evidence for supposed resurrections in other religions, the late reports of the alleged events, and the fact that opposing theories can account for them makes any claims of true resurrection implausible. On the other hand, the strong evidence and the fact that opposing theories completely fail to account for all of the evidence places Jesus' resurrection in an entirely different category. The fact that many of the miracles in other religions have been disproved does nothing to undermine Jesus' miracles and resurrection. Jesus' miracles have not been disproved, and the accounts of them suffer from few of the weaknesses that bring miracle accounts of other religions into question.[32] Furthermore, if the New Testament faithfully reports Jesus' words, he predicted that false christs and false prophets would come and deceive others.[33] Based on his words, competing resurrection claims in non-Christian religions should not be a surprise.

Although some skeptics today would like us to believe that resurrection claims in other religions cancel out Jesus' resurrection, when we look more closely at them we note that the accounts themselves are unclear, that they lack evidence for the event, and that they fail to explain the known historical data concerning Jesus' resurrection.[34]

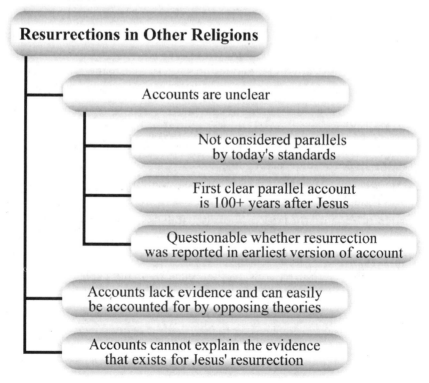

Resurrections in Other Religions

- Accounts are unclear
  - Not considered parallels by today's standards
  - First clear parallel account is 100+ years after Jesus
  - Questionable whether resurrection was reported in earliest version of account
- Accounts lack evidence and can easily be accounted for by opposing theories
- Accounts cannot explain the evidence that exists for Jesus' resurrection

Fraud theories assume the story was a deception

Claiming that something is true is a long way from *establishing* that something is true. The disciples, Paul, and James claimed to have seen the risen Jesus, but why should we believe them? A skeptic might propose that a motive for inventing the story of Jesus' resurrection can certainly be found. For three years the disciples had placed their normal lives on hold and followed Jesus with total dedication. Most of them were peasants who had not formally studied religion. Yet they were teaching that the well-educated Jewish religious leaders of the day were wrong and that Jesus, a carpenter, had it right. Then Jesus was arrested, and within twenty-four hours he was dead. Bewildered and without a leader, they came to the realization that they had made an embarrassing mistake. So they invented the story of Jesus' resurrection in order to save face, or to promote their own views or causes.

Fraud appears to be the first opposing theory proposed by Jesus' critics. The gospel of Matthew reports that the Jewish leaders in the first century spread the story that Jesus' disciples had stolen the body.[35] In A.D. 150, in his *Dialogue with Trypho*, Justin Martyr writes that the Jewish leadership was still spreading the same rumor in his day.[36]

There are two general types of fraud theory. We will refer to these as *Fraud 1* and *Fraud 2*. Fraud 1 charges that the disciples invented the appearance accounts and stole the body from the tomb. Fraud 2 proposes that someone other than the disciples stole the body, leading the disciples to believe mistakenly that Jesus had risen from the dead.

Fraud 1: "Disciples lied or stole the body . . ."

Did the disciples lie about the appearances and possibly steal the body from the tomb? This is the central idea of *Fraud 1* theories. The data we have strongly suggest that this was not what happened.

First, we established earlier that the disciples of Jesus claimed to have seen the risen Jesus because they really believed that they had seen him. Shortly after Jesus' crucifixion, their lives were radically transformed to the point that they were willing to endure imprisonment, sufferings, and even martyrdom. This indicates that their claim of seeing the risen Jesus was the result of a strong and sincere belief that they truly had seen him. In all the political scandals that occurred over recent generations, one or more from the guilty party was often willing to tell the truth rather than face a lengthy prison term. The disciples of Jesus, on the other hand, boldly proclaimed the risen Christ in the face of severe persecution and death. They faced dungeons, torture, and brutal executions—not the white collar prisons that hold today's corrupt politicians. And yet, we are not aware of a single disciple who recanted. An accomplice to the 1972–73 Watergate scandal that toppled U.S. President Richard Nixon, Charles Colson elaborates:

> Watergate involved a conspiracy to cover up, perpetuated by the closest aides to the President of the United States—the most powerful men in America, who were intensely loyal to their president. But one of them, John Dean, turned state's evidence, that is, testified against Nixon, as he put it, "to save his own skin"—and he did so only two weeks after informing the president about what was really going on—two weeks! The real cover-up, the lie, could only be held together for two weeks, and then everybody else jumped ship in order to save themselves. Now, the fact is that all that those around the President were facing was embarrassment, maybe prison. Nobody's life was at stake. But what about the disciples? Twelve powerless men, peasants really, were facing not just embarrassment or political disgrace, but beatings, stonings, execution. Every single one of the disciples insisted, to their dying breaths, that they had physically seen Jesus bodily raised from the dead. Don't you think that one of those apostles would have cracked before being beheaded or stoned? That one of them would have made a deal with the authorities? None did.[37]

Skeptics many times respond that people often convert to other faiths and even die for those faiths, so this proves nothing. One need only think of the devotion of Islamic terrorists. But this misses the point. It is not being argued that the sincerity of the apostles proves that Jesus rose from the dead. The point is that their sincerity to the point of martyrdom indicates that they were not intentionally lying. No one holds that the Muslims enlisted for the horrible suicide missions of September 11, 2001, sat in front of their recruiters and thought, "Okay, Muhammad is a false prophet and Islam is a false religion. If I do this, I'm going straight to hell when the plane crashes. Sounds good! Where do I sign?" They *really believed* in their cause. Deceived? Yes. Liars? No.

Remember that in the Fraud 1 theory, the skeptic is claiming that the disciples lied about the risen Jesus. Their willingness to suffer continuously and die for the gospel points to their sincerity, and points out a fatal flaw in the Fraud 1 theory.[38]

Second, a mere story propagated by the disciples would not have convinced Paul, who was an enemy of the church. Fraud on their part would have been the first thing he would have suspected, just as we would be suspicious today if someone claimed that a recent cult leader like David Koresh of the Branch Davidians had risen from the dead after dying in the 1993 fire when federal officers attacked their Texas compound. Instead of rejecting the claims of Jesus' resurrection as fraud, Paul was convinced by what he described as the risen Jesus appearing to him.

Third, it is doubtful that fraud on the part of the disciples would have convinced James who, even though he may have heard of Jesus' miracles, had rejected him prior to his resurrection. Jesus' resurrection from the dead would likely have been perceived merely as another lie from Jesus' disciples. Like Paul, James appears to have been convinced by what he believed was an appearance of the risen Jesus to himself.

In summary, the strong and abiding conviction of the disciples that the risen Jesus had appeared to them, shown in their willingness to suffer continuously and even die for these beliefs, speaks strongly against lies and theft of Jesus' body on their part. Moreover, the skeptics Paul and James would have been looking for fraud on the part of the disciples. For these reasons and others, only a small number of critical scholars have opted for this view during the last 200 years.[39]

Fraud 2: "Someone other than the disciples stole the body."

Since the disciples must have sincerely believed that they had seen the risen Jesus, perhaps someone else who stole the body from the tomb duped them. When the disciples discovered that the tomb was empty, they simply concluded that Jesus had risen from the dead. This is the *Fraud 2* option, which is flawed because it cannot account for the vast majority of the known historical facts. Virtually all critics recognize this. That is why very few scholars held it during the twentieth century. Here are some reasons why.

First, an empty tomb by itself would not have convinced the church persecutor Paul. Instead, he would have suspected foul play. If it were reported today that the grave of Mormonism's founder Joseph Smith was empty, would those of us who

Fraud

Fraud 1 (Disciples Lied/Stole Body)

- Disciples really believed resurrection
- Conversion of the church persecutor Paul based on appearance
- Conversion of the skeptic James based on appearance

Fraud 2 (Someone Else Stole Body)

- Conversion of the church persecutor Paul based on appearance
- Conversion of the skeptic James based on appearance
- Beliefs of the Disciples based on appearances
- At best, only questions cause of empty tomb

do not embrace Mormonism rush to become Mormons, or would we presume that someone had moved the body? Paul converted because he believed the risen Jesus had appeared to him. Fraud 2 fails to account for the appearance to Paul, which is far stronger evidence for Jesus' resurrection than is the empty tomb.

Second, an empty tomb by itself would not have convinced the skeptic James, who, like Paul, appears to have been convinced by an appearance of the risen Jesus to him.

Third, the empty tomb did not appear to lead any of Jesus' followers except John to believe that he had risen from the dead.[40] Indeed, the gospel of John reports that Mary Magdalene immediately jumped to the conclusion that someone had stolen the body upon discovering the empty tomb. Her first thought was not that Jesus had risen.[41] The gospels further report that Peter, upon seeing the empty tomb, was unconvinced as well.[42] Thomas was unconvinced by reports of an empty tomb and reports of appearances by the risen Jesus to the others.[43] It was the appearances that led to the disciples' belief that Jesus had risen from the dead.[44] Fraud 2 fails to account for these appearances.

Fourth, *even if true*, Fraud 2 could only call into question the cause of the empty tomb, not the Resurrection itself. This is because the strongest evidence for Jesus' resurrection is the appearances to the disciples, Paul, and James. But the theory that a non-disciple stole Jesus' body does nothing to disprove the claim that many persons had actually *seen* the risen Jesus. So Fraud 2 is so weak that additional theories are needed to explain the most crucial data.

The empty tomb convinced no one. Rather, it was the appearances that brought about belief in friend and foe alike, and Fraud 2 cannot account for these. All Fraud 2 can account for is the empty tomb. Jesus' resurrection can account for all of the facts and, therefore, is a better explanation than theft.

"Witnesses went to the wrong tomb."

The *wrong tomb theory* states that the women and the disciples went to the wrong tomb and, having discovered it empty, concluded that Jesus had risen from the dead. Can we be certain that they remembered where the tomb was? Furthermore, can we know whether the burial account found in the Gospels is accurate?

At least six major problems beset the wrong tomb theory:

First, even if the disciples went to the wrong tomb, this does not account for their belief that they had *seen* the risen Jesus. Since this approach cannot account for the strongest evidence for Jesus' resurrection, the appearances, an additional opposing theory is necessary.

Second, the testimony of the Gospels is that the empty tomb convinced no one but John. Mary concluded that the gardener stole the body. The disciples did not believe upon seeing the empty tomb, but rather were confused.

Third, the church persecutor Paul converted based on the appearance of the risen Jesus, not on an empty tomb. Paul would have assumed that someone had stolen the body or that the wrong tomb was visited. Rather, he was convinced based on the appearances of the risen Jesus, not the empty tomb. So even if the wrong tomb had been visited or the burial accounts in the Gospels are inaccurate, these do nothing to call into question Jesus' resurrection. This theory only offers to remove the empty tomb from the collection of historical facts we have.

Fourth, the skeptic James would not have been convinced merely by an empty tomb. Like Paul, James was convinced by an appearance.

Fifth, no sources support the wrong tomb theory. If the women and disciples had gone to the wrong tomb, all that the Roman and Jewish authorities would have had to do would have been to go to the right tomb, exhume the body, publicly display it, and clear up the misunderstanding. Yet, not a single critic is recorded to have even thought of this explanation for the Resurrection during the first few centuries of Christianity.

Sixth, the evidence suggests that the tomb's location was known, because a well-known man, Joseph of Arimathea, buried Jesus in his own tomb. If the burial by Joseph was an invention, then we might expect ancient critics to state that Joseph denied this version of the story. Or the critics could have denied the existence of Joseph if he had been a fictitious character. After all, Joseph was allegedly on the Sanhedrin, the highest Jewish ruling body in the time of Jesus, and was therefore a public figure. Instead of questioning the place of burial, however, this group resorted to claiming that the disciples had stolen the body.

Considering the above six refutations, we can note that our argument for Jesus' resurrection is not weakened, even if the disciples had gone to the wrong tomb, because it was not the empty tomb that led to the belief held by friends and foes of Jesus that he was risen. It was the appearances. Moreover, there is no evidence that his disciples went to the wrong tomb. In fact, there is good reason to believe the disciples went to the correct tomb. Finally, by all accounts, the empty tomb failed to convince anyone of the Resurrection except John. Thus, that the tomb of Jesus was empty remains a fact that believer and unbeliever alike can agree upon.

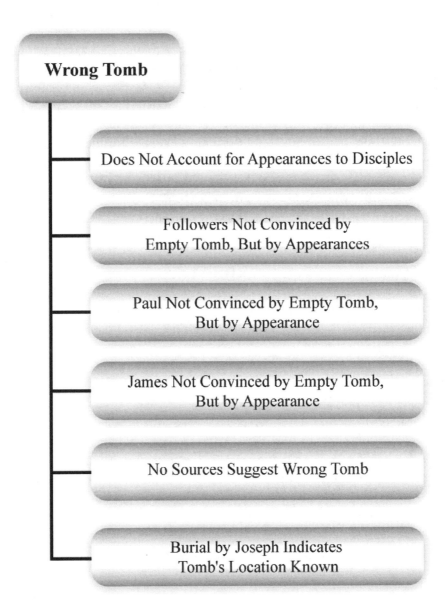

Apparent Death Theory

That Jesus was crucified is certain.[45] Notwithstanding, how can we be certain that he actually died while on the cross? We have all heard of cases in which someone who had been declared dead started breathing again a few hours later. If this can happen in our modern society, what would have prevented it from happening two thousand years ago? Perhaps Jesus never died to begin with, so there was no Resurrection. Could it have been that the soldiers at the cross mistook him for being dead when he had actually fallen into a coma? Jesus had many followers. Certainly some of them must have been affluent. Could they have bribed the soldiers to take him off the cross while he was still alive? Then Jesus could have recuperated and showed his nail-scarred hands and feet so that some believed him to be risen from the dead. This apparent death theory has been referred to as the "swoon theory," and there are at least three major problems with it.[46]

First, such an occurrence seems highly unlikely, given the nature of scourging and crucifixion. We now understand these processes much more than we did even fifty years ago. In the March 21, 1986 issue of the Journal of the American Medical Association, a team of three, including a pathologist from Mayo Clinic, studied the procedures of scourging and crucifixion and their effects on the victim. The following is an excerpt from that article and begins by describing the process of scourging:

> The usual instrument was a short whip . . . with several single or braided leather thongs of variable lengths, in which small iron balls or sharp pieces of sheep bones were tied at intervals . . . the man was stripped of his clothing, and his hands were tied to an upright post. . . . The back, buttocks, and legs were flogged. . . . The scourging . . . was intended to weaken the victim to a state just short of collapse or death. . . . As the Roman soldiers repeatedly struck the victim's back with full force, the iron balls would cause deep contusions, and the leather thongs and sheep bones would cut into the skin and subcutaneous tissues. Then, as the flogging continued, the lacerations would tear into the underlying skeletal muscles.[47]

Keep in mind that this procedure is just the preparation for crucifixion. Regarding the actual crucifixion, each wound was intended to cause intense agony. The team reported that when the condemned man had his wrists nailed to the cross, "the driven nail would crush or sever the rather large sensorimotor median nerve. The stimulated nerve would produce excruciating bolts of fiery pain in both arms."[48] Another doctor compares the sensation to using pliers to crush the nerve that causes intense pain when you hit your elbow—what we commonly call the "funny bone."[49]

The many physicians who have studied crucifixion over the years have invariably concluded that the major problem faced by victims of crucifixion was breathing, or more precisely—asphyxiation. Once on the cross, the victim would want to take the pressure off his nailed feet. To do this, he would allow the weight of his body to be held up by his nailed hands. However, in this "down" position, certain muscles would be in the inhalation position, making it difficult to exhale. Thus, the victim would have to push up on his pierced feet in order to exhale. However, the first several times he did this would cause intense pain, since it would cause the nail to tear through the flesh in the feet until it enlodged itself against one of the bones. Thus, the crucifixion victim would be seen pushing up quite often and returning to the down position. Severe muscle cramps and spasms would also make breathing all the more difficult and painful.[50]

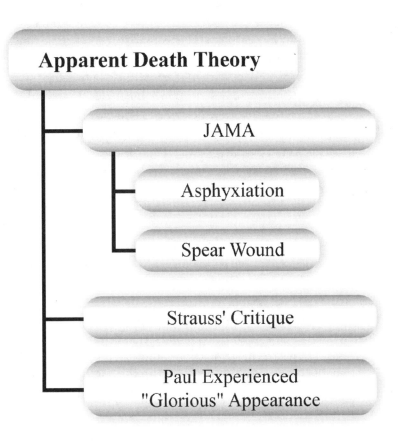

Apparent Death Theory

JAMA

Asphyxiation

Spear Wound

Strauss' Critique

Paul Experienced "Glorious" Appearance

It was typical for a person to hang on the cross for days. However, on occasion when the Romans desired to speed up the process they would employ the *crurifragium*, the act of breaking the legs with a heavy club or mallet. This would prevent the victim from pushing up and exhaling. The cause of death for the crucified victim was simple—he could not breathe.

That inability to breathe was the cause of death by crucifixion is a fact supported by an ancient writing composed around the middle of the second century A.D.: the Gospel of Peter. Although all but a handful of the most radical of critical scholars maintain that this writing was composed much later than the canonical Gospels and was certainly dependent on them, it does provide us with insight regarding why the practice of breaking the legs of crucified victims was done: "And having become irritated at him, they ordered that there be no leg-breaking, so that he might die tormented."[51] To the victim of crucifixion, shattering the legs, painful as it was, was, in an ironic sense, a merciful act, because it shortened their time on the cross. The soldiers had seen hundreds of men executed by crucifixion. It was routine to know when the victim was dead. He was not pushing up any longer for air. The team writing the article concluded, "Accordingly, interpretations based on the assumption that Jesus did not die on the cross appear to be at odds with modern medical knowledge."[52]

Moreover, if the spear wound described in John 19:34–35 was inflicted on Jesus, the blood and water that were described as flowing from his body were probably due to the rupturing of the sac that surrounds the heart (called the pericardium). This would produce the water and, if the right side of the heart was pierced, blood would likewise flow (as attested by our medical sources above). The Roman author Quintilian (A.D. 35–95) reports of this procedure being performed on crucifixion victims.[53] No question remained concerning the status of the victim afterward.

Second, over a century before this study, one liberal scholar who thought hallucinations accounted for the appearances of the risen Jesus ended up decimating the swoon theory. The German scholar D. F. Strauss wrote that it was not plausible that, having been scourged and crucified, Jesus pushed the heavy stone away from the tomb with pierced hands and walked blocks on pierced and wounded feet. Even if such a ridiculous scenario were possible, when he appeared to his disciples in his pathetic and mutilated state, would this convince them that he was the risen Prince of life?[54] Alive? Barely. Risen? No.

So even if Jesus got off of the cross while he was still alive, the disciples would not have been convinced that he had risen from the dead, since the sight of his body and his slow and careful movements would have clearly indicated that he was a horribly hurting man. Upon seeing a swooned Jesus who was limping, bleeding, pale, and stooped over in pain, Peter would not have responded, "Wow, I can't wait to have a resurrection body just like that!" Rather the disciples would have said, "Let's get you a doctor. You need help!"[55] One of my acquaintances chuckles as he imagines Jesus grimacing when Thomas touches him and responds, "Wait! That still hurts! Ouch!"[56] But we have established that the disciples really believed that he rose from the dead.

Third, the apparent death theory cannot account for Paul's dramatic reversal of worldviews. Paul claimed that his conversion was the result of experiencing a glorious appearance of the risen Jesus.[57] A swooned Jesus, even if healed, would not appear gloriously. Therefore, it looks as if the swoon theory is "dead" with no hopes of a resurrection.[58]

When discussing the Resurrection with others, remember that in most instances you will not need to go over all of the reasons presented here as to why a particular opposing theory is inadequate. One or two refutations will usually be sufficient. Articulating every one of them may be an overload of information, causing the other person to lose interest in the process.

Chapter 6

Mind Games

Psychological Phenomena

B efore we look at the following opposing theories of hallucinations and delusions, it may be helpful to get a clear understanding of what these phenomena are. A fun and easy way of doing this is to contrast illusions, delusions,
and hallucinations. Let's start by looking at the picture below.

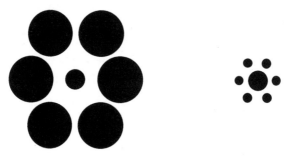

Which center dot is larger? The center dot in the group on the right appears
to be. This is an *illusion*, because a distorted perception is caused by the size of
the surrounding dots. If you measure both center dots, you will discover that
they are exactly the same size. Now let us suppose that you measure the dots
and have twenty other people measure them too and everyone comes to the
same conclusion that the center dots are the same size. Nevertheless, you still

strongly hold your belief that the center dot in the group on the right is larger, in spite of incontrovertible evidence to the contrary. You are now experiencing a *delusion*. Finally, if you have not been to bed for the past three nights, suffer from sleep deprivation, and see a third set of dots, you are experiencing a *hallucination*, because you see something not there.

Psychological phenomena theories look to the mind for an explanation

Now let's go to the real world, formally define these phenomena, and provide more realistic examples. Then we'll show how hallucinations and delusions can be applied to Jesus' resurrection. *A delusion is a false belief held with the conviction that it is true in spite of evidence that invalidates its truth.*[1] A grieving widow may become delusional if she refuses to accept that her husband of sixty years has died, despite the fact that she has his death certificate, went to his funeral, and is unable to see him. *A hallucination is a false perception of something that is not there.*[2] The grieving widow who believes that her recently deceased husband is talking to her may be experiencing a hallucination, because she believes that she hears or sees something that in reality is not there. *An illusion is a distorted perception of something that is there.* It is a deceptive appearance.[3] The grieving widow is tricked by her senses and experiences an illusion when she sees a man in the distance who looks like her husband and who has similar mannerisms. She thinks she sees her husband. This differs from a hallucination because she experiences a distorted picture of an object that is really there, whereas in a hallucination she sees something that is not there. She may experience the illusion of her husband momentarily without believing that it is actually him, because she has evidence to the contrary, much as we know the appearance of water ahead of us on the sunlit highway is an illusion.

Put succinctly: An illusion is a distorted perception. A hallucination is a false perception. A delusion is a false belief.

"Hallucination explains the accounts."

If the disciples believed they were telling the truth when they testified that the risen Jesus had appeared to them, perhaps other explanations could better account for these appearances. Could hallucinations be responsible for the appearances to the disciples? It is common for a person to experience grief hallucinations following the death of a loved one. No different than us moderns, the ancients used wine and drugs to soothe emotional pain. Too much of either might cause people to see things that are not there.

Although the hallucination theory enjoyed some popularity over a hundred years ago and still has a few adherents, it suffers from a number of problems.

First, today we know that hallucinations are private occurrences, which occur in the mind of an individual. They are not collective experiences.[4] In a group, all of the people may be in the frame of mind to hallucinate, but each experiences hallucinations on an individual basis. Nor will they experience the same hallucination. Hallucinations are like dreams in this way. Imagine that it is the middle of the night. You wake up your wife and say, "Honey, I just had a dream that we were in Hawaii. Come back to sleep and join me in my dream and we'll enjoy a free vacation together." It would be impossible for her to do so, since a dream exists only in the mind of the individual. It cannot be shared with another person. Likewise, a hallucination cannot be shared.

Let us suppose that a group of twenty people is sailing across the Atlantic Ocean when the ship sinks. After floating on the ocean for three days with no sleep, food, or fresh water, and with the strongest desire for rescue, one member points to a large ship on the horizon that he is hallucinating. Will the others see it? Probably not, since hallucinations are experienced only in the mind of the individual. However, let us suppose that three others in the group are so desperately hopeful of rescue that their minds deceive them into believing that they see the ship as well. As their imaginary ship approaches, will they all see the same hull number? If they do, it is time for the entire group to begin yelling at the top of their lungs because the ship is real.

U.S. Navy SEALS are arguably the most elite fighting force in the world. Before becoming a SEAL, the candidate must complete a grueling "Hell Week." All of the candidates are put through intense exercises and experience extreme stress during the week on only a total of three to five hours of sleep. As extreme fatigue and sleep deprivation quickly set in, most of the candidates experience hallucinations.[5] According to several SEALS interviewed, most hallucinations occur while the candidates, as a team, paddle in a raft out in the ocean. One believed that he saw an octopus come out of the water and wave at him! Another thought he saw a train coming across the water headed straight toward the raft. Another believed that he saw a large wall, which the raft would crash into if the team persisted in paddling. When the octopus, train, and wall were pointed out by the candidates to the rest of the team, no one else saw them, even though they were all in the same frame of mind. Most of them hallucinated at some point, but none of them participated in the hallucination of another.

The disciples of Jesus claimed that as a group they saw the risen Jesus. This is stated in the earliest tradition of the Christian church: "He appeared to Cephas, then to the twelve" (1 Cor. 15:5).[6] Since Cephas was one of the Twelve, the creed is certainly referring to a group appearance to the Twelve. Otherwise, the creed may have read, "He appeared to Cephas, then to the rest of the twelve." Paul reports that "he appeared to more than five hundred brethren at one time" (verse 6). Finally, he reports that he appeared "to all the apostles" (verse 7). The appearance to "all the apostles" is certainly a group appearance, since as with Cephas and the Twelve, James was an apostle and witnessed an appearance prior to "all the apostles" (verse 7). Three group appearances are mentioned in this creed: the Twelve; five hundred plus; all of the apostles. This creedal material seems to have been a list of some of the appearances (e.g., Cephas, the Twelve,[7] five hundred plus, James, all of the apostles, and then Paul adds himself to the list as the last to whom Christ appeared). Finally, group appearances are mentioned in the Gospels[8] as well as Acts.[9] Therefore, the earliest witnesses, and indeed all of them we know of, taught that several of Jesus' post-mortem appearances were to groups.

Second, hallucinations do not account for the empty tomb. Even if the Twelve, Paul, and James had all experienced hallucinations of the risen Jesus, his body would still have been in the tomb.

Third, hallucinations do not account for the conversion of the church persecutor Paul. Even if hallucinations could account for the appearances to the disciples, how do we account for the life-changing appearance to Paul? He did not appear to have been in the frame of mind to experience a hallucination, since it seems he hated both Jesus and his followers and believed it was God's will to stop them.[10] He was far from grieving over Jesus' death.[11]

Fourth, hallucinations do not account for the conversion of the skeptic James. Although we do not have as much information about James and his frame of mind after Jesus' death as we do for Paul, there is no indication that James was stricken by grief over his brother's death. As discussed earlier, during Jesus' life, James did not believe that his brother was the Messiah. In fact, it seemed that he was among those who thought that Jesus was even deluded.[12] It is unlikely that a pious Jewish unbeliever—who would have viewed his crucified brother as a false Messiah who had been cursed by God[13]—was in the frame of mind to experience a life-changing hallucination of the risen Jesus, a hallucination so powerful that it would motivate him to alter his religious beliefs in an area that he believed would cost him his eternal soul if he was mistaken.

Fifth, there are too many incident variances. Let us suppose that a UFO hovering one thousand feet above the ground is seen by a group of Boy Scouts in the country one evening. When they report it to the police, the sergeant thanks them and tells them that they have received numerous calls during the past week from individuals and groups reporting similar phenomena, even a couple of individuals who are known to be skeptical of aliens. We may not necessarily conclude that the UFO is an alien spaceship. But we can know for certain that all of these individuals could not have been hallucinating. Likewise, individuals and groups, friends as well as foes saw Jesus not once but many times over a period of forty days. We are told that these numbers in-

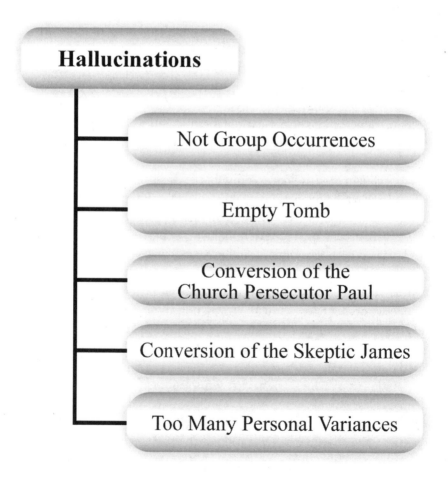

cluded both men and women, hardheaded Peter and softhearted Mary Magdalene, indoors and outdoors, and so on. Not all these persons would be in the same state of mind. It pushes credulity beyond reason to regard every last one of these appearances as hallucinations. Other serious problems plague the hallucination theory. In fact, there are probably more refutations of this theory than any other.[14]

"Delusion explains the accounts."

While group hallucinations may be impossible, it cannot be denied that groups of people sometimes do embrace shared false beliefs, to their own demise.[15] One need only remember Marshall Applewhite of the Church of Venus, who committed suicide with thirty-eight followers in 1997, believing that a spaceship hiding behind the Hale-Bopp comet would pick them up after the event. Cult members led by Jim Jones (Peoples Temple, 1978) and David Koresh (Branch Davidians, 1993) also willingly died with the hope that their leader would lead them to a better place in eternity. One does not need to employ hallucinations to account for these events. Charismatic leaders misled their followers, resulting in tragedy. Therefore, why not employ delusions as an explanation to account for the appearances and the rise of Christianity? Could the charismatic leader Peter have convinced the others that they had seen the risen Jesus and, thus, explain the beliefs of the disciples?[16]

Delusions are a highly problematic explanation for Jesus' resurrection, since they fail to explain much of the known data. First, they do not explain the conversion of the church persecutor Paul. Second, they do not explain the conversion of the skeptic James. People who are candidates for delusions believe something that overrides their logic. While some may accuse the disciples of being in this frame of mind because they really wanted Jesus to be with them, neither Paul nor James appear to have had any desire to see Jesus alive. Paul was having Christians arrested and beaten. He threatened to kill them.[17] He did not want to become one of them, following someone he perceived to be a false Messiah cursed by God. He did not want to forfeit his own soul.[18] He did not exhibit the mental instability required for such an enduring delusion of a risen Jesus. James appears to have been a skeptic before the Resurrection. There is no hint that he wanted Jesus back. He was a pious Jew, committed to the Jewish law, who viewed Jesus as Paul did. Paul and James do not fit the profile of someone who would suffer a delusional experience resulting in conversion to

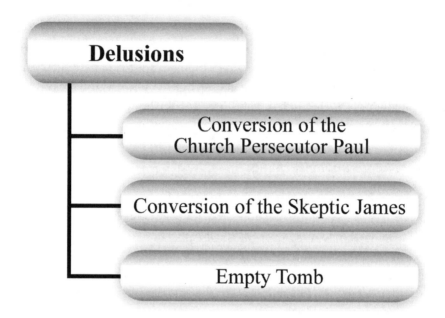

Christianity. Therefore, the position that delusion can account for both of their conversions is highly implausible.

Third, delusions do not explain the empty tomb. In fact, no psychological cause suggested in order to account for the appearances can explain the empty tomb. Thus, although delusion can adequately account for the rise of various cults, it fails as a plausible opposing theory to account for the known facts surrounding Jesus' resurrection.

"Vision explains the accounts."

In order to avoid the tremendous pitfalls of the hallucination theory, it is common today for critics to claim that the appearances were a type of vision.[19] Many religious writings, from antiquity through today, speak of visionary appearances of the divine. Some critics hold that the appearances of the glorified Jesus to his disciples fall into this category and are no more credible than those mentioned in these other writings.

What exactly does the term *vision* mean? Its definition can be somewhat hazy. In fact, a skeptic who suggests a "vision" to explain the appearances to the disciples seldom defines whether the vision is like a dream, a hallucination, an epiphany, or a real experience of something without a body. Getting a solid definition from a critic for what he means by "vision" can sometimes be as dif-

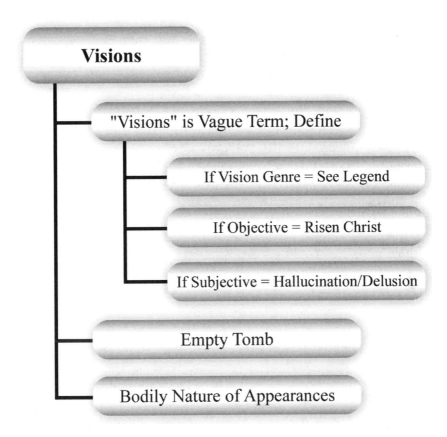

ficult as nailing jello to a wall. Ask a skeptic who suggests such visions to specify what he means by the term "vision."

If the skeptic defines vision in terms of "vision literature" or a literary style, this has already been answered above in the discussion of legends and the nonhistorical genre. It may be best to ask the skeptic if the vision is objective or subjective in nature.

An *objective* vision is seen without the use of natural senses. However, the object seen is real, not imaginary. There is a reality and cause of the phenomenon outside of the mind. Christians might regard Stephen's experience of seeing Jesus in heaven as an objective vision, since nothing in the text hints that any of those present also saw him.[20] Of course, an atheist rejects the possibility that appearances of Jesus might be objective visions. Claiming an objective vision is claiming that the risen Jesus actually appeared to others in some sort of glorified body from heaven, rather than in a material one, though others in the same location might not have seen him.[21] Such a visionary meaning would admit that Jesus rose from the dead. So, the atheist must say that the disciples' visions of Jesus were subjective in nature.

A *subjective* vision is a product of our minds and has no cause or reality outside of our mind, so it is much like a hallucination or dream.[22] It could be said that a subjective vision is a hallucination or a dream that has a religious subject. Thus, the skeptic who claims that the appearances can be accounted for by subjective visions believes they were hallucinations or dreams. This makes subjective visions susceptible to all of the problems faced in regard to hallucinations (see p. 106–8), among others.

Therefore, objective and subjective visions as explanations for the appearances of the risen Jesus are problematic: If the vision was objective, we still have a risen Jesus. The most an "objective vision" theory can do is to try to avoid a bodily resurrection. But we still have a resurrection.[23] If the vision was subjective, this implies that the vision was the result of some sort of hallucination. Yet, hallucinations are unpalatable.

Visions cannot account for the empty tomb. If the disciples only saw visions of the risen Jesus, objective or otherwise, the tomb should still have been occupied. Thus, vision theory fails to account for the facts surrounding Jesus' resurrection.

The bodily nature of the appearances also testifies against a vision, since a body of Jesus that occupied space and time is described. Many times critics will cite the appearance of Jesus to Paul in Acts 9. In contrast to what was reported by the disciples, only a blinding light in the sky and a voice is mentioned. There was no body to touch or even see.

Thus, these critics usually argue for at least one of three positions. First, Paul saw a vision (i.e., hallucination). Second, since Paul includes his encounter with the risen Christ in a list of the appearances to the disciples (i.e., the creed in 1 Corinthians 15:3–8), he regarded the nature of the appearances to the disciples to be the same as his own (i.e., visionary). As atheist New Testament critic Gerd Lüdemann argues, "Isn't it reasonable to grant that Paul . . . had the same experience that the others had—and to conclude from his statement that the others had visionary experiences too?"[24] Third, since Paul's writings appear to be earlier than the Gospels, which certainly report bodily appearances, the Gospels must reflect legendary development that occurred in the early oral traditions of Jesus, circulating after Paul's testimony but before being written in the Gospels.

How would we address these objections to the vision theory? The answer is important because, if the Resurrection appearances can be downgraded to events that occurred only in the minds of the disciples, Paul and James, the reality of the appearances can be undermined. First, we must determine what our skeptic means by vision. Lüdemann would claim that it was a subjective vision. So we would provide all the refutations to hallucinations: (1) They are not group occurrences; (2) they do not account for the empty tomb; (3) they do not adequately explain the conversion of Paul; (4) they do not adequately explain the conversion of James; (5) there are too many personal variations. In addition, we would cite the physicality of the appearances described by Paul, since our critics here are focusing on him.[25] For example, we might point out that the very experience cited by the skeptic in support of a subjective vision (Acts 9) contains details that rule out such an experience (e.g., Paul's traveling companions saw the same light, heard the same voice, and even fell to the ground). Why should critics accept some details in the Acts texts but not others? Remember that subjective visions have no cause or reality outside the mind. If others saw the light and heard the voice, there must have been a cause and reality to the vision outside of Paul's mind.[26] The skeptic cannot arbitrarily pick and choose which details to believe and which to ignore because they do not fit into his view.

"Conversion disorder explains the accounts."

Conversion disorder is a psychological problem in which a person experiences symptoms or deficits to one's senses that are not intentionally produced and may have a neurological origin.[27] Let us suppose that the year is 1968. A young American named Rick has been drafted into the U.S. Army for a tour in Vietnam. Shortly after he receives his letter from the Department of Defense, Rick begins to feel a sharp pain all the way down his right leg. The pain worsens, and by the time he goes for his military physical he is limping severely. In this case, Rick is not faking the pain in order to get out of going to Vietnam. He may have conversion disorder. Typical symptoms of conversion disorder are blindness, paralysis, loss of voice, pain, uncontrolled vomiting, tics, and seizures. The term *conversion* is not used here in a sense related to a religious conversion, but we may ask if Paul's religious conversion from Judaism to Christianity was a result of conversion disorder. Perhaps the bright light that blinded him could have been the result of a neurological malfunction or other medical causes rather than a divine visitation.

A conversion disorder on Paul's part does not refute Jesus' resurrection because of the following crucial reasons:

First, even if plausible, at best a conversion disorder could only account for the single appearance to Paul. It cannot adequately account for the appearances to the disciples or the appearance to James.

Second, conversion disorder cannot account for the empty tomb.

Third, Paul does not fit the profile of one who is likely to experience a conversion psychosis. According to the *Diagnostic and Statistical Manual of Mental Disorders: DSM-IV*,[28] the primary source used by professional psychologists and psychiatrists for diagnosing psychological conditions, women are more likely than men to experience conversion psychosis by as much as a 5:1 ratio. Adolescents, military persons in battle, those of a low economic status, and those with a low IQ are likewise more prone to experience the phenomenon. Paul does not fit into any of these categories.[29] This does not mean that he could not have experienced the disorder. Men still experience depression, although women are much higher candidates for it. However, combined with other challenges to the theory, the fact that Paul does not fall into any category of those likely to experience a conversion disorder renders the condition all the more unlikely as the cause of his experience of the risen Jesus.

Fourth, conversion disorder cannot explain other details of Paul's account of the risen Jesus appearing to him, such as the voice and his belief that God wanted him to tell others something. This would require an additional auditory hallucination, since he claimed that he heard a voice speak to him. Remember, as discussed under the hallucination theory, Paul hated Christians and saw the enterprise as a movement against God. He did not appear to be in the frame of mind to hallucinate a risen Jesus. Similarly, the same mindset would make conversion disorder difficult.

Conversion disorder also requires Paul's experience to include another psychosis often referred to as a "messiah complex." Here, a person really believes that God spoke to him and told him to tell others something. Now, of course, we can find examples of people who have experienced visual hallucinations, auditory hallucinations, and a messiah complex. It is highly uncommon to find someone who has experienced all three simultaneously. Did Paul experience all three during the same period? The data suggests that he did not, since he does not fit into the psychological profile for conversion disorder, and he does not appear to have been in the frame of mind to hallucinate a risen Jesus.

It would not benefit the critic to say that he does not trust the accounts in

Acts of the appearance of Jesus to Paul, and so the voice and command to tell others a message from God is irrelevant. The only accounts of the bright light, the voice, and the command are found precisely in these accounts in Acts. Therefore, in rejecting the Acts accounts, the critic would also reject any data he has for claiming conversion disorder.

A fifth and final problem with conversion disorder as an explanation to account for Paul's experience of Jesus is that it requires the adding of multiple explanations to account for the event. Such a combination theory appears *ad hoc*, that is, it appears to have been manufactured in order to make everything fit, not because this appears to have been what happened.

Therefore, conversion disorder is implausible as an explanation for the appearances. Paul does not fit the profile of someone who is a candidate for conversion disorder. Conversion disorder cannot explain the other details of Paul's account of the risen Jesus appearing to him. Other explanations must be employed in order to do this, such as hallucination and messiah complex. However, this is problematic as well. Not only does it appear from what we know of Paul that he was not in the frame of mind to experience a hallucination of the risen Jesus, but the number of additional theories required in order to make conversion disorder explain Paul's experience makes it strongly suspect of being *ad hoc*. More damaging to conversion disorder theory, however, is that even if the evidence suggested that Paul experienced one, it still does not account for the appearances to the disciples, the conversion of the skeptic James, or the empty tomb. Therefore, conversion disorder does not adequately explain all of the known facts. In fact, it hardly explains any of them.

In a nationally televised debate in April 2000 between atheist philosopher Antony Flew and Habermas, conversion disorder was one of Flew's main objections to Jesus' resurrection. However, when Habermas brought up the above problems, Flew commented that he was glad to give up the objection and never found it very helpful anyway.[30]

Other psychological theories target Paul

Most scholars today believe that Paul's letters precede the writing of the Gospels, and admit that he saw what he believed was an appearance of the risen Jesus. Moreover, Paul preserves many earlier creedal traditions regarding the gospel message. Thus, his testimony of Jesus' rising from the dead is believed to be the most reliable account of Jesus' resurrection. Paul had been an enemy of Jesus and the church. He was glad Jesus was dead, and he was trying to finish the job the Jewish leaders had started by destroying the church, which he believed was a gross heresy. Then to the amazement of many, he suddenly changed his mind and became a member of the church he had sought to destroy. What caused this change in Paul? His testimony is that the risen Jesus appeared to him personally. The opposing theories we have observed thus far have failed to account for the appearances of the risen Jesus to others. But what if we were to focus only on Paul for a moment? Are there any possibilities we should consider that might account for his sudden change of mind? Let's look at three.

Just as we can imagine a Nazi soldier feeling great remorse after the Holocaust and converting to Judaism, we can imagine Paul on his way to persecute Christians feeling great remorse over his recent actions of destroying Christian families and consenting to the death of Stephen. Could it be that Paul experienced such pain over his actions that it motivated him to convert to Christianity?

Several serious problems beset the *guilt theory.*

First, there is not a shred of evidence from Paul's writings or Luke's account of Paul's actions in Acts that he experienced guilt while conducting his persecution. However, even if he did, this would more likely have led to the cessation of his terrorism toward Christians ("I'm sure they learned their lesson."), rather than his becoming one. His interpretation of the Scriptures prohibiting Jesus from being the Messiah would simply have been too strong.

Second, Paul's own testimony indicates the very opposite—that he was very content in Judaism and confident of his actions. In Philippians 3:5–6 he provides his resume as a Jew: He was the Jew's Jew and a zealous teacher of the Law in which he was blameless. He gives no indications of experiencing guilt while in that position.

Third, even if guilt could account for Jesus' appearance to Paul, it does not account for his appearances to the others. Finally, guilt does not account for the empty tomb.

Could it be that Paul was *hungry for power* and converted to Christianity with the hope that he might come to lead the church from one of its most prominent positions? According to his own testimony, Paul was moving up within the Jewish leadership more quickly than his colleagues. Perhaps it wasn't fast enough for him. Filled with confidence and ambition, he believed that the new Christian church would be filled with pride and empowered if he became a Christian. Christians would cite the name of this former powerful

Pharisee as one of Christianity's trophies. Perhaps he had dreams of having a large platform of influence within the church and of being respected for bringing peace between Christian Jews and non-Christian Jews, between whom there were bitter relations.

In a critique of Habermas, New Testament critic Evan Fales writes concerning Paul's motivation, "What Paul absolutely needed . . . was to legitimate a claim of independent authority. . . . I would suggest that he had the vision because he needed the authority."[31] For whatever reasons we might speculate, perhaps ambitious Paul converted because he believed he could realize his goals for power faster in the church than in Judaism.

Yes, it was a change. But we must remember that since the early church was comprised almost entirely of Jews who continued worshiping in the synagogues for some time, at the time of Paul's conversion it would not have been the major leap that it would be today. Rather it would have been more like the relatively minor switch from major league baseball's National League to its American League.

While we are all aware of the ambition for power possessed by some, the "power theory" applied to Paul seems unlikely for a number of reasons.[32] We present three:

First, if Paul was looking for quick power through a prominent position of authority in the church, his actions certainly provide no indication that this was the case. According to Paul's own testimony, even after being a Christian for seventeen years, he visited Jerusalem in order to compare the gospel he was preaching with that preached by the apostles. He wanted to insure that his labors had not been in vain and that he was not preaching a false gospel. It may be that at this time the apostles first fully accepted him into fellowship as a leader in the church.[33]

Second, if Paul was looking for more power, being a Roman citizen, why didn't he pursue a place of power within the Roman government?

Third, the hard life that Paul cheerfully lived as a Christian did not reflect a person who was out for self-gratification. Paul accepted multiple beatings, imprisonments, put his life in danger continuously, and lived a life close to poverty for the sake of the gospel.

An *epiphany* is a sudden perception of reality caused by an intuitive breakthrough. For example, let's suppose you were brought up in a family with atheist parents and have been an atheist since childhood. One night you are looking up at the stars and say to yourself, "How could all of this be here by chance?

There must be a God!" Irrespective of the soundness of your reasoning or the truth of your conclusion, you have experienced an epiphany.

How would an epiphany be employed in an attempt to account for Paul's change of mind concerning Jesus? Let's consider the following scenario: Paul had already started his aggressive persecution of Christians as reported by Luke in Acts 6:8–8:3. He consented to the execution of Stephen and began persecuting Christians in Jerusalem, dragging men and women from their homes and throwing them into prison. He then went to the high priest, asking for and receiving permission to arrest Christians in Damascus and bring them bound to Jerusalem (9:1-2). While on his way to Damascus, Paul and his traveling companions engage in discussions concerning why Jesus could not have been the Messiah. One of his colleagues raises the point that the Scriptures clearly state that anyone hanged on a tree is cursed by God and that crucifixion met that criterion (Deut. 21:23). God would exalt his Messiah; not curse him. They all nod in agreement. Then Paul experiences an epiphany. He suddenly understands what Christians mean when they say that the Messiah became cursed by God for us and in doing so paid the penalty for our sins. The Messianic prophecies in Isaiah 53 of a suffering Messiah now make sense to him. As a result of this epiphany, Paul is now convinced that Christianity is true and converts.

What about the details of Paul's experience reported by Luke in Acts, such as the bright light and the voice from heaven? From the viewpoint of a skeptic, we might explain these by saying that they are metaphors for the epiphany itself. For example, today when we have an epiphany or a new idea we say, "A light came on in my mind," or "I now see the light!" Those in antiquity of course did not have electricity and light bulbs but the metaphor was the same. The New Testament uses the metaphor of light many times.[34] Jesus himself said, "I am the light of the world."[35] Non-Christian Jewish writings of the time use the word "light" as a metaphor for wisdom, knowledge, insight, and both physical and spiritual life.[36] So it appears that this metaphor was used in Jesus' day in much the same manner it is employed today.

Was Paul saying he now saw the light of the gospel and that he saw it very clearly? What about the voice from heaven? Today it is very common for Christians exiting a worship service where they were affected, to say, "God spoke to me today." The language sounds like they are claiming that they heard the audible voice of God. However, what they mean is they believe that God communicated something to them through the music or sermon. Paul and his traveling companions heard the voice from heaven, but his companions did not understand the words.[37] Paul's metaphor here is that God's Word concerning the Messiah was discussed among them. Paul heard from God through his new understanding of the Messianic prophecies applied to Jesus. But the others just didn't get it.

While the epiphany theory sounds interesting at first look, it is plagued with many serious difficulties. First, even if all of these conjectures were true, it only accounts for the appearance to Paul. It does not account for the appearances to the disciples, nor does it account for the appearance to the skeptic James.[38]

Second, an epiphany experienced by Paul does not account for the empty tomb. Jesus' body should still have been lying there. Third, Christianity's critics responded to a literal interpretation of Jesus' resurrection rather than to an epiphany, implying this is what the witnesses were proclaiming. The Jewish leaders claimed that the disciples stole the body.[39] The accounts of the bright light and voice do not come from the early writings of Paul. Rather, they come from Acts which scholars date after the writing of Matthew, Mark, and Luke. Thus, an evolution of the story of Jesus' resurrection going from an epiphany in Paul to the bodily appearances in the Gospels seems to be going in precisely the opposite direction, since it is the Gospels that teach bodily resurrection and the later Acts that provides certain details that might be used to support the notion of a Pauline epiphany.[40]

Fifth, there is something helpful to remember when considering the differences between Paul's encounter with Jesus and what the disciples experienced: Paul's experience of the risen Jesus occurred after Jesus' ascension. That could account for the difference in the glorified nature that Christ showed to Paul from what the disciples experienced.

No psychological phenomena—such as hallucinations, delusions, visions, conversion disorder, grief, guilt, epiphany, or Paul's lust for power can adequately account for all of our five facts. Serious problems stand in the way of these theories.

Chapter 7

Stopping at Nothing
More Critical Comebacks

Even if all of the opposing theories conjectured by skeptics fail to account for the collection of historical data on an individual basis, what if a few of these explanations were combined? As an example, let us make up a combination theory and call it the "theft/multiple psychosis theory." In this theory, someone other than the disciples stole the body from the tomb (i.e., Fraud 2). Peter experienced a hallucination of the risen Jesus and subsequently deluded the disciples into believing that they saw him as well. Paul had a conversion disorder, and James also experienced a hallucination of Jesus. Would this account for all of the historical data and be as good an explanation, if not better, of the data than a resurrection?

"A combination of theories can explain the Resurrection."

At least four major problems beset all combination theories.

First, combinations of theories generally lead to higher *improbability*, not a more probable solution. If a combination theory is to be true, all of its subtheories must be true. If one is not, then the theory fails to account adequately for all of the data. If one subtheory fails, the combination fails. Why does this lead to higher improbability? Suppose we flip a nickel into the air. The chance that it will land with the head side up is *50 percent*. Then we add a second nickel and flip both into the air. The chance that both will come up on heads is *25 percent* (.5 x .5). If we add three more nickels and flip all five into the air, the chances that all will come up on heads is 3 percent. Likewise, five theories, each having a *50 percent* probability, lead to a combined probability of *3 percent*. That is a *97 percent* chance that things did not happen according to that combination theory.[1] Of course probabilities here are subjective estimations assigned by the person who is considering the force of the argument. However, some may find it helpful. Realizing that all of the theories must be true in a combination theory, even if one assigned an *80 percent* probability to each of the five opposing theories posited in our example (such would be straining it to say the least), the probability of the combination of all of these theories being true is much less likely (.8 x .8 x .8 x .8 x .8 = .328 or *33 percent*) than the theory being false (*67 percent*).

Second, while combination theories do a better job of accounting for more of the data, many of the problems that are present when considered individually remain when considered together. For example, in our "theft/multiple psychosis theory" above, a conversion disorder on Paul's part remains highly unlikely, and there is no indication that James was in a frame of mind to hallucinate.

Third, it ends up sounding *ad hoc*. Even if there were no remaining problems, five component theories must be employed in order to account for the data in our "theft/multiple psychosis theory." So it appears that the theory was contrived to make everything fit. The person who has been caught in a lie and then fabricates new lies in an attempt to defend his original lie is acting in an *ad hoc* manner. The liar is contriving new excuses to support the initial lie. Applied to Jesus' resurrection, the *ad hoc* nature of combination theories creates suspicion that the critic offering it is not interested in knowing what really happened. Fewer than five theories could be combined, but the challenge is to explain *all* of the relevant data regarding Jesus' resurrection.

Now of course if there were evidence that Paul experienced a conversion disorder and that James hallucinated, the *ad hoc* nature of our combination theory would be eliminated. However, no such evidence exists.

Fourth, even if no problems remained and no signs of an *ad hoc* component were present, the mere stating of an opposing theory does nothing to prove that this is what really happened. The burden lies on the shoulders of the one with the opposing theory to demonstrate that this is not only possible but that each component is a probable explanation of the facts.[2]

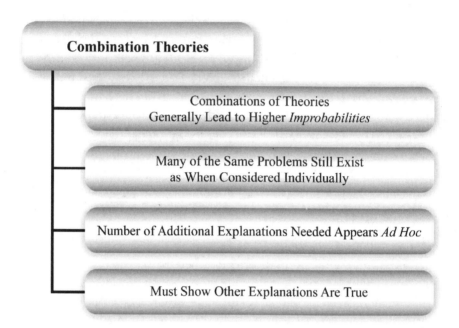

Combination Theories

Combinations of Theories
Generally Lead to Higher *Improbabilities*

Many of the Same Problems Still Exist
as When Considered Individually

Number of Additional Explanations Needed Appears *Ad Hoc*

Must Show Other Explanations Are True

"There are discrepancies among resurrection accounts."

It is often suggested by critics that the Gospel writers themselves cannot seem to agree on some details surrounding the resurrection of Jesus. For example, were there one (John 20:1), two (Matt. 28:1), or three women who visited the tomb (Mark 16:1)? Did they see one (Matt. 28:2–7; Mark 16:5) or two angels (Luke 24:4; John 20:12)? Did they see the angel(s) before they told the disciples that Jesus' body was gone (Matt. 28:7; Mark 16:4–7; Luke 24:9) or after (John 20:1–9)? Because of such tensions, some critics suggest that we cannot know what really happened if the Gospel writers contradict themselves and the alleged eyewitnesses cannot even correctly report the events. In fact, they assert, these contradictions render the whole resurrection story as dubious.

There are several problems with this conclusion:

First, discrepancies in the Gospels concerning Jesus' resurrection, at most call into question the issue of the complete accuracy of the Gospels, but not their general trustworthiness when recording historical events.

Second, historians do not conclude that an event did not occur because the accounts contain discrepancies.[3] Ancient accounts vary on the details pertaining to the burning of Rome. How big was the fire? Who started it? Do these discrepancies nullify the general report that Rome indeed burned?[4] If eyewitnesses to an automobile accident at a busy intersection differ as to which car first entered the intersection, how many cars were involved, and how many people were in each car, is it reasonable to conclude that no accident occurred?[5] An insurance company may want to argue in this manner, but would you buy this assertion as a member of the jury? Therefore, one could even grant that all of these discrepancies were unsolvable and still hold to the general trustworthiness of the Gospel accounts.

Third, the discrepancies in the Gospels may indicate that they were independent accounts, since copiers would have been more unified on the facts. From a historian's vantage point, this diversity adds to their credibility, since it indicates that the event is being attested by more than one source.[6]

Fourth, while a discussion of alleged discrepancies is not part of our task here, coherent and plausible explanations exist that account for many if not all of the discrepancies.[7]

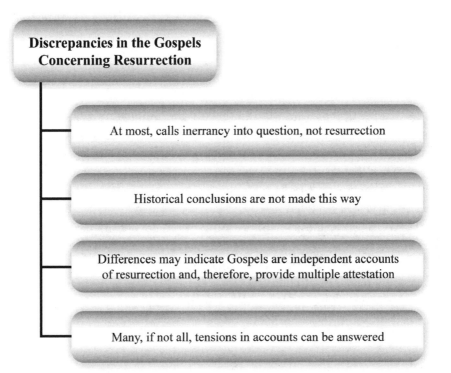

"The Resurrection accounts are biased."

Another criticism offered by skeptics is that all we have are the testimonies of Christians, who most likely transferred their personal biases and traditions into their writings. Therefore, these writings must be considered biased. Thus, we must suspect that they do not accurately report what really occurred.

This objection is plagued with several difficulties.

First, Paul's testimony is stronger than that of a neutral witness of the risen Jesus, since his bias ran in the *opposite* direction. He was certainly not sympathetic to the Christian cause. Rather he viewed Jesus as a false Christ and severely persecuted his followers. The skeptic may reply, "Yes, but after he became a Christian, he lost his standing as an unbiased source."

Granted that Paul lost his status as a hostile source *after* he became a Christian. However, he maintained hostility toward Christianity right up to the time when he believed. So we still have an appearance of the risen Jesus as the reason for the belief of a hostile source.

With one who persists in asserting that Christians still lack the testimony of someone who saw Jesus risen and did not convert, we might ask, "If someone actually witnessed the risen Jesus and was not changed by the experience, wouldn't this indicate that the person was too biased against Jesus to act on the facts? Biases go both ways." We would question the testimony of a person who really saw the raised Jesus and still rejected him.

Second, the biases of James the brother of Jesus also ran contrary to Christianity. The Gospels report that he was an unbeliever during the life of Jesus. Later we find reports of the risen Jesus appearing to James (1 Cor. 15:7a) and of his death for his belief that Jesus was the risen Messiah (see pp. 67–69). So with testimonies in our hands from the disciples Paul and James, we have examples of friends and foes who believed that the risen Jesus had appeared to them.

Third, recognizing the bias of an author does not automatically merit the conclusion that he or she has distorted the facts.[8] Modern Jewish historians of the Nazi holocaust have very carefully chronicled Nazi atrocities because they are passionately committed to exposing what really occurred, whereas revisionist historians (mostly Gentile) tend to downplay the facts. In this case, personal bias encourages historical accuracy.[9]

Fourth, if we reject the testimony of all interested parties, we will have to reject most of our standard historical sources. The authors of such works often would not be writing unless they had a personal interest. It is the role of the historian to comb through the literature and attempt to see past the writer's personal biases to ascertain what really happened. A good example of this is found in the writings of the ancient Roman historian, Tacitus (A.D. 55–117). He opens his *Annals* with the claim to write "without anger or partiality, from whose motives I am far removed."[10] However, obvious statements to the contrary are present in his work.[11] Yet these biased remarks do not disqualify much of what Tacitus writes as history. Today's historians usually can evaluate bias and separate questionable material from the core material of the events described. As a result of our employment of historical-critical procedures, Tacitus may still be regarded as our most reliable source for Roman history during the period about which he writes.[12]

Fifth, the skeptic must be careful not to commit the *genetic fallacy*. We must recognize the difference between understanding why something is true versus understanding why something is believed or how one came to believe that it is true. There is no problem if the latter is the reason for the former. For example, Bill is presenting evidence for Jesus' resurrection to Steve. Steve attempts to cast doubt on Bill's evidence by saying that the reason Bill believes Jesus' resurrection is because he was brought up as a Bible believing Christian. Steve is committing the genetic fallacy. He is shifting the issue onto why Bill may have initially believed that Jesus rose rather than the truth of that belief. He's not answering Bill's evidence.

Likewise, to claim that we cannot rationally believe Jesus rose because the New Testament authors were biased toward Jesus is to commit the genetic fallacy. Such an argument fails to address the data they provide. The prominent New Testament historian N. T. Wright comments, "It must be asserted most strongly that to discover that a particular writer has a 'bias' tells us nothing whatever about the value of the information he or she presents. It merely bids us be aware of the bias (and of our own, for that matter), and to assess the material according to as many sources as we can."[13]

Sixth, the skeptic must also avoid arguing *ad hominem*, a tactic that focuses on the person rather than on the content of the argument being considered. Someone who claims that the arguments of an atheist are invalid because the atheist has a bias against God is using an *ad hominem* argument. Here, the critic focuses on the person and not on the arguments presented by the atheist. The atheist may be very biased against God. But this says nothing in terms of the legitimacy of the arguments, which must be evaluated on their own merits.

Bias does not mean lying. Someone may be biased and correct. Likewise, even if the testimony that Jesus rose from the dead came from those who would benefit from the miraculous reappearance of their teacher, this does not necessarily mean that they lied about it, especially since the data indicate that they were not (see discussion on Fraud 1, p. 93–95).

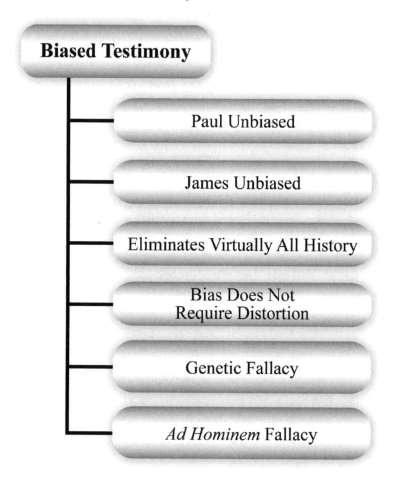

"A risen Jesus would have made a greater impact."

If Jesus performed all the miracles that are claimed, especially his resurrection from the dead, why isn't he mentioned in the first century beyond a few Christian sources? A risen Jesus would have made more of an impact on his culture.

In the first century, people did not have access to all of our convenient ways to record and preserve the facts about events. Further, we know that much of what was recorded in the past has been lost. New Testament scholar Craig Blomberg, who served as an editor for and contributor to a large scholarly work on the Gospels,[14] provides four reasons why more was not written on Jesus in his time: "the humble beginnings of Christianity, the remote location of Palestine on the eastern frontiers of the Roman empire, the small percentage of the works of ancient Graeco-Roman historians which have survived, and the lack of attention paid by those which are extant to Jewish figures in general."[15] We know that about half of what the Roman historian Tacitus wrote is no longer available. Only a fragment of what Thallus wrote in the first century about ancient Mediterranian history has survived. Suetonius is aware of the writings of Asclepiades of Mendes, yet, his writings are no longer available. Herod the Great's secretary, Nicholas of Damascus, wrote a *Universal History* in 144 books, none of which have survived. Livy, the great Roman historian, has suffered a similar fate. Only his early books and excerpts of the rest survive.[16]

We also know of several early Christian writings that are no longer available. For example, an influential church leader of the early part of the second century named Papias wrote five books that are quoted by several early church fathers.[17] However, none of these books has survived. Only a few citations and slight summary information remain.[18] Quadratus was a Christian leader who wrote a defense of the Christian faith to the Roman Emperor Hadrian around 125. However, if Eusebius had not quoted a paragraph and mentioned his work, we would be totally unaware of its composition.[19] The five books of *Recollections*, written by Hegesippus in the second century, have likewise been lost. Only fragments have been preserved, mostly by Eusebius.

What we have concerning Jesus actually is impressive. We can start with approximately nine traditional authors of the New Testament. If we consider the critical thesis that other authors wrote the pastoral letters and such letters as Ephesians and 2 Thessalonians, we'd have an even larger number. Another twenty early Christian authors[20] and four heretical writings mention Jesus within 150 years of his death on the cross.[21] Moreover, nine secular, non-Christian sources mention Jesus within the 150 years: Josephus, the Jewish historian; Tacitus, the Roman historian; Pliny the Younger, a politician of Rome; Phlegon, a freed slave who wrote histories; Lucian, the Greek satirist; Celsus, a Roman philosopher; and probably the historians Suetonius and Thallus, as well as the prisoner Mara Bar-Serapion.[22] In all, at least forty-two authors, nine of them secular, mention Jesus within 150 years of his death.

In comparison, let's take a look at Julius Caesar, one of Rome's most prominent figures. Caesar is well known for his military conquests. After his Gallic Wars, he made the famous statement, "I came, I saw, I conquered." Only five sources report his military conquests: writings by Caesar himself, Cicero, Livy, the Salona Decree, and Appian.[23] If Julius Caesar really made a profound impact on Roman society, why didn't more writers of antiquity mention his great military accomplishments? No one questions whether Julius did make a tremendous impact on the Roman Empire. It is evident that he did. Yet in those 150 years after his death, more *non-Christian authors alone* comment on Jesus than all of the sources who mentioned Julius Caesar's great military conquests within 150 years of *his* death.

Let's look at an even better example, a contemporary of Jesus. Tiberius Caesar was the Roman emperor at the time of Jesus' ministry and execution. Tiberius is mentioned by ten sources within 150 years of his death: Tacitus, Suetonius, Velleius Paterculus, Plutarch, Pliny the Elder, Strabo, Seneca, Valerius Maximus, Josephus, and Luke.[24] Compare that to Jesus' forty-two total sources in the same length of time. That's more than four times the number of total sources who mention the Roman emperor during roughly the same period. If we only considered the number of secular non-Christian sources who mention Jesus and Tiberius within 150 years of their lives, we arrive at a tie of nine each.[25]

"The disciples experienced 'something.' What it was will never be known."

Surely the disciples did have some kind of experience. The prevalent reaction among critical scholars today who reject Jesus' resurrection is to agree that something happened, but add that we will never know exactly what transpired. A few points may help us address this type of response.

First, this response is a *rejection of the conclusion* that Jesus rose from the dead, rather than a *rejection of the evidence*. It is not even a denial of the evidence.

Second, it is not what we do not know that is the issue here. It is what we do know. The facts are pieces of a puzzle that when assembled looks only like a resurrection. These facts cannot be ignored, especially since we have chiefly used only the minimal data that are so well evidenced that virtually all critical scholars who address these issues admit them. Two thousand years of attempts by critics to account for these facts by natural causes have failed. Most modern critics even grant this. Therefore, Jesus' resurrection from the dead is the only plausible explanation for the known facts.

Third, the context in which the evidence for Jesus' resurrection appears increases the likelihood that it occurred. This context includes Jesus' claims to divinity,[26] that he was known as a powerful miracle-worker,[27] and other data that support God's existence.[28] In the absence of a valid reason for rejecting Jesus' resurrection, nothing prevents a rational person from concluding that Jesus' resurrection from the dead was an event in history.

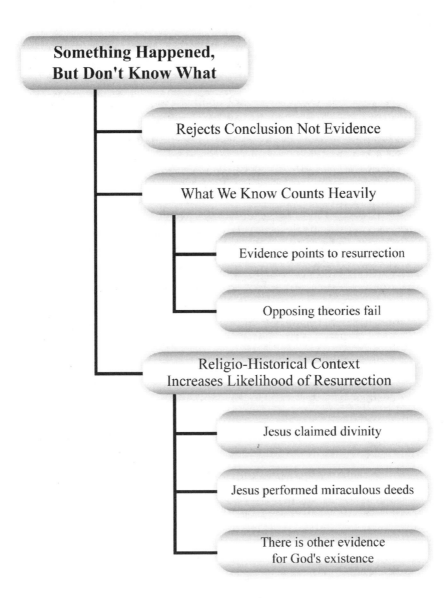

Something Happened, But Don't Know What

- Rejects Conclusion Not Evidence
- What We Know Counts Heavily
  - Evidence points to resurrection
  - Opposing theories fail
- Religio-Historical Context Increases Likelihood of Resurrection
  - Jesus claimed divinity
  - Jesus performed miraculous deeds
  - There is other evidence for God's existence

"Jesus was an extraterrestrial alien."

Even if Jesus rose from the dead, this does not mean that he was who he claimed to be. Perhaps he was an alien from another planet who was playing some sort of cosmic joke on humankind and led us to believe that he died on a cross and rose from the dead. While this objection may be heard on a popular level, it is never raised in a scholarly context.

A skeptic who brings up an objection like this may be grasping for any argument. If you believe that the person is not truly seeking the truth at this point, smile and say something like, "It may be better to deal with the academic criticisms first, and if there is any time left over, we can look at the fun ones." This lets the person know that such a theory should not be given much merit, without being insulting.[29] Or you could answer with a smile, "Yes, I agree. Jesus was an alien. As the Son of God, he was certainly not from this world!"

But what if the alien theory comes from someone who views it as a serious opposing theory? How will we answer the charge that Jesus may have been an alien?

Alien theory does not deny Jesus' resurrection, only God as the cause of it.

We observe that the life of Jesus differs substantially from typical alien accounts. Aliens usually arrive in a spaceship; Jesus was born on earth. Aliens usually appear for a very short time; Jesus was on earth for over thirty years. The usual report of an encounter with aliens describes them as abusive; Jesus was loving and compassionate.

The supposition that life exists in the universe outside Earth is questionable. Contrary to the popular media's portrayal of aliens in movies like *ET, Cocoon,* and *Contact,* the scientific evidence from astrophysics within the past thirty-five years makes it seem increasingly improbable that life exists anywhere else in the cosmos.

Cosmic constants are factors in our universe that if altered just a little, would make life impossible. Many factors must be within an extremely narrow range in order for a planet to meet just the most basic criteria for sustaining life. Constants relate to planet-star relationships, planet-moon relationships, the degree which a planet rotates on its axis, and many other conditions.

It is frequently stated that there must be life somewhere else in such a vast universe. Even if cosmic constants require that a planet meet an extremely narrow range of conditions to support life, given the immensity of our universe and the number of planets, wouldn't the existence of life elsewhere be probable? The estimated number of galaxies in the cosmos is a little fewer than 1 trillion. Each galaxy has an average of 100 billion stars (10^{22}). An average estimate of the number of planets is one planet per 1,000 stars (10^{19}). The existence of 10,000,000,000,000,000,000 planets would seem almost to require that the conditions for life to exist must come together somewhere other than Earth. Or does it?

The required constants for planet-star relationships themselves would eliminate 99.9 percent of all potential planets. When additional constants are considered, the odds of the existence of a planet capable of sustaining life are $1:10^{25}$. Since the total estimated number of planets in the universe is 10^{19}, it seems that we would not expect life to exist on even one planet, much less any others.[30]

There is good evidence that God exists.[31] Not only does the resurrection of Jesus provide strong evidence for the existence of God, but new understandings of complexity make recent arguments for an intelligent Designer of the universe very compelling. Scientific discoveries made during the past thirty-five years in the fields of molecular biology and astrophysics have increased awareness of the intelligence behind creation.[32] In addition, many have found compelling the arguments for an eternal first Cause of everything.[33] Therefore, this interconnected account involving Jesus' resurrection is better explained as God's confirmation of his claims to divinity than an alien playing a cosmic joke.[34]

Chapter 8

Naturally Speaking

The Challenge of Naturalism

Naturalism views the natural world as the sum of reality, usually holding that scientific investigation is the best or even the only path to knowledge and that only material phenomena are real. Those who embrace naturalism hold that there is no such thing as a supernatural realm. God cannot be tested empirically (i.e., by observation and experiment) or by any other means. Some naturalists think that matters that cannot be resolved scientifically have little value. What is nonscience is nonsense. This view is prevalent in Western society and has permeated the scientific community, spilling over into other disciplines.[1] Therefore, additional space will be given here to address the various objections offered by naturalists and others who reject miraculous events, in spite of the evidence that might be raised in their favor.

The arguments offered by naturalists are a major departure from the other opposing theories we have discussed thus far. You will notice that the objections included in this chapter are made apart from any investigation of the historical facts that may argue in favor of miracles, or Jesus' resurrection. In other words, they are philosophical considerations that are made without viewing the available evidences. Philosophers refer to these as *a priori* arguments. An example of an *a priori* argument would be to say, "No matter what evidence you are going to use in favor of miracles, such events never occur because they would contradict the laws of nature." In contrast, the opposing theories we have discussed in the two previous chapters attempt to address the known data and provide an alternate explanation for the observed phenomena. Philosophers refer to these as *a posteriori* arguments because they take a scientific or historical angle, entertaining the available facts. An example of an *a posteriori* argument would be to say, "I can explain all of your evidence for the Resurrection without resorting to anything supernatural," followed by the attempt to defend a particular opposing theory like those we have seen in this volume.

This may not seem like a big difference at first look. However, it will not take long for you to recognize that the way you respond to an *a priori* argument is quite different from the manner in which you answer an *a posteriori* argument. For example, if I desired to argue on behalf of miracles, I might challenge the philosopher taking the *a priori* argument above by saying, "How do you know that miracles are impossible? The historical evidence that I am presenting may just be what we need to refute your theory." Better yet, I might walk onto the philosopher's home turf and challenge the reasons for holding such a philosophical position in the first place. In this chapter we will use both approaches. On the other hand, we have already learned to challenge *a posteriori* arguments by saying, "Your alternative approach does not explain the data I am presenting. In fact, it fails by a large margin."

Most skeptics still respect the results of scientific research, continuing an outlook that has blossomed over the last century or two. We have learned a remarkable amount of information through the process of observation and testing known as the scientific method. What can science tell us about the possibility of a person rising from the dead? Has science shown that resurrections are impossible? Of what relevance are the laws of nature? Are there philosophical reasons why Jesus' resurrection was impossible or that, even if it occurred, we can never know it was a miracle, since science cannot verify it?

Let's look now at the general objections to miracles offered by naturalists. You may encounter them frequently from more sophisticated skeptics, such as some of those on the Internet and especially college students. Therefore, it is worth the effort to familiarize yourself with the following objections and their refutations.[2]

"Only what science can prove is true."

Some skeptics hold that scientific research is the only means of achieving new knowledge and assert that miracles such as Jesus' resurrection simply do not pass the test. So there is no way to verify that Jesus rose from the dead, since science has no tools with which to verify such an event.

This basic objection may be posed in many guises. For instance, it might simply be said that Christians do not have enough quality evidence for the Resurrection, or that, unlike scientific data, the historical evidence for miracles is not predictable or repeatable. Others think that scientific testing supersedes historical research and that history has no test for gullibility, so again we must rule out the Resurrection. These various responses have in common the belief that, somehow, the standards of the scientific method outweigh any historical data that may possibly exist for the Resurrection.

The first major problem with this objection is that the scientific method is limited in its ability to observe and test. Like history, this is simply part of the rules of research. Scientists regularly concede this. Popularly, it might be said that we can't measure love with a Geiger counter. Perhaps some examples would be helpful. Biology is frequently unable to predict outcomes. Geology and paleontology, like history, involve many situations that are not repeatable. As much as we might like to do so, we can't relive the dinosaur era.[3] Lastly, the scientific method cannot totally eliminate gullibility, other misrepresentations of the data, or plain old mistakes made by scientists. As with history, we must always inspect research results and require careful reporting practices. Thus, science has its own limitations that cannot serve as an excuse to rule out the supernatural.

Second, to claim that truth is found only in what science can test and "prove" is self-refuting. "There is no such thing as truth; and that's the truth" is a self-refuting statement. If it is true that truth does not exist, then the statement itself is false—because that comment professes to be true. If it is false that there is no such thing as truth, then at least some truth exists because the statement itself is true. Either way, some things are true and the statement that denies it is false.[4]

But what is not as easily recognized is that the person who claims that truth is found only in what science can prove makes the same sort of self-refuting claim. Using only the scientific method, can the skeptic show that truth is found only in what science can demonstrate? The answer is obviously, no. There is no way to test the claim that only science yields truth. Lock a scientist in a room with all of the latest hi-tech equipment and ask for proof that only what science proves is true. The scientist will not succeed. The *rule* that science is the only way to know something is itself unscientific; it cannot be tested. So the claim that only science can demonstrate truth actually flunks its own test, since it cannot validate itself! Therefore, it is illegitimate to require that religion be proved in a test tube.[5]

Third, to require that historical events be predictable or repeatable also turns out to be self-refuting, since these are just different ways of stating that science is the only way to know something. Few historical events of any kind are truly predictable in the sense a scientist means, and none are, strictly speaking, repeatable. But once again, we have the same dilemma. The rule that levels these sorts of requirements is not scientific, hence it fails its own test. Further, should we reject the veracity of statements that Julius Caesar crossed the Rubicon River or that George Washington was the first president of the United States? These events are not repeatable. Even worse for the scientist, unless the historical enterprise is reliable, science as we know it could not even proceed, since scientists must build on the shoulders of those who have made past discoveries. There is insufficient time in one's life to retest all former experiments before moving onward. Little progress could be made without historical assumptions. So we have a host of problems if historians must work only according to the scientific method. The system would be self-defeating for the scientist and an unscientific requirement that fails its own criteria.[6]

Fourth, while science perhaps cannot measure God's activity, there is no reason why we cannot consider non-supernatural portions of claims concerning the Resurrection. For example, did Jesus die? Was he seen alive at some later time? The scientist or historian could evaluate the conclusion: "Jesus was seen alive after his death." However, *in his capacity as a scientist or historian*, he perhaps could not draw the conclusion: "God raised Jesus from the dead," since he is unable to detect God's actions with the tools of his trade.[7]

Of course, this would not prohibit the scientist or historian from *believing* that God raised Jesus, and many of them do.[8] On the other hand, the philosopher or theologian can argue that God raised Jesus based on other well-founded data (see pp. 174–81).

"Science proves that people do not come back to life."

Let's look at another specific example or extension of the previous objection. A resurrection requires dead cells to come back to life. Hasn't science determined that such a state of affairs is clearly impossible? Through observation and testing, scientific laws are formulated in order to state what normally happens under certain circumstances. These laws have been observed throughout the past. We get similar results most of the time. The historian must employ his or her knowledge of scientific laws as they currently exist in order to determine whether something happened in the past. It may make sense that these laws, which produce consistent results today, produced the same results in the past. By understanding the laws of nature and how living cells work, we know that, when humans die, they stay dead. Their cells do not just regenerate, allowing them to return to life.

Therefore, assuming that the laws of nature are consistent, many skeptics claim that it is irrational to believe that Jesus rose from the dead, since science has proven that resurrections are impossible. But does scientific investigation really show that resurrections are impossible—period? Not at all. First, what science has shown is that a person is not going to rise from the dead by *natural causes*. But this does not apply to Jesus' resurrection, since we are not claiming that Jesus came back to life naturally.[9] The writers of the New Testament asserted that it was God who raised Jesus from the dead.[10]

Second, the Resurrection is not an isolated event; it occurred in an interconnected religio-historical context that helps to provide meaning. This context includes such facts as Jesus' personal claims to divinity,[11] his deeds that appeared miraculous in nature,[12] and possibly even his predictions concerning his resurrection.[13] Jesus' life and claims happened within a context in which his resurrection is right at home.

If someone reported that they had seen Mike's grandfather walking around after being dead for over twenty years, we would have no context in which to believe them. Mike's grandfather never claimed divinity, never performed a miracle, and did not predict that he would rise from the dead. Obviously, we would rightly have many serious questions. It is much more likely that some sort of misunderstanding has taken place. But if we also saw Mike's grandfather, especially in groups and on several occasions, in contexts where we could check out the circumstances, we might begin to wonder.

Now if, unlike Mike's grandfather, these events *did* occur in a religiously significant environment, as in Jesus' case, the situation would differ on another level. We might even begin thinking about the possibility that God was at work. It seems that this is what happened to Jesus' disciples, as well as to James, the brother of Jesus, and Paul. The evidence overwhelmed them all.[14]

Thus, this objection does not apply to Jesus' resurrection unless a naturalistic theory is workable, and we've already seen how difficult it is to find one that works. We should also remember that, as we have said, this objection is an extension of the previous scientific response. As such, it is additionally burdened by many of those objections, as well as a few that we will now list.

"Science can explain everything, so we don't need a God."

"Science will one day explain everything, so we don't need a God," says the naturalist, who may argue that often "God" has been suggested as the cause of everything a culture cannot understand. God was handy to fill in the holes in current knowledge. This is sometimes referred to as a "God of the gaps" theory. For example, prior to a scientific understanding of weather phenomena, some may have described thunder and lightning as the audible and visible indications of God's anger. An eclipse might have signaled even greater wrath. Further, since science can explain much more today, there is a good chance that, as we learn still more in the future, science will be able to one day explain everything, including Jesus' resurrection. Then there will be no need to appeal to "God of the gaps" explanations.

First, the existence of "God of the gaps" explanations in the past no more undermines current arguments for God than discarded scientific theories and medical beliefs undermine today's science and medicine. The mistakes in each should only drive us to more careful theorizing in the future.

Second, the criticism that God is simply a way to explain unknown phenomena commits the informal logical error known as the *genetic fallacy*. Remember, this occurs when it is assumed that discovering how a belief originated (e.g., God of the gaps) is sufficient to explain that belief. However, it is a fallacy because it attacks the origin of a view instead of the view itself, which could still be correct. For example, that some ancient Romans may have thought that Jupiter was responsible for their victory over the Gauls, does not nullify the historical factuality of the battle or Rome's great victory.

Third, what we already know from respected disciplines like medical science, history, and psychology is precisely what renders the conclusion of Jesus' resurrection so compelling. Conversely, these same disciplines disprove natural explanations of this event, as we have seen. Interestingly enough, without a workable opposing theory, the skeptic must be careful not to substitute a "naturalism of the gaps" view. This occurs when critics have little ground on which to oppose the Resurrection, yet they conclude that it still could not have happened (which is a mere denial). Or they simply refuse to believe in spite of not having a viable counter response. We must not suspend judgment when adequate evidence is available upon which to make a decision. The Resurrection challenges nature's laws, and there does not seem to be a way to incorporate it within nature.

Fourth, it is an unjustified leap to proclaim that at some future point in time we will find a scientific answer for the resurrection of Jesus. This could be said about almost anything. For example, would it be permissible for someone to proclaim that at some undisclosed future point we will overturn some well-founded scientific or historical position and then begin acting as if this hope already is a reality? Miracle-claims are always subject to future investigation, so what is the issue? If the Resurrection is attacked at some future date, Christians will research and respond accordingly. In the meantime, we should not over-rule the possibility of the Resurrection *without* a viable reason.

"If God exists, he cannot intervene in natural laws."

"If God exists, he is not stronger than the laws of nature, or he may choose not to act in our world." This might be the position of a deist who holds that God exists and created the world, but does not get involved in his creation. It is also held by one who thinks that God is unable to overrule his laws. Of course, these are not natural-istic positions, but someone with this view of God agrees with the naturalist that God does not act in history, so he did not perform Jesus' resurrection.

This view is beset with a number of problems. First, where do these questioners receive their information? This conclusion would not seem to be arrived at through scientific means, since we are regularly told that science can know nothing about God. Therefore, these philosophical beliefs that God cannot supersede the laws of nature must be justified some other way.

If God created the universe, including the natural laws that govern it, what would prohibit such a Being from suspending or temporarily overriding those same laws to perform a miracle? God cannot perform logically impossible acts such as making a married bachelor or a square circle. However, there is nothing logically impossible about God suspending the physical laws he set up, especially if he wished to send a message. And if he acted miraculously to create the world, it would certainly seem that he can work further in nature. In the end, it does not seem there is any reason, either scientific or philosophical, why God could not intervene in the world he created if he chose. In the absence of any compelling reasons to reject this possibility, we must be open to it.

Third, Jesus' resurrection is an excellent reason for concluding that God not only *could* act miraculously in the world, but that he actually *did*.

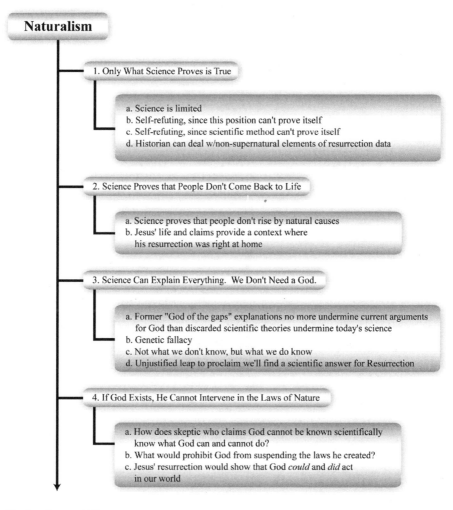

Naturalism

1. Only What Science Proves is True

    a. Science is limited
    b. Self-refuting, since this position can't prove itself
    c. Self-refuting, since scientific method can't prove itself
    d. Historian can deal w/non-supernatural elements of resurrection data

2. Science Proves that People Don't Come Back to Life

    a. Science proves that people don't rise by natural causes
    b. Jesus' life and claims provide a context where
       his resurrection was right at home

3. Science Can Explain Everything. We Don't Need a God.

    a. Former "God of the gaps" explanations no more undermine current arguments
       for God than discarded scientific theories undermine today's science
    b. Genetic fallacy
    c. Not what we don't know, but what we do know
    d. Unjustified leap to proclaim we'll find a scientific answer for Resurrection

4. If God Exists, He Cannot Intervene in the Laws of Nature

    a. How does skeptic who claims God cannot be known scientifically
       know what God can and cannot do?
    b. What would prohibit God from suspending the laws he created?
    c. Jesus' resurrection would show that God *could* and *did* act
       in our world

(Continued on pg. 145)

"Science must assume a naturalistic explanation for everything."

Not wishing to abandon a scientific demeanor, the skeptic might continue along a related path to explain, "Science must assume that all events have natural causes." A scientist would most likely assume that, even if there were good evidence that a dead man had been seen later, this would have to be explained in a natural manner. Once again, this objection to the Resurrection could be expressed variously, using one or more of the theories that we discussed in chapters 6 and 7.[15]

Or a person might allow that such an occurrence as someone returning to life did occur as a freak event of nature, a one-of-a-kind set of occurrences that, in spite of appearances, was really quite natural as the result of an unusual confluence of natural properties we do not yet understand. After all, strange things do happen. Or maybe a specific strategy would be proposed: "We should expand our concept of nature's laws to make room for such an event that is otherwise unexplainable in natural terms." Or someone could charge that, as long as something occurs in nature, we will simply call it a natural event.

The force of all such strategies is to keep scientific reasoning in control of the explanation, to avoid the idea of divinity superseding nature. These responses are really quite creative. But they still face a number of serious problems such as the following.

First, although natural causes should be considered first, a supernatural cause may be considered when all natural theories fail, and there is credible evidence in favor of divine intervention. True, we should be careful that this not become a "God-of-the-gaps" solution, where God becomes the default answer whenever we cannot think of something else. Nevertheless, when the facts seem to point strongly to the divine, and all natural explanations appear highly improbable, a supernatural explanation should be strongly considered. Another reason to keep an open mind is that we cannot apply the scientific method to a supernatural occurrence if one comes along. That is a limitation on science, not on our ability to know.[16] Molecular biologist, Michael Behe, clearly states the dilemma for the scientist:

> Imagine a room in which a body lies crushed, flat as a pancake. A dozen detectives crawl around, examining the floor with magnifying glasses for any clue to the identity of a perpetrator. In the middle of the room, next to the body, stands a large, gray elephant. The detectives carefully avoid bumping into the pachyderm's legs as they crawl, and never even glance at it. Over time the detectives get frustrated with their lack of progress but resolutely press on, looking even more closely at the floor. You see, textbooks say detectives must "get their man," so they never consider elephants.[17]

When it comes to Jesus' resurrection, Behe's elephant may represent God. The complete inability of opposing theories to account for the disciples' beliefs that they had seen the risen Jesus, coupled with supporting evidence favoring the truthfulness of their beliefs, leaves Jesus' resurrection as the best explanation to account for our collection of historical data.[18] In fact, it is the only plausible explanation that accounts for it.

Second, the laws of nature would be no match for an omnipotent God who chooses to act by superseding those laws. Thus, the entire naturalistic mindset misses the forest for the trees. The issue here is not whether everything can be explained by the laws of nature. The crucial question is whether there is a God who may have superseded nature by a superior power. Scientific reliance upon natural processes to explain everything does not answer the question of whether all things that happen are controlled only by natural processes. God may have momentously stepped in to do something that nature cannot explain. Further, if we had evidence that such an event occurred, this data would actually be *superior* to the natural working of nature's laws, since that would mean that God performed an act for which nature cannot account. The result of this critique is that historical evidence might, for a brief time, actually supersede scientific evidence, since it means that, *at that very moment*, God intervened in nature.

Third, certain miracles have characteristics that show that they are actually caused by interferences with the laws of nature. Philosopher Richard Swinburne suggests that the best case for recognizing a miracle would include all of the following: (1) It has never happened before or since; (2) the event definitely cannot be accounted for by a current law of nature; and (3) no foreseeable revision of our statement of a law of nature could explain the event in natural terms. Swinburne claims that a resurrection meets these criteria.[19] Intriguingly, resurrection claims in other religions are not well-attested.[20] Will the naturalist say that dead men do not rise, except for Jesus Christ?

Fourth, when a naturalist *insists* on assuming that all events *must* be interpreted naturally, or that nature must always be made to allow only natural events, he is arguing in a circle because he *assumes* his naturalistic stance in order to pronounce judgment on other conceptual issues. But how does he know that naturalism is correct, especially when good evidence for a divine miracle exists?

"Even if a miracle occurred, we could never know that it was a miracle."

This objection does not so much question the evidence for a miracle, but wonders how we can trace it to God. Like other objections we have examined in this chapter, this can be raised from various directions. Events do not come with nametags on them identifying their cause, so, short of such a signature, how could we ever know that God performed it? Besides the event itself, we need a pointer that will help to indicate its significance. Otherwise, even if we discover an incredibly strange event, we could treat it like a "natural miracle"—a one of a kind natural oddity (like a group hallucination) instead of an act of God.

At least three problems exist with this view. First, if God exists, then we have a good reason to consider a link between some events and a divine cause.[21]

Second, signs exist that identify an act as a miracle. It is true that a historical event, by itself, could never be labeled as a miracle without additional criteria. We need another yardstick, besides the event itself, to indicate that God performed it. And we have just these sorts of pointers in the case of the Resurrection. In addition to the outstanding evidence for Jesus' resurrection, we have the religio-historical context of his claims to divinity (see chapter 10). He was known as a powerful miracle-worker.[22] He claimed that how people responded to him would determine where they spent eternity. Further, no plausible natural explanations can account for all of the known facts regarding the resurrection of Jesus. Never in history has there been such a unique combination of events, along with additional criteria.

Third, expanding the laws of nature in order to eliminate the miraculous nature of the data surrounding Jesus' resurrection creates more problems. For example, some will argue that it is preferable to accept that there were "natural miracles," or exceptional oddities like mass hallucinations, to accepting the existence of real supernatural miracles. But a huge problem is that no single natural option, however unusual, can explain all of the evidence for the Resurrection, even if we stretch to this further position of referring to it as a natural miracle.

On the one hand, such an adjusted hallucination theory would still leave facts like the empty tomb, Paul's conversion, James's conversion, and other facts unexplained. But on the other hand, this revised theory is even more problematic than it first appears. It does not simply require one group hallucination, but several of them. A separate group hallucination would be required for every time Jesus appeared to a group of people. Instead of a single group hallucination, which is foreign to modern psychology, we need *several* of these "natural miracles" in a row. Should we conclude, then, that mass hallucinations do not occur, except among Jesus' followers, and then they did so *repeatedly?* Certainly, this would seem to be a highly problematic admission for naturalists, since it appears in itself to border on a real miracle. And even if we accepted that possibility, we *still* would not have resolved several of the critically acknowledged historical facts.

A resurrection looks more plausible than these repeated rational contortions.

"Miracles in other religions count against Christian miracle claims."

Some critics may charge that Christians must disprove miracles in all other religious traditions in order to let their examples stand. Or they complain that non-Christian miracle claims somehow make Christian claims less likely. Although popular, this sort of response is opposed by a host of issues that are frequently overlooked.

First, genuine miracles could happen among unbelievers and still be entirely compatible with Christian belief. Thus, Christians have no obligation to disprove miracle claims in other religious traditions. Even in Scripture, God acted supernaturally among unbelievers, such as healing Naaman's leprosy.[23] If Scripture is correct, it may even be the case that demons can perform actual supernatural wonders or counterfeit illusions designed to confound people.

Second, miracles in other religions tend to be rather poorly attested. Their questionable factuality as historical events cannot rule out the possibility that a real miracle with good attestation could occur.[24] Miracle stories involving founders of major world religions such as Buddha or Krishna, appear centuries after the events they are said to record. In other cases, like the lives of Confucius and Lao-Tzu, there are no serious miracle claims. Historian Edwin Yamauchi, one of the foremost scholars on ancient world cultures and religions, argues that the reports relating to miracles by Jesus and the accounts of his resurrection are unique.[25]

Third, miracles in other religions usually can be dismissed with a plausible opposing theory, whereas we have seen that opposing theories fail to answer the facts regarding Jesus' resurrection.[26]

"There is a huge mountain of probability against an event ever being an act of God."

Another major scruple stands behind many naturalistic objections to miracles. The critic says, "Even before investigating a claimed miracle, we know that there is a huge mountain of probability against it ever being an act of God."

To say that corpses stay dead much more often than they come back to life is a wild understatement. In short, the world we inhabit does not make room for the miraculous. It is simply not that kind of universe. So even if we cannot explain what happened to Jesus after his crucifixion, this reasoning would insist that there could not have been a resurrection. The technical name for the issue that is being raised by this sort of objection is *antecedent probability*. Even before an investigation, miracles are so improbable because of the evidence against miracles from past experience, that they are considered highly unlikely, if not practically impossible.[27]

This mindset seems to make sense and is a thoughtful approach, but it has serious problems:

First, if the sort of God described in the Christian Scriptures exists, there is no reason to reject the possibility of miracles as the explanation of well-attested events for which no plausible natural explanations exist.[28]

Second, to say that we should deny Jesus' resurrection, no matter how strong the evidence, is to be biased against the possibility that this could be the very case for which we have been looking.[29]

Third, the entire foundation on which this objection is based is fatally flawed. We learn about the nature of this world by our experience of reality. Our knowledge of the world around us is gained by gathering information. When we cast our net into the sea of experience, certain data turn up. If we cast our net into a small lake, we won't be sampling much of the ocean's richness. If we make a worldwide cast, we have a more accurate basis for what exists.

Here is the crunch. If we cast into our own little lakes, it is not surprising if we do not obtain an accurate sampling of experience. However, a worldwide cast will reveal many reports of unusual occurrences that might be investigated and determined to be miracles. Surely most of the supernatural claims would be found to be untrustworthy. But before making the absolute observation that no miracles have ever happened, someone would have to investigate each report.

It only takes a *single justified example* to show that there is more to reality than a physical world. We must examine an impossibly large mountain of data to justify the naturalistic conclusion assumed in this objection. When data relating to the supernatural are examined, unwanted evidence is cast aside. This point does not claim that we actually have such evidence.[30] Rather it is simply a straightforward challenge to naturalistic methods.

Evidence exists that there have been (and perhaps still are) supernatural phenomena. Although not as well-attested as Jesus' resurrection, to the extent that they can be confirmed, they should significantly change our ideas concerning the nature of this world. Consequently, not only would the backdrop for the entire naturalistic objection disappear, but also it would actually turn the subject in the opposite direction. If other miracles do occur, then the Resurrection is far more plausible. Although we cannot defend such specifics here, we do

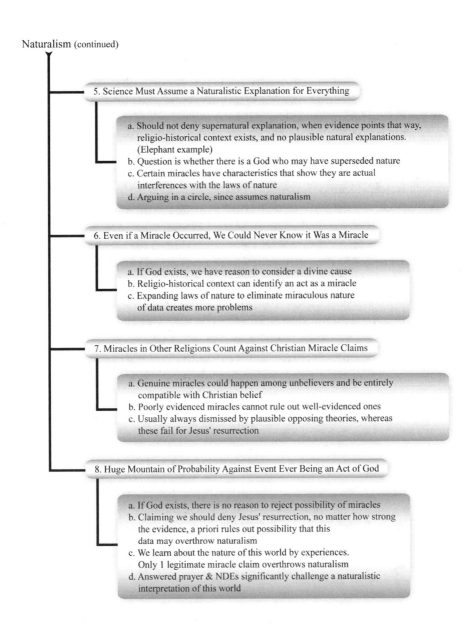

Naturalism (continued)

5. Science Must Assume a Naturalistic Explanation for Everything

a. Should not deny supernatural explanation, when evidence points that way, religio-historical context exists, and no plausible natural explanations. (Elephant example)
b. Question is whether there is a God who may have superseded nature
c. Certain miracles have characteristics that show they are actual interferences with the laws of nature
d. Arguing in a circle, since assumes naturalism

6. Even if a Miracle Occurred, We Could Never Know it Was a Miracle

a. If God exists, we have reason to consider a divine cause
b. Religio-historical context can identify an act as a miracle
c. Expanding laws of nature to eliminate miraculous nature of data creates more problems

7. Miracles in Other Religions Count Against Christian Miracle Claims

a. Genuine miracles could happen among unbelievers and be entirely compatible with Christian belief
b. Poorly evidenced miracles cannot rule out well-evidenced ones
c. Usually always dismissed by plausible opposing theories, whereas these fail for Jesus' resurrection

8. Huge Mountain of Probability Against Event Ever Being an Act of God

a. If God exists, there is no reason to reject possibility of miracles
b. Claiming we should deny Jesus' resurrection, no matter how strong the evidence, a priori rules out possibility that this data may overthrow naturalism
c. We learn about the nature of this world by experiences. Only 1 legitimate miracle claim overthrows naturalism
d. Answered prayer & NDEs significantly challenge a naturalistic interpretation of this world

note that scientists have occasionally found ways to measure and discern a possible correlation between prayer and healing.[31] We might be able to find other potential avenues for looking at the possibility of supernatural intervention into today's history.[32] Due to its evidential nature, we will take a more-detailed look in the next section at one of these areas, "near-death" experiences.

Near-death experiences challenge naturalistic understandings.

The phenomenon that has come to be called a "near-death experience" (NDE) also provides a substantial challenge to naturalism. It might even be said that, by themselves, NDEs offer evidence that naturalism is mistaken at a key point— that of life after death. We are not interested here in the thousands of reports by those who have claimed simply to have experienced tunnels, lights, and meetings with deceased loved ones, angels, and even God. During the past few decades, however, dozens of more credible reports have been documented of individuals who returned to consciousness after being comatose or at the point of clinical death. Some of these individuals have described in amazing detail, facts about their physical surroundings that they should not have been able to know. Some have described details of medical procedures performed on them. Some have related memories of conversations that others had during their medical emergencies or even described the jewelry and clothing worn by those around them. Some accounts have given verified details about what happened outside the immediate room, down the hallway, or even miles away. The amount of verification is sometimes staggering. People blind from birth have correctly recalled visual details of things around them and outside their presence. Many of these near-death details were of events occurring when the individual had no heartbeat or brain wave activity, as indicated by "flat" EKG and EEG readings, sometimes over lengthy periods of time.[33]

A nine-year-old girl had a swimming accident and was under water for nineteen minutes. She was given very little chance of surviving. Hooked up to machines to keep her alive, she surprised everyone by regaining consciousness three days later. She took almost one hour to explain her experiences during that time. Even though Melvin Morse, the pediatrician who resuscitated her in the emergency room, reported that she was "profoundly comatose" with "fixed and dilated pupils" and without brain activity, she accurately described several details from the emergency room. Then she said that she visited heaven with an angel and had spoken with her deceased grandfather. She said that she also looked in on her family at home, and accurately described what her father, brother, and sister were doing, as well as their clothing. She knew that her mother had cooked roast chicken and rice for dinner. Since she claimed that these conditions had occurred only a couple of days before, Morse was able to verify these details with the family.[34]

Interviews with those who claim to have visited heaven often are very moving. However, these comments do not contain the verifiable landmarks possible with NDEs that describe events or conditions in this world. Only evidential reports concern us here.

Many of these reports are so well-documented that some naturalists have been forced to take them seriously, even admitting the possibility they pose of life beyond the grave. John Beloff, writing in *The Humanist*, argued that the evidence for an afterlife was so strong that humanists should just admit it and attempt to interpret it in naturalistic terms.[35] Amazingly, the well-known atheist philosopher A. J. Ayer experienced an NDE that he could not explain in natural terms: "On the face of it, these experiences, on the assumption that the last one was veritical, are rather strong evidence that death does not put an end to consciousness."[36] Ayer concluded, "My recent experiences have slightly weakened my conviction that my genuine death, which is due fairly soon, will be the end of me, though I continue to hope that it will be."[37] Atheist philosopher Antony Flew attests that NDEs "certainly constitute impressive evidence of the possibility of the occurrence of human consciousness independent of any occurrences in the human brain. . . . This evidence equally certainly weakens if it does not completely refute my argument against doctrines of a future life."[38]

The challenge provided by NDEs is just an example of numerous indications we might cite that this is most likely not a naturalistic universe. Of course, we have been arguing throughout this book that Jesus' resurrection is another evidence that needs to be answered by naturalists. Strong evidence for an afterlife as well as other pointers mentioned above, challenge naturalism's attempt to explain reality.[39] So strong is the totality of evidence that the assumption of naturalism needs to be abandoned. If naturalism is no longer tenable, the most influential backdrop for rejecting miracles is itself an illegitimate avenue.

We have seen that the naturalistic worldview fails to account adequately for the known facts that surround Jesus' resurrection. Often dressed up with scientific jargon, some naturalists appear to think that science and religion cannot coexist. The skeptic asks us to come to our senses and realize that Jesus' resurrection is shown to be nonsense by the same science that has taken us to the moon and created technology that leaves our minds reeling in amazement. When we examine the naturalist's claims, however, we discover no wedge between science and religion. Indeed the approach of the naturalist fails to disprove miracles. We also find that naturalism fails to account for some crucial phenomena regarding the nature of the world in which we live. This is indeed distressing to the critic, since what it fails to explain sheds an entirely new light on the question of Jesus' resurrection. The world is a more complicated place than some critics have thought. Strong data suggests it is a world where God has acted.

Conclusion

We have taken a good look at the major theories that oppose the proposition that Jesus rose from the dead. Over the last two thousand years, critics have developed and proposed these alternatives to account for the collection of strongly attested data. We have seen that, one by one, they have all suffered mortal blows from the known data.

Nothing can ruin an otherwise interesting argument like the facts.

Although several opposing theories have been posited, it seems to us that most of them can be traced to one difficulty. Each critic is committed to a particular worldview that cannot permit Jesus' resurrection without their worldview being overturned. This applies to atheism and deism, both of which hold that supernatural events like a resurrection from the dead cannot or do not occur. The Muslim must likewise reject Jesus' resurrection for theological reasons, since this event would confirm the Christian worldview and expose Muhammad as a deceiver or as one deceived.[40] If one does not start out with a philosophical or theological bias against the Christian God, there are no good reasons to reject the resurrection of Jesus, particularly because the evidence for it is so good. As the prominent atheist scholar Antony Flew commented, "Certainly given some beliefs about God, the occurrence of the resurrection does become enormously more likely."[41]

In spite of the strong evidence and the fact that opposing theories fail to explain it adequately, critics of Jesus' resurrection abound today within scholarship. As stated in the introduction to part 3 (See also pp. 118–9), the prevalent view among sophisticated critics today is that the disciples seemed to have experienced "something," but what it was that they experienced will never be known. The general bias is against resurrections because of the widespread acceptance of naturalism. However, we have seen that naturalism is besieged with problems. Therefore, when we consider what we do know historically about Jesus' resurrection, there simply are no opposing theories that can account for the facts.

Let's sum up where we are at this point. We have seen that the resurrection of Jesus is the cornerstone of Christianity, which stands or crumbles depending on whether this event actually occurred.

The "minimal facts approach" considers only those historical data that are so strongly attested that virtually all scholars who study the subject grant them as facts, even the majority of nonbelieving scholars. Therefore, one cannot object to Jesus' resurrection because he rejects the Bible, since in our argument nothing hinges on the trustworthiness of the Bible.

Using this approach, we have observed four minimal facts, plus a fifth fact that is granted by an impressive majority, though not virtually all of scholars. We refer to these five facts as "4+1."

We have seen that (1) *Jesus died due to crucifixion.* Subsequent to his death, (2) *the original disciples sincerely believed that Jesus rose from the dead and appeared to them.* Since the disciples themselves claimed to be eyewitnesses to the resurrected Jesus, a legend developed over time cannot account for the story. Since there is good evidence that they believed that what they said was fact, deliberate lies cannot account for it either.

We have also seen that there is good evidence to support the credibility of the disciples' claims about the resurrection of Jesus. (3) *We have credible testimony from one enemy of Christianity* and (4) *one skeptic,* both of whom converted to Christianity based on their beliefs that the risen Jesus had appeared to them. Therefore, not only did Jesus' friends believe that he had risen and appeared to them, one of his foes did as well, as did a skeptic. Moreover, (5) *the tomb was empty,* a fact totally consistent with a resurrection.

We have seen that, to date, no opposing theories have developed that can adequately account for the collection of facts we have. That leaves us with good reason to hold Jesus rose from the dead and no good reasons for rejecting it.

Therefore, Jesus' resurrection is more than the most plausible explanation to account for the data. It is the only explanation that accounts adequately for all of the facts.

Before we wrap up our studies on Jesus' resurrection, it will be beneficial to cover a few topics that are likely to come up in discussions with others. These will be the focus in the next four chapters. However, since these issues are not of primary importance, if you are feeling quite challenged or overwhelmed by all of the new information, feel free to skip over those chapters for now and proceed to chapter 13. You can return to them later.

It is time again to improve your skills. Take your second quiz using the software that came with this volume. The first quiz reinforced your knowledge of the evidence. This second quiz will help you remember how to answer objections to Jesus' resurrection. We would appreciate hearing from you when you have passed both quizzes with a minimal grade of *80 percent*. A hyperlink will be provided. Click and go to the special web site. This will let us know that another person has successfully passed both quizzes. You will also be able to download a "Certificate of Completion." Once you have completed the quizzes successfully, congratulations on your good work! We encourage you to move to Part 4 after completing the quiz. We pray that our Lord will use you more effectively than ever to share his good news with others.

Part 4

Wait! There's More!

Introduction to Part 4

Other Issues

Some issues have an importance in our discussion of Jesus' resurrection because, although they are minor points in the overall argument, they may end up playing a role in the course of our discussions with a skeptic. Because they are minor points, we should not focus on them in our discussions with skeptics. However, we should be prepared to address them. In addition, sometimes in the course of our discussions with others, the person will bring up a topic that may seem important to that person and yet really does not refute the Resurrection. When you recognize this occurring, you can simply state, "I appreciate your question. However, are you aware that no matter how it is answered, it has no impact on whether Jesus rose from the dead?" This pulls the focus back on the important issues. Address the issue if he still desires and then return to the Resurrection. Let's look at a few of these issues in chapters 9–12.

In addition, there is more to sharing Jesus' resurrection with others than providing facts. Good relational skills are essential if we are to gain the ear of others. Chapter 13 will provide practical tips for relating well with others.

Chapter 9

Heavenly Vision or Bodily Appearance?

The nature of Jesus' resurrection body is not discussed within a minimal-facts argument. However, it is very important. It is common today for critics to claim that the original disciples believed that he rose in a nonbodily form and that the story of his bodily resurrection, as found in the Gospels, was the result of embellishments added as the event of Jesus' resurrection faded into the past. The appearance of Jesus to Paul is of particular importance. While few scholars would dispute that the Gospels clearly speak of Jesus' bodily resurrection, many critics claim that Paul contradicts them on this issue. Since Paul was an eyewitness, and his writings are thought to be the earliest in the New Testament, his letters precede the Gospels. If Paul taught something other than a bodily Resurrection, the Gospels may reflect a tradition that had developed over time. These critics claim that the bodily resurrection of Jesus became part of the story about Jesus as it was embellished.[1]

Some critics also hold that the original disciples' account of Jesus' resurrection was an example of ancient *vision literature* (i.e., the nonhistorical genre). Thus, when they spoke of Jesus having a glorified body in which he appeared, this resurrection body was not his physical body coming back to life.

We have addressed the issues of embellishment and nonhistorical genre in chapter 5.

Still some other scholars think that the early Christians were correct that Jesus really appeared to them, but his body was other than physical. Jesus was raised from the dead in some seldom-defined sense, but they favor a nonphysical notion that they believe they find in Paul's writings over the Gospels' bodily depiction. This is sometimes referred to as the *objective* vision view, in that these were real perceptions of Jesus.[2] This position is *not* a naturalistic theory, since it holds that Jesus was raised in some *supernatural* sense.

Keep in mind a major distinction: Even though this topic is employed frequently by critics, we need to note carefully that the chief question in this chapter is *not* whether Jesus was raised, but the form in which the New Testament writers claimed he appeared.

What do the writers of the New Testament say regarding the nature of Jesus' resurrection body? Did Paul view Jesus' resurrection differently than did the original disciples? Let's look first at what he claimed. Then we will compare his views to those presented throughout other New Testament writings. Finally, we will address some of the responses offered by critics on the subject.

Paul preached the bodily resurrection of Jesus

If Paul also believed in Jesus' bodily resurrection, then the Gospels certainly do not reflect later tradition on the matter.

Paul's use of the early creed in 1 Corinthians 15:3–5 implies bodily resurrection. After mentioning the death of Jesus, the creed states, "and that he was buried and that he was raised." It is implied that what goes down in burial, comes up in resurrection. In verses 42–44 of this same chapter, Paul uses the metaphor of a seed four times to make the same point: "It is sown. . . . It is raised. . . . It is sown. . . . It is raised. . . ." What goes down in burial comes up in resurrection.

Paul writes that when Christ returns, he "will transform our *lowly bodies* so that they will be like his glorious body" (Phil 3:21 NIV). It is our lowly and mortal body that will be "transformed," not eliminated. The apostle could easily have said we would be like Jesus' glorious *spirit*. But instead, he used the word *body*. Paul claims that the believers' future body will be like the body of the risen Jesus. So if Paul's view is that the future state of the believer involves a body, his view is also that Jesus has a body in his risen state. If our transformation from mortal to immortal is similar to his, a bodily resurrection for Jesus by default would seem to be Paul's view. We will see below that this is supported by Paul elsewhere.

Paul writes, "But if the Spirit of Him who raised Jesus from the dead dwells in you, He who raised Christ Jesus from the dead *will also give life to your mortal bodies* [our emphasis] through His Spirit who dwells in you" (Rom. 8:11). This does not say much about the nature or appearance of a glorified body. It does indicate that Paul seems to have held that a transformation was made to Jesus' mortal body. It was not left in the tomb.[3]

In Colossians 2:9, Paul writes that in Christ, "all the fullness of Deity dwells in bodily form."[4] We may notice that Paul here uses the present tense. For him, the very essence and nature of God not only belongs to Jesus; it presently dwells in *his body*.

Paul is reported in Acts as saying that Jesus' body did not decay in the grave as had the body of Israel's king David, but rather it was raised up by God (Acts 13:34–37). Moreover, this bodily resurrection was viewed as a fulfillment of prophecy.[5] It is difficult to think of a more definite manner in which Paul could speak of the literal and bodily resurrection of Jesus.

The account of Paul's conversion in Acts is insufficient for concluding that Paul believed that Jesus did not rise bodily. In Acts, Luke describes the appearance to Paul differently than what the Gospel writers reported occurred with the disciples. For example, the Gospels report that the disciples touched Jesus,[6] but Paul saw Jesus in the sky as a blinding light.[7] However, there are at least four reasons why this distinction does not rule out a bodily resurrection.

First, other details in the account indicate that it was not merely an experience that occurred only in the mind of Paul. For example, Paul saw a bright light and heard Jesus' distinct words, while the bystanders fell to the ground in fear, saw the light, and heard a voice but did not understand the words.[8] Since others were included in this event, Paul's appearance was no subjective experience such as a hallucination.[9] The critic cannot consider only details that may support his view while ignoring those that do not.

Second, if the critic brings up Paul's conversion experience in Acts in order to say that it is different than the disciples' experience, he must also take this in light of Paul's sermon in Acts 13. In it he clearly implies bodily resurrection.

Third, it should be noted that the disciples' experiences occurred prior to Jesus' ascension to the throne of God. Paul's experience occurred after this event. Whether the critic believes in the ascension is irrelevant. The account of the appearance of a *post-ascension, glorified* Jesus to Paul is sufficient to explain why Paul's experience was different than those of the disciples.

Fourth, Luke apparently did not think there was a problem between Paul's encounter with Christ and Christ's appearances to the disciples (Luke 24; Acts 1:1–11), since he records *both*.

Finally, Acts was written *after* Matthew, Mark, and Luke. These Gospels portray a bodily resurrection of Jesus in the plainest of terms. Thus, if any evolution of the nature of the appearances is occurring, it's going in the opposite direction; bodily to vision. This observation is strengthened all the more when we consider that the earliest of those commenting on Jesus' resurrection, Paul, strongly hints at its bodily nature.

Peter preached the bodily resurrection of Jesus

According to Acts, Peter, like Paul, claimed that Jesus' body did not decay in the grave as did David's, but rather was raised up by God (Acts 2:25–32).

Peter also claimed that the risen Jesus ate and drank with his disciples. [10] Luke and John claimed the same thing (John 21; Acts 10:39–41).

The Gospels present the bodily resurrection of Jesus

The Gospel of Matthew viewed Jesus' resurrection appearances as physical. The women touched Jesus (Matt. 28:9). The Jewish leadership accused the disciples of stealing the body (v. 13). This accusation implies an empty tomb and, therefore, bodily resurrection.

The Gospel of Mark viewed Jesus' resurrection as bodily. The empty tomb implies a bodily resurrection (Mark 16:6). After saying Jesus had been raised, the angel draws attention to the "place" where Jesus body had been laid. [11]

The Gospel of Luke viewed Jesus' resurrection as bodily. "And as the women were terrified and bowed their faces to the ground, the men said to them, 'Why do you seek the living One among the dead? He is not here, but he has risen.'" The "dead" were the corpses, since they were among tombs, and the women wanted to place spices on the corpse of Jesus. The angel contrasts Jesus as "the living one" and said, "He is not here" (Luke 24:5–6). This states an empty tomb and strongly implies bodily resurrection.

Luke reports that Jesus' resurrection body had flesh and bones, could be touched, and could eat (Luke 24:36–43). [12]

The Gospel of John viewed Jesus' resurrection as bodily, including Jesus' prediction that he would rise bodily: "The Jews then said to him, 'What sign do you show us as your authority for doing these things?' Jesus answered them, 'Destroy this temple, and in three days I will raise it up.' The Jews then said, 'It took forty-six years to build this temple, and will you raise it up in three days?' But He was speaking of the temple of his body" (John 2:18–22).

John reports that Mary Magdalene, Peter, and John noticed the empty tomb (John 20:1–15). Thomas's experience is described plainly as a physical appearance of Jesus as he invites Thomas to touch him (vv. 24–28). The risen Jesus speaks to his disciples, eats with his disciples, and converses with them in a walk along the beach (21:19–30).[13]

The bodily resurrection of Jesus was proclaimed at the earliest stages of Christianity (i.e., Paul and the Acts sermon summaries) and is multiply attested. Moreover, no first-century Christian writer presents a contrary view.

"But what about texts used to deny a bodily resurrection?"

Critical scholars rarely question the physical nature of the Resurrection appearances as they are described in the Gospels. However, some have suggested that a few biblical passages describe the appearances of the risen Jesus as visions or subjective experiences. Let's look at a few of these passages.

"John 21:12 hints that the disciples didn't recognize Jesus."

John reports that when the risen Jesus prepared breakfast for his disciples on the beach, "None of the disciples ventured to question Him, 'Who are you?' knowing that it was the Lord" (John 21:12). This can be interpreted as an odd statement concerning those who had lived with Jesus for three years. Why would they think of asking him who he was?

Although John testifies that Jesus' body was raised from the dead and had scars from his crucifixion, there is reason to believe that there were some differences in the way Jesus looked, since he also claims that Jesus' body was now immortal. These differences may explain a degree of uncertainty, yet his disciples knew it was him. But we must also remember that John relays this appearance in light of clearly speaking of a bodily resurrection just one chapter earlier, when reporting the empty tomb and Jesus' invitation to Thomas to touch his resurrection body (20:27–28).[14]

"Matthew 28:16–17 indicates that there were doubts."

Jesus' disciples went to Galilee to meet him. Matthew writes, "When they saw him, they worshiped Him; but some were doubtful." If they saw the risen Jesus with their own eyes, why would some of the disciples doubt? There are a few issues for consideration: (1) What is the meaning of the Greek word translated "doubt"? (2) Who were the "some" who doubted? (3) Why did they doubt?

New Testament scholars differ on the answers and there seems to be no majority position. Regarding the meaning of the word translated "doubt," several scholars comment that the word distazō may more accurately be translated in this instance as "hesitate." In its only other occurrence in the New Testament, also in Matthew, it is used to describe Peter as he began to hesitate or doubt in his belief while walking on water toward Jesus (14:31).[15] The fact that Peter was out walking on water shows that Peter was not in total disbelief. Faith was mixed with doubt.[16]

Regarding the identity of the "some" who doubted, there is no agreement. Some scholars hold that different groups of people also were present on this occasion. Perhaps the group surrounding Jesus and the Eleven included other followers of Jesus. Paul would testify that Jesus on one occasion had appeared to more than 500.[17] Others hold that those who doubted must have been some of the eleven remaining disciples.[18] If the former is correct, we must remember that this appearance was reported to have taken place in Galilee, where most people had only *heard* that Jesus had been crucified and may have doubted whether he really had. If the latter is correct, then it may be that a few of the Eleven had mixed thoughts that led to hesitation on their part. They could have had the same thoughts that many of us would have if some loved one died and then suddenly appeared before us.

This leads us to the third issue: Why did they hesitate? While we may not have enough information to be clear on this matter, it could have been for any of a number of reasons. For example, based on other accounts, Jesus' post-resurrection body could have been different enough that he was difficult to recognize at first.[19] Could they, like Peter when walking on water, have experienced two simultaneous thoughts: "Jesus is risen! But how is this possible? Is this really happening or am I experiencing a dream, vision, or hallucination?"[20]

We can see that several plausible explanations exist for this verse without having to resort to requiring that the disciples experienced visions, which does not appear to be plausible. Just a few verses earlier, Matthew 28:5–10 certainly presents a bodily resurrection. Jesus is not where he was laid, he rose from the dead (lit. "dead ones"), and the women touched him.

"Galatians 1:16 seems to say Paul's experience was not physical."

Paul writes that God was pleased "to reveal His Son in me." Some interpret Paul as saying here that Jesus' resurrection appearance to him was something that was an inward experience rather than how it is described in Acts. This is not the most plausible interpretation, since Paul elsewhere strongly hints at bodily resurrection, and Acts 13:30–37 portrays Paul with a strong belief in Jesus' bodily resurrection. The majority view seems to be that Paul is here referring to how he learned about Jesus and grew spiritually during the three years after his Damascus road experience. This interpretation also is much more at home with Paul's strong teaching of a bodily resurrection.

"First Peter 3:18 says Jesus' spirit was made alive, not his body."

Peter writes that Jesus died for our sins, "having been put to death in the flesh, but made alive in the spirit." Some hold that Peter is saying that Jesus' spirit was made alive, not his body. One of the things that may be pointed out here is that these same critics usually deny that Peter wrote this letter and assign its composition toward the final quarter of the first century. If this is true, we have a letter that by critical dating is written contemporary with or after the Synoptic Gospels, Matthew, Mark, and Luke, which certainly claim Jesus' bodily resurrection. Therefore, it would be difficult to claim theological evolution in 1 Peter, since the purported theological evolution would be going in the opposite direction; from bodily resurrection to spiritual.

"Mark 16:7 could say that Jesus' spirit will meet the disciples."

Virtually every English translation of this verse portrays an angel instructing the women to tell Jesus' disciples, "He is going ahead of you to Galilee; there you will see Him, just as He told you." Some critics make the point that the Greek word Mark uses for "going ahead" (*proagō*) can also be translated "leading." They interpret Mark as saying that Jesus' spirit will lead them to go to Galilee where they will see a vision of Jesus.

However, this view is plagued by problems. First, even if proagō is to be translated in this manner, it does not follow that the disciples will experience Jesus in a *vision* rather than bodily upon reaching Galilee. Second, in the preceding verse, the same angel tells the women that the Jesus who was crucified is not there in the tomb. Rather he has been raised, and the women are invited to see the place where his body used to be. Thus, it is very poor exegesis to have the angel clearly speak of bodily resurrection in verse 6 and then in verse 7 use an alternate definition of a word to claim that the future appearance would be a vision. Third, "leading" is only a possible translation of the word. "Going ahead" is more common. That is how the majority of translators render it.

One further point should be mentioned in reference to the passages discussed thus far: Difficult passages should be interpreted in light of clear ones.[21] If Matthew is clear that Jesus rose bodily in one passage and then a few verses later he writes in a manner that is unclear and that invites a number of interpretations, the interpretation most compatible with his clear passage is to be preferred. The same may be said of Paul. If he has hinted strongly for the bodily resurrection of Jesus in a number of passages and then a couple of unclear passages are open to differing interpretations, including one that paints the post-resurrection appearance of Jesus to Paul as a vision, we should adopt the interpretation that is more closely aligned to his clearly stated views.

"First Corinthians 15:37–50 contrasts the natural physical body with the spiritual."

Skeptics frequently appeal to 1 Corinthians 15:37–50 to challenge the bodily nature of Jesus' resurrection. Throughout 1 Corinthians, Paul is answering questions raised in a letter by the church at Corinth. After discussing the resurrection of Jesus, he makes a transition to questions concerning whether there is a physical resurrection of believers from the dead on the final day and the nature of the immortal body. Since comparisons are made between the risen Christ and the future state of believers in 1 Corinthians 15,[22] it would seem that if the nature of our future resurrection body is immaterial and not physical, then so was Jesus' resurrection body. On the other hand, if the nature of our future resurrection body is material and physical, then so was Jesus' resurrection body. The critic claims that Paul is here promoting an immaterial body.

Paul begins his answer by using the analogy of a seed. "When you sow, you do not plant the body that will be, but just a seed" (1 Cor. 15:37a NIV). "So will it be with the resurrection of the dead" (v. 42a NIV). "It is sown a natural body, it is raised a spiritual body" (v. 44). "Now I say this, brethren, that flesh and blood cannot inherit the kingdom of God, nor does the perishable inherit the imperishable" (v. 50).

Is Paul here saying that Jesus' resurrection body was not a physical body? A "spiritual body" could refer to a ghost-like or nonphysical body? Notice that at first look he also seems to contradict Luke blatantly by writing that "flesh and blood cannot inherit the kingdom of God." Jesus makes a point in Luke 24:39 that, unlike a spirit, his body has "flesh and bones" (cf. vv. 36–43). Is Paul's view of the resurrection body different than what is taught in the Gospels? Several reasons militate against this conclusion.

For one thing, we have already shown that Paul strongly implies Jesus' bodily resurrection elsewhere (see pp. 155–57). Second, in 1 Corinthians 15, Paul clearly is not contrasting a material body with an immaterial one. Rather, he's contrasting a body that is holy with its spiritual appetites, with one that is weak with both its fleshly and sinful appetites.

Let's consider two words of interest that Paul employs in this passage, *psychikos*[23] and *pneumatikos*.[24] Speaking of our body, Paul writes, "it is sown a natural [psychikos] body, it is raised a spiritual [*pneumatikos*] body" (1 Cor. 15:44). What does Paul mean by these terms? In answer, let's first look earlier in his same letter. In 2:14–15, Paul writes, "But a natural [*psychikos*] man does not accept the things of the Spirit of God, for they are foolishness to him; and he cannot understand them, because they are spiritually appraised. But he who is spiritual [*pneumatikos*] appraises all things, yet he himself is appraised by no one." Here Paul contrasts the natural and spiritual man, i.e., the unsaved man who is lead by his soulish or fleshly nature and the Christian who is led by the Holy Spirit.[25] Now these are the same two words Paul employs in 15:44 when, using a seed analogy, he contrasts the natural (*psychikos*) and spiritual (*pneumatikos*) body. In other words, Paul answers the question of the Corinthians concerning the nature of our future body by saying that our body is sown with its fleshly and sinful appetites and raised holy with spiritual appetites.

Paul elsewhere speaks of our future bodies as being connected to the one we now possess. Later in 1 Corinthians 15 he says that our current bodies will be "changed" (v. 52).[26] He also states this clearly in Philippians 3:21a that Christ "will transform the body of our humble state." In Romans 8:11b, the Holy Spirit "will also give life to your mortal bodies."[27] Thus, at least three other verses in Paul's writings teach that our "mortal" and "humble" bodies will be "changed," "transformed," and "raised." This affirms that Paul is not speaking of a disembodied future existence of believers in his use of the term "spiritual body" in 1 Corinthians 15. Thus, it is poor exegesis to interpret Paul as saying that Jesus rose spiritually, implying an immaterial body.

If Paul meant to contrast a physical body with an immaterial one, he had a better Greek word available to him, one he had used earlier in a similar contrast, even using a seed analogy (1 Cor. 9:3-10; cf. Rom. 15:27). In 9:11 Paul writes, "If we sowed spiritual [*pneumatikos*] things in you, is it too much if we reap material [*sarkikos*] things from you?" *Sarkikos* means fleshly, material, physical.[28] It comes from its root, sarx, meaning "flesh." Paul had started the topic of sowing and reaping in the verses that precede 9:11. He then asks rhetorically if it is inappropriate to reap fleshly, material, physical things like food, clothing, and lodging for the spiritual blessings the apostles had sown in the Corinthian church.

Summary

In 1 Corinthians 15, there are no good reasons at all for holding that Paul is making a contrast between the material and immaterial. Paul strongly implies bodily resurrection elsewhere. The terms he employs were used in an earlier contrast in the letter and mean a body that is weak with both its fleshly and sinful appetites and one that is holy and with spiritual appetites. Moreover, if it was Paul's intention to contrast a material and immaterial body, the term *sarkikos*, which he employed just a few chapters earlier, would have gotten the point across. Finally, Paul says our current body will be changed.

But what about Paul's statement that "flesh and blood cannot inherit the kingdom of God?" Every language has its figures of speech. For example, in the U.S. when we refer to a "red-blooded male," we aren't contrasting him with someone who has green blood. The phrase "flesh and blood" is found five times in the New Testament and twice in the Old Testament Apocrypha.[29] It was "a common Jewish expression referring to man as a mortal being"[30] and each occurrence of the seven references reflects this. Therefore, the term, "flesh and blood," should not be understood as referring to a physical body but rather to our bodies in their current "mortal" form. Thus, Paul's statement does not contradict Luke's. Our future bodies will be physical in nature, yet immortal.

Accordingly, we have seen that, rather than challenge bodily resurrection,

Paul's statements in 1 Corinthians 15 point to a physical, material (yet immortal) body of the risen Jesus. The atheist New Testament scholar Gerd Lüdemann writes, "Let me hasten to add that I do not question the physical nature of Jesus' appearance from heaven. . . . In the rest of chapter 15 Paul develops his idea of a bodily resurrection, which according to the apostle can be deduced directly from the proclamation in 1 Corinthians 15:3–5."[31] In addition, the highly critical New Testament scholar John Dominic Crossan admits, "For Paul . . . bodily resurrection is the only way that Jesus' continued presence can be expressed."[32]

The Risen Jesus: Casper or Corporeal?

Many critics appeal to 1 Corinthians 15:44–50 in order to support their view that Paul, the earliest author we know to have written about Jesus' resurrection, says that he was raised as a *spirit* rather than with a *physical body*. To support this view, these scholars appeal to Paul's contrast of a resurrection body with our current mortal one by using the terms *spiritual* and *natural*. Some translations, like the *New Revised Standard Version,* use *spiritual* and *physical.* If this is correct, Paul is saying that the earthly body is material while the resurrection body is spiritual or immaterial.

A more careful look at the two Greek words Paul uses reveals that this interpretation is incorrect. Outside of this passage in 1 Corinthians, Paul uses the word translated "spiritual" (pneumatikos) in the sense of the spiritually mature in this world (2:15; 3:1; 14:37; cf. Galatians 6:1), or of something that has to do with, or has as its origin, the Holy Spirit (2:13–14; 9:11; 10:3–4; 12:1; 14:1). With the *possible* exception of Ephesians 6:12, *the term is never used in the Pauline letters either to refer to or describe a being as immaterial.*

But what about the term often translated "natural" and "material" (psychikos)? Paul uses the term a total of four times in his writings, all in 1 Corinthians (2:14; 15:44 [2x]; 15:46). Granted, four times is not a large sampling. When we observe how other New Testament writers as well as intertestamental writings employ the word, we observe that *neither Paul nor any other New Testament author nor the writers of intertestamental books ever use* psychikos *to refer to or describe something as being material.*

Accordingly, any attempts to use this passage to support an immaterial resurrection body are mistaken. Paul is also clear in other texts that Jesus was raised bodily.

Chapter 10

Who Did Jesus Think He Was?

I f we were to investigate the Bible to find out what Jesus claimed of himself, the answer would be easy to determine: Jesus claimed to be the uniquely divine Son of God. However, what if we were to approach the Bible through the eyes of a skeptic? What if we denied that the Bible is the Word of God, concluding that its original stories were embellished to the form in which they were passed down to us? What if we believed the legendary influences in the first-century were so strong that we can only guess what the original sources said?

Is there any way that we can answer these specific beliefs by reaching some specific conclusions concerning what Jesus claimed about himself? Did he claim he was divine? Let's look at two titles the New Testament ascribes to Jesus and attempt to establish reasonable historical certainty concerning whether Jesus actually used these of himself.

Jesus referred to himself as "Son of Man"

In the Gospels, "Son of Man" is Jesus' favorite self-designation. Even most skeptical scholars accept this as an authentic title that Jesus used of himself for three reasons: first, the title appears as a reference to Jesus in the New Testament only three times outside the Gospels[1] and only three other times in early Christian writings during the first 120 years following Jesus.[2] How likely is it that the church invented the title "Son of Man" as Jesus' favorite self-description, when the church itself rarely referred to him in this manner? There is almost a total absence of such language in Paul and the other epistles. Second, the title as used in the Gospels is multiply-attested, being found in *all* of the Gospel sources. Third, the title seems to lack the signs that it was a result of theological evolution, since at first glance it appears to be a title that places more emphasis on Jesus' humanity than on his divinity. For these reasons and others, we can have confidence that Jesus indeed referred to himself as "Son of Man."[3]

What did Jesus mean? It is generally agreed that Jesus used the phrase in three senses: (1) as a reference to his earthly ministry; (2) as a reference to his death and resurrection; and (3) as a reference to a future coming in judgment and glory.

A key passage concerning the title is found in the Old Testament. In Daniel 7:13–14, it is written:

> I kept looking in the night visions, and behold, with the clouds of heaven One like a Son of Man was coming, and He came up to the Ancient of Days and was presented before Him. And to Him was given dominion, glory and a kingdom, that all the peoples, nations and men of every language might serve Him. His dominion is an everlasting dominion which will not pass away; and His kingdom is one which will not be destroyed.

Daniel saw "one like a Son of Man" coming "with the clouds of heaven." God gave this Son of Man eternal sovereignty over everything.[4] For example, this "preexistent" and "superhuman" figure delivers God's judgment against evil.[5]

With this in mind, consider the words of Jesus during his trial before the high priest: "Again the high priest was questioning him, and saying to him, 'Are you the Christ, the Son of the Blessed One?' And Jesus said, 'I am; and you shall see the Son of Man sitting at the right hand of power, and coming with the clouds of heaven'" (Mark 14:61b–62).[6] We should not miss that Jesus replied directly and affirmatively to the high priest's question. The phrase "coming with the clouds of heaven" clearly reveals that Jesus thought of himself as the "Son of Man" referred to by Daniel.[7] It is also interesting that Jesus seems to refer to the "Son of Man" and the "Son of God" as two titles for the same person. Notice that when the high priest asks him if he is the Christ (i.e., Messiah), the Son of God, Jesus says, "Yes, and you will see me, *the Son of Man*, seated next to God and coming with the clouds." Since the responses of the high priest and those around him were to accuse Jesus of blasphemy and demand the death penalty,[8] it seems clear that when Jesus referred to himself as the Son of Man, he thought of himself as divine.[9]

Jesus referred to himself as "Son of God"

Three questions must be asked concerning the title "Son of God": (1) What is usually meant by it? (2) Did Jesus claim to be the Son of God? (3) If so, what did *he* mean by it?

Philosopher John Hick states that there are two problems with calling Jesus "Son of God" in a divine sense. First, Hick believes that early believers did not give divine status to Jesus. Rather, this idea developed toward the end of the first century.[10] Hick further states that the title "Son of God" was applied to human beings in the ancient world, so it does not necessarily refer to a divine being. Political leaders, religious leaders, and great philosophers were sometimes called a "son of God."[11] Angels were likewise referred to as "sons of God."[12] The nation Israel was referred to as God's son.[13] Accordingly, the Messiah or any outstandingly pious Jew could be referred to as a "son of God." Hick continues that Gentiles were not familiar with the Jewish meaning behind certain terms. "Son of God" came to be interpreted in the Gentile sense of a a divine being. Therefore, theological evolution took place and Jesus became divine.

Likewise, Jesus Seminar cofounder John Dominic Crossan states that the title "Son of God" was used in the first century in a lesser sense than for a divine being. He claims that the early second-century Roman historian, Suetonius, portrays the Emperor Augustus as having a divine father. He was, therefore, a "son of God." Since Jesus is likewise portrayed as having a divine paternity, this was simply a literary device to honor a great person.[14] Thus, for Crossan, the title "Son of God" applied to Jesus simply meant he was a great man. If Hick and/or Crossan are correct, neither Jesus nor his disciples thought of him as Son in a divine sense.

Such an interpretation loses sight of the fact that Jesus and the Gospel writers claimed specific things in relation to His title as the "Son of God." Let's look at Mark 13:32, a verse that most scholars admit contains an authentic saying of Jesus. Speaking in reference to his return, Jesus states, "No one knows about that day or hour, not even the angels in heaven, nor the Son, but only the Father" (NIV).

Earlier we learned about the Principle of Embarrassment as applied to the women as primary witnesses to the empty tomb. It is unlikely that an author would invent an account so as to include details that are embarrassing and potentially discrediting. In Mark 13:32, the Gospel writer states that there is something that Jesus does not know, the time of his coming. One would think that in an evolving theology where Jesus was assigned a divine status, even of being God himself,[15] a statement emphasizing his limitations of knowledge would not be included.[16] This is why most scholars agree that this verse is an actual statement of Jesus.[17]

If Jesus claimed to be the Son of God, what did he mean by it? In the passage we just considered, Mark employs a figure of speech called *anabasis*, an ascending scale with increasing emphasis. An example of anabasis would be my saying, "I wouldn't do such and such for a thousand dollars. I wouldn't do it for a hundred thousand dollars. I wouldn't even do it for a million dollars." Here we see an ascending scale in the amounts of money that could theoretically be offered. We also see an increasing emphasis, stressing the idea that I will not do such a thing.

In Mark 13:32, we also see the use of anabasis. Jesus says that no human knows the time of his coming. Not even the angels in heaven know, who are greater than humans. The Son does not know either, even though he is higher than the divine angels. Thus, this Son of God is higher than humans (including kings, prophets, and pious followers of God), higher than the angels in heaven, and is only lower than the Father.[18] Therefore, in this verse that is regarded as an authentic saying of Jesus, he claims that he is the Son—the divine Son of God.

But Mark 13:32 isn't the only text where a large number of critics agree that we are told that Jesus claimed divinity by claiming to be the Son of God. Another is Matthew 11:27 (cf. Luke 10:22), a famous early passage attributed to the so-called "Q" sayings of Jesus.[19] Here he claims to be God's Son, the only one who has exclusive knowledge of his Father.[20] Critical scholars also generally agree that in Mark 14:36 Jesus refers to his Father by a term (*Abba*) that is so intimate it is seldom applied to God by ancient Jews. Prominent New Testament critical scholar Joachim Jeremias asserts that this term is an "authentic and original utterance of Jesus . . . the claim of a unique revelation and unique authority."[21] We have already looked at Jesus' strong and direct affirmation in Mark 14:61–62 that he was the Son of God.

These are further indications that Jesus' use of the word *Son* has nothing in common with general usage in the ancient world. He claimed to occupy a unique sonship with the God of the universe, a relationship not shared with others.[22] Thus, Hick's view—that the title was applied to Jesus as a result of theological evolution and that if Jesus claimed he was the Son of God, he did not mean it in a divine sense—is false.

But what about Crossan's view that the Gospel writers merely employed a literary device to honor Jesus, as did others of their day? First, we have already established that Jesus himself claimed that he was the divine Son of God. If Jesus viewed himself as divine, then the disciples were not fabricating claims simply to honor him.

Second, as pointed out earlier under the concept of resurrections in other religions (see pp. 90–92), miracle accounts in other religious writings are unanimously inferior in historical credibility to the New Testament reports of the appearances of the risen Jesus. They are not usually multiply attested, and the records are normally very late when compared to the time the miracle was supposed to have taken place. The first reports of these miraculous events were written long after the time when the alleged events took place.

Crossan's appeal to Suetonius is a good example. Suetonius admits that he received his information from a single source, a book called *Theologumena* by Asclepiades of Mendes. We know nothing of this book. All we know of Asclepiades is that he may have written another book about Egypt.[23] So, concerning the phenomenal birth account of Augustus, we have one source who cites an unknown book by an unknown author. So we know nothing of Asclepiades' reliability. But most damaging is that Suetonius wrote about 183 years after Augustus was born.

This is a far cry from the Christian account of Jesus' miraculous birth. The birth account of Jesus has two independent sources, Matthew and Luke and, thus, there is *multiple attestation.*[24] If Matthew was one of the original disciples of Jesus or if there are other firsthand sources behind this writing, material from eyewitnesses would probably be present, and Luke claims that he received his information from the eyewitnesses.[25] We know that both accounts have been accurately preserved in the manuscripts.[26] Further, there are no credible grounds for claiming influence from pagan accounts.[27] And Jesus' life is marked by the miraculous, establishing a *context* in which a miraculous birth is more at home than an isolated event within someone's life, as was the case with Augustus. Finally, simply because some authors employed a rhetorical device in order to honor someone, this does not merit the conclusion that the Gospel writers did so.

Thus, Crossan's view, like Hick's, fails to provide a sound skeptical position for rejecting the title "Son of God" as one referring to divinity when applied to Jesus.

We can, therefore, establish that Jesus not only claimed to be the Son of God, but that when he did so he meant it in a divine sense. Moreover, Jesus claimed to be the Son of Man, a reference to the divine and sovereign Son of Man in Daniel 7. Remember again that we are coming to these topics by chiefly using a minimal facts approach. It is interesting that, even after using strict criteria, one can arrive at many of the same conclusions as someone who accepts the inspiration of the Bible.

Context Counts

If a number of credible witnesses testified that Joseph Stalin had risen from the dead last year and walked around Russia for two months, we would not be quick to believe, even if some evidences were present and no plausible naturalistic theories were available. Why is it different for Jesus? This is where context counts.

Stalin never claimed divinity for himself, never performed miracles, and never predicted that he would return from the grave. His resurrection from the dead would be completely out of place. Jesus' life, on the other hand, created a context in which his resurrection from the dead would not be a surprise. He claimed that he was divine. He performed deeds that were interpreted as miracles. And he predicted his resurrection.

This context is not evidence for Jesus' resurrection. However, it presents an additional perspective when someone says, "People just don't come back to life after being dead." The context of Jesus' life and claims cannot be ignored. For if God exists, there is no reason why the Author of life could not raise the dead. And Jesus was just the sort of person we might expect God to raise.

Chapter 11

What Does God Have to Do with This?

A theist Frank Zindler asks what are we to do with the Wizard of Oz once we realize that there is no Oz?[1] In terms of Jesus' resurrection, one could argue, "What are we to do with the risen *Son of God* once we realize that there is no God?" If God does not exist, neither does his son. All talk about a risen Son of God is ridiculous.

"If atheism is true, then Jesus did not rise."

The resurrection of Jesus would actually provide strong evidence for the existence of God. Therefore, to have an effective argument against the resurrection of Jesus, the atheist must first successfully tear down the evidence for Jesus' resurrection and then present strong reasons why God does not exist. Unless and until he does both of these, this argument is ineffective as a refutation of Jesus' resurrection.

We have seen that there simply are no compelling arguments against the resurrection of Jesus. But what about arguments against the existence of God? Space does not permit us to go into great detail regarding all the arguments for and against God's existence that have developed over the millennia. However,

172

we will look briefly at the major contemporary argument that is used by atheists to bring into question the Judeo-Christian concept of God. This line of reasoning revolves around the problem of evil:

> If God is all-good, he would prefer a world where no evil exists to one where it does. If God is all-powerful, he could create such a world. If he would prefer such a world and could create it, why do we have evil in our world? Perhaps he is willing but unable and, therefore, not all-powerful. Perhaps he is able but unwilling and, therefore, not all-good. Either way, an all-good and all-powerful God does not exist.[2]

Only a few of the problems with this argument can be mentioned here. First, this argument does not call into question God's existence. Rather it could question only his character and power. Atheism does not necessarily follow from this argument. The only conclusion for consideration is that an all-good and all-powerful God does not exist. Even if the argument is sound, there still might be a Creator of the universe who loves us but who is not omnipotent. Therefore, this also fails to rule out the resurrection of the Son of God.

Second, it may be that we currently live in the best of all possible worlds where free beings are involved.[3] God cannot accomplish logical absurdities. Is it possible for God to create a married bachelor in the strictest sense of these terms? Can God "smell the color nine"[4] or draw a square circle? If God is unable to accomplish logically contradictory actions, this does not limit his omnipotence. But how does this relate to the problem of evil? Perhaps it is logically impossible to have a world in which all free beings always freely choose to live righteously. As long as there is a reasonable possibility, one cannot claim that the matter has been decided.[5] We may very well live in a world that has an optimized balance of the greatest amount of good with a minimal amount of evil. Thus, evil does not render impossible the existence of an all-good and all-powerful God.

Third, some defenses that have been proposed rely upon natural law and the inability to propose a better state of affairs than the one in which we find ourselves. One variation of this argument concentrates on the "soul-making" aspects of suffering. It sometimes seems that this is the optimal way to grow as human beings.[6]

Fourth, if the Bible is correct, God did create a world where no evil existed. Humans chose to do evil and evil usually carries with it certain consequences. Therefore, God is not responsible for the evil in the world; human beings are.[7]

Could he rid the world of all evil tonight at midnight? If he did, which of us would be left at 12:01? Or how many of us would push a button to eliminate all of our pain and suffering if, by so doing, we *also* eliminated all of our free choices? It is interesting to see how God has dealt with the problem of our evil. He sent his Son to take the sins of the world on himself, to die for those sins, to rise from the dead, and to offer eternal life to everyone who comes to him in belief and repentance.

We have briefly looked at what is currently the most popular argument for atheism. It is fraught with problems, only some of which we have mentioned. Now let us look at some of the arguments *in favor* of the existence of God, since these also frustrate arguments against Jesus' resurrection based on God's non-existence.

Evidence is strong that God exists

Let us look briefly at two major arguments (other than Jesus' resurrection) that are advanced by theists in support of the existence of God.[8] Antony Flew, regarded by many professional philosophers as one of the twentieth century's most influential atheist philosophers, once stated the following regarding Jesus' resurrection: "Certainly given some beliefs about God, the occurrence of the resurrection does become enormously more likely."[9] Why? In Flew's mind, the philosophy of naturalism discussed in chapter 8 provides the major tension to Jesus' resurrection. Naturalism is true if God does not exist and false if he does. If naturalism is false, then there would be no reason to dismiss Jesus' resurrection since the evidence for this event is strong. Therefore, although arguments for God's existence are not necessary in order to establish Jesus' resurrection, a strong case for God's existence does render Jesus' resurrection more likely, especially since the known facts strongly support it.

The scientific evidence points to an Intelligent Designer of the universe and life

Before determining whether our universe and life itself are products of an intelligent Designer, we must ask, "How do we recognize when something has been designed?" Philosopher and mathematician William Dembski offers two criteria for identifying design. First, the thing under consideration must be so complex that it is extremely unlikely to have occurred by chance. Second, the thing under consideration must exhibit a sort of pattern that is normally associated with a cause that possesses intelligence. Dembski refers to these criteria as *specified complexity*.[10]

If we were to drive out into the country and pass by a cornfield with its neat and numerous rows, we would be justified in concluding that the field was the result of a designer. Why? Because the cornfield meets the two criteria for identifying design. First, although the design of the rows is simple to the eye, it is complex in that it is extremely unlikely to have occurred by chance. Our background knowledge tells us that, given wild seeds and the wind, the undirected processes of nature would produce a field of mixed plants and there would be no neat arrangement. This sort of pattern of rows and pure corn is what we might expect only if an intelligent source is present.

What distinguishes our cornfield from the neat surf lines on the beach produced from the receding tide and the complex combination of dust particles within a whirlwind at a given moment? Natural causes can produce these; thus, they aren't complex. Therefore, both are disqualified from being the result of the actions of an intelligent or personal agent. The specific combination of dust particles in a whirlwind doesn't meet the second criteria either, since the particular combination of dust particles is quite arbitrary. It has no functional difference than if a slightly different combination had occurred. Thus no pattern is present that we might normally associate with design.

Dembski adds that we already use *specified complexity* in various scientific disciplines in order to identify when an intelligent cause is present. Two examples are forensic science and the search for extraterrestrial intelligence (SETI). By searching for certain types of patterns normally associated with an intelligent cause, detectives can many times determine if a personal agent was involved in a crime. Regarding SETI, scientists listen to sounds in space, seeking to identify a sort of pattern that is too complex to be the result of an undirected natural process and that would normally be the product of some sort of intelligence. In the science fiction movie *Contact*, a scientist discovers a signal from space and identifies a pattern of beats and pauses in it that correspond to a sequence of prime numbers between two and 101. Such a pattern would meet both criteria for identifying something with an intelligent source behind it.

Now that we have an idea of how to identify design, is it possible to conclude scientifically that the universe and life itself are products of an intelligent Designer? Let's look at some examples from astrophysics and molecular biology. In 1965, two Bell Laboratory scientists, Robert W. Wilson and Arno A. Penzias, discovered a blanket of microwave radiation in the center of our universe. This indicated that at some point in the distant past the universe was extremely hot and dense. Moreover, the fact that the universe is expanding outward from that point in the center has led most astronomers to conclude that a massive explosion sent all matter hurtling out through space at some point. We will not discuss here whether what has been called the "Big Bang" actually occurred, but if it did, the theistic implications are tremendous.[11] It would almost be a fingerprint of the Creator.[12] With the acceptance of the Big Bang, some scientists jumped to the conclusion that the idea of a Creator God was no longer needed to explain the origin of the universe, since it currently appears that the universe began with a bang.

In the years that followed the development of the theory of an expanding universe, further research in astrophysics revealed that certain conditions would have to be present for the possibility of life to exist. These conditions are referred to as *cosmic constants*. These conditions must be present within an extremely narrow margin. Given any composition of matter outside these extremely narrow parameters, no life could be produced. Based on this observation, Donald Page, a Nobel Prize winning astronomer, calculated that given all of the possible ways in which the constants could have obtained in a Big Bang, the odds of getting a universe capable of sustaining life is 1 in $10^{10(124)}$; that is one chance in ten followed by 1,240 zeros![13] Given these odds, it is enormously more probable that, in an undirected "Bang," the constants would not have obtained in favor of life. Thus, the first criterion for *specified complexity* has been met.

It is only natural to note that vastly improbable events occur all of the time, and ask why the constants indicate design any more than an improbable natural event. Imagine that four people are playing cards. One of them shuffles and deals out all the cards. One person notices that he has been dealt all hearts in the order of ace through king. The next person has been dealt all spades in ace through king order, the next all diamonds, ace through king. The dealer has all clubs in the same order. One of the players asks the dealer, "How did you do that?" The dealer responds by saying, "What do you mean? This happened by pure chance." Although this is remotely possible, the players who have been dealt these cards will not believe the dealer, because there is a strong appearance that the deck has been stacked.

Even so, the complexity of cards doesn't compare to the complexities of the universe. When it comes to the origin of the universe, it appears that the deck was stacked in order for life to occur. It is not that one configuration of the universe isn't just as improbable as another. But, given undirected processes, a life-prohibiting universe is astronomically more probable than a life-permitting one. Agnostic physicist Robert Jastrow of NASA's Goddard Institute for Space Studies calls the life-permitting constants of the universe "the most theistic result ever to come out of science."[14] Paul Davies, a Templeton laureate and prominent physicist moved from promoting atheism in 1983,[15] to conceding in 1984 that "the laws [of physics] . . . seem themselves to be the product of exceedingly ingenious design,"[16] to in 1988 saying that there "is for me powerful evidence that there is something going on behind it all. The impression of design is overwhelming."[17]

With the turn of the twenty-first century and more years of research and understanding, the data pointing to an intelligent Designer has only increased. Astrophysicist Hugh Ross explains that more cosmic constants are still being discovered. In 1998, Ross listed twenty-nine constants that pertained to specific values in the universe and forty-five additional constants related to planet, moon, star, and galaxy relationships.[18] In June 2002, Ross updated the list to forty-five constants pertaining to specific values in the universe,[19] and 118 constants related to planet, moon, star, and galaxy relationships.[20]

Arno Penzias, a Nobel laureate in physics and one of the two scientists who in 1965 discovered the strong evidence in favor of the Big Bang, comments, "astronomy leads us to a unique event, a universe which was created out of nothing, and delicately balanced to provide exactly the conditions required to support life. In the absence of an absurdly-improbable accident, the observations of modern science seem to suggest an underlying, one might say, supernatural plan."[21] A recent paper entitled "Disturbing Implications of a Cosmological Constant" by physicists Lisa Dyson, Matthew Kleban, and Leonard Susskind of Stanford University and MIT concludes that, aside from assistance from an unknown agent outside the universe, the appearance of life in the universe requires "statistically miraculous events" and is incomprehensibly unlikely. It is *not* as though one threw a deck of cards into the air and they fell onto the floor into the only arrangement that would make life possible. It is more as though one threw a deck of cards into the air and they landed as a tidy and perfectly balanced house of cards.

Thus, the second criterion of *specified complexity* has been met. The universe exhibits a pattern that speaks of an intelligent cause. The three scientists just mentioned do not consider the possibility of a Creator. Rather they suggest that there is something fundamentally incorrect with the physics used by scientists today.[22] While we can and should be open to future discoveries that would change our current understanding of physics, it is safe to say that what we have been discovering within astrophysics since 1965 certainly points to an intelligent Designer as the external agent who fine-tuned the universe so that life might appear.

The constants in our universe are more at home in a designed universe than in one that exists by chance.[23] If an intelligent Designer created the universe, we expect such a balance of forces. On the other hand, if the universe is the result of undirected natural processes, the odds that it will possess such a strong appearance of design are incomprehensibly unlikely. Thus, the most reasonable explanation for the appearance of design in the universe is that an intelligent Designer exists. While it is admitted that this does not conclusively prove the existence of God, it is certainly a "face card" in the hand dealt to the one who believes that God exists.

Some of the more recent results of molecular biology have likewise impressed many scientists and philosophers that there must be an intelligent Designer behind life. The odds against life forming by chance chemical evolutionary scenarios have brought a new argument to the table for an intelligent Designer that skeptics have been unable to answer adequately to date.

The cell once was viewed as a very simple entity, containing fluid and a small dot in the middle called the nucleus. However, with the advent of the electron microscope, scientists can now look deep into the cell, and what they have discovered has left them in awe. Each cell is like a city, with a city hall, a transportation department, a hospital, a fire department, and a police department. Mechanisms within the cell act to fulfill their individual purposes and all work interdependently. Some excellent studies are available to explain this work of monumentally complex organization.[24] Here we will just introduce one very important component of cellular design, DNA. DNA is contained in the nucleus. Of many amino acids in the body, only twenty types are useful for life. Of those, only four types are found in DNA. These are arranged in an extremely complex pattern that tells the rest of the cell what to do. These instructions amount to a blueprint for the entire organism, determining eye color, hair color, athletic capabilities, natural intelligence, and even vulnerability to specific diseases.

This complexity poses a significant challenge to anyone proposing that undirected processes of nature are responsible for such complexity. This complexity is discovered on one of the most basic levels of life. Given the maximum estimated age of our Earth, 4.5 billion years, there was little time for chemical evolution to produce the type of complex and functioning information we observe in DNA. Consider the words of Flew who writes, "Indeed, again and so far as I know, no one has yet produced a plausible conjecture as to how any of these complex molecules might have evolved from simple entities."[25] Francis Crick is one of the two scientists who discovered DNA. Crick is an atheist. Yet, having observed the complexity of DNA, Crick estimates the odds that intelligent life exists on the Earth as the result of nondirected processes to be around $1:10^{2,000,000,000}$. Thus, the first criterion of *specified complexity* is met. DNA is too complex to have occurred by chance.

But does DNA exhibit a pattern that we would normally associate with an intelligent cause? The functional orderliness of DNA and life itself would seem to require an answer in the affirmative. Consider what else Crick writes when commenting on this functional orderliness present in life: "Biologists must constantly keep in mind that what they see was not designed, but rather evolved."[26] Elsewhere Crick writes, "An honest man, armed with all the knowledge available to us now, could only state that in some sense, the origin of life appears at the moment to be almost a miracle, so many are the conditions which would have to be satisfied to get it going."[27]

Crick is one of many scientists and philosophers who have made statements like these. Thus, even many who don't embrace a belief in God would grant the second criterion of *specified complexity*. There is a pattern exhibited in DNA that we normally associate with intelligent causation.

In summary, we have observed that fairly recent discoveries in the disciplines of astrophysics and molecular biology have provided a strong foundation for a scientific understanding of the universe and the life it contains to be products of an intelligent Designer. This is referred to in contemporary terms as the "Intelligent Design Argument" or ID. ID does not argue for any particular God. Nor does it claim anything about the nature of God. It does not even require that the Designer be God. It simply states that the appearance of design in the universe and in life itself is best explained as being the result of a Designer who planned it, rather than the result of natural causes. In relation to our discussion on Jesus' resurrection, evidence for an intelligent Designer is consistent with the existence of God and, thus, provides one more reason for belief in his existence and a further refutation of the arguments against it, removing a philosophical barrier to belief in Jesus' resurrection.

A First Cause is required, given the evidence collected by science

Many astronomers believe that the universe is all there is and that nothing exists outside of it. As we discussed in the previous section, most astronomers today believe that the universe began with a huge explosion that has popularly come to be called the "Big Bang." Astronomers likewise believe that all there was prior to the Big Bang was a small point of incredible density they refer to as the "singularity." However, this singularity did not exist prior to the Big Bang. At that time, nothing existed. So if we were to invite some friends over, make some popcorn, turn on the television, place a special DVD into our player, and watch an actual history of the universe in reverse, starting from today and going all the way back to just moments prior to the Big Bang, what we would see is all of the stars and galaxies simultaneously arriving at a single point, which would then disappear. In the words of the late prominent astronomer Fred Hoyle, the universe was "shrunk down to nothing at all."[28] Moreover, most astrophysicists believe that space and time likewise began at the moment of the Big Bang.[29] Thus, there was not a place where someone could have witnessed the Big Bang or filmed it for our DVD, since space did not exist prior to the Big Bang. When it happened, everything exploded into existence. In another sense, nothing exploded into everything.

Why does the Big Bang raise serious questions for the atheist's consideration? It seems to require a beginning of the universe and a beginning seems to require a cause of some sort, at least for the vast majority of people who agree that everything that begins to exist has a cause. What then caused the Big Bang?

If nothing existed prior to the Big Bang, not even space or time, then the cause of the Big Bang must be spaceless (i.e., immaterial) and timeless (i.e., infinite or eternal).[30] It seems to be impossible to get something from nothing, at least by natural causes.[31] And yet, if atheism is true, the Big Bang requires that the universe came *out of nothing* and *was not caused.* This places the atheist in the difficult position of embracing a highly questionable philosophy, since science and all of human experience lead to the conclusion that things do not just come into existence without a cause.

Now there are atheists who disagree. Philosopher Quentin Smith unashamedly asserts, "The fact of the matter is that the most reasonable belief is that we came from nothing, by nothing and for nothing. . . . We should . . . acknowledge our foundation in nothingness and feel awe at the marvelous fact that we have a chance to participate briefly in this incredible sunburst that interrupts without reason the reign of non-being."[32] When we read statements like this, our faith may be increased due to the rather *ad hoc* explanations that skeptics make in order to rationalize the data.[33]

It seems, then, that the existence of the universe is impossible without an eternal and immaterial cause. Thus, the scientific argument for some sort of first cause looks like this:

1. Everything that begins to exist has a cause.
2. The universe began to exist.
3. Therefore, the universe was caused.[34]

When we reflect on the nature of the cause, we find that it must be immaterial and timeless. From the nature of the complexity it would seem that the Designer would have to be extremely intelligent. Some would just call this cause God. Although we can't argue this issue further at this point, what we see certainly seems to favor the case for theism over the case for naturalism.

Keep in mind that the above arguments for God do not prove the Christian God. However, the Creator is strikingly consistent with him.[35] Remember what atheist Flew stated: "Certainly given some beliefs about God, the occurrence of the resurrection does become enormously more likely."[36] It appears likely that God exists. Thus, Jesus' resurrection becomes "enormously more likely," since the known facts support the occurrence of such a resurrection anyway.

In a world where God probably exists, there are no good reasons for rejecting the possibility of the Resurrection. It is Jesus' resurrection that reveals that the God apparently disclosed by the philosophical and scientific arguments above is the Christian God, as we will briefly point out in the next chapter.

Chapter 12

Some Final Issues

S ome skeptics object that Jesus' resurrection does not prove God's existence. Jesus' resurrection is often used as an argument for the existence of God. "However," the skeptic responds, "even if Jesus rose from the dead, this does not prove that God exists. A very powerful being about whom we know nothing may have raised Jesus. Perhaps a natural occurence for which no scientific explanation yet exists (i.e., an anomaly) brought Jesus back to life. Therefore, God's existence is not proved by Jesus' resurrection, even if it occurred."

"The Resurrection doesn't prove God's existence."

When such a complaint is raised as a rebuttal, it means that the skeptic has become frustrated in the lack of a good opposing theory. After all, this objection does nothing to disprove Jesus' resurrection. Rather, it questions *who* raised Jesus or *how* he was raised, not *whether* he was raised.

Are there any strong *reasons* to believe that someone other than God raised Jesus from the dead? No one else has claimed responsibility, and there is no evidence that someone else did it. Yet we do have Jesus' claim that his resurrection would be evidence that he had divine authority.[1] We do have the claims of alleged eyewitnesses who were taught by the risen Jesus and claimed that *God* raised him.[2] These individuals, especially Jesus were certainly in the best posi-

182

tion to identify the cause of his resurrection. Unless the skeptic can produce stronger data in support of another cause, the most rational explanation is that God raised Jesus from the dead.

Another way of looking at this is to say that the cause of Jesus' resurrection was either natural or supernatural. From what we know today from science, a natural cause is not a viable option. The decomposing cells of a deceased person are not going to regenerate themselves back to any sort of life. Thus, just as it is unlikely that science will someday overturn the law of gravity, it seems even more improbable that a natural cause will someday explain Jesus' return to life. Therefore, given that Jesus claimed to be divine and that those who saw him after his resurrection claimed that God raised him from the dead, a supernatural God as the cause of Jesus' resurrection is the most plausible explanation for it.

Can the historian establish that it was God who raised Jesus? The historian can conclude that Jesus rose from the dead. But the historian cannot conclude from historical inquiry alone that God raised Jesus from the dead. This is not to say that we are unjustified in concluding that God raised Jesus. It is simply to admit that historical inquiry alone cannot answer the question of the *cause* of Jesus' resurrection. It can only address whether the event occurred.[3] Nevertheless, after looking at the data for the existence of God, Jesus' claims about himself, his prediction of the resurrection, his miracles and fulfilled prophecy, the limits of historical inquiry do not keep us from concluding that God raised Jesus from the dead. This interpretation of the facts is a far better option than to subscribe to another theory that lacks any credible data.

So we might summarize our case:

Due to Jesus' own teachings, his listeners concluded that his resurrection was an act that only God was capable of performing. Why? Jesus had the best perspective from which to interpret the significance of this event. Jesus made various, amazing claims to divinity. He performed miracles and predicted future events. He lived an exemplary life. Further, we can read into his words the expectation that the Resurrection would be his chief miracle. It would be an extraordinary act performed by the God of the universe to approve and establish the truth of his entire person and message.

This combination of an extraordinary life, extraordinary claims, and an extraordinary event composed the earliest Christian proclamation. The Resurrection confirmed the Christian message about God.

Jesus' own claims, especially regarding his divinity would have been heresy unless they were true. But then Jesus was raised from the dead! What did such an event mean, especially in a Jewish context? Since dead men have no such power to act, it would certainly be reasonable to conclude that God was involved. After all, God wouldn't have raised a heretic. Yet, the only time that an evidenced resurrection has ever happened,[4] it occurred to the very person who made these amazing, unique claims regarding himself and his part in salvation.

So the verdict is in: Jesus' resurrection justified both his life and his claims.[5]

"Jesus never died, so there was no Resurrection."

Muslims, like the gnostics who preceded them by 500 years, object that Jesus never died. If he never died, he did not rise from the dead. The Muslim accounts are highly problematic in defending this proposition. Two sources, the Qur'an[6] and the *Gospel of Barnabas,*[7] state that when the mob came for Jesus, God made someone else, perhaps Judas, look like him. The mob arrested the look-alike and crucified him instead.

This view is plagued by two major problems: First, since we can establish that Jesus' disciples sincerely believed he had risen from the dead and had appeared to them, what caused their beliefs if Jesus was never crucified? The Qur'an claims that God raised Jesus up to himself, apparently at the time of the rescue.[8] So who or what did the disciples see three days later? We have observed that opposing theories cannot account for the appearances. Second, most scholars regard the Gospel of Barnabas as a Muslim forgery composed no earlier than the fifteenth century. Our earliest manuscript is from that era, nor is there any earlier mention of such a book.[9] If Muslims were aware of such a supportive account, they certainly would have appealed to it in their frequent interactions with Christians. If the book was really written by Barnabas, it would have been cited by the early church Fathers. None do. The book also contains a striking contradiction that would rule out Barnabas as its true author. It refers to Jesus as "Christ" on at least two occasions in the beginning, only to later deny that he is the Messiah.[10] This demonstrates an ignorance of the original languages, since *Christ* is the Greek equivalent to the Hebrew/Aramaic word *Messiah.* This is not a mistake that Barnabas as a first-century Jew would have made, since he would have been well acquainted with both Hebrew/Aramaic and Greek. Several anachronisms also occur in the book, indicating a late composition. One indication of its date is that the *Gospel of Barnabas* mentions the year of Jubilee as occurring every hundred years.[11] Yet, the year was celebrated every fifty years until a papal decree by the Catholic Church in 1343.[12] Barnabas also mentions systems of medieval feudalism,[13] a medieval court procedure,[14] and wooden wine casks. Wineskins were used in first-century Palestine.[15]

While the Qurʾan is much earlier, it is a seventh-century composition, that still dates it over five full centuries after all of the New Testament sources, plus at least five full centuries from our best secular references to Jesus' death on the cross. If the Muslim objects that the Qurʾan is inspired, we might respond that we are making no such assumptions in our use of the New Testament concerning Jesus' resurrection in our minimal facts approach, and we will not make them with the Qurʾan. The Muslim references that deny the death of Jesus are far from being credible sources in this matter.

"Reports of Jesus' appearances differ little from the reports of the angel's appearance to Joseph Smith."

What's the difference between Mormonism's founder Joseph Smith and his eleven witnesses to the golden plates and Jesus' disciples experiencing the appearances? Joseph Smith claimed that an angel appeared to him and directed him to golden plates, which he showed to eleven others.[16] Smith claimed to have translated these plates and the translation was called *The Book of Mormon.*

Like Jesus' apostles, Smith willingly suffered and died for his beliefs. Thus, if I am going to claim that a person's willingness to suffer for his beliefs indicates that he sincerely regarded those beliefs as true, why not accept the testimony of Joseph and his eleven witnesses?

A few factors distinguish the case of Jesus' disciples from that of Joseph Smith.

While all of the apostles were willing to suffer and die for their beliefs, six of the eleven witnesses to the gold plates left the Mormon Church. Imagine what we would think about the credibility of the testimonies of Jesus' resurrection if Peter, Paul, James, John, and two other disciples had left Christianity within a few years. However, they clung to their faith to the very end of their lives.

Even if several persons did see gold plates, this says *absolutely nothing* about the viability of their content. The issue is not whether there actually were eyewitnesses to the plates, but whether the plates contained revealed truth from God. Of that, we really have no evidence at all.

There is no evidence that the *Book of Mormon* is true. For example, no specific archaeological findings have been linked to events and places described in *The Book of Mormon.* There is considerable evidence outside of the testimony of the disciples to support the claim of Jesus' resurrection. Here we have stressed the empty tomb and the conversion of the skeptics Paul and James.

There is, however, evidence that the Mormon documents are not true, including the lack of archaeological evidence where it should be and problems with the Book of Abraham.[17]

"Reports of the Resurrection are no more believable than today's reports of Elvis and alien sightings."

Why believe the eyewitness accounts of the risen Jesus while rejecting numerous reports of encounters with Elvis Presley and aliens?

"Elvis sightings are like those of Christ."

It is possible to find people who honestly believe that there is no body in the tomb of Elvis Presley or that he rose from death but no one has found the evidence convincing enough to dig up the casket to see what it contains. Jesus' tomb, however, was demonstrably empty.

Elvis sightings are best explained by various opposing theories such as mistaken identity, especially since many Elvis impersonators are about. It is also conceivable, if highly unlikely, that Elvis faked his death. All such explanations of Jesus' resurrection fail.[18]

The religio-historical context for a resurrection is not present with Elvis as it was with Jesus. Elvis never claimed divinity; Jesus did. Elvis did not perform deeds that appeared miraculous; Jesus did. Elvis never predicted his resurrection; Jesus did.

"Extraterrestrial sightings are like post-Resurrection appearances."

We can establish that multiple believers and even a couple of hard-core skeptics believed that the risen Jesus had appeared to them. No good reasons exist for doubting the testimonies of the disciples, since they are also supported by a couple of hard-core skeptics, James and Paul, who were also convinced that they saw him. The tomb was empty. These even occurred within the historical context of Jesus' claims,[19] his miracles,[20] and the probable existence of God.[21] There are no plausible explanations that can account for the known historical data.

Therefore, Jesus' resurrection is not only the most plausible explanation to account for the known data; it also fits into a context charged with theological significance that increases its evidence as well as explanatory power.

Eyewitness testimony of alien activity is often questionable on its own grounds. Plausible opposing theories abound to account for the phenomena (e.g., weather balloons, military aircraft, hallucinations, and poor reporting techniques). There is strong data from science that renders the chances of life elsewhere in the universe as extremely unlikely.

The fact that these same UFO testimonies frequently attest that these phenomena regularly break the laws of nature requires a rejection of *material* entities, as concluded by scientists who have researched this phenomenon. So we must consider a *spiritual* reality as a possible cause.[22] Certain UFO reports may actually be true and don't have to be explained away, but we must still inquire as to the *cause* for these data.

Ad hominem arguments

At one time or another, almost everyone has argued in an *ad hominem* manner. *Ad hominem* argumentation comes in different forms, but in general it can be said to attack the individual rather than the issues. One candidate for public office says of the opponent, "You cannot trust his reasoning for opposing import car taxes because he owns a Toyota dealership." That is an example of arguing *ad hominem*. Motives are irrelevant to the content of an argument. The dealership owner may have selfish motives for holding his position, yet his arguments not to impose import taxes may still be valid.

When discussing Jesus' resurrection, a skeptic may say, "Well, Christianity was responsible for the atrocities of the Crusades." This is an *ad hominem* argument, since it attacks the position but does not address the evidence. You might respond, "Politically motivated people may have advanced the Crusades in the name of Christ, but that does not necessarily make those activities Christian. Certainly Jesus would not have approved of the Crusades. This doesn't come close to answering the evidence I have presented."

"Extraordinary claims require extraordinary evidence."

Skeptics occasionally cite the maxim that the more radical the claim, the stronger the requirement of evidence to justify belief. This would be the case with Jesus' resurrection. It requires more evidence to justify belief in the Resurrection than evidence required to justify belief that he was crucified.

This imposed rule possesses a common sense appeal, but there are problems with it.

We believe that we have enough evidence to satisfy such a requirement. We have a collection of historical data that is consistent with Jesus' resurrection and in fact strongly attests to it. The risen Jesus appeared to individuals and to groups. His appearances are attested by friends, an enemy, and a skeptic. His tomb was empty and opposing theories to account for the collection of data fail. Therefore, Jesus' resurrection from the dead is the *most* plausible explanation to account for the historical data.

The requirement for extraordinary evidence cuts both ways. If Jesus did not rise from the dead, one must explain the known data. Let's say that the critic suggests group hallucinations in an attempt to account for the group appearances. We know from psychology that group hallucinations, if not impossible, require certain circumstances of expectation and ecstacy, both of which were absent from the groups of disciples he allegedly appeared to. Therefore, the skeptic's assertion that group hallucinations account for the appearances to the disciples is an extraordinary claim and, therefore, requires extraordinary evidence in order to justify our belief. We have observed that all opposing theories to Jesus' resurrection are extremely improbable, if not practically impossible. Accordingly, they face the same challenge for extraordinary evidence.[23]

Unsubstantiated issues may be a tactic of avoidance

A very common tactic of some skeptics is to raise a number of objections without substantiating them, because they think that as long as a question can be raised against something, one is justified in dismissing the data. Michael Licona once had a very involved discussion on the Internet with a skeptic over the matter of Jesus' resurrection. It was an extremely beneficial discussion, during which time the skeptic was able to expose weaknesses in Licona's arguments for Jesus' resurrection that he gladly acknowledged and corrected. The skeptical friend also came to the realization that there is some pretty good evidence for Jesus' resurrection that neither he, nor anyone else he knew of, had been able to answer.

During the course of a lengthy discussion that ended up being 260 typed pages, the skeptic raised many questions and possibilities. However, as was pointed out to him, "You have to do more than raise issues. You must also support them. You can't just say, 'Well what about this or that' without supporting those theories, and then claim that you have effectively undermined the data I provided."

Why is it important that the other guy provide support for his view? Without supporting data, the view is considerably weaker. We'll call this the "Plutonian Fowl Principle." Let's suppose that someone named Bert proposes that invisible purple polka-dotted geese from Pluto are responsible for all of the unexplained phenomena in the universe. Bert appeals to a dream he had about these colorful Plutonian fowl and adds that if they are indeed invisible, we wouldn't see them, and since they are from a planet we are not yet capable of exploring, this would explain why so many phenomena have not yet been explained. However, if and when we can explore Pluto, he believes that we may discover these geese and, consequently, all of the unexplained phenomena in the universe will be solved. Finally, Bert challenges you, "Now I think this is a pretty good argument that accounts for the unexplained phenomena in our universe. Try and disprove it!"

I might respond to Bert by saying, "If you want to hold that view, be my guest. But you really need to provide some reasonable data in its support. I have no responsibility to refute your theory until you can provide evidence to support it. The burden of proof is on you, since you make the positive claim."

Another problem with this strategy of proposing an opposing theory without support is that many of these types of objections are sometimes raised simultaneously. Here are some suggested responses.

"If historians dismissed data merely because a doubt could be raised in opposition, then virtually nothing could be held as knowable history."

"One cannot just say, 'Well what about this? . . . or that? . . . or still that?' without providing good reasons for embracing those ideas. The ideas in themselves cannot undermine the case for Jesus' resurrection."

Skeptics sometimes try to raise more questions than can be fairly answered in the allotted time available. Throw it back on them: "If you want to speculate with an opposing theory, the burden of proof is upon you to show that your theory is plausible. Why should I be stuck with the responsibility of thoroughly researching and refuting every possible unsubstantiated assertion that can be thrown at me? Do the work yourself; then give me something credible to consider and I will consider it. Until then, such a theory should fall upon deaf ears." This response cuts both ways. We could also respond to the skeptic with far more objections to their position or theory than they could possibly answer in the allotted time. You could even raise a string of your own objections and then say, "Where does this get either one of us? Let's agree to raise objections one at a time and only when we have some data to discuss.

Conclusion

We have spent a considerable amount of time discussing the evidence for Jesus' resurrection and how to answer skeptics who provide opposing theories that attempt to account for the known facts. It should be noted that, just because someone asks, "Why couldn't the disciples have experienced hallucinations rather than having actually seen the risen Jesus?" does not necessarily mean that person is a skeptic. Many times people who are seeking the truth, including believers, will ask the same questions in order to see if there is a good answer and a reason why they should believe. There is nothing wrong with this. Many believers have been encouraged in their relationship with God upon learning that their Christian faith has a rational foundation.

We have seen that Jesus' resurrection is strongly attested historically and is the most plausible explanation for the facts. In fact, it is the *only* plausible explanation for them. We have also looked at preferred ways of communicating the truth. When dialoguing with skeptics and those who are seeking truth, we must not have the objective of "winning" the debate. Our goal should be to show the love of Christ through compassion, gentleness, and respect (1 Peter 3:15). In the next two chapters, we will discuss how you may do this and then pull everything together and show how it can play out in real life.

Chapter 13

People Skills

The Art of Sharing

Who you are speaks more loudly than what you say. We have all been around difficult people. One person constantly talks without allowing you to get a word in. Another is only interested in talking about himself. Still another always has bad breath, frequently has food stuck between his teeth, and smells like his shower only works on Saturdays. Many of these people are brilliant. But sometimes it seems that no one wants to listen to you in return. It is important that, in addition to having solid evidence in support of Jesus' resurrection, we present ourselves in a manner that helps others to be open to what we have to say. So here are a few tips that may enable you to be more effective when talking with others.

Be loving

What are you like around others? My family and I (Licona) were together in a car that was struck by another vehicle. The bumper of our car was banged up pretty well, and the car that hit us had buckled its hood in the event. As I was waiting for the police and talking with the driver of the car who hit us, a young man with his hair slicked back, wearing a white shirt, dress trousers, and a tie, walked up to us both, handed each of us a gospel tract and said, "Here. Read this while you wait." He smiled and walked off into the sunset, never asking if anyone was hurt or if there was anything he could do to help. If I were a skeptic, that well-meaning brother would have become the subject of ridicule in future conversations. He left no positive impression of love behind the gospel of Christ.

If we want others to take our message seriously, we need to become credible messengers. Perhaps we can do this best by reflecting the love of Christ in our lives, the very thing we desire to communicate with others. What are you communicating? Are you so concerned about offending others that you refuse to take a stand on virtually any issue? This is far from the way Jesus was. Many were offended by his teachings.

On the other hand, are you the company preacher who walks around with a scowl? Do people smell your brimstone aftershave as you pass by? This was not Jesus' general approach either. While he did not hesitate to confront the Jewish leaders of his day who were more concerned with their position, power, and traditions than with an intimate relationship with God, Jesus appears to have spent most of his time ministering to people and sharing the gospel with them. If we allow the world to see that the Christian worldview has much to offer over a secular worldview, perhaps nonbelievers will be more interested in what we have to say. Don't forget that beyond truth itself, we want to model the changed life that is present by the grace of Jesus Christ.

Be humble

Having learned the evidences presented thus far, it is easy to gain a confidence when dialoguing with others that can turn to arrogance. The apostle Paul wrote, "Knowledge makes arrogant, but love edifies" (1 Cor. 8:1b). Keep a check on your heart. It is certainly thrilling to experience new confidence in sharing your faith as you obtain new knowledge and skills. We may start out with the right motives, only to have them change in the process without our even realizing it. Pretty soon we find that all we want to do is win an argument. We have been there and speak from experience. Such an attitude is not glorifying to God and may bring about failure in your discussions with skeptics. The object is *not* to win an argument but rather to lead a sincere person to the truth. Present the evidence in a humble, patient, and loving manner.

The Bible teaches us about the attitude we should have while sharing our faith. Consider the following verses (emphasis added):

A *gentle answer* turns away wrath. But a harsh word stirs up anger. The tongue of the wise makes knowledge acceptable. (Prov. 15:1–2a)

Let your speech *always be with grace*, as though seasoned with salt, so that you may know how you should respond to each person. (Col. 4:6)

And the Lord's bond-servant *must not be quarrelsome*, but be *kind to all*, able to teach, patient when wronged, *with gentleness* correcting those who are in opposition, if perhaps God may grant them repentance leading to the knowledge of the truth, and they may come to their senses and escape from the snare of the devil, having been held captive by him to do his will. (2 Tim. 2:24–26)

But sanctify Christ as Lord in your hearts, always being ready to make a defense to everyone who asks you to give an account for the hope that is in you, *yet with gentleness and reverence.* (1 Peter 3:15)

Have mercy on some, who are doubting. (Jude 22)

Notice that God urges us to be kind, gentle, and merciful toward those who hold views other than our own. Unfortunately, too many of the Christians whom skeptics and seekers encounter are unprepared and become extremely defensive and unpleasant. This, of course, is not the response that will encourage someone to become a Christian. Many will embrace the truth if someone will simply show it to them. That someone may be *you*. Dare to be different by having a response that is both sound and loving.

Even with the best intentions, it is easy to become upset with someone who disagrees with you on the subject of God. A few years ago, I (Licona) really failed in a discussion with a Jehovah's Witness who came to my door. She was going around the neighborhood with her teenage daughter and I invited them in. Our time together turned into a heated discussion, and I had to ask her to leave. Although she was initially quite unpleasant when I told her that we disagreed on the issue of who Jesus is, my attitude was bad from the start. I was more interested in winning the argument than compassionately sharing the truth and patiently attempting to reveal the errors of the organization to which she belonged.

How often do we listen with an open mind when someone angrily or arrogantly tells us that we are wrong? Rarely or never. We shut off our minds to whatever that person tells us, even if deep down inside, we have a feeling that what he is saying is true. Skeptics and seekers are people too, of course. If our attitude is bad, they may close their minds to us as well. We will get nowhere and mistakenly blame their unreceptiveness on a disinterest in truth. Remember that Satan has led many down the wrong path. Lead them to the right path. Many of these are sincere and committed people, just the kind you want in your church.

Christian philosopher Terry Miethe writes, "I have known several famous Christian debaters who won the 'argument,' but lost the 'debate'! They had the best content *and* the worst personality. Consequently, the audience went away with more emotional sympathy for the atheist opponent, and therefore for his position!"[1] It has been said that people do not care how much you know until they know how much you care. Your genuine love will have a greater positive impact on a person than any other character quality.

Be a good listener

Have you ever been in a conversation with someone who would not let you say a word? Was it more of a monologue than a dialogue? Did you begin thinking of ways to excuse yourself graciously? When sharing the evidence with others, do not make the mistake of doing the very thing that turns you off in a discussion. Let the other person fully express his or her views and feelings. Do not interrupt. In fact, ask questions to provide the speaker additional opportunity to expound on his views. Have a genuine interest in the person. By listening to his views, you can learn a lot about what issues are really bothering him. If the person believes that you truly understand the issue(s) with which he struggles, he is more likely to listen to your answer.

Stay on the subject of Jesus' resurrection

It is easy to be drawn off the subject of Jesus' resurrection. Frequently this can occur when your skeptical friend does not have an answer to what you presented. For example, let's say your friend begins the dialogue by saying that she could never become a Christian because it is a first-century fairytale with no evidence to support it.

Sara: "This is the twenty-first century. We know that people don't come back from the dead. It's ridiculous to believe that Jesus did. There's no evidence, either, to support your belief."

You: *"I can appreciate what you're saying. However, a strong case can be made in favor of Jesus' resurrection."*

Sara: "I find that hard to believe. How?"

So you begin to share how several facts surrounding the event can be established, even from non-Christian sources. In Sara's experience, no one has been able to do this before. Confused, she realizes that she cannot keep up with you on this discussion. So she changes her objection:

Sara: "Well, if God is so loving as you say he is, why does he allow all of the evil in the world?"

If you elect to switch course in the discussion and now go with the problem of evil, you may be treading on ground on which you are not as familiar and, most importantly, you move away from your central subject. Stay on the subject of Jesus' resurrection:

"That's a great question. And I think it would be enjoyable to discuss it with you sometime. But an unanswered question does not nullify the resurrection of Jesus. You mentioned that you were unaware that there is strong historical evidence for Christ's resurrection. What do you think about the evidence I've just provided?"

Then continue the discussion. This type of response will keep the issue in perspective and keep you on track.

During one of my (Licona) email discussions with a skeptic, the latter brought up a number of objections with Christianity. For example, he claimed that God contradicted himself when he said "Thou shalt not kill" when giving the Ten Commandments, and shortly afterward commanded the Israelites to kill their enemies. Moreover, he brought up occasions when God commanded that enemy women and children be killed as well. I attempted to answer these problems for him. But he either did not like my answers or had decided to be difficult. So I finally said:

As I consider your thoughts, it sounds like we will continue to quibble over issues that are not of great importance to our discussion since they do not invalidate Christianity. Remember this: If you accept the inspiration and trustworthiness of the Bible, you have no argument against Christianity's being true, because the God-inspired Bible says it is. On the other hand, if you reject the inspiration and trustworthiness of the Bible, you have no argument against Christianity, either, since your objections about a horrid God depend on the accounts being true! Either way, the issues that trouble you about Christianity do not invalidate it. This is because the truth of Christianity is not tied to the inspiration of the Bible, since I can demonstrate the truth of Christianity apart from accepting the inspiration or even the general trustworthiness of the Bible.

I suggested to him that we limit our discussion for the moment to whether Christianity is true by looking at Jesus' resurrection, since Christianity stands or falls on that event. I continued, "If Jesus' resurrection did not occur, then we can just laugh at the problem passages in the Bible. However, if you decide that Christianity is true, then we can discuss these passages later that are troubling you."[2]

This focused the discussion back on the most important issue already before us, instead of moving into smokescreens that obscure the main point. A smokescreen is precisely what many of these introduced objections are, barriers behind which the skeptic can hide the true reason for rejecting Jesus' resurrection. Many times this is simply an objection of the will rather than of the intellect. Perhaps this person simply does not want to have a relationship with God. Some enjoy the position of unbelief too much to want to give it up. A familiar position in which pride is invested would be lost if the questions about God really found answers. There are often motives behind our beliefs.

Some of these motives may seem far-fetched to those who have not spent much time sharing their faith with others. But those who have know how often people have a stake in their own unbelief. I used to struggle when I read about Jesus' account of the rich man and Lazarus in Luke 16. In it, the rich man who is in hell asks Abraham to send Lazarus from paradise to warn his brothers lest they, too, end up in hell and be tormented. Abraham answered, "If they do not listen to [the writings of] Moses and the Prophets, they will not be convinced even if someone rises from the dead."[3]

I used to wonder how that could be. If someone really appeared from the dead with a message from God, would others look at this person and not accept what he had to say? Then I developed a friendship with an atheist. As we became closer friends, we discussed the topics of God and Christianity more often. He moved slowly from atheism to agnosticism. Then he became a skeptical theist. Finally, he admitted that he was certain God existed, that Jesus rose from the dead, and that God was offering him eternal life. Nevertheless, he still refused to accept Jesus into his heart because he wanted to be the master of his own life. His rejection of Jesus was not due to a lack of any evidence. Rather this was a refusal on the part of his will. He was very straightforward about his real reasons.

We may never know the motives in the people we dialogue with. Nevertheless, in order to help prevent us from getting discouraged when the person remains an unbeliever, it can be helpful to remember that the majority of the people we talk to will reject Christ, not because of any lack of evidence, but because they simply want to do so. One way to recognize this is when the person clearly has no more questions about the facts of the gospel. Yet they still are not ready to go further. The skeptic in the e-mail dialogue mentioned above, agreed to focus on Jesus' resurrection. I presented the evidence, answered a few objections, and I never heard back from him.

So stay focused on the topic of Jesus' resurrection. Not only will this help you to concentrate on the most important topic, but it will also prevent you from wasting a lot of time with those simply seeking a sparring partner for debate. "When you wrestle a pig in the mud," runs the old farm saying, "sooner or later you realize that the pig is enjoying it." [4] Jesus said, "Do not throw your pearls before swine."[5]

Anchor a conclusion before moving on

Conclude one matter with your skeptical friend before moving on to another topic. Once you have engaged in several dialogues with skeptics, you will discover that because of human nature he will rarely acknowledge that you have effectively answered his objection. He will often simply move on to still another objection. It is easy for this to go on over a period of time. It can be helpful to bring closure to a matter before moving on to the next. This assists in preventing your skeptical friend from coming back later and saying, "Yes, but remember it still could have been . . . ," even though you answered that objection fifteen minutes prior. Let's look at an example of how anchoring works.

"So you can see from the reasons I've just provided, hallucinations fail to explain Jesus' resurrection."

Rick: "Well, maybe Jesus didn't really die on the cross and he later just came out of a coma and some who thought he had died now thought he had risen."

"Hey, that's an interesting point, Rick. But before we go there, will you agree with me that hallucinations fail to account for all of the data that we have, or should I give you some more reasons why scholars have rejected that theory?"

Learn common objections and be comfortable answering them

In the process of inquiry, it is normal to question the claim that a supernatural event occurred and to raise other potential explanations for the data. After talking with a number of skeptics, you will realize that the same opposing theories to the Resurrection are raised most of the time. These were covered in part 3. Review the information in that section, especially the charts, until you have a good grasp of the facts that refute various opposing theories. The more experience you gain fielding common objections, the more comfortable you will become in responding to them.

Be prepared to address objections for which you do not know the answer

No matter how much you have read on a subject or how often you have discussed it, occasionally someone will bring up something you have never heard before. If you do not know how to answer it, what should you do? Our natural reflex is to "wing it" and say something that may not be altogether true, or it may be hard to defend. By doing this, you dig yourself into a hole that will be more difficult to get out of if the skeptic decides to probe further.

Our recommendation is to be honest. There is no shame in admitting that you do not know the answer to something. Moreover, by doing this you establish credibility about the answers you do provide, since your listeners will know that you were not winging it when you provided them. Honesty may also encourage the person with whom you are talking to be just as candid about what he or she does not understand. By admitting that you do not know all of the answers and would be willing to research further, you may facilitate a more open discussion, whereas "winging it" may begin to shut down communications.

You may want to say: "That's a good question. I honestly don't know the answer. So rather than say something that may not be totally right, I'll have to look into it, and I'll be happy to get back to you if you like." Then return to where the discussion left off before the question.

Before you do this, however, you may surprise yourself with a good answer. Here's a two-step approach that may be of help: (1) Ask yourself whether this objection, if true, would refute Jesus' resurrection. If it does not, point this out to your skeptical friend. For example, suppose someone were to object that he does not like all the "dos and don'ts" in the Bible. I might respond by saying, "Even if these are present, how does that answer or refute the historical evidence for Jesus' resurrection I have just presented?" You will find that many objections actually do nothing to call Jesus' resurrection into question and are unrelated. However, if his objection to Jesus' resurrection *would* refute it if true, proceed to the second step. (2) Quickly reflect on your minimal facts approach and determine whether any of the five major facts $(4 + 1)$[6] you presented remain unexplained if this objection is true.

For example, let's suppose you have presented the evidence for Jesus' resurrection when your skeptical colleague asserts that the Gospels were not written by the four authors to whom they have been attributed. Thus, your claim that the original disciples taught that Jesus rose cannot be supported. Perhaps you haven't involved yourself in matters of New Testament higher criticism and are unprepared to discuss the authorship issue. That's okay. You may be surprised that you can still answer your colleague. Remember that in a minimal facts approach you do not have to defend theological positions such as the inspiration or trustworthiness of the New Testament or the traditional authorship of the Gospels. Doing so may even detract from the more important issue of Jesus' resurrection.

So you quickly reflect through your five facts that are strongly attested and granted by the majority of scholars who study the subject of Jesus' resurrection, even the rather skeptical ones. Then you can reply with the following: "I haven't based my argument that the disciples saw the risen Jesus on a specific authorship of the Gospels. Rather I have presented nine sources in three categories that provide early, multiple, and even nonbiblical testimony that they were making this claim."[7]

For this objection, we did not even have to reflect on the facts. We only needed to understand the minimal facts approach.

Let's try another one. It may be suggested that Jesus' disciples gave him something to drink that contained some common herbs prior to being crucified. Shortly afterward, the herbs in the drink made him appear dead and substantially reduced his oxygen needs. The soldiers mistook him for dead and removed him from the cross. The disciples, perhaps Luke the physician, then gave Jesus some other herbs that restored his health. The disciples then proclaimed that he had risen from the dead.

Now let's think through our minimal facts and see if these alone can provide a formidable defense. The death of Jesus by crucifixion is our first minimal fact. Thus, this theory is dead from the outset.

Second, we have the sincere belief of the disciples that they had seen the risen Jesus. Remember that their continual willingness to suffer and even die for those beliefs indicates that they sincerely regarded their beliefs as being true. Yet our conjectured Swoon-Fraud 1 theory earlier presents the disciples as deceivers and does not seem compatible with the known data. Remember that people may die for what they believe is true. But it is not reasonable to think that an entire group of men would be willing to suffer horribly and die for something they all knew was false.

Another problem with this theory is that it does not take into account the conversion of the church persecutor Paul, who himself claimed to have seen Jesus risen. If the herbs were common as suggested, then an educated Paul should have been aware of their existence and would have multiple doubts in his mind, especially given his beliefs that a crucified man was cursed by God and could not possibly be the Messiah. We also might ask ourselves if these herbs had such powerful healing powers, why they are not employed today in modern medical treatment for knife wounds, gun wounds, and injuries sustained from serious car accidents. Besides, Paul's description of Jesus' appearance to him was glorious. Thus, the normal appearance of a Jesus who had swooned and been healed will not do. Paul would probably have remained skeptical, and a glorious appearance would, of course, eliminate a swooned Jesus.

Notice that in these examples we simply focus on whether the objection really calls into question Jesus' resurrection. We apply the minimal facts approach.

In many instances these minimal facts alone provide decisive refutation to objections with which we are unfamiliar.

Skeptics will always come up with theories that attempt to explain Jesus' resurrection in natural terms. Most if not all of these are simply nuances on old theories. If you understand the minimal facts approach and the five facts (4+1), you should be able to refute many if not all of those new theories without prior knowledge of them.

Don't be taken in by false information

In 2001, I (Licona) was asked to debate a mystic who claimed that Christianity was invented by some pagans and Jews who got together and concocted the whole account of Jesus and his disciples, all of whom are mythical figures. She also claimed that the Christian fish was not invented for Christians to identify themselves secretly when being publicly identified as a Christian could have meant death. Rather, she asserted, these conspirators invented it to signify the inauguration of the age of Pisces.

A secular radio talk show host thought a debate between the two of us would make an interesting show. However, the mystic declined the opportunity, and I was instead invited to answer her claims on a show that followed one where she appeared as a guest. When I researched her major claims, I found that they were completely without merit. I would not claim that she invented the data. But it became clear that someone in the past had done precisely that.

For example, regarding the Christian fish representing the ushering in of the age of Pisces, I contacted a professor of astronomy at a prominent university who specialized in the practice of astronomy in antiquity. When I informed him of her claim, he replied that her claims were not worth answering. He added that her claim that those in antiquity formed the Christian fish as a symbol for the age of Pisces was an obvious anachronism. Although constellations were recognized in antiquity, the method employed by astrologers for recognizing an astrological age did not develop to the point of identifying an "age of Pisces" until the twentieth century. Checking revealed that a number of her claims had similar serious flaws in foundation or evidence. However, for the average listener, who will not investigate claims such as those the mystic was making, this false information can have devastating results. It can cause severe doubts concerning the validity of Christianity.

On another occasion on the radio, the talk show host, a guest who was an atheist, and I (Licona) were discussing the evidence for Jesus' resurrection. We began to take calls. Halfway through the program, a man called and claimed that Licona was making up this whole thing about ancient sources such as Josephus, Tacitus, and others mentioning Jesus. He claimed that he was a serious student and writer of ancient history and that no ancient sources mentioned Jesus, so these citations were lies. He went on saying this for a good three minutes or so. Finally, I said that it was one man's word against another. I provided the locations in these sources and said that anyone who wanted to check it out could go to their nearest bookstore and purchase the works of any of these ancient authors for under $15 and read them personally.

The man responded with several new false assertions that may have been believable to the uninformed. A commercial break followed and when we came back a new call was taken and the opportunity to respond to the previous guest was gone. Some people oppose Christianity so much that they will do whatever they can to thwart attempts to articulate the truth.

Most of us will never be involved in a public debate for which we spend months in preparation. Therefore, if the skeptic shares false information that he has innocently received, or if he decides to stretch the truth on a certain matter, there is very little chance that we will have had an opportunity to research the views of our opponent in order to see if what he is saying is true. What should we do? First, recognize that people often stretch the truth and treat it as an objection to which you have no answer. Second, if you are suspicious of the skeptic's response, ask for evidence: "That's new to me. What are your sources?" After all, you have to provide sources to support your view. Why not require that your opponent do likewise?

Prepare for the battle in prayer

The other author of this book, Gary Habermas, has represented the Christian view in several public debates. He is fond of pointing out that anyone who has argued the Christian view in a public debate setting realizes that it is more of a spiritual battle than an exercise in logic. Paul wrote that our battle "is not against flesh and blood, but against the rulers, against the powers, against the world forces of this darkness, against the spiritual forces of wickedness in the heavenly places" (Eph. 6:12). Our main struggle is not against humans (i.e., flesh and blood), but against spiritual forces.

Therefore, it only makes sense that we should prepare ourselves for this kind of battle. Paul says that the way to do this is to put on the proper spiritual armor: truth, righteousness, peace, faith, salvation, and God's words. We must remain alert and pray both for the words to say and the courage to say them (see Eph. 6:10–20). So, study and prepare as though it all depends on you; pray as though it all depends on God, because it does. The main reason for this is simple: Changing hearts is God's business. In fact, it is not even within our power to "convince" someone to trust Jesus Christ as Lord and Savior, so we need to rely on the work of the Holy Spirit.

Resist the temptation to overstate your case

You may be very excited about your new knowledge. It can be extremely uplifting to discover that what the Holy Spirit revealed to you is largely supported by historical investigation. Moreover, as you discover that most people cannot effectively address the issues you present, it is easy to give in to the temptation to claim more than is accurate by saying something like, "I will prove to you beyond any doubt that Jesus rose from the dead." As discussed earlier, virtually nothing can be proved with that degree of certainty. The problem with making this type of statement is that if the person walks away with any doubts after you have claimed you would prove Jesus' resurrection beyond all doubt, you have failed to support your view in his eyes. It is much better to state your case accurately or even understate it: "I believe there is good evidence for Jesus' resurrection" or "There is enough evidence for Jesus' resurrection that the Christian is rationally justified in accepting it." When the person with whom you are having dialog realizes that you have fulfilled your promise, he or she may be more inclined to consider the matter further.

Always be calm

It is easy to become defensive when someone attacks your beliefs. Our natural impulse is to respond with anger. The result is a heated argument. You must resist the temptation to do this at all costs. Not only will anger hurt your Christian testimony, your "opponents" also will lose whatever receptivity and good will they had to begin with, and you will feel badly afterward. Do not be offended when someone brings up an opposing theory. As you have seen, there are good answers to these. Each opposing theory is an *opportunity* to show the strength of the argument for Jesus' resurrection. I (Licona) find it effective to respond to an objection as though the person wants to believe and simply has a few questions that stand in the way: "That's a great question [or point]. In fact, there are some scholars who once raised that same issue. Here are some things for your consideration. . . ."

Remember the words of Solomon in Proverbs 15:1: "A gentle answer turns away wrath."

To be proficient, practice

As with anything else in life, if you want to excel, you cannot do it without practice. The more you present the evidence, the more proficient you will become. To become a good hitter at slow-pitch softball, one must practice in a batting cage with a pitching machine, as well as on the field with the team. However, even with all the practice, a real game is different. The opposing pitcher will throw much the same as did the machine in batting practice. However, the emotional setting of a game makes a big difference, and it takes experience to become more comfortable.

When I (Licona) played softball, I practiced diligently, going to the batting cage several times a week. By the time the season began, I was hitting the ball very well. However, in the game, I produced a slew of weakly tapped ground balls until I was greatly frustrated. One hot afternoon during a tournament game, I stepped up to the plate, my confidence gone. Then a teammate encouraged me with the words, "You're at the batting cage, Mike." The mental image of the cage immediately relaxed my body and I hit a long ball to the outfield, and got on base. The batting slump was over when I realized that it was the tension of a live game that caused the problem. It took the experience of playing the game to lead to new levels of competence.

It is the same with sharing your faith with others. Work on mastering the information. Practice alone in the car. Imagine that there is a skeptic sitting in the passenger's seat and have a discussion as you drive. What would you say? How would you defend the truth of Jesus' resurrection? How would you answer specific objections? How can you say it succinctly? Practice.

Then get in the game. There is nothing like a real conversation with a skeptic to show where you need improvement. It was discussions with the toughest skeptics that prompted the authors to study further and find better answers and ways of communicating. When confronted with a weakness, return to this book and CD. Study the relevant sections and take a look at relevant endnotes and the detailed outline in the appendix to become better prepared for the next conversation.

Now it is time to pull everything together. How does our argument for Jesus' resurrection look? And how do we share it with others? Answers to these questions will be our focus in the next chapter.

Conclusion

Putting It All Together

We have covered a lot of information in this book. In order to keep from overwhelming those you talk to, have a simple outline of a basic presentation in mind. This will help you stay on track and avoid fumbling for words.

As discussed in the last chapter, many times it is better to understate your conclusion. A friend from Scotland described Germany's bombing of London in 1940 as a "bit of a nuisance."[1] We may hold that Jesus' resurrection can be established with a reasonable degree of historical certainty. When talking with unbelievers, though, on many occassions it may be better to understate this conclusion.

Suppose we make the claim to an unbeliever that we can "prove" that Jesus rose from the dead with "a reasonable degree of historical certainty." The person we are talking to may have a much tougher set of criteria for proving something to that degree of certainty than we do. The average person has never given any thought to the nature of historical truth and the various degrees of historical certainty, as we considered them in chapter 1 (pp. 30–33). In this person's eyes, something must be either proven with *100 percent* certainty, or it is not proven at all. In the end we inevitably will be perceived by such a person as failing to "prove" Jesus' resurrection. The unbeliever may not reflect on the fact that there is pretty good evidence for it. All he or she thinks about is that we didn't live up to his or her standard for proof.

Now suppose that we say instead to the unbeliever, "I think there's some pretty good evidence for Jesus' resurrection." The person is still going to ask for some of this evidence, and we still will have to respond to his opposing theories. The difference is that, at the end of our discussion, the person is more likely to think, "Not only did they provide some good evidence for Jesus' resurrection as they promised, but it almost looks to me that they may have even proved it."

Using this approach, we may start off by saying, "I believe there's some pretty good evidence for Jesus' resurrection." When asked to provide that evidence, we respond by saying, "Because not everyone believes the Bible in its entirety, how about if I use only facts that are so strongly evidenced historically that they are granted by nearly every scholar who studies the subject, even the rather skeptical ones?" This usually solicits the skeptical friend's attention. We can then follow up by providing something like the following argument:

- The disciples sincerely believed that Jesus rose from the dead and had appeared to them.
- A number of outside evidences support the truth of their belief in his resurrection.
- Since no opposing theories can adequately account for all of the historical evidence. Therefore, Jesus' resurrection is the only plausible explanation.

This argument has proven effective. For one thing, it makes the conversation more interesting for the skeptic who probably thought we were going to say, "The Bible says it. I believe it. That settles it!" Furthermore, this argument is simple and can be stated in about twenty seconds.

The argument also follows logically. Suppose we know a fact designated as "X." Let's also say that there are a total of four possible explanations for X: explanation 1, explanation 2, explanation 3, and explanation 4. Finally, there is good evidence that 1 accurately explains X, while 2, 3, and 4 are extremely unlikely, if not impossible. In this instance, 1 is the most reasonable explanation for X.

Johnny's mother finds the cookie jar open, several of the chocolate chip cookies are missing, and the clean floor is marred by small muddy human footprints that lead up to and away from the jar. We will refer to this collection of facts as "X." Let's also say that we conclude that there are only four plausible explanations to account for X:

Explanation 1: Johnny stole the cookies.
Explanation 2: Johnny's mother ate the cookies and forgot.
Explanation 3: Johnny's sister stole the cookies.
Explanation 4: Johnny's father stole the cookies.

We might be able to think of other explanations. Perhaps an alien, wearing shoes much like Johnny's, stole the cookies. While this cannot be ruled out altogether, it would not be an explanation we'd include among the most reasonable or plausible. We decide to confine the possibilities to 1–4, as the most plausible. The size of the footprints by the cookie jar seem to mean that Johnny's mother and father are unlikely candidates. Besides, Johnny's father has been at work the entire time. His sister has been at a friend's house all day and is allergic to chocolate, making her unlikely as well. Moreover, Johnny loves cookies and had just told his mother that he was hungry. Given that there is strong evidence in support of 1 (the theory that Johnny stole the cookies), and given that 2, 3, and 4 are all unlikely, Johnny's mother is justified in believing—with a reasonable degree of confidence—that 1 is true, and she can act accordingly.

This logical reasoning applies to the resurrection of Jesus. X is the proposition that the disciples of Jesus sincerely believed that he rose from the dead and appeared to them. Let's say that there are only five initially plausible explanations that account for these claims on the part of the disciples:

Explanation 1: Jesus rose from the dead.
Explanation 2: Fraud was involved on the part of the disciples.
Explanation 3: The disciples sincerely believed they saw the risen Jesus, but were hallucinating or delusional.
Explanation 4: Jesus never really died, so when he appeared to his disciples they thought he had risen from the dead, when he had really only revived from a coma.
Explanation 5: The entire story was a legend that developed over time.

Now consider the additional factors of the empty tomb and the conversions of the church persecutor Paul and the skeptic James because they both believed that the raised Jesus had appeared to them. These provide evidence that explanation 1 is true. One might speculate that explanation 2 (that the disciples stole the body and were lying about the appearances) may also account for the empty tomb. But it does not adequately account for the disciples' transformed lives and willingness to die. Nor does it adequately explain the appearances of the risen Jesus to the skeptics Paul and James.

Similarly, let's consider that explanations 2–5 have all been demonstrated to be extremely unlikely, if not impossible, by several reasons each. Given that there is strong evidence in support of explanation 1, and explanations 2 through 5 are extremely unlikely, if not impossible, Jesus' resurrection from the dead is the most reasonable explanation of the historical data.

Granted, the scenario is more complicated than this exceptionally brief synopsis, but it summarizes the principles used throughout this volume.

How about showing me how to do it?

How could we use the above argument in practice? Your company has announced that it is sponsoring a night out at the ballpark to see the local minor league baseball team. On the night of the game, you get to your seat and find that you are sitting next to Tom, the guy in accounting. Tom is very logical, and, although he has not been hostile toward the religious beliefs of others in the office, he has made it clear that he does not embrace a belief in God. He views religious beliefs as perhaps helpful to others, but not for a thinking person. It is now the third inning, and your conversation has been sporadic. Both of you have been up for pizza, hot dogs, french fries, cotton candy, and conversation with a few of the other employees. He now asks you what you enjoy doing when away from the office. For the past year you have spent much time with the visitation ministry of your church, dropping by the homes of those who have visited the church. You know that Tom is an atheist and will not think highly of your volunteer work. However, you want to use this as an opportunity to share the new information you have just acquired on the evidence for Jesus' resurrection.

So you confidently say to him,

> I'm part of the visitation team at our church. We follow up with those who visit us for the first time on a Sunday morning. We ask them if there is anything we, as a church, can do to meet their needs. I also ask them if they're aware of the historical evidence for Jesus' resurrection. Most aren't, so I briefly share some of the evidence with them. I've been doing it for about a year now, and I really find fulfillment investing time in a worthwhile cause.

You have not pushed your message on him or put him on the defensive. However, you have answered him in a manner that will probably produce curiosity on his part. He may respond by saying something like, "What do you mean by 'historical evidence for Jesus' resurrection'? There's no real evidence. You have to believe the Bible."

Now you begin your case for the resurrection of Jesus. It is not an academic debate where you will possibly need to cover each point in depth. It is a casual discussion with a person who most likely knows much less than you do on the subject. This is not a time to show off your knowledge or to test yourself on how much of this book you remember. You have to get right to the point and be brief. You are confident that you know the truth, and you are compassionate, gentle, and respectful toward your friend. So you respond,

> I understand where you're coming from. Many people are where you are and think that you have to believe that the Bible is the inspired Word of God in order to believe in Jesus' resurrection. However, I have found that the evidence that Jesus rose from the dead is pretty good, even if we only consider those facts that are so strongly attested historically that even most skeptical scholars grant them.

Now your coworker is really curious. He's a logical person and a thinker. No one has ever told him that there are good reasons to believe. Yet you have just informed him that there is "evidence." You are talking his language and he becomes more interested in what you have to say. "What do you mean by historical facts?" he asks.

You are excited about his interest, yet you remain relaxed. You present your basic argument for Jesus' resurrection:

> Well, to state it briefly: we know that Jesus' disciples sincerely believed that he rose from the dead and appeared to them, especially since they were willing to die specifically for this message. Moreover, a number of outside data strongly suggest that their beliefs were true. Considering the fact that there are no viable opposing theories that can account for the disciples' beliefs, Jesus' resurrection is the only plausible explanation for the historical data.

You have made your case in a nutshell. If your coworker is interested in religious issues, you can expect him to respond with some questions. "Wait a minute. Back up the trolley! Apart from believing that the Bible is God's Word, how do you know that the disciples really believed that Jesus rose from the dead?" He has asked you a reasonable question. And you are ready.

You present your *POW!* response:[2]

> That's a great question. Let me give you three categories of evidence. First, we have the eyewitness Paul, who claims to have known and fellowshipped firsthand with the disciples. He repeats their testimony. Second, we have some very early oral tradition that was circulating within the church *before* the New Testament was even written, and it reports that the disciples were saying it. Finally, we have a number of written sources that all portray the disciples teaching that Jesus had appeared to them after he rose from the dead. In all, we have nine independent sources. Several of them are not even biblical writings. So you can see why there is a virtually unanimous consensus among scholars today, even among skeptics, that Jesus' original disciples said that he appeared to them risen from the dead.

Again, do not think that you have to provide all nine sources in order to establish that the disciples claimed that Jesus rose from the dead. They are all there if you need them. But you probably will not need them and will be giving too much information for a casual conversation if you do use them. Give him the three categories and unpack them if the need arises. Then mention that the disciples' willingness to suffer for their beliefs establishes that they sincerely regarded their beliefs to be true.

If we are talking to a person who is rather educated on the subject, we'll focus on Paul and the oral traditions, since scholars consider these to be the strongest reasons. However, if we are talking with the average layperson, we have found that many prefer to hear what nonbiblical sources say. In this case we will focus on the oral traditions and the apostolic fathers, demonstrating that the former predate the New Testament and are, therefore, extrabiblical sources. Let's assume that our friend here is an informed skeptic. You might answer,

> First, we have Paul. Today we have the New Testament as one volume. However, the New Testament is comprised of twenty-seven books and letters from several different authors. It was not until the middle part

of the second century that these books and letters began to be collected into a single volume that was considered to be sacred. My point is that Paul's writings are independent of those of Jesus' disciples. All scholars who study the subject regard Paul as a contemporary of Jesus' disciples. Paul wrote that both he and the disciples were claiming that Jesus rose from the dead and had appeared to them. Second, we have an early Christian creed that predates the writing of the New Testament, probably dating within five years of Jesus' crucifixion, that lists a number of times that the risen Jesus appeared to his disciples, to groups of people, and even to skeptics. Most agree that Paul received this material in Jerusalem from two other eyewitnesses, just a very few years after Jesus' crucifixion. Although this cannot be determined with great certainty, Paul quotes it and since he knew the disciples, the source of the creed was either the disciples themselves or from someone Paul deemed credible.

If he objects that these are all from the Bible, a book filled with errors and contradictions, you can add,

Even critical scholars accept these facts by using the New Testament as no more than books of ancient literature. But if you don't like them, we still have the writings of two church leaders from about the same time as the New Testament writers, who knew the apostles and were trained by them.[3] Both of them imply that Jesus' disciples were claiming that he had risen and had appeared to them. So we have eyewitnesses outside of the Bible who also say that the disciples claimed that Jesus rose from the dead.

Furthermore, it's important to remember that oral tradition predated the New Testament. So to the extent that it can be demonstrated, and it certainly can, that creeds and sermon summaries exist in the New Testament and predate it, these can be regarded as nonbiblical sources.[4] Nonbiblical sources are quoted in other parts of the New Testament. This does not make them 'biblical.'[5] But for the sake of our discussion on Jesus' resurrection, your charge that the Bible is filled with errors and contradictions is beside the point here, since I am not basing my argument for Jesus' resurrection on the inerrancy of the Bible or even on its general trustworthiness. I'm only considering strongly attested historical facts that are granted by the vast majority of scholars who study the subject, even the rather skeptical ones.

"Well, that's fine," responds your colleague. "I can accept that they were claiming that he rose from the dead. But that doesn't mean that he did. Maybe they were lying." This is a thoughtful response on the part of your colleague. And you acknowledge it:

> I agree with you that merely claiming something says nothing about its being true. However, we can go a step further and establish that, not only did they claim it, they really believed it. Both a secular historian from the first century and Christian historians from the first through fourth centuries report how the disciples were all willing to suffer to the point of dying for their belief that Jesus had risen from the dead. While this does not prove that what they believed *was* true, since people have suffered and died for various causes, it does indicate that they *sincerely regarded their belief* in Jesus' resurrection to be true. Liars make poor martyrs. So now that we know that the disciples truly believed that Jesus rose from the dead, we have to account for their beliefs. What caused them to come to this conclusion?

Your skeptical friend now thinks about other possibilities, such as hallucinations, Jesus never died, the disciples never intended for us to believe that Jesus rose in a literal sense, and so on. You respond, "Yes, those are interesting possibilities. Let's consider them for a moment." Then, one by one, provide the reasons why these opposing theories fail to account for the data. You will need to bring up the other evidence in the process such as the empty tomb, the conversion of the church persecutor Paul, and the conversion of the skeptic James. Try not to inundate your friend with too much data. Keep it simple and let him ask for more if he needs it. Again, do not provide all of the reasons why each opposing theory should be abandoned. Rather give him one or maybe two reasons for each, unless he inquires further.

As the progression of the conversation begins to slow down, sum up what you have discussed:

> So we know that the disciples sincerely believed that Jesus rose from the dead and appeared to them. We've seen that there is good evidence

to support their claims, namely the conversion of the church persecutor Paul, the conversion of the skeptic James, and the empty tomb. And
finally, the complete inability of opposing theories to account for the
data leaves Jesus' resurrection as the only plausible explanation to account for the known historical facts. And it seems that if Jesus rose
from the dead, we have good evidence that God exists and has actually
revealed himself to mankind in Jesus Christ.

You have now given your friend quite a bit to chew on. Don't be pushy. If he
continues to ask questions, this may be a good time to transition to the gospel:

"I'm curious, Tom. Do you know what the main teaching of Jesus was?"
"That we should love each other?" he answers.

His main teaching is that God's kingdom has arrived and we can have
salvation through believing in his Son. As it is now, we all stand condemned before God for failing to live up to his standard of perfection.[6]
He taught that there is a penalty for failing to meet his standard and
that is an eternal separation from God, quarantined in a place he calls
hell.[7] However, he loved us all so much that he left his divine lifestyle
in heaven to come and pay the penalty for our sins by his death on a
cross.[8] Finally, by putting our faith in him alone as risen Lord of the
universe and in his ability to save us, he promises to extend his mercy
and grant us eternal life.[9] It is not something that we can earn through
our good deeds, but through faith in what he has already done for us. [10]

Tom now has a lot to think about. Everyone has a different personality. Don't
expect Tom to break down and cry at this point and ask how he can become a
Christian. Someone like Tom is going to need some time without being pres-
sured by you or others to make a decision. Allow God to work in his heart as
you consistently pray for him. Casually invite him and his family to go to church
with you, then to go out to lunch afterward. Be available to answer his questions and do not be afraid to admit when you do not know the answer: "That's
a really good question and I don't know the answer. But now I'm curious. I'll see
what I can find out and get back to you." Don't be afraid to let Tom talk and
fully express his questions and concerns. You will be surprised at how many
times a person who is searching for answers, simply needs to air his concerns

and have someone acknowledge them as fair questions, more than he needs an actual answer!

Notice the five points of the gospel presented to Tom:

1. We all stand condemned before God for failing to live up to his standard of perfection.
2. There is a penalty for sin and that is eternal separation from God, quarantined in a place he calls hell.
3. However, Jesus loves us all so much that he left his divine lifestyle in heaven in order to satisfy the penalty for our sins through his death on the cross.
4. By putting our faith in Jesus alone as risen Lord, he promises to grant us mercy and give us eternal life.
5. It is not something that we can earn through our good deeds. Otherwise, he would not have had to die on the cross. It is through faith in what he did for us on the cross.

It is helpful to notice the Bible verses used to support the five points, found in the endnotes, connected to the conversation with Tom (Romans 3:23; 6:23; 5:8; 10:9). These constitute what has come to be popularly known as the "Romans Road to Salvation" and is an easy way to present the gospel to others. It is helpful to have these references memorized, so that they will be on the tip of your tongue when you need them.

The fictional conversation with Tom was just an example. Every conversation will be a different experience. I (Licona) saw a good illustration of this just a few days after teaching a course on Jesus' resurrection. I received the following e-mail from one of those who had attended:

> Hey! How are ya? I'm doing great and really trying to keep my head up. I feel like I am losing a "debate" with a friend of mine. I presented the argument for the Resurrection and then he responded: "Sounds like a second Superman. First point: people who were killed on the cross only had their hands nailed. Second point: none of the people who wrote the *JAMA* article [i.e., against the theory that Jesus didn't really die] were there. So how would they know? Third point: taking the word of a book that contains mystical animals and things that can be explained with drug usage (i.e., manna) or over-exaggerations, and using it as fact is absurd." Fourth

point: he says I can't be a self-respecting person and base my life on something that I can't hold with 100% certainty. He says that would be a violation of who I am. Thus, I'm turning to you because I'm stuck. Oh, and are there more Muslims than Christians? He threw that at me as well. Anyways, I really, really, really appreciated your course these past seven weeks. I have learned a lot, but I'm still wanting to learn more. Thank you again for your time and for your help.

Keeping the Faith,
Brayden

I appreciated that e-mail. Brayden was out in the trenches sharing his faith. Without a doubt, on occasions we will be given objections we have not previously heard or have an objection presented in a manner somewhat differently than what we have presented in this book. However, that's okay. Remember what we discussed in the previous chapter under "Tips." There is no shame in admitting to not knowing an answer and volunteering to research it and come back with an answer if it may make a difference in whether that person will accept that Jesus' resurrection occurred. This is what I wrote back to Brayden:

Dear Brayden,

Thanks for your e-mail. It doesn't sound like he's very open-minded. If this is the case, no amount of logic will be of use to him. So don't be discouraged. Nevertheless, you do well to engage him in dialogue. Here are some responses that correspond to his points.

He is gravely mistaken in his assertion that victims of crucifixion in the first century had only their hands nailed. Archaeological findings in Jerusalem in 1968 revealed that the biblical accounts of crucifixion are correct for that period. Besides, whether Jesus' feet were nailed is not a major point. He was executed by crucifixion, and this is attested by multiple ancient sources outside of the New Testament who did not share Jesus' convictions (see Josephus, *Antiquities* 18.3; Tacitus, *Annals* 15.44).

Of course none of the writers of the *JAMA* article were there. However, if we conducted historical research in the manner your friend seems to be suggesting, we couldn't know anything about the American Civil War, Julius Caesar, or even World War 2. Was your friend there to witness any of these events or people? Does your friend deny the Holocaust because he wasn't there? If he says "of course not," ask him why not. When he says we have eyewitnesses who were there and documents that attest to it, answer that we have that also for Jesus' crucifixion! We not only have sympathizers of Jesus, but we also have secular historians of the period who write of his crucifixion. Even some of the most critical of scholars affirm that Jesus died due to being crucified. The strength of the *JAMA* article is that those in the medical community who have considered the effects of crucifixion on the body, claim that one cannot survive the full process.

You have nothing to be ashamed of when it comes to the Bible. However, remember Brayden that you can use your "minimal facts approach." You are basing your argument primarily on historical data that can be established and is accepted by virtually all scholars who study the subject. So he cannot simply say, "I don't believe the Resurrection, because I don't believe the Bible." He is going to have to address the data you provide. You can begin to see why the minimal facts approach is powerful.

He says, "I can't be a self-respecting person and base my life on something that I can't be *100 percent* certain that it's true. That would be a violation of who I am." Really? Ask him if he can have *100 percent* certainty that all of us were not created by an alien just 5 minutes ago with our memories and the food in our stomachs. He cannot be *100 percent* certain. Therefore, using his own logic, he is not "a self-respecting person" who can base his decisions as though the past events of his life are real! No one makes decisions based on *100 percent* certainty. The wise person chooses probabilities.

I do not know if there are more Muslims than Christians. I believe estimates show that there are more Christians at present. However, what does that matter? In the first century there were certainly more Jews and pagans than Christians. Does that do anything to undermine the truth of a faith? Whenever questions you may not have thought through are thrown at you, don't be afraid to ask him how his question refutes Jesus' resurrection. Let him give you a reason. In many instances like this one, he may become confused himself over why he even mentioned it to begin with.

Reply to him with some of these things I've shared with you and feel free to e-mail me back with his response if you need more help. I'm proud of you, Brayden, for getting out there and sharing your faith. I've had experiences just like the one you are now having. Don't flee from these opportunities. They will strengthen you and prepare you to be even better the next time you engage in a dialogue with a skeptic. In time, you will have heard it all—and you'll smile when you hear it again because you will be prepared and confident in your response.

Remember to answer with "gentleness and respect" (1 Peter 3:15). "Let your speech always be with grace, seasoned as it were with salt, so that you may know how you should respond to each person" (Col. 4:6). Love this guy and pray for him. Stand before this guy in humility before God, and answer him with gentleness and respect. But let him sense your confidence in your relationship with Christ.

Very truly yours,
Mike

Brayden's skeptical friend raised several objections that were covered in this book—Jesus did not die on the cross, the disciples hallucinated, and the Bible has discrepancies—and questioned the nature of proof and historical certainty. However, his objection that Jesus did not die on the cross was not spelled out clearly in those terms, and that confused Brayden. But this skeptical friend also raised an objection that we did not cover by claiming there are more Muslims than Christians in the world today. Of course, this objection has no bearing whatsoever on whether Jesus rose from the dead. With experience, Brayden will develop the ability to recognize flaws in the arguments of the person with whom he's talking.

Be patient and develop your skills. There are no substitutes for study and experience. Be careful not to go off onto other subjects. Stay on Jesus' resurrection.[11] Don't get discouraged when someone seems unmoved by your presentation. When someone maintains their radical views after you have shared the evidence with them, this is not necessarily the result of any shortcomings of your efforts or weakness in the evidence. He may continue to shake his head in disagreement with you. But that is far from refuting the evidence you presented. In time, sharing your faith will become a lot of fun and you will be amazed at how God will use you to spread his Word.

Appendix

A Detailed Outline of Arguments

The following outline summarizes the ideas and arguments presented by the authors. It can be used as a convenient way to review and learn the arguments and as a quick reference. Page numbers after main points indicate where to find the full discussion.

I. Introductory Information
   A. Importance of Jesus' Resurrection (pp. 26–29)
      1. It was the focal point of the disciples' preaching.
         a. Many doctrines were based upon it.
         b. Belief in it is required for salvation (Rom. 10:9).
         c. It secured for us an inheritance in heaven (1 Peter 1:3–4).
         d. If it did not occur we are lost (1 Cor. 15:17).
      2. It was the evidence that Jesus provided to validate his teachings (Matt. 12:38–40; 16:1–4; John 2:18–21; Cf. Mark 14:58; Luke 11:29–30). The Resurrection was also the chief evidence provided by the apostles that Christianity is true (Acts 17:2–3, 18, 31; 2:22–32; 3:15; 1 Cor. 15:17).
      3. Therefore, Jesus' resurrection largely confirms Jesus' claims, much of Christian doctrine, and the truthfulness of Christianity (1 Cor. 15:14).

B. At least four reasons support the likelihood that Jesus actually predicted his resurrection: (pp. 29–30)

   1. These predictions are denied, usually because the Resurrection itself is denied as an historical event. If, however, the Resurrection occurred, the reason for rejecting Jesus' predictions concerning it fails.

   2. The Gospels provide embarrassing testimony concerning the disciples and the women in relation to Jesus' resurrection. They either were truly distraught or didn't believe (Mark 8:31–33; 9:31–32; 14:27–31; Luke 24:13–24; cf. Luke 24:10–11; John 20:2, 9, 13–15, 24–25). The principle of embarrassment supports authenticity; it seems highly unlikely that the disciples—or early Christians who highly respected them—would invent predictions of Jesus, which, in hindsight, casts them in such a negative way.

   3. Jesus' use of the title "Son of Man" in reference to his predictions of his own resurrection (Mark 8:31; 9:31; 10:33–34) heavily supports authenticity. The New Testament Epistles never refer to Him in this manner, nor did the Jews think of *Son of Man* in the sense of a suffering Messiah (see Dan 7:13–14). Thus, the principle of dissimilarity may be employed, which "focuses on words or deeds of Jesus that cannot be derived either from Judaism at the time of Jesus or from the early Church after him" (Meier).

   4. Jesus' predictions concerning his resurrection are multiply attested to: Matthew 12:38–40; 16:1–4, 21; 17:23; 20:19; Mark 8:31–32; 9:31; 10:33; Luke 9:22; John 2:18–21. Cf. Mark 14:58; Luke 11:29–30.

C. Minimal Facts Approach:
   Considers only those facts that are both strongly supported by evidence and are conceded by almost every scholar, even those who are skeptical. We present five facts (4 + 1). Four meet the minimal facts criteria and one closely meets it.

D. Argument for Jesus' Resurrection

   1. Jesus' disciples sincerely believed he rose from the dead and appeared to them.

   2. External evidence and events support the authenticity of their belief in his resurrection: the conversion of the church persecutor Paul, the conversion of the skeptic James, and the empty tomb.

   3. Since no plausible opposing theories exist that can account for the historical facts, Jesus' resurrection is the only plausible explanation.

II. The Facts (4 + 1)

  A. Jesus' death by crucifixion (p. 48)

    1. Reported in all four Gospels

    2. Reported by a number of non-Christian sources

      a. Josephus (*Ant.* 18:3)

      b. Tacitus (*Annals* 15:44)

      c. Lucian (*The Death of Peregrine,* 11 – 13)

      d. Mara bar Serapion (Letter at British Museum)

  B. Disciples believed Jesus rose from the dead (p. 49)

    1. They claimed it. *(POW!)*

      a. Paul

        (1) Paul said that disciples claimed Jesus rose

          (a) 1 Corinthians 15:9–11

          (b) Galatians 2:1–10

        (2) Paul's authority

          (a) Claimed by Paul (2 Cor. 10:8; 11:5; 13:10; 1 Thess. 2:6; 4:2; 2 Thess. 3:4; Philem. 1:21)

          (b) Acknowledged by Apostolic Fathers (Clement of Rome [1 Clem. 5:3–5], Polycarp [Pol. *Phil.* 3:2; 12:1], Ignatius [Ign. *Rom.* 4:3])

      b. Oral Tradition

        (1) Early Creed (1 Cor. 15:3–8)

          (a) How do we know it's a creed?

            i. "Delivered" and "received" communicates that Paul is giving them the tradition he received.

            ii. It contains indicators of an Aramaic original:

              a. Fourfold use of the Greek term *hoti* is common in creeds

              b. "Cephas," is Aramaic for Peter, but Paul wrote in Greek.

              c. Text's content is stylized, containing parallelisms

              d. Non-Pauline terms

          (b) When is origin of creed dated? Very soon after Jesus' crucifixion (probably within five years).

            i. Crucifixion dated A.D. 30 by most scholars

            ii. Paul's conversion dated A.D. 31 – 33

            iii. Paul goes away for three years after his conversion,

> then visits Peter and James in Jerusalem (Gal. 1:18–19). Most scholars believe that Paul received the creed from them at this time.

    iv. The other option is that he received it in Damascus at conversion (three years earlier). Either way he probably received it within two to five years of Jesus' crucifixion (which places the origin of the creed even earlier) from someone whom he, as an apostle, deemed to be a trustworthy source.

    v. Very latest dating of the creed would be prior to A.D. 51, since Paul writes that what he had received, he delivered to them while visiting Corinth (1 Cor. 15:3), which visit scholars date around A.D. 51. So Paul had the creedal information prior to that time and received it still earlier from a source he considered trustworthy.

(c) Biblical vs. extrabiblical

    i. Paul quotes secular writers in New Testament (1 Cor. 15:33; Titus 1:12; Acts 17:28), but this does not make them New Testament sources.

    ii. Evidence that demonstrates that the creed existed prior to Paul's writings and was not originated by him, can be claimed as a non-New Testament source. Such evidence includes the terms "delivered" and "received," and the non-Pauline terms.

(d) Important points concerning this creed:

    i. Early testimony to Jesus' resurrection

    ii. Probably eyewitness testimony to Jesus' resurrection

    iii. Multiple testimonies to Jesus' resurrection: Cephas (Peter), the Twelve, more than five hundred at one time, James, all of the apostles, Paul.

    iv. Post Resurrection appearances: the 12, 500+, all of the apostles.

(e) Sermon Summaries (Acts 1–5, 10, 13, 17)

    i. When is origin of sermons dated? Probably within twenty years of Jesus' crucifixion

    ii. Important points concerning the sermon summaries:

    a. Early testimony to Jesus' resurrection

    b. Possible eyewitness testimony to Jesus' resurrection

    c. Group appearances: Acts 10, 13

  (2) Written Tradition

    (a) All four Gospels. Regardless of critics' skepticism concerning the Gospels, they contain multiple claims by disciples, written within seventy years of Jesus, that Jesus rose from the dead.

    (b) Apostolic Fathers

     i. Clement of Rome (A.D. 95, 1 *Clem.* 42:3)

     ii. Polycarp (A.D. 110, Pol. *Phil.* 9:2)

2. They believed it.

 a. Their transformation is strongly documented—from men who abandoned and denied Jesus at his arrest and execution to men who, to their own harm, boldly and publicly proclaimed him risen from the dead.

  (1) Luke (Acts 7; 12)

  (2) Clement of Rome, a contemporary of the apostles, reports the sufferings and deaths of the apostles Peter and Paul (1 Clem 5:2–7).

  (3) Ignatius, who likely knew the apostles, reports that the disciples were so encouraged by seeing and touching the risen Jesus, they were unaffected by the fear of martyrdom (Ign. *Smyrn* 3:2–3).

  (4) Polycarp was instructed and appointed by the apostles and attests that Paul and all of the apostles suffered (Pol. *Phil.* 9:2).

  (5) Dionysius of Corinth (cited by Eusebius in *EH* 2:25:8)

  (6) Tertullian (*Scorpiace* 15).

  (7) Origen (*Contra Celsum* 2:56, 77)

  (8) Important points:

    (a) The willingness of the apostles to suffer and die for their testimony of the risen Jesus is evidence of their sincerity. They truly believed that Jesus rose from the dead.

    (b) It's not implied that their sincerity verifies the truth of their beliefs; people have long been willing to suffer and die for various religions and causes. It does, however, demonstrate that they were not deliberately lying. Liars make poor martyrs.

(c) The fact is strongly attested to, then, that Jesus' disciples sincerely believed that he rose from the dead and appeared to them. Thus, legend and lies fail to account for the appearances, because the original apostles both claimed and believed that the risen Jesus had appeared to them.

C. Conversion of the church persecutor Paul (pp. 64–65)
   1. His conversion
      a. Paul (1 Cor. 15:9–10; Gal. 1:13–16; Phil. 3:6–7)
      b. Recorded in Acts (9; 22; 26)
      c. Early oral tradition circulating in Judea (Gal. 1:22–23)
   2. His suffering and martyrdom
      a. Paul (2 Cor. 11:23–28; Phil. 1:21–23)
      b. Luke (Acts 14:19; 16:19–24; 17:5; 17:13–15; 18:12–13; 21:27–36; 23:12–35)
      c. Clement of Rome (1 Clem 5:2–7)
      d. Polycarp (Pol. *Phil.* 9:2)
      e. Tertullian (*Scorpiace* 15; also cited by Eusebius in *EH* 2:25:8)
      f. Dionysius of Corinth (cited by Eusebius in *EH* 2:25:8)
      g. Origen (Commentary on Genesis cited by Eusebius in *EH* 3:1)
D. Conversion of the skeptic James (pp. 67–69)
   1. His conversion
      a. The Gospels report that Jesus' brothers were unbelievers prior to Resurrection (Mark 3:21, 31; 6:3–4; John 7:5)
      b. Early creed reports appearance to James (1 Cor. 15:7)
      c. Paul and Acts identify James as a leader in the church (Gal. 1:19; Acts 15:12–21)
   2. His suffering and martyrdom
      a. Josephus (*Ant.* 20:200)
      b. Hegesippus (quoted at length by Eusebius in *EH* 2:23)
      c. Clement of Alexandria (quoted by Eusebius in *EH* 2:1; mentioned in *EH* 2:23)
E. Empty tomb (pp. 69–74)
   1. *Jerusalem factor.* Impossible for Christianity to survive and expand

in Jerusalem if body still in tomb. The enemies would have only to produce the corpse.

2. *Enemy attestation.* In claiming that Jesus' disciples stole the body, his enemies (Matt. 28:12–13; Justin Martyr, *Trypho* 108; Tertullian, *De Spectaculis* 30) indirectly affirmed an empty tomb; they would not have claimed such if the body were still in the tomb.

3. *Testimony of women.* Women are listed as primary witnesses to empty tomb. It's unlikely that the disciples would have invented the story, since in their a woman's testimony was not highly regarded and, in fact, would have been damaging to their claim (Luke 24:11; Josephus, *Ant.* 4:8:15; *Talmud:* J Sotah 19a; Rosh Hashannah 1:8; Kiddushin 82b; Origen, *Contra Celsum* 2:59; 3:55; Suetonius, *The Twelve Caesars,* Augustus 44).

III. Opposing Theories

    A. Legend (pp. 84–92)

        1. Embellishments to the story over time

            a. The story of the Resurrection can be traced back to the original disciples. Critics can accuse them of lying or hallucinating, but claiming that a resurrection legend developed after the time of the disciples is not an option; the disciples themselves made the claim.

            b. Paul came to believe in Jesus' resurrection apart from the testimonies of the disciples.

            c. James came to believe in Jesus' resurrection apart from the testimonies of the disciples.

            d. While it's true that embellishments occur over time, the issue is, Has such occurred with the Resurrection claims. Merely making an assertion of embellishment is not evidence.

        2. Non-historical genre, that is, disciples wrote in a literary style of the time to honor their teacher , and their writings were not meant to be historical accounts of a literal resurrection.

            a. Empty tomb, which is attested to apart from New Testament (e.g., Jerusalem factor, enemy attestation).

            b. The skeptic Paul, who was hostile to Christians, was educated (Pharisee) and would be well acquainted with Jewish fable. He wouldn't have been persuaded by—in his perception—a feeble

Christian attempt at Jewish Midrash, nor would he have followed someone he considered to be a false Messiah, thereby jeopardizing his soul.

c. The same applies to James. Sources tell us that James remained pious toward the Jewish law even after becoming a Christian (Hegesippus quoted by Eusebius). It is extremely unlikely that, merely over a story he would have considered fiction, he would change his worldview, follow a false Messiah who was cursed by God (since Jesus had been crucified), and jeopardize his soul.

d. It is true that fable genre existed. It is also true that historical genre existed. Merely pointing out mystical accounts does nothing to demonstrate that the Christian accounts are of the same genre. A separate argument must be presented.

e. When we come to the Resurrection accounts, a historical genre seems likely:

(1) Acts 2:13, where David is contrasted with Jesus: David's body decayed, Jesus' did not.

f. The responses of early critics imply that the early church believed that the resurrection of Jesus was an historical event (e.g., Celsus, Jewish leaders). These responses presented arguments against the view of a literal and bodily resurrection. Why argue against it, if a literal and bodily resurrection was not what was being claimed?

3. Resurrections in other religions

a. The accounts of rising gods in other religions are unclear.

(1) Today's scholars would not regard the stories as parallels, since the details of the accounts are vague and are not similar to Jesus' resurrection.

(a) Aesculapius was struck by lightning and ascended to heaven.

(b) Baccus and Hercules and a few other sons rose to heaven on the horse Pegasus, having died violent deaths.

(2) First clear parallel is 100+ years after Jesus

(3) That a resurrection was reported in the earlier accounts of these pagan deities is questionable.

(a) No clear death or resurrection of Marduk.

(b) In the earliest versions of Adonis, no death or a resurrection is reported.

> > > (c) In no version is there a clear account of Osiris rising from the dead.
> > b. Accounts of rising gods in other religions lack evidence and can easily be accounted for by opposing theories.
> > c. Opposing theories cannot explain the evidence that exists for Jesus' resurrection.

B. Fraud Theory (pp. 93–97)

> 1. Fraud 1 (Disciples lied and/or stole body)
> > a. Disciples sincerely believed that they saw the risen Jesus.
> > b. Does not explain conversion of Paul, who, as an enemy of the church, would have concluded fraud was responsible for the empty tomb. He was converted because of an appearance of Jesus.
> > c. Does not explain conversion of James, who apparently disbelieved reports of Jesus' miracles prior to his death. Resurrection would simply have been another of the disciples' lies.
> 2. Fraud 2 (Someone else stole body)
> > a. Does not explain conversion of Paul, who would have suspected fraud and who converted because of an appearance.
> > b. Does not explain conversion of James, who would have suspected fraud and who converted because of an appearance.
> > c. Does not explain beliefs of the disciples, which were based on the appearances. Moreover New Testament indicates Jesus' followers did not expect Resurrection and did not respond with belief in Resurrection when they saw empty tomb (John 20:2, 13–15; 24–25; Luke 24:10–12).
> > d. *Even if true,* could only call into question the cause of the empty tomb.
> 3. Being willing to die for one's beliefs does not verify that those beliefs are true; many who embrace beliefs contrary to Christianity's have also died for their beliefs.
> > a. The claim is that a person's willingness to suffer and die for his or her beliefs strongly indicates that person sincerely thought those beliefs to be true.
> > b. This willingness on the disciples' part strongly indicates that they sincerely believed that Jesus arose. In other words, they were not lying.
> > c. Examples of adherents to other religions who were willing to die

for their beliefs differ from the case of the disciples. Muslims, Buddhist monks, Christians, and others who die for their beliefs may be deceived by false teachings. But the disciples claimed that they themselves saw the risen Jesus.

C. Wrong Tomb Theory (pp. 97–98)
1. Even if true, the appearances to the disciples cannot be accounted for.
2. The testimony of the Gospels is that the empty tomb convinced no one but John.
   a. Mary concluded that the gardener stole the body.
   b. Disciples did not believe upon seeing the empty tomb.
3. Paul was not convinced by the empty tomb but by an appearance of Jesus. Without it, he would have concluded that the body was stolen or that the disciples went to the wrong tomb.
4. James would have been unconvinced by the empty tomb. As with Paul, an appearance convinced James.
5. No sources exist that they went to the wrong tomb.
6. Burial by Joseph of Aramethea indicates tomb's location was known.

D. Apparent Death Theory (Jesus survived the cross) (pp. 99–103)
1. JAMA (3/21/86) says such is impossible, considering the pathological effects of scourging and crucifixion.
   a. Asphyxiation generally believed to be cause of death with crucifixion.
   b. Spear wound (John 19:34–35) indicates that the blood and water that flowed probably issued from the sac surrounding the heart (the pericardium), it being ruptured, produced the water, and the right side of the heart being pierced produced the blood. (The Roman author Quintilian [A.D. 35–95] reports this procedure being performed on crucifixion victims.)
2. Strauss' critique. Implausible to believe the wounded Jesus pushed the stone away with nail-pierced hands, then beat up the guards, walked blocks on pierced and wounded feet, appeared to his disciples in his pathetic and mutilated state, and convinced them he was the risen prince of life.
3. Cannot account for Paul's dramatic reversal of worldviews. Paul claimed that he experienced a glorious appearance of the risen Jesus.

E. Psychological Phenomena
1. Definitions

     a. Illusions are distorted perceptions.

     b. Hallucinations are false perceptions of something that is not there.

     c. Delusions are false beliefs, when evidence to the contrary is known.

2. Hallucination Theory (pp. 105–109)

     a. Not group occurrences, but individual (like dreams)

     b. Does not explain empty tomb

     c. Does not explain conversion of Paul, who was not in the mindset

     d. Does not explain conversion of James, who was not in the mindset

     e. Too many variances in incidences

          (1) Included men and women

          (2) Seen by individuals and groups

          (3) Attested by friend and foe

          (4) Hard-headed Peter and soft-hearted Mary Magdalene

          (5) Indoors and outdoors

          (6) Seen not once but many times over a period of forty days

3. Delusion Theory (pp. 109–110)

     a. Does not explain empty tomb

     b. Does not explain conversion of Paul. People who are candidates for delusions believe something to the extent that it overrides their logic. Paul was a Jew committed to his current faith and even hostile toward Christians. No reason can be offered for his motivation to leave his faith for a dead man, whom he would have viewed as a false prophet rightly put to death for blasphemy.

     c. Does not explain conversion of James for the same reason as Paul.

4. Vision Theory (pp. 110–113)

     a. Determine what is meant by vision

          (1) If vision genre, such is refuted above (see Legend/Non-historical genre).

          (2) If visions were objective, Christ, then, is risen. "Objective" vision means Jesus was really seen but not in a physical state. If Jesus was seen, then he survived death and the ramifications are the same as Resurrection; God exists and Christianity is true. The issue then becomes the nature of Jesus' resurrection body, not whether or not he was raised.

          (3) If visions were subjective, the appearances were hallucinations/delusions. Such is problematic, however, for the reasons above.

      b. Does not explain empty tomb.

      c. Bodily nature of appearances. New Testament writers spoke of physical, material body of risen Jesus, rather than an immaterial one.

   5. Conversion Disorder (pp. 113–115)

      a. At best, only accounts for Paul's experience

          (1) Cannot account for the appearances to the disciples

          (2) Cannot account for the appearance to James

      b. Cannot account for the empty tomb

      c. Paul does not fit the profile of a person with conversion disorder

          (1) Woman by 5:1

          (2) Adolescents

          (3) Low economic status

          (4) Low IQ

          (5) Military persons in battle

      d. Paul's conversion, too, would require more than a conversion disorder.

          (1) Visual hallucination

          (2) Auditory hallucination

          (3) Messiah Complex

      e. Since multiple explanations are required in order to account for Paul's experience, a new combination theory (see below) appears *ad hoc.*

F. Target: Paul (pp. 115–119)

   1. Guilt

      a. No evidence that Paul felt guilt at the time of his experience

      b. Paul's writings indicate the very opposite—he was very content in Judaism and confident of his actions (Phil. 3:5–6).

      c. Even if guilt could account for the appearance to Paul, it does not account for Jesus' appearances to the others.

      d. Does not account for the empty tomb

   2. Desire for power

      a. If Paul was looking for power through a prominent position of authority in the church, his behavior provide us no indication of such. During the first seventeen years of his Christian life He had little contact with those who could have empowered him.

    b. If Paul was looking for more power, being a Roman citizen, he could have pursued a position of power within the Roman government.

    c. The difficult life that Paul cheerfully lived as a Christian did not reflect a person whose goal was self-gratification.

3. Epiphany

    a. Even if true, it only accounts for the appearance to Paul.

       (1) Does not account for the appearances to the disciples

       (2) Does not account for the appearance to the skeptic James

    b. Does not account for the empty tomb

    c. Christianity's critics responded to a literal Resurrection rather than to an epiphany, which implies that literal Resurrection was being proclaimed by the witnesses.

       (1) The Jewish leadership claimed that the disciples stole the body.

       (2) Celsus claimed that either Jesus never really died on the cross or that trickery was used.

    d. The accounts of the bright light and voice appear in Acts, which dates after Paul's conversion and the Gospels of Matthew, Mark, and Luke. It's unlikely, then, that the story of Jesus' resurrection evolved from epiphany to bodily appearances.

G. Combination Theories (p. 121)

1. Combinations of theories lead to higher improbabilities. Two theories, each having a 50 percent probability, lead to a combined probability of 25 percent.

2. Remaining are many of the same problems that face individual opposing theories.

3. Even if no problems remained, the number of opposing theories that must be employed in order to account for all of the facts screams of being *ad hoc.*

4. The mere stating of an opposing theory does nothing to prove that the theory is true. Evidence must be provided.

H. Discrepancies in the Gospel accounts of Resurrection make entire story dubious. (p. 122)

1. At most, calls into question inerrancy.

2. Historians do not conclude that, because individual accounts contain

discrepancies, an event did not occur. Other works of antiquity are not rejected when discrepancies exist. Rather, the data is more closely examined. Thus, the "minimal facts" approach is valuable in this discussion.

3. Differences in the Gospels may indicate that they were independent accounts, thus, from an historian's perspective, adding to their credibility because of the existence of multiple witnesses.

4. Plausible explanations exist for many if not all of the discrepancies.

I. Biased Testimony (p. 124)

1. Paul who was actually biased against Jesus.

2. James appears to have been biased against Jesus.

3. If testimony is dismissed because it comes from an interested party, most of our historical sources would have to rejected, since the author wrote about the events because he or she has an interest in the subject.

4. Recognizing the bias of an author does not automatically merit the conclusion that the author has distorted the facts. Jewish historians who write about the Holocaust have reason to report what happened. This works in favor of historical accuracy.

5. *Genetic fallacy.* We must recognize the difference between understanding *why* something is believed verses understanding why something is true.

6. *Ad hominem fallacy,* that is, attacking the source rather than the argument.

J. A risen Jesus would have made a great impact on his culture and, thus, we would have more records on him. (p. 126)

1. Few records survive from two thousand years ago.

   a. Non-Christian writings

   (1) About 50 percent of the writings of Tacitus have been lost.

   (2) The writings of Thallus have been lost.

   (3) The writings of Asclepiades of Mendes have been lost.

   (4) Herod the Great's secretary Nicolas of Damascus wrote a *Universal History* of 144 books. None have survived.

   (5) Only the early books of Livy and excerpts from some of his other writings have survived.

   b. Christian Writings

   (1) Papias. Only fragments remain, referenced by others.

(2) Quadratus. Only fragments remain, referenced by others.
(3) Hegesippus. Only fragments remain, referenced by others.
2. The accounts that now exist concerning Jesus are impressive.
   a. Forty-two authors mention Jesus within 150 years of his life:
     (1) Nine traditional authors of the New Testament: Matthew, Mark, Luke, John, Paul, Author of Hebrews, James, Peter, Jude.
     (2) Twenty early Christian writers outside the New Testament: Clement of Rome, 2 Clement, Ignatius, Polycarp, Martyrdom of Polycarp, Didache, Barnabas, Shepherd of Hermas, Fragments of Papias, Justin Martyr, Aristides, Athenagoras, Theophilus of Antioch, Quadratus, Aristo of Pella, Melito of Sardis, Diognetus, Gospel of Peter, Apocalypse of Peter, and Epistula Apostolorum.
     (3) Four heretical writings: Gospel of Thomas, Gospel of Truth, Apocryphon of John, Treatise on Resurrection.
     (4) Nine secular non-Christian sources: Josephus (Jewish historian), Tacitus (Roman historian), Pliny the Younger (Roman politician), Phlegon (freed slave who wrote histories), Lucian (Greek satirist), Celsus (Roman philosopher), Mara Bar-Serapion (prisoner awaiting execution), Suetonius, Thallus.
   b. Ten authors mention Tiberius Caesar—the Roman emperor during Jesus' ministry—within 150 years of his life: Josephus, Tacitus, Suetonius, Seneca, Paterculus, Plutarch, Pliny the Elder, Strabo, Valerius Maximum, and Luke.
   c. The ratio of sources mentioning Jesus compared to those mentioning the Roman emperor at the same time and during the same period is 42:10! Even if only secular non-Christian sources who attest to Jesus are considered, the ratio is 9:9.
K. The disciples seemed to have experienced something. What it was will never be known. (p. 128)
1. Rejects the *conclusion* rather than the *evidence*.
2. What we do not know is not the issue; rather, the issue is what we do know: facts that are pieces of a puzzle and that when put together looks like only a resurrection.
3. The religious context in which the evidence for Jesus' resurrection appears increases the likelihood that it occurred, i.e., Jesus' claims

to divinity, that he was known as a powerful miracle-worker, and evidence for God's existence.

L. Alien Theory (p. 130)

1. Alien theory does not deny Jesus' resurrection; only God as its cause.

2. The life of Jesus differs substantially from typical alien accounts.

   a. Aliens usually arrive in a spaceship. Jesus was born on earth.

   b. Aliens usually appear for a very short time. Jesus was on earth for 30+ years.

   c. Aliens usually are abusive. Jesus was loving.

3. The evidence that aliens exist is questionable. Scientific evidence, namely cosmic constants, indicates the high improbability for life to exist anywhere in the universe except on earth.

4. There is good evidence that God exists (e.g., intelligent design and argument for a final eternal cause of the universe). Therefore, Jesus' resurrection is better explained as confirmation of his claims to divinity than as an alien playing a cosmic joke.

5. The Christian might say to the skeptic posing the alien theory, "Let's stick with the academic arguments for now. Once we're done with those, we'll get back to some of the fun ones." Or "Yes, Jesus as Son of God was an alien and not of this world."

M. Naturalism (comes in several forms) (p. 132)

1. "Only what science proves is true."

   a. Science relates to only what can be observed and tested. Some things lay outside of empirical science. Love, for instance, cannot be measured. The limitations of science, however, are not a reason to deny Jesus' resurrection.

   b. Self-refuting. A scientist placed n a room with the latest technology would be unable to prove that only what science proves is true. Thus, naturalism fails its own test.

   c. Self-refuting again. To require that historical events be predictable or repeatable is self-refuting, just a restatement that science is the only way to know something. I.e., the rule that establishes these sorts of requirements is not scientific, hence it fails its own test.

   d. There is no reason why the historian cannot determine the non-supernatural portions of claims concerning the Resurrection. E.g., Did Jesus die? Was he seen alive at some later time? The scientist or historian could conclude that "Jesus was seen alive after his death."

2. "Science proves that people do not come back to life."
   a. Science proves that people do not come back to life—*by natural causes.* Scripture does not claim that Jesus rose by natural causes.
   b. The Resurrection occurred in an interconnected religio-historical context that includes Jesus' claims to divinity, his deeds that appeared miraculous, and his predictions concerning his resurrection. In other words, Jesus' life and claims provide a suitable context for his resurrection.
3. "Science can explain everything. We don't need a God."
   a. "God of the gaps" explanations of the past no more undermine current arguments for God than do discarded scientific theories and medical beliefs undermine today's science and medicine.
   b. *Genetic fallacy.* This is the assumption that discovering how a belief originated (e.g., god of the gaps) is sufficient to explain that belief. It is fallacious, however, because it attacks the origin of a view instead of the view itself, which could still be correct.
   c. Jesus' resurrection as the best explanation of the data results not from what we don't know from science, but from what we do know from science
   d. It is an unjustified leap to proclaim that in the future we will find a scientific answer for the resurrection of Jesus. This could be said about almost anything.
4. "If God exists, he cannot intervene in the laws of nature."
   a. How does the skeptic know what God can and cannot do?
   b. If God created the universe, including the natural laws that govern it, it is neither logically impossible nor inconsistent for him to override those same laws at will.
   c. Jesus' resurrection would show that God *could* and *did* act in our world.
5. "Science must assume a naturalistic explanation for everything."
   a. While science must look for a naturalistic explanation, there is no need to deny a supernatural one, when both evidence and a religio-historical context is present, and no plausible naturalistic explanations exists. (Elephant example)
   b. The issue is not whether everything can be explained by the laws

of nature. The more crucial question is whether there is a God who may have superseded nature by a superior power.

c. Certain miracles demonstrate characteristics of actually interfering with the laws of nature.

d. When a naturalist *insists* on assuming that all events *must* be interpreted naturally, or that the laws of nature must have been expanded to allow an events, that person is engaging in circular argumentation because he or she *assumes* a naturalistic stance.

6. "Even if a miracle really occurred, we could never know that it was a miracle."

a. If God exists, then we have good reason to consider a link between a qualified event and a divine cause.

b. A religio-historical context helps to identify an act as a miracle.

c. Expanding the laws of nature in order to eliminate the miraculous nature of the data surrounding Jesus' resurrection creates more problems. One must propose unreasonable natural theories that are highly improbable to impossible.

7. "Miracles in other religions count against Christian miracle claims."

a. Genuine miracles could occur among unbelievers and still be entirely compatible with Christian belief.

b. Miracles in other religions are for the most part poorly evidenced and are scarcely able to rule out a well-evidenced one.

c. Miracles in other religions are usually always dismissed by a plausible opposing theory, whereas these theories fail regarding Jesus' resurrection.

8. "Even before investigating a claimed miracle, there is a huge mountain of improbability against it ever being an act of God."

a. If God exists, there is no reason to reject miracles as the explanation of well-attested events for which no plausible natural explanations exist.

b. To say that we should deny Jesus' resurrection, no matter how strong the evidence, is to be biased against the possibility that this could be the very case for which we have been looking

c. We learn about the nature of this world by our experiences. Arriving at the "mountain of improbability" conclusion rules out many claims of supernatural experiences.

d. Evidence exists for contemporary supernatural phenomena (e.g., answered prayer, NDEs). To the extent that they can be confirmed, this phenomena significantly challenge a naturalistic interpretation of this world. If other miracles subsequently occur, the Resurrection would become enormously more plausible.

IV. Other Issues
    A. Bodily Resurrection (p. 154)
        1. Paul preached a bodily resurrection.
            a. First Corinthians 15:4. "He was buried . . . he was raised" signifies what goes down in burial comes up in resurrection. Just a few verses later, Paul says the same, four additional times (15:42–44). In other words, what goes down comes up.
            b. Philippians 3:21. Christ will *transform* our lowly bodies, not eliminate them.
            c. Romans 8:11. The Holy Spirit will give life to our mortal bodies as he did to Jesus' mortal body at his resurrection.
            d. Colossians 2:9. Paul says that the fullness of God's nature and essence presently dwells in Jesus' body. Jesus has a body now. He is not a disembodied spirit.
            e. Acts 13:34–37. Paul is reported to preach that, contrary to king David's body, which decayed after death, Jesus' body, as a fulfillment of prophecy, did not decay (Ps. 16:10). Rather, God raised it and there were eyewitnesses.
            f. Acts 9; 22; 26. Although the appearance to Paul is described differently than what we read in the Gospels, the discrepancy is insufficient to conclude that Paul believed that Jesus was not raised bodily.
                (1) Other details in the account indicate that the experience occurred not only in the mind of Paul (others saw the light and heard the voice).
                (2) If critics use Paul's testimony in Acts in order to conclude vision, they must consider the other words of Paul in Acts 13:34–37 that clearly speak of bodily resurrection.
                (3) Paul's experience was post-ascension and may explain how Jesus' appearance after death was different than in the Gospels.
                (4) Luke apparently was not troubled by the difference between Paul's appearance and those made to the disciples (Luke 24; Acts 1:1–11); he records *both*.

(5) Acts was written after Matthew, Mark, and Luke, which are clear regarding bodily resurrection. Thus, if an evolution is taking place, it one that has devolved rather than evolved.

2. Peter preached bodily Resurrection
   a. Acts 2:25–32. Peter is reported preaching that Jesus' body did not decay in the grave as did David's, but rather was raised up by God as a fulfillment of prophecy (Ps. 16:10).
   b. Acts 10:39–41. Peter is reported to preach that Jesus ate and drank with his disciples.

3. All four gospels clearly speak of a bodily resurrection of Jesus.
   a. Empty tomb implies bodily Resurrection.
   b. Matthew, Luke, and John testify that people touched the risen Jesus (Matt. 28:9; Luke 24:39–40; John 20:24–8).
   c. Luke and John attest that Jesus ate in front of or with his disciples (Luke 24:41–3; John 21:19–30).
   d. Luke said Jesus' resurrection body had "flesh and bones" (Luke 24:39).
   e. John reports Jesus saying that if his enemies destroyed his body, he would raise that body in three days (John 2:18–22).

4. Thus, the bodily resurrection of Jesus was proclaimed at the earliest stages of Christianity (i.e., Paul and the Acts sermon summaries) and is multiply attested to.

5. No Christian writer of the first century presents a contrary view.

6. But critics use a few New Testament verses to support a non-bodily Resurrection.
   a. John 21:12. "None of the disciples ventured to question Jesus: "Who are you?" knowing that it was the Lord.
      (1) Jesus' immortal body may have been slightly different.
      (2) The same author who writes this verse clearly spoke of a bodily Resurrection just one chapter earlier (20:27).
   b. Matthew 28:17. "When they saw him, they worshiped Him; but some were doubtful."
      (1) The word for "doubt" *(distazo)*
      may more accurately be translated "hesitate."
      (2) The some who hesitated may have been other than the Twelve and were seeing Jesus for the first time. Or they could be some of the Twelve having the same thoughts many of us

would have today if someone we loved had died and then suddenly appeared before us. We would rejoice greatly and yet we would have questions: "Is this really him [or her]? How can this be? People do not come back from death."

    (3) Just a few verses earlier, Matthew clearly speaks of a bodily Resurrection (28:5–10).

    (4) Appearance reported in Galilee (a few days walk from Jerusalem), where most would only have heard about Jesus' crucifixion. Thus, upon seeing him, many may have doubted he had been crucified.

c. Galatians 1:16. "to reveal His Son in me."

    (1) Paul strongly hints at bodily resurrection elsewhere.

    (2) Acts 13:30–37 portrays Paul with a strong belief in Jesus' bodily resurrection.

    (3) Paul here probably refers to his spiritual growth in the three years following his Damascus road experience.

d. First Peter 3:18. Jesus was "put to death in the flesh, but made alive in the spirit."

    (1) Critics who cite this verse usually deny that Peter wrote this letter and assign its composition to the final quarter of the first century. If true, the passage is contrary to what we know the apostles were teaching. Therefore, to support critics' belief that spiritual resurrection was first proclaimed, evolution of the story would be devolving rather than evolving.

e. Mark 16:7. "He is going ahead of you" could be translated "he is leading you," thus, could hint at an inward (i.e., visionary) experience at their destination.

    (1) If Greek "proagō" is translated in this manner, it does not follow that disciples will experience a vision in Galilee.

    (2) In the verse that immediately precedes, the angel is clear that a bodily resurrection has occurred (empty tomb). Thus, it's poor exegesis to assign an alternate definition to a word to make it fit with a visionary appearance and heavily strains the text.

    (3) While "leading" is a possible translation, "going ahead" is more common, which is how the majority of translations render it.

   f. First Corinthians 15:37–50. Natural vs. Spiritual body

     (1) Paul is *not* contrasting a material body vs. an immaterial one. Rather, he's contrasting a body that is holy and has spiritual appetites to one that is weak and has both fleshly and sinful appetites.

     (2) Paul used the same two Greek terms earlier in 2:14–15, where he contrasts the spiritual or godly man with the lost man who thinks only of worldly things.

     (3) If Paul was contrasting a physical body with an immaterial one, a better Greek word was available to him, one which he had just used a few chapters earlier in a similar contrast, even using a seed analogy as he does in chapter 15 (1 Cor. 9:3–10)! In 9:11 Paul writes, "If we sowed *spiritual* things in you, is it too much if we reap *material [sarkikos]* things from you [such as food, clothing, and lodging]?" Thus, in 1 Corinthians 15, no basis exists for holding that Paul is making a contrast between the material and immaterial.

     (4) Elsewhere in the New Testament and the intertestamental writings, the Greek term Paul uses in chapter 15 for "natural" is used to refer to the fleshly nature of man as opposed to the spiritual. In fact, *neither Paul, nor any other New Testament author, nor the writers of intertestamental books ever use the term* psychikos *in the sense of something that is material.* The word does not appear in the writings of the Apostolic Fathers.

       (a) James uses *psychikos* to contrast a Christian's state of heart that is not from God (described as "earthly, natural *[psychikos]*, demonic") verses the spirit-filled Christian's state of the heart (James 3:15).

       (b) Jude uses the word of the lost who live by "natural instinct" *[psychikos]*, not having the Holy Spirit (Jude 1:19).

       (c) In 2 Maccabees 4:37 and 14:24 it means "heartily" in reference to feelings of grief and warmth.

       (d) In 4 Maccabees 1:32 it is used of a bodily appetite.

     (5) Paul uses the same Greek word for "spiritual" *(pneumatikos)* four other times in all of his writings: three

times in 1 Corinthians and once in Galatians (2:15; 3:1; 14:37; Gal. 6:1). In each case he is referring to the spiritually mature. *Paul never uses the term to mean an immaterial body.* Only three times elsewhere in the New Testament (1 Peter 2:5 [2x's]; Rev. 11:8), none of which mean "immaterial." Not found in LXX or intertestamental writings. The word appears twenty-one times in the Apostolic Fathers (1 Clem. 47:3; 2 Clem. 14:1, 2, 3; Barn. 1:2; 4:11; 16:10; Ign. *Eph.* 8:2 [3x's]; 5:1; 7:2; 11:2; 10:3; Ign. *Mag.* 13:1,2; Ign. *Smyr.* 3:3; 12:2; Ign. *Polycarp* 1:2; 2:2; Didache 10:3). Of these, six may be considered candidates for a meaning of "immaterial," although it is not clear (Ign. *Eph.* 7:2; 10:3; 2 Clem. 14:1–3; Barn. 16:10). In each case, however, the sense of being of God is always present and it is never used of Jesus' resurrection in the sense of the body being immaterial.

    (6) When Paul states that "flesh and blood cannot inherit the kingdom of God," "flesh and blood" was a common Jewish expression for a mortal body (Matt. 16:17; 1 Cor. 15:50; Gal. 1:16; Eph. 6:12; Heb. 2:14; Ecclesiasticus 14:18; 17:31).

B. Claims of Jesus about Himself (p. 166)
  1. Son of Man. Mark 14:61–62 (cf. Dan 7:13–14).
    a. Its Authenticity
      (1) The term appears in the New Testament only three times outside of the Gospels (Acts 7:56; Rev. 1:13; 14:14) and only three times in Christian writings during the first 120 years following Jesus (Ign. *Eph.* 19; Ign. *Trall.* 9; *Barn.* 12). Is it unlikely that the church originated the title Son of Man as Jesus' favorite self-description, when the church itself did not refer to him in this manner.
      (2) The title as used in the Gospels is found in *all* of the Gospel sources.
      (3) The title seems to lack indications that it was a result of theological evolution, since at first glance it appears to be a title that places more emphasis on Jesus' humanity.
    b. Its Meaning. Jesus' use of it in Mark 14 seems to make reference to himself as the divine the Son of Man in Daniel 7. This person is

given eternal authority, glory, power, and is worshipped. He rides the clouds of heaven, something deity does (Ps. 104:3; Isa. 19:1).

   2. Son of God. Mark 13:32

      a. Its Authenticity. Principle of Embarrassment in Mark 13:32. When claiming the view that Jesus is divine, Mark would not say there is something that Jesus does not know.

      b. Its Meaning

         (1) In antiquity, the term Son of God could be used of a divine being, leaders, philosophers, angels, and the nation Israel. But what did Jesus mean when he referred to himself as "Son of God"?

         (2) Mark 13:32. Anabasis (ascending scale with increasing emphasis). Jesus is greater than all humans and all angels. Thus, he understood himself as Son of God in a divine sense.

      c. Other texts where "Son of God" claims have good evidence: Matthew 11:27; Mark 14:36.

C. If atheism is true, Jesus did not rise: *Problem of Evil* (p. 172)

   1. Does not call into question God's existence; only his character

   2. It may be that we currently live in the best of all possible worlds, at least worlds wherein free beings are involved. If it's true that God cannot engage in logical absurdities, perhaps he cannot *make* someone *freely* choose to do right all of the time.

   3. Suffering may be the optimal way for us to grow.

   4. If the Bible is correct, God created a perfect world in which humans chose to sin and that such produced moral and natural consequences. Therefore, God is not responsible for the evil in the world—humans are.

   5. Good evidence exists for God (p. 174)

      a. Scientific argument for an intelligent Designer of the universe

         (1) Identifying design

            (a) Extremely unlikely to have occurred by chance

            (b) Exhibits a pattern normally associated with an intelligent cause

         (2) Cosmic constants: Factors in the universe, which, if varied only a little, would make the universe a life-prohibiting place.

            (a) Improbable: Given all the possible ways in which the universe could have obtained as a result of the Big Bang, the ratio of life-permitting universes to life-prohibiting ones is 1 in $10^{10(124)}$ (Nobel Laureate Donald Page).

       (b) Pattern: A 2002 paper titled "Disturbing Implications of a Cosmological Constant" by physicists Dyson, Kleban, and Susskind of Stanford University and MIT concludes that, aside from assistance from an unknown agent outside the universe, the appearance of life in the universe requires "statistically miraculous events" and is incomprehensively unlikely.

     (3) Scientific argument for a First Cause

       (a) Everything that begins to exist has a cause.

       (b) The universe began to exist (Big Bang).

       (c) Therefore, the universe was caused.

D. Other Challenges

  1. Jesus' resurrection does not prove the existence of God. (p. 182)

    a. The question has become *who* raised Jesus or *how* was he raised; not whether the Resurrection occurred.

    b. There are no claims from or evidence for another cause that could be responsible for Jesus' resurrection.

    c. The one who was raised claimed that God raised him.

    d. The Resurrection was not an isolated event. It occurred to one whose entire life was charged with religious significance (e.g., miracles and claims to divinity).

  2. Muslims claim that Jesus was never crucified and, therefore, was never risen. Based on two sources: *Qur'an* (sura 4:157–158) and *Gospel of Barnabas* (Section 217) (p. 184)

    a. *Qur'an*

     (1) It can be established historically that Jesus' disciples believed he rose from dead and appeared to them.

     (2) If Jesus not crucified, what caused them to believe that he rose? The *Qur'an* claims that God raised Jesus up to himself, apparently at the time of the rescue (4:157–158). So who or what did the disciples see three days later?

     (3) The *Qur'an* was written is six hundred years after Jesus, too late to provide valuable information.

    b. *Gospel of Barnabas*

     (1) Appears to be Muslim forgery composed no earlier than fifteenth century

      (a) No evidence that it existed prior to then

      i. No manuscript prior to fifteenth century

     ii. Prior to the fifteenth century, not cited by anyone. Nor mentioned by the early church Fathers or by Muslim apologists who were engaged in constant debates with Christians throughout the first eight centuries of Islam's existence. (Only mention relating a *Gospel to Barnabas* is in a fifth-century document (The Gelasian Decree, by Pope Gelasius, A.D. 492–495). Only its name is mentioned and that it was a spurious book rejected by the church. Given the medieval anachronisms in the *GoB* we have today, however, this reference is probably referring to a different *GoB*.

    iii. Contains a striking contradiction that would rule out Barnabas as its true author. The Hebrew/Aramaic word "Messiah" was translated "Christ" in Greek. The *GoB* makes the mistake of referring to Jesus as "Christ" on at least two occasions in the first two sentences of the gospel only to later deny that he is the Messiah (chaps. 42; 70; 82; 96; 97; 198; 206). Barnabas would certainly not have made this mistake, since he would have been well acquainted with Hebrew/Aramaic and Greek.

    iv. Contains several anachronisms, indicating a later date

       a. Year of Jubilee every 100 years. It was, however, celebrated every fifty years until papal decree in A.D. 1343 (*GoB* 83).

       b. Medieval feudalism (*GoB* 122)

       c. Medieval court procedure (*GoB* 121)

       d. Wooden wine casks instead of wineskins used in first-century Palestine (*GoB* 152)

3. Joseph Smith and eleven witnesses vs. Jesus and twelve disciples. They all said they experienced supernatural appearances. (p. 185)

    a. While all of the apostles were willing to suffer and die for their beliefs, six of the eleven witnesses to the gold plates left the Mormon Church!

    b. *Even if* several persons witnessed the gold plates, this says *absolutely nothing* concerning the viability of their content.

    c. There is no evidence that the *Book of Mormon* is true (e.g., specific archaeological findings, which link the events and places to the *Book of Mormon*), while other evidence exists outside of the testimony of the apostles to support Jesus' resurrection (e.g., empty tomb, conversion of the skeptics Paul and James).

    d. Evidence exists, however, against Mormonism (e.g., the severe problems with the

Book of Abraham, no archaeological evidence for the *Book of Mormon* where it should be), while no viable evidence exists against Christianity.

4. What about Elvis and alien sightings? (p. 186)

    a. Elvis Sightings

      (1) Elvis' body is still in his tomb. Jesus' tomb, however, was empty.

      (2) Elvis sightings may be best explained by various opposing theories, such as Elvis faked his death or mistaken identity (since many impersonators). All such explanations of Jesus' resurrection fail.

      (3) The religio-historical context for a resurrection is not present with Elvis as it was with Jesus. Elvis never claimed divinity; Jesus did. Elvis did not perform deeds that appeared miraculous; Jesus did. Elvis never predicted his resurrection; Jesus did.

    b. Alien Sightings

      (1) Eyewitnesses of Jesus' resurrection

        (a) It can be established that multiple believers and at least two hard-core skeptics believed that the risen Jesus had appeared to them.

        (b) No good reasons exist for doubting the testimonies of the disciples since those testimonies are supported by hard-core skeptics, who were also convinced that they saw him; the tomb was empty, Resurrection occurred within the context of Jesus' claims, his miracles, and the probable existence of God, and no plausible explanations can account for all of the known historical data.

        (c) Therefore, Jesus' resurrection is the only plausible explanation to account for the evidence.

     (2) Eyewitnesses of alien activity

        (a) Many of the testimonies are questionable.

        (b) Many plausible opposing theories exist (e.g., weather balloons, military aircraft, hallucinations, poor reporting techniques, etc.)

        (c) Strong data from science renders the chances of life elsewhere in the universe as extremely unlikely.

        (d) UFO testimonies frequently attest that these phenomena regularly break the laws of nature, requiring a rejection of *material* entities. So we must consider a *spiritual* reality as a possible cause. In other words, certain UFO reports may actually be true, and don't have to be explained away.

  c. Extraordinary claims require extraordinary evidence. (p. 187)

     (1) Extraordinary evidence exists.

        (a) Jesus appeared to individuals and groups.

        (b) Jesus appeared to friends and foes.

        (c) His tomb was empty.

        (d) Opposing theories fail.

        (e) Jesus' resurrection is the only plausible explanation of the data.

     (2) The requirement for extraordinary evidence is reciprocal. If Jesus did not rise from the dead, one must explain the evidence. Explanations such as group hallucinations are extraordinary and must be supported by extraordinary evidence.

E. How to have eternal life (p. 215)

  1. We all stand condemned before God for failing to live up to his standard of perfection (Rom. 3:23).

  2. There is a penalty for missing the mark, and that is an eternal separation from God, quarantined in a place he calls hell (Rom. 6:23; 2 Thess. 1:9; Rev. 20:15).

  3. He loves us all so much, however, that he left his divine lifestyle in heaven to come die for our sins (Rom. 5:8; Phil. 2:7).

  4. If we put our faith in him alone as risen Lord of the universe and in his ability to save us, he promises to extend his mercy and grant us

eternal life. Salvation cannot be earned through good deeds, but through faith in what he has already done for us (Rom. 10:9; Eph. 2:8–9; Titus 3:5).

Notes

Introduction to Part 1: Let the Discussion Begin

1. On a National Public Radio program that one of the authors heard some years ago, the editor of a popular magazine was asked why his magazine and several others had recently published controversial articles on Jesus as Christmas approached. The gentleman chuckled and replied, "Jesus sells."
2. David Van Biema, "The Gospel Truth," *Time* Magazine, 8 April 1996, 57.
3. Craig Blomberg, "Where Do We Start Studying Jesus?" *Jesus Under Fire*, Michael J. Wilkins and J. P. Moreland, eds. (Grand Rapids: Zondervan, 1995), 43.
4. Seven New Testament scholars were interviewed by Jennings for a total of sixty-five comments. Of these, seventeen comments (26 percent) were made by Crossan.
5. Paul Copan, ed., *Will the Real Jesus Please Stand Up? A Debate between William Lane Craig and John Dominic Crossan* (Grand Rapids: Baker, 1998), 54. Compare Craig's comments about the *Chicago Tribune* statement regarding Crossan on page 68 and Crossan's response on page 71.
6. Evangelical responses to Jennings's program have included the volume by D. James Kennedy with Jerry Newcombe, *Who Is This Jesus: Is He Risen?* (Fort Lauderdale, Fla.: Coral Ridge Ministries, 2002), and the video *Jesus: The Search Continues*, produced by The Ankerberg Theological Research Institute, Chattanooga, Tenn., in 2001.
7. Van Biema, "The Gospel Truth," 57.
8. Ibid., 59.
9. The English noun *defense* translates the Greek word apologia, from which we get the term *apologetics*. Apologetics is normally used in a Christian context, so

it can be defined as the discipline of presenting arguments for the Christian faith. See the range of meaning in Acts 22:1; 25:16; 1 Corinthians 9:3; 2 Corinthians 7:11; Philippians 1:7, 16; 2 Timothy 4:16.

Chapter 1: Unwrapping the Gift

1. On its Web site, *Barna Research Online*, the Barna Research Group reports the results of a 1994 study that nine out of ten American adults (86%) cannot accurately define the meaning of the Great Commission, seven out of ten do not know what John 3:16 means. Less than one-third (31%) know the meaning of the expression "the gospel." "Only 4% of adults could define the 'Great Commission,' quote John 3:16, and define 'the gospel.'" "The basic understanding of evangelism," barna.org/cgi-bin/PageCategory.asp?CategoryID=18. Accessed 16 December 2003.

2. Acts 1–5, 10, 13, 17.

3. Romans 1:2–4; 10:9; 1 Corinthians 15:3ff; 2 Timothy 2:8–9.

4. Romans 10:8–9 NIV. New Testament historian N. T. Wright points out that in the Greco-Roman world the word *Lord* (kyrios) had two meanings that were quite distinct from each other. The term could be used in polite direct address, like the English *sir*, or it could be used "to denote *the* social superior above all: the emperor. Ultimately, for the Roman point of view; there was only one Lord of the world. According to Paul, he now had a rival." N. T. Wright, *What Saint Paul Really Said: Was Paul of Tarsus the Real Founder of Christianity?* (Grand Rapids: Eerdmans, 1997), 56.

5. First Peter 1:3–4.

6. Romans 10:9.

7. First Corinthians 15:17–18.

8. First Corinthians 15:32 (NIV).

9. Matthew 12:38–40; 16:1–4; John 2:18–21; cf. Mark 14:58; Luke 11:29–30. Elsewhere Jesus predicted his resurrection, without commenting on the issue of confirmation (Matt. 16:21; 17:23; 20:19; Mark 8:31–32; 9:31; 10:33; Luke 9:22). See "Did Jesus Predict His Resurrection?" on page 29 for reasons to believe that Jesus did predict his resurrection. Because of one or more of these reasons, a number of critical scholars now accede to these claims. See, for example, Pheme Perkins, "The Resurrection of Jesus of Nazareth," *Studying the Historical Jesus: Evaluations of the State of Current Research*, Bruce Chilton and Craig A. Evans, eds. (Leiden: Brill, 1994), 431, and Gerald O'Collins, *Inter-*

preting Jesus (London: Geoffrey Chapman, 1983), 85–87. They hold that Jesus predicted his vindication or resurrection. For further discussion of these points, see Gary R. Habermas, *Jesus' Resurrection and Future Hope* (Lanham, Md.: Rowman & Littlefield, 2003).

It has also been objected that in the Matthew 12 passage, Jesus' prediction that he will be in the tomb for three days and three nights does not reconcile with the accounts in the Gospels that he was probably buried Friday evening and raised Sunday morning (i.e., one day and two nights). The late Muslim apologist, Ahmed Deedat, argued this in his article, "What Was the Sign of Jonah?" www.islamworld.net/jonah.html. Accessed 16 September 2003. Deedat's argument against Jesus as Christ is flawed for several reasons:

1. Deedat assumes that every part of an analogy must match in order for it to be an analogy. For example, he points out that Jonah was alive in the fish while Jesus was dead in the tomb. This by no means destroys Jesus' prediction, since his emphasis is primarily on the fact that he would be buried and then raised and secondarily on the duration of his "tomb time."

2. Deedat's argument is somewhat vague. Perhaps he is assuming that the New Testament must be inerrant in order for Christianity to be true. This, of course, would follow from Muslim dependance on the complete inerrancy of the Qurʾan in order for Islam to be true. So his argument might be restated: "Since the New Testament is incorrect on the 'sign of Jonah' prophecy, it is not inerrant. Therefore, we can reject Christianity." This is a non-sequitur argument. In other words, the conclusion does not follow from the premises. If this is his point, he would be saying: "Some of the Bible is inaccurate. Therefore, all of it is inaccurate." This does not follow, since attempting to demonstrate that some things in the Bible are false does not justify the conclusion that all of it is. It would be like arguing, "Some politicians are liars. Therefore, all politicians are liars." Many scholars have argued for the historicity of the Resurrection without believing at all in the inspiration of Scripture.

3. Our own method below will not argue from the truth of inspiration. The critic who thinks that the Resurrection depends on the truth of inspiration is mistaken.

But perhaps Deedat is not arguing this at all. Instead, he may be arguing, "If Jesus' prophecy about his resurrection is incorrect, then he did not rise from the dead." But this, too, is problematic, since it likewise assumes that the New Testament must be inerrant in recording Jesus' words in order for Christianity to be true. If

Matthew is wrong, Jesus still predicted his resurrection elsewhere (see Mark 14:58; John 2:19). These prophecies do not contain the "three nights" portion that is problematic for Deedat.

So, Deedat's argument does nothing to debunk Christianity. What it does is challenge the inerrancy of the New Testament. If Matthew was wrong in recording Jesus' words, then the New Testament cannot be inerrant. Can the three days and three nights (i.e., seventy-two hours) component of this prediction be reconciled with the position that Jesus was buried around 6 p.m. Friday and raised before 6 a.m. Sunday (i.e., about thirty-six hours)? Deedat's problem is answered in Norman Geisler and T. A. Howe, *When Critics Ask: A Popular Handbook on Bible Difficulties* (Wheaton, Ill.: Victor, 1992), 343:

> Most biblical scholars believe that Jesus was crucified on Friday. They take the phrase "three days and nights" to be a Hebrew figure of speech referring to any part of three days and nights. They offer the following in support of their position. First, the phrase "day and night" does not necessarily mean a complete 24-hour period. The psalmist's reference to meditating "day and night" on God's Word does not mean one has to read the Bible all day and all night (Ps. 1:2). Second, it is clear from the use of the phrase "three days and three nights" in the Book of Esther that it does not mean 72 hours. For, although they fasted three days and nights (4:16) between the time they started and the time she appeared before the king, the passage states that Esther appeared before the king "on the third day" (5:1). If they began on Friday, then the third day would be Sunday. Hence, "three days and nights" must mean any part of three days and nights. Third, Jesus used the phrase "on the third day" to describe the time of His resurrection after His crucifixion (Matt. 16:21; 17:23; 20:19; cf. 26:61). But, "*on* the third day" cannot mean "*after* three days" which 72 hours demands. On the other hand, the phrase "on the third day" or "three days and nights" can be understood to mean within three days and nights. Fourth, this view fits best with the chronological order of events as given by Mark (cf. 14:1), as well as the fact that Jesus died on Passover day (Friday) to fulfill the conditions of being our Passover Lamb (1 Cor. 5:7; cf. Lev. 23:5–15)."

(Cf. *Hard Sayings of the Bible* by Walter C. Kaiser Jr., Peter H. Davids, F. F. Bruce, Manfred T. Brauch [Downers Grove, Ill.: InterVarsity, 1996], pp. 380–81.)

10. The apostle Paul wrote that Jesus' resurrection vindicated him as the Son of God (Rom. 1:4). The event was God's endorsement of Jesus and his teachings.
11. Sura 2:23; cf. suras 10:37–38; 17:88.
12. Moroni 10:4–5.
13. The Muslim who objects that the beauty of the Qur'an is only realized in Arabic should wonder at the soundness of this objection, since a Jew might argue for the superiority of the linguistic and structural beauty of the Hebrew Psalms.
14. Michael Licona accepted the frequent Mormon challenge to read the *Book of Mormon* while sincerely asking God to reveal whether it is true. He remains unpersuaded, especially given the many textual and historical difficulties. For a critique of Mormonism, see Michael Licona, *Behold, I Stand at the Door and Knock* (Virginia Beach, Va.: TruthQuest, 1998). To find out more about the book, go to www.risenjesus.com. See also Francis J. Beckwith, Carl Mosser, and Paul Owen, eds., *The New Mormon Challenge* (Grand Rapids: Zondervan, 2002).
15. Gary R. Habermas, *The Resurrection,* vol. 1, *Heart of New Testament Doctrine* (Joplin, Mo.: College Press, 2000), Gary R. Habermas. *The Resurrection: Heart of the Christian Life* (Joplin, Mo.: College Press, 2000).
16. Historical Jesus scholar Graham Twelftree comments, "[The historical approach] does not mean that if I cannot prove historicity in any particular case, the story—or elements of it—must be discarded as necessarily historically unreliable. It must be stressed: We cannot move from '*unproven*' to '*disproven*.'" Graham H. Twelftree, *Jesus: The Miracle Worker* (Downers Grove, Ill.: InterVarsity, 1999), 250.
17. For more information, see Licona, *Behold, I Stand at the Door and Knock,* 17–24; Craig Blomberg, *The Historical Reliability of the Gospels* (Downers Grove, Ill.: InterVarsity, 1987); F. F. Bruce, *The New Testament Documents: Are They Reliable?* (Downers Grove, Ill.: InterVarsity, 1984); Paul Barnett, *Is the New Testament Reliable? A Look at the Historical Evidence* (Downers Grove, Ill.: InterVarsity, 1993).
18. A similar graph with explanations is presented in Gary R. Habermas and J. P. Moreland, *Beyond Death* (Wheaton, Ill.: Crossway, 1998), 16–18.
19. We will look at a few of these principles in chapter 2.
20. Annette Gordon-Reed. *Thomas Jefferson and Sally Hemings: An American Controversy* (Charlottesville, Va.: University Press of Virginia, 1997), xix–xx (emphasis added).
21. Twelftree, *Jesus: The Miracle Worker,* 248. Twelftree summarizes a discussion of historical method provided by Robert J. Miller. See Robert J. Miller, "Historical

Method and the Deeds of Jesus: The Test Case of the Temple Demonstration,"
Forum 8 (1992): 5–30.

22. Philosophers Peter Kreeft and Ronald K. Tacelli write, "We believe Christ's resurrection can be proved with at least as much certainty as any universally believed and well-documented event in ancient history." Peter Kreeft and Ronald
K. Tacelli, *Handbook of Christian Apologetics* (Downers Grove, Ill.: InterVarsity,
1994), 181.

23. First Peter 3:15.

24. In 1 Corinthians 15:33 Paul quotes the Greek poet Menander (c. 342–291 B.C.),
"Evil associations ruin upright morals." Also see Acts 17:28, where Paul quotes
from the Cretan poet Epimenides (c. 600 B.C.), "For in him we live and move and
are" and the Cilician poet Aratus (c. 314–240 B.C.), "For we are indeed His off-
spring." In Titus 1:12 he quotes the Cretan poet Epimenides (sixth century B.C.),
"Cretans are always liars, evil beasts, lazy gluttons."

25. In Paul's first letter to the Corinthian church, he wrote: "To the Jews I became as a
Jew, so that I might win Jews; to those who are under the Law, as under the Law
though not being myself under the Law, so that I might win those who are under
the Law; to those who are without law, as without law, though not being without
the law of God but under the law of Christ, so that I might win those who are
without law. To the weak I became weak, that I might win the weak; I have become
all things to all men, so that I may by all means save some" (1 Cor. 9:20–22).

Chapter 2: History 101

1. For purposes of this book, the term *principle* is used, since it is a less technical
term than that used in academia, where the term *criterion* is employed. Moreover, instead of "History 101," it would be more accurate to title the chapter
"Historiography 101," since historiography studies the philosophy and methods
of collecting and writing history, including the entire procedure of gathering
data, critical interaction, and interpretation, as we attempt to achieve the best
explanation of what occurred.

2. For additional criteria, see Graham H. Twelftree, *Jesus: The Miracle Worker*
(Downers Grove, Ill.: InterVarsity, 1999), 247–53 (Twelftree credits Robert J.
Miller's "Historical Method and the Deeds of Jesus: The Test Case of the Temple
Demonstration," *Forum* 8 [1992], 5–30 for his eighteen theses for historicity);
John P. Meier, *A Marginal Jew: Rethinking the Historical Jesus*, 3 vols. (New
York: Doubleday, 1991–2001), 1:167–95; C. Behan McCullagh, *Justifying His-*

torical Descriptions (Cambridge: Cambridge University Press, 1984), 19. For a demonstration of how historical criteria of authenticity are sometimes abused, see Ben Witherington III, *The Jesus Quest: The Third Search for the Jew of Nazareth* (Downers Grove, Ill.: InterVarsity, 1995), 46–48.

3. See Harold C. Syrett, ed., *Papers of Alexander Hamilton*, vol. 25 (New York: Columbia University Press, 1974), 169–234. This information is contained in David McCullough, *John Adams* (New York: Simon & Schuster, 2001), 549–50. We thank Debbie Licona for providing this example.

4. The statement "Communism fails as an economic system" would be much stronger coming from Mikhail Gorbachev than Ronald Reagan, and would provide another example of enemy attestation.

5. Meier, *Marginal Jew*, 1:168.

6. Annette Gordon-Reed, *Thomas Jefferson and Sally Hemings: An American Controversy* (Charlottesville, Va.: University Press of Virginia, 1997).

Introduction to Part 2: The Minimal Facts Approach

1. Quoted from Jerry Newcombe, *Coming Again* (Colorado Springs, Col.: Chariot Victor, 1999), 45.

2. Gary Habermas has developed this approach in some detail. See, for example, Gary R. Habermas, "Evidential Apologetics," *Five Views on Apologetics*, Steven B. Cowan, ed. (Grand Rapids: Zondervan, 2000), 99–100, 186–90.

3. Both Christians and skeptics have been guilty of illogical arguments in the debate over the inspiration of the Bible. One type of fallacious argument is referred to as *non-sequitur reasoning* in which a conclusion is unsupported by the premises. Let's look at an example: "The native American Indians did a raindance. It rained. Therefore, the dance caused the rain." The conclusion that the dance caused the rain is unjustified, since there are other potential causes, some of which may be more likely. Non-sequitur reasoning is easily spotted in the inspiration debate. Many times the Christian states, "Archaeology and the writings of secular historians have corroborated much of what the Bible says about peoples, places, and events. Therefore, *all* of the Bible is true." This is non-sequitur reasoning. The conclusion that the entire Bible is true is not justified by evidence that some of it is true. This, of course, does not mean that the Bible is not the inspired Word of God, only that this argument fails to prove it. The skeptic is, likewise, often guilty of the same type of argument. Quick to point out apparent errors and contradictions in the Bible, some skeptics concludes, "Therefore, *all* of the

Bible is false." This, too, is non-sequitur reasoning, since the conclusion that the entire Bible is false is not justified by evidence that some of it may be false. Moreover, the fact that at least some of what the Bible says has been corroborated independently falsifies the allegation that the entire Bible is false. The *minimal facts approach* bypasses the discussion on inspiration and directs the focus more directly to the issue of Jesus' resurrection. Since we are establishing that Jesus rose from the dead from facts that have strong historical foundation and that are acknowledged by the majority of scholars, one could bypass *for the sake of discussion* whether the Bible is inspired. We can avoid the rabbit trail issues of whether Scripture has errors without having any negative impact on our minimal facts approach for establishing Jesus' resurrection. It is important to discuss the historicity and plenary inspiration of Scripture, but such discussions do not belong in the middle of considering the Resurrection.

4. Romans 10:9; 1 Corinthians 15:1–5.

5. Stephen R. Covey, A. Roger Merrill, and Rebecca R. Merrill, *First Things First* (New York: Simon & Schuster, 1994), section 2.

6. Moses Hadas, "Introduction," *The Complete Works of Tacitus*, Moses Hadas, ed.; Alfred John Church and William Jackson Brodribb, trans. (New York: Random House, 1942), xvi–xviii.

Chapter 3: A Quintet of Facts (4 + 1): The First Two

1. Gary R. Habermas, *The Historical Jesus* (Joplin, Mo.: College Press, 1996), 158–67. Gary R. Habermas and J. P. Moreland, *Beyond Death* (Wheaton, Ill.: Crossway, 1998), 115. Antony Flew, considered by many to be the most influential philosophical atheist of the late twentieth century, granted all twelve of these facts in a televised debate with Habermas on the Resurrection in April 2000. See *The John Ankerberg Show* "Did Jesus Rise from the Dead?" The debate is currently available in video format at www.johnankerberg.org/TV/ankjasrd.html or by calling 423-892-7722. A published volume with the debate transcript is forthcoming.

2. Elsewhere, Habermas has broken some of the facts presented here into separate points and presented them in a slightly different manner. See Habermas, *Historical Jesus*, 158–61.

3. Gerard S. Sloyan, *The Crucifixion of Jesus: History, Myth, Faith* (Minneapolis: Fortress, 1995), 18–20. Also see Martin Hengel, *Crucifixion* (Philadelphia: Fortress, 1977).

4. "When caught, they resisted, and were then tortured and crucified before the walls as a terrible warning to the people within. Titus pitied them—some 500 were captured daily—but dismissing those captured by force was dangerous, and guarding such numbers would imprison the guards. Out of rage and hatred, the soldiers nailed their prisoners in different postures, and so great was their number that space could not be found for the crosses." Josephus, *Jewish Wars*, 5.451; quoted from Paul L. Maier, *Josephus: The Essential Works* (Grand Rapids: Kregel, 1994), 358.

5. Sloyan, *Crucifixion of Jesus*, 13, citing M. Tullius Cicero in *Against Verres* 2.5.64. In 2.5.165, Cicero refers to crucifixion as "that most cruel and disgusting penalty." Cited in Hengel, *Crucifixion*, 8.

6. Cicero, *Pro Rabirio* 9–17.

7. Cornelius Tacitus, *The Annals* 15.44. For more on crucifixion in antiquity, see Hengel, *Crucifixion*.

8. Josephus, *Antiquities* 18.64. *Josephus in Ten Volumes*, vol. 9, *Jewish Antiquities*, Loeb Classical Library, Louis H. Feldman, trans. (Cambridge, Mass.: Harvard University Press, 1981).

9. Tacitus, *Annals* 15.44 (c. A.D. 115).

10. Lucian of Samosata, *The Death of Peregrine*, 11–13 (c. mid-second century).

11. This document is currently at the British Museum, Syriac Manuscript, Additional 14,658 (c. late first–third century). The translation is from Logos Protestant Edition of the early church fathers, A. Roberts, J. Donaldson, and A. C. Coxe, eds. and trans., *The Ante-Nicene Fathers: Translations of the Writings of the Fathers Down to A.D. 325* (Oak Harbor, Ore.: Logos Research Systems, 1997).

12. Talmud, Sanhedrin 43a (probably late second century). Unless otherwise indicated, all citations from the Talmud are from *The Babylonian Talmud*, I. Epstein, ed. and trans. (London: Soncino, 1935–1952). The Talmud was written too late to provide evidence for Jesus that is independent of earlier sources. It should be noted that Jewish writings of antiquity never denied the existence, miracles, and execution of Jesus. See John P. Meier, *A Marginal Jew: Rethinking the Historical Jesus*, 3 vols. (New York: Doubleday, 1991–2001), 1:96–97.

13. Pronounced "ee-ay-soos."

14. Livy 1:26:6ff; Luke 23:39; Galatians 3:13.

15. See John Dominic Crossan, *Jesus: A Revolutionary Biography* (San Francisco: HarperCollins, 1991), 145; see also 154, 196, 201.

16. For an in-depth look at the disciples' claims that have come to us through Paul and other sources, see the helpful chart in R. Douglas Geivett and Gary R.

Habermas, eds., *In Defense of Miracles* (Downers Grove, Ill.: InterVarsity, 1997), 266.

17. Second Corinthians 10:8; 11:5; 13:10; 1 Thessalonians 2:6; 4:2; Philemon 1:21; cf. 2 Thessalonians 3:4. On Paul's apostolic authority, see pp. 263–64 and chapter 4, n4 in this volume.

18. Paul's writings are cited twenty-one times by five of the apostolic fathers and perhaps alluded to on several other occasions. Clement of Rome refers to Paul's first letter to the Corinthians (1 Clement 47). The author of 2 Clement cites him once (19:2). Polycarp (c. 110) cites him sixteen times (*To the Philippians* 1:3; 2:2; 4:1 [three times, the second may be a dual reference to 2 Cor. 6:2]; 5:1, 3; 6:1–2 [two times]; 9:2; 11:1, 2, 4; 12:1 [two times]). Papias, who probably heard the apostle John teach and who wrote in the early part of the second century, cites Paul twice (*Fragments:* Traditions of the Elders 2, 5). Eusebius, *Chronicle,* is also found in *Fragments* 1; also see *Fragments* 5, 7, 9. In *Fragment* 3, Eusebius provides a contrary opinion concerning the personal encounters of Papias with the apostle John. However, Eusebius is certainly incorrect in his reasons. For a detailed discussion of Papias, see Robert H. Gundry, *Mark: A Commentary on His Apology for the Cross* (Grand Rapids: Eerdmans, 1993), 1026–45. Ignatius of Antioch (c. 107), who was the second to succeed the apostle Peter as head of the church in Antioch (Eusebius, *Ecclesiastical History* 3.36.3–4), cites Paul once (*To Polycarp* 5:1), and the author of *The Martyrdom of Polycarp* cites him once (1:2). The following letters traditionally attributed to Paul are certainly cited by the Apostolic Fathers: Romans, 1 Corinthians, 2 Corinthians, Galatians, Ephesians, Philippians, 1 Thessalonians, 2 Thessalonians, 1 Timothy. Finally and most interesting, is how these authors viewed Paul. From Polycarp's letter to the Philippians (3:2; 9:1; 11:2–3; 12:1), we learn in the first reference that Paul "accurately and reliably taught the word concerning the truth." If Irenaeus is correct in claiming that Polycarp was "instructed" and "appointed" by the apostles, had "conversed with many who had seen Christ" (*Against Heresies,* 3.3.4), and that he had fellowshipped with John and those who had seen the Lord (*To* Florinus, cited in Eusebius, *Ecclesiastical History* 5.20), his testimony of Paul has huge significance. He knew what the apostles taught, and he believed Paul's writings were accurate and reliable when compared to their teachings. Moreover, in *To the Philippians* 12:1, Polycarp cites Ephesians two times, calling it part of the "sacred Scriptures." If Ephesians was truly written by Paul, then we know that his writings were considered to be sacred Scripture. Clement of Rome and Ignatius both mention Paul as though he

were on equal par with, and carried the same apostolic authority as, Peter, one of the original apostles (Clement in 1 Clem. 5:3–5; Ignatius in *To the Romans* 4:3). See more information on Paul on pp. 263–64 and chapter 4, n4.

19. Galatians 1:18–19; 2:2–20. Paul also says that these three approved his gospel message (Gal. 2:1–12). Virtually every scholar admits that Paul wrote about twenty years after Jesus' death and had multiple interactions with Jesus' brother and two of his lead disciples. All three of these went to their deaths, and two suffered martyrdom, claiming that Jesus had risen and had appeared to them.

20. Acts 9:26–30; 15:1–35.

21. As a few examples, Clement (1 Clem. 5, c. A.D. 95); Polycarp (*To the Philippians* 9–c. 110); Ignatius (*To the Romans* 4, c. 110); and Papias (Fragment 5, c. 100–7 [The traditional date for Papias is 125, but Gundry, *Mark*, 1026–45, argues convincingly for a date of between 100 and 107]). All of these may very well have known one or more of the apostles (see pp. 53–55).

22. In Galatians 2:1–10, Paul says that he went to the apostles so that they could confirm that the gospel he preached was correct and right in line with the gospel they preached. The gospel always included the resurrection of Jesus (1 Cor. 15:3–5). Therefore, since Paul's gospel was the same as the apostles', and the gospel included the resurrection, it is safe to say that Paul's words here in Galatians support the proposition that the disciples claimed that Jesus rose from the dead. As noted above, in 1 Corinthians 15:11 Paul claims this directly. So we have reports that the disciples approved Paul's preaching of the Resurrection and that Paul acknowledged that they preached the same message.

23. It is agreed by most scholars who study the subject that verses 3–5 are from a creed and that the end of verse 5, "then to the twelve," through the end of verse 7 also is creedal material, it is not necessarily from the same creed.

24. First, Paul's introductory comment, "I delivered to you . . . what I also received," denotes the imparting of oral tradition (cf. 11:23). Paul is saying that he delivered to the Corinthian church information he received from others. Second, since the first Christians were Jews, we would expect that the early creeds and hymns would appear in their primary spoken language, Aramaic. There are indications that verses 3–5 had an Aramaic origin, such as the four-fold use of the Greek term for "that" *(hoti)* common in Aramaic narration and the name, *Cephas*, which is Aramaic for Peter (see John 1:42). Third, the text's content is stylized and contains parallelism. In Greek, the first and third lines are longer, have the same construction, and contain the phrase "according to the Scriptures" at the end, followed by a short sentence beginning with "that." (a) "That Christ died

for our sins according to the Scriptures (b) and that he was buried (c) and that he was raised on the third day according to the Scriptures (d) and that he appeared to Cephas. Fourth, non-Pauline terms indicate that he probably did not form the creed but got it elsewhere, as he states in verse 3. For a detailed analysis of this creed and the early, eyewitness tradition behind it, see John Kloppenborg, "An Analysis of the Pre-Pauline Formula 1 Cor 15:3–5b In Light of Some Recent Literature," *The Catholic Biblical Quarterly* 40 (1978): 351–67; William Lane Craig, *Assessing the New Testament Evidence for the Historicity of the Resurrection of Jesus* (Lewiston, N.Y.: Edwin Mellen, 1989), 1–49, esp. 1–6; Gary R. Habermas, "Evidential Apologetics," *Five Views on Apologetics*, Steven B. Cowan, ed. (Grand Rapids: Zondervan, 2000); and Habermas, *Historical Jesus*, 152–57.

25. How is the creed dated? Jesus' crucifixion has been dated at A.D. 30 by most scholars, who also date Paul's conversion to between 31 and 33. Paul went away for three years after his conversion, afterward visiting Peter and James in Jerusalem (Gal. 1:18–19). Many scholars believe Paul received the creed from Peter and James at this time. One reason for this is Paul's use of the Greek term *historēsai* to describe his visit with Peter. The term means "to gain a historical account." See its use in Esther 8:12 (LXX); Esdras 1:33 (two times), 40; 2 Maccabees 2:24, 30, 32 (2 times); 4 Maccabees 3:19; 17:7. Thus, when Paul visited Peter, he went with the intent of learning firsthand from Peter about Jesus. Paul says he also saw James while there (Gal. 1:19). Accordingly, even if Paul was not given the creed at this time, he learned information from two of the most prominent disciples who had known Jesus. Thus, he would know if the content in the creed was their testimony. Another option is that he received it in Damascus at the time of his conversion (which places the origin of the creed even earlier). Either way he received it within two to five years after Jesus' crucifixion from the disciples themselves. Another possibility is that he received it at a later date. But this could have been no later than 51, since Paul visited Corinth around that time. First Corinthians, in which Paul said that he delivered the creed to them (1 Cor. 15:3), was probably written between 53 and 57. Thus, Paul says he delivered this creed to the Corinthians when he saw them (51 or earlier) and that he received the creed earlier ("I delivered to you . . . what I also received"). The creed would have originated earlier still. At minimum, Paul must have received the creed from someone he, an apostle, deemed to be a trustworthy source. We've already seen that in both of his early discussions with the most prominent apostles all agreed upon the content of the gospel (Gal. 1:16–2:10).

Critics grant this fact too. It should also be noted that just a few verses after the creed, Paul said that the other apostles were currently teaching the same message concerning Jesus' resurrection appearances (1 Cor. 15:9–11, 14–15).

26. Most scholars also recognize Luke 24:34 as an early proclamation that reports a post-mortem appearance of Jesus to Peter. This is because it is somewhat of an awkward insertion that lacks an accompanying story. This may be the appearance mentioned in 1 Corinthians 15:5 in the creed.

27. Quoted in Richard N. Ostling. "Who Was Jesus?" *Time* Magazine, 15 August 1988, 41.

28. See Acts 1–5, 10, 13, 17 and note the claims to group appearances in 10:39–43 and 13:29–31.

29. Additional reasons why scholars believe that they can identify these summaries as oral tradition include their possession of Jewish words and traits, referred to as Semitisms (C. H. Dodd, *The Apostolic Preaching and Its Developments* [repr., Grand Rapids: Baker, 1980], 17–31). Also see chapter 9 note 10. Moreover, some of these sermon summaries, Acts 10 for example, are written in rough Greek (e.g., how some people sound who speak English as a second language), unlike the rest of Acts, which is written using the Greek of an educated person. These traits may well reflect that the summaries were from an original source in Aramaic, a common language known by first century Jews that was very similar to Hebrew, and later translated into Greek. The author was an educated Gentile writer who also claimed to have received his information from the original disciples: "just as they [i.e., the stories about Jesus] were handed down to us by those who from the beginning were eyewitnesses and servants of the word" (Luke 1:2). The succinct sermons record only basic doctrines, compared to more detailed theology in the writings of the later church fathers (Habermas and Moreland, *Beyond Death*, 131–32). Although some scholars hold that the sermon summaries in Acts reflect what the specified person said at the specified place and time, the majority today hold that Luke was following a common practice of writing history in the format of a story and invented the speeches/sermons. In this practice, he would convey what early Christians, perhaps the very Christians to whom the sermons are attributed, were communicating by importing a summary of their content in the sermons. In this option, the particular sermon and the time and place of its delivery were invented. Perhaps even someone other than the person specified may have delivered it. But the content was authentic of what was being proclaimed by early Christians. This is not to say everything about the sermon,

including even its content were inventions of Luke. Few scholars today take
that view. See Colin J. Hemer, *The Book of Acts in the Setting of Hellenistic
History* (Winona Lake, Ind.: Eisenbrauns, 1990), 415–43.

30. Although most scholars, including most scholars who identify themselves as
evangelicals, hold that the final verses of Mark (16:9–20) are not part of the
original text, they still hold that Mark knows of the post-mortem appearances of
Jesus. Mark predicts Jesus' resurrection five times (8:31; 9:9, 31; 10:32–34;
14:28). In addition, Mark reports the testimony of the angel (16:5–7), which
includes the Resurrection, the empty tomb, and the imminent appearance of
Jesus in Galilee. Notice that Mark sees this as a fulfillment of 14:28. Furthermore, the reference to Peter in 16:7 may be the appearance reported by the creed
in 1 Corinthians 15:5 and Luke 24:34. The majority of scholars hold that the
omission of the actual appearances was an intentional literary device employed
by Mark, although a good number hold that the original ending has been lost.
See R. T. France, *The Gospel of Mark*, New International Greek Testament Commentary, I. Howard Marshall and Donald A. Hagner, eds. (Grand Rapids:
Eerdmans, 2002), 670–74.

The main reasons why scholars hold that 16:9–20 were not part of Mark's
original are: (1) External evidence: (a) These last twelve verses do not appear in
the two oldest Greek manuscripts or the oldest translations in antiquity. (b) The
early church fathers, Clement of Alexandria, and Origen show no knowledge of
them. (c) Eusebius and Jerome (fourth century) testify that the verses were absent from almost every Greek manuscript of Mark known to them. (2) Internal
evidence: (a) The vocabulary and style of verses 9–20 are not typical of Mark.
(b) The connection between verse 8 and verses 9–20 is awkward. For example,
although Mary Magdalene had just been mentioned in 15:47 and 16:1, she is
mentioned in 16:9 as though for the first time. The other women mentioned in
16:1–8 seem to have been forgotten in 9–11. New Testament scholar Bruce
Metzger writes, "it is more likely that the section was excerpted from another
document, dating perhaps from the first half of the second century" (Bruce M.
Metzger, *A Textual Commentary on the Greek New Testament* [Stuttgart:
United Bible Societies, 1975], 125).

31. Critical scholars have always proclaimed that there were sources behind various
Gospels (for example, Mark and the alleged documents Q, M, L) plus John. Luke
admits he used other sources (Luke 1:1–4). See chapter 10 note 19.

32. As with Ignatius, a friend of Polycarp who knew some of the apostles. Ignatius
was the bishop of the churches in Antioch. He was arrested and on his way to

face execution in Rome when he penned seven letters, six to various churches and one to Polycarp. In his letter *To Polycarp*, Ignatius says he saw Polycarp in person (1:1). He knew Polycarp was praying for his church in Antioch (7:1). He approves or encourages Polycarp to "convene a council" to select someone to go to Smyrna to congratulate and encourage them (7:2; 8:2; see also Ignatius, *To the Smyrnaeans* 11:2–3).

33. Irenaeus, *Against Heresies*, 3.3.3, c. 185. Taken from A. Roberts, J. Donaldson, and A. C. Coxe, eds. and trans., *The Ante-Nicene Fathers: Translations of the Writings of the Fathers Down to A.D. 325* (Oak Harbor, Ore.: Logos Research Systems, 1997).

34. Tertullian, *The Prescription Against Heretics*, 32. In ibid.

35. First Clement 42:3. (author's translation).

36. Irenaeus, *Against Heresies*, 3.3.4. Elsewhere, Irenaeus mentions that he had heard from someone who had been a disciple of the apostles, although the person is not named (4.27.1). Thus, Irenaeus appears to offer firsthand testimony. Although Irenaeus based the purity of his doctrine and that of the church in his time on the line of relation to the disciples (i.e., he heard from those who heard the apostles), apparently some groups of heretics did this as well. For example, in the early third century, Clement of Alexandria wrote that one group of heretics was claiming that Peter taught Glaucias who taught Basilides. Another, he says, claimed that Paul taught Theudas who taught Valentinus the Gnostic. Clement of Alexandria writes,

> And that of the apostles, embracing the ministry of Paul, ends with Nero. It was later, in the times of Adrian the king, that those who invented the heresies arose; and they extended to the age of Antoninus the elder, as, for instance, Basilides, though he claims (as they boast) for his master, Glaucias, the interpreter of Peter. Likewise they allege that Valentinus was a hearer of Theudas. And he was the pupil of Paul. For Marcion, who arose in the same age with them, lived as an old man with the younger [heretics]. And after him Simon heard for a little the preaching of Peter. Such being the case, it is evident, from the high antiquity and perfect truth of the Church, that these later heresies, and those yet subsequent to them in time, were new inventions falsified [from the truth]. (*The Stromata*, 7.18 in Roberts, Donaldson, and Coxe, eds. and trans., *The Ante-Nicene Fathers*)

Clement points out that, although they made claims to having received their teachings from the apostles, the teachings of the heretics were "new inventions." This seems to be confirmed by the earliest Christian writings. Paul and John appear to be refuting an incipient form of Gnosticism in some of their writings. The earliest Christian writings we have outside of the New Testament (i.e., those of the apostolic fathers) seem to be battling a more developed form of the same heretical teachings. This fits with the position that the heretics were continuing the practices of their teachers. Accordingly, it seems most reasonable to conclude with Clement that they were inventions of the heretics. Indeed, Irenaeus traces Marcion's line to Cerdon and then to Simon the sorcerer of Acts 8:9–24 (*Against Heresies*, 1.27. 1–2; 3.4.3). Around 200, the African church father, Tertullian, wrote:

> But if there be any [heresies] which are bold enough to plant themselves in the midst of the apostolic age, that they may thereby seem to have been handed down by the apostles, because they existed in the time of the apostles, we can say: Let them produce the original records of their churches; let them unfold the roll of their bishops, running down in due succession from the beginning in such a manner that [that first bishop of theirs] shall be able to show for his ordainer and predecessor some one of the apostles or of apostolic men,—a man, moreover, who continued stedfast with the apostles. For this is the manner in which the apostolic churches transmit their registers: as the church of Smyrna, which records that Polycarp was placed therein by John; as also the church of Rome, which makes Clement to have been ordained in like manner by Peter. In exactly the same way the other churches likewise exhibit [their several worthies], whom, as having been appointed to their episcopal places by apostles, they regard as transmitters of the apostolic seed. Let the heretics contrive something of the same kind. For after their blasphemy, what is there that is unlawful for them [to attempt]? But should they even effect the contrivance, they will not advance a step. For their very doctrine, after comparison with that of the apostles, will declare, by its own diversity and contrariety, that it had for its author neither an apostle nor an apostolic man; because, as the apostles would never have taught things which were self-contradictory, so the apostolic men would not have inculcated teaching different from the apostles, unless they who received their instruction from the apostles went and

preached in a contrary manner. To this test, therefore will they be submitted for proof by those churches, who, although they derive not their founder from apostles or apostolic men [as being of much later date, for they are in fact being founded daily], yet, since they agree in the same faith, they are accounted as not less apostolic because they are akin in doctrine. Then let all the heresies, when challenged to these two tests by our apostolic church, offer their proof of how they deem themselves to be apostolic. But in truth they neither are so, nor are they able to prove themselves to be what they are not. Nor are they admitted to peaceful relations and communion by such churches as are in any way connected with apostles, inasmuch as they are in no sense themselves apostolic because of their diversity as to the mysteries of the faith. (*Prescription Against Heretics*, 32)

Tertullian posited two tests: (1) He challenged the heretics to produce the same sort of succession lines back to the apostles with credible records that the churches possessed. (2) He said that a comparison of the writings of the heretics to those of the apostles reveals that the former do not have the latter as their source.

37. Irenaeus, *To Florinus*, cited by the fourth-century church historian, Eusebius, who regarded Irenaeus as a reliable source (*Ecclesiastical History* 5.20). See *To Florinus* in Roberts, Donaldson, and Coxe, eds. and trans., *The Ante-Nicene Fathers*. See Eusebius, *Eusebius: The Church History,* Paul L. Maier, ed. and trans. (Grand Rapids: Kregel, 1999), 195–96.

38. Tertullian, *Prescription Against Heretics*, 32.

39. *The Martyrdom of Polycarp* 9:3. Also known as the *Encyclical Letter of the Church at Smyrna.*

40. *To the Philippians* 9:2. (author's translation).

41. Ibid., 1:2; 2:1–2; 9:2; 12:2. Ignatius also provides early confirmation but he cannot be directly tied to the apostles. Ignatius was bishop of the church in Antioch in Syria. He knew Polycarp and wrote a letter to him while en route to his execution in Rome in about 110. Since the apostles trained Polycarp, Ignatius is certain to have been well acquainted with apostolic teachings. In addition to his letter to Polycarp, Ignatius wrote letters to six churches. These have been of immense value in revealing beliefs of the early church. In his letter to the church at Smyrna, Ignatius writes that the disciples were so encouraged by seeing and touching the risen Jesus that "they too despised death" and that after his resurrection,

"he [i.e., Jesus] ate and drank with them like one who is composed of flesh" (3:2–3). In the same letter, he writes, "Do pay attention, however, to the prophets and especially to the Gospel, in which the Passion has been made clear to us and the resurrection has been accomplished" (7:4). In his letter to the Philadelphians, Ignatius writes concerning the gospel, which of course was at the center of Christian preaching, "But the Gospel possesses something distinctive, namely, the coming of the Savior, our Lord Jesus Christ, his suffering, and the resurrection" (9:2). In his letter to the Magnesians, he writes, "I want to forewarn you not to get snagged on the hooks of worthless opinions but instead to be fully convinced about the birth and the suffering and the resurrection, which took place during the time of the governorship of Pontius Pilate. These things were truly and most assuredly done by Jesus Christ" (11:2–4). These translations are from *The Apostolic Fathers: Greek Texts and English Translations of Their Writings*, Michael W. Holmes, ed. and rev.; J. B. Lightfoot and J. R. Harmer, eds. and trans., 2d ed. (Grand Rapids: Baker, 1999).

42. It is possible that the first-century Jewish historian Josephus reports that the disciples claimed that the risen Jesus had appeared to them. Josephus was born in A.D. 37 in Jerusalem to Matthias, a popular Jewish priest. See Edwin M. Yamauchi, "Josephus and the Scriptures," *Fides et Historia* 13 (1980), 42; F. F. Bruce, *Jesus and Christian Origins Outside the New Testament* (Grand Rapids: Eerdmans, 1974), 32–34; Robert E. Van Voorst, *Jesus Outside the New Testament: An Introduction to the Ancient Evidence* (Grand Rapids: Eerdmans, 2000), 81–83. This places Josephus geographically and chronologically in a position to know about Jesus, since he is growing up where and when the disciples were preaching of Jesus and his resurrection. He became a Jewish priest in his early twenties, hated the Romans, fought the Romans, was defeated by the Romans, and later joined the Romans as the court historian for the Emperor Vespasian. See *Ante-Nicene Fathers*, vol. 10. In *Commentary on Matthew* (2.10.17), Origen in about A.D. 200 comments on Josephus: "And the wonderful thing is, that, though he did not accept Jesus as Christ, he yet gave testimony that the righteousness of James was so great; and he says that the people thought that they had suffered these things because of James" (*Ante-Nicene Fathers*, vol. 10). In *Contra Celsum* 1.47, Origen reiterates that Josephus was not a believer.

In *Antiquities of the Jews* (A.D. 95), extant manuscripts of Josephus include a remarkable passage on the disciples' claims that Jesus rose from the dead, which has come to be referred to as the *Testimonium Flavianum*:

About this time there lived Jesus, a wise man, if indeed one ought
to call him a man. For he was one who wrought surprising feats and was
a teacher of such people as accept the truth gladly. He won over many
Jews and many of the Greeks. He was the Messiah. When Pilate, upon
hearing him accused by men of the highest standing amongst us, had
condemned him to be crucified, those who had in the first place come
to love him did not give up their affection for him. On the third day he
appeared to them restored to life, for the prophets of God had proph-
esied these and countless other marvelous things about him. And the
tribe of the Christians, so called after him, has still to this day not disappeared. (18.3.63–64, Feldman trans., 49–51)

It is questionable whether all of the *Testimonium* contains the authentic
words of Josephus. Origen's testimony that Josephus was not a Christian creates
a problem. If Origen is correct, it would be odd that a non-Christian Jew would
make statements such as Jesus was "a wise man, if it be lawful to call him a man,"
"He was the Christ," and "he appeared to them alive again the third day, as the
divine prophets had foretold these and ten thousand other wonderful things
concerning him." Unfortunately, the question cannot be answered by textual
criticism, since no early manuscripts of the works of Josephus still exist. The
earliest of three manuscripts of Book 18 where the passage is found is from the
eleventh century, a difference of one thousand years between the original and
our first manuscript. However, this is not unusual for a work of antiquity. The
earliest manuscripts of the works of Julius Caesar, Plato, and Aristotle are all at
least seven hundred years removed from the originals. Origen quotes this passage of Josephus much earlier—in c. 246, and Eusebius quotes it about 325. Thus,
the questionable reading appeared relatively early.

If Josephus was not a Christian, how do we explain his laudatory statements
about Jesus, even referring to him as the "Christ" (i.e., Messiah) and
acknowledging his resurrection? The majority of scholars hold that a Christian
editor doctored the original text sometime between the second and fourth
centuries. This is referred to as "interpolation." The majority of scholars also agree
that there was an original form of the *Testimonium* in which Josephus says of
Jesus that he was a miracle worker, that he gained followers, that Pilate crucified
him, and that Jesus' followers remained loyal to him. Several reasons support
this conclusion and three are compelling: (1) The term, *wise man* is typical for
Josephus and less than we would expect from a Christian editor (Van Voorst,

Jesus Outside the New Testament, 88. Van Voorst adds, "Josephus says the same about Solomon [Ant. 18.5.2 §53] and Daniel [Ant. 10.11.2 §237], and something similar about John the Baptizer, whom he calls 'a good man' [Ant. 18.5.2 §116–9]"; cf. Yamauchi, *Jesus Under Fire*, 213). (2) The style belongs to Josephus (Meier, *Marginal Jew*, 1:62; Van Voorst, *Jesus Outside the New Testament*, 90. Yamauchi, *Jesus Under Fire*, 213). (3) The Greek word for "tribe" is not a typical Christian expression (Van Voorst, *Jesus Outside the New Testament*, 91–92; Yamauchi, *Jesus Under Fire*, 213). Still, the three laudatory parts saying "if indeed one should call him a man," "he was the Messiah," and "for he appeared to them alive again the third day, as the divine prophets had foretold these and ten thousand other wonderful things concerning him" may be the additions of a later Christian editor.

We just do not have enough data to know with certainty whether Josephus included the resurrection claims in this passage. Louis Feldman, one of the most informed Josephus scholars, comments that "until unquestionable proof is found, in the form of a manuscript containing the genuine version of Josephus' passage, no decisive answer can be given, and the entire matter remains in the domain of sheer speculation" (Louis H. Feldman and Gohei Hata, eds., *Josephus, the Bible, and History* [Detroit: Wayne State University Press, 1989], 339). For more on the *Testimonium*, see Meier, *Marginal Jew*, vol. 1, ch. 3. Feldman expressed agreement with Meier in a personal e-mail to one of the authors (Aug. 28, 2001). Zvi Baras writes that the "more plausible" position is "accepting parts of the passage and rejecting others" (Louis H. Feldman and Gohei Hata, eds., *Josephus, Judaism, and Christianity* [Detroit: Wayne State University Press, 1989], 339). Morton Smith, professor emeritus of ancient history at Columbia University, is pessimistic about a reconstruction of the passage, but concludes that Josephus certainly mentions Jesus (ibid., 252).

Uncertainty about parts of the passage does not justify rejection of it in its entirety, and most scholars do not go that far. Although no formal research has determined the percentage of Josephus scholars who accept parts of the passage versus those who reject it in its entirety, Feldman is perhaps the most qualified to make an informed assessment. In *Josephus and Modern Scholarship: 1937–1980* (New York: Walter de Gruyter, 1984), Feldman surveys more than one hundred scholarly writings on Josephus. In a personal e-mail to one of the authors (Nov. 26, 2001), Feldman admitted that his list for the period 1937 to 1980 is incomplete and that much on Josephus has appeared since 1980. Asked to make a rough assessment of where contemporary scholarship stands on the authenticity of the *Testimonium* as a whole, he responded, "My guess is that the ratio of those who in some manner accept the *Testimonium* would be at least 3 to 1. I would not be surprised if it would be as much as 5 to 1."

An old Arabic version of the disputed passage that is quite toned down from the Greek text may more accurately resemble what Josephus originally wrote. This Arabic text comes from an Arab Christian named Agapius and omits statements like "if it be lawful to call him a man." The text also contains statements which appear less embellished, such as "he was perhaps the Messiah" or "he was the so-called Messiah" rather than "he was the Christ" and that the disciples "reported that he had appeared to them three days after his crucifixion and that he was alive" rather than "he appeared to them alive again the third day, as the divine prophets had foretold these and ten thousand other wonderful things concerning him." However, there are reasons to reject the Arabic text as representing a more accurate rendering of Josephus's original words. Feldman comments, "the fact that the order of statements in Agapius differs from that in Josephus [Greek text] would seem to indicate that we are dealing here with a paraphrase. Furthermore, Agapius declares that according to Josephus, Herod burned the genealogies of the tribes, whereas there is no such passage in Josephus, but there is in Eusebius (*Historia Ecclesiastica* 1.7.13). This is further indication that Agapius did not consult Josephus directly" (Feldman and Hata, *Josephus, the Bible, and History*, 433). This book is an excellent source for those interested in reading the arguments for and against the genuineness of the passage. He now certainly views the three questionable parts as interpolations while accepting the rest as authentic (e-mail to author, Aug. 28, 2001). Josephus scholar Paul Maier is more optimistic than Feldman. Maier once wrote to Paul Winter, the ranking authority on Josephus at the time, to ask whether he thought *any* part of the *Testimonium Flavianum* was genuine, and if he did, how he thought the original passage ran. "He wrote me back with a yes for 1) and a reconstruction on 2) that *closely resembles the Agapian text*! Tragically, he died before the AT [*Agapian Text*] was announced by Schlomo Pines" (correspondence with author, March 7, 2003). Thus, a tone-downed version of the *Testimonium* as proposed by Maier and Winter is certainly a plausible reconstruction. Gerd Theissen and Annette Merz allow this reconstruction in *The Historical Jesus* (Minneapolis: Fortress, 1996), 72.

Van Voorst writes, "In sum, Josephus has given us in two passages [18:3; 20:200] something unique among all ancient non-Christian witnesses to Jesus: a carefully neutral, highly accurate and perhaps independent witness to Jesus, a wise man whom his persistent followers called 'the Christ'" (Van Voorst, *Jesus Outside the New Testament*, 103–4). Yamauchi comments, "Josephus knew that Jesus was the brother of James, the martyred leader of the church in Jerusalem, and that he was a wise teacher who had established a wide and lasting following, despite the fact that he had been crucified under Pilate at the instigation of some of the Jewish leaders" (Yamauchi, *Jesus Under Fire*, 213–14).

43. Norman Perrin, *The Resurrection According to Matthew, Mark, and Luke* (Philadelphia: Fortress, 1977), 80.

44. Someone might argue that to claim that the disciples suffered because they believed in the risen Christ is to claim too much, because they died for Christian teachings, of which the Resurrection was only one. After all, the Romans and Jews charged the early Christians with atheism and breaking the law. The Roman complaint was that they were atheists because they did not believe in the nation's gods. However, whatever reasons the authorities had, if Paul, James, and the original disciples had not believed that they had seen the risen Lord, there would have been no transformation in their lives. They would not have preached Jesus and his resurrection to the world, so they would not have suffered and faced death for their evangelistic actions. Christianity would not exist today. We will provide evidence for this view.

45. See Acts 4, where Peter and John are arrested and imprisoned; Acts 5, where the apostles are arrested, imprisoned, and flogged; and Acts 12, where James, the brother of John is martyred and Peter is imprisoned. Other persecutions are reported in Acts but not targeted specifically against the original disciples. We are specifically told that the Resurrection was their central message (Acts 4:2, 33).

46. First Clement 5:2–7 (author's translation). Clement reports that Peter and Paul suffered multiple attacks, and likely refers to their martyrdoms, although the latter is not without question. *Unto death* is the Greek, heōs thanatou. This construction appears sixteen times in Jewish writings in the Septuagint, Old Testament apocrypha, and New Testament and can mean dying or almost dying (2 Chron. 32:24; Isa. 38:1; 39:1; Jon. 4:9; Zech. 5:3 (two times); 4 Macc. 1:9; 14:19; Sir. 4:28; 18:22; 34:12; 37:2; 51:6; Odes Sol. 16:6; Matt. 26:38; Mark 14:34). Observe how heōs thanatou is used in Matthew 26:38, where Jesus says, "My soul is deeply grieved, to the point of death." Jesus did not die at the moment of this grief, but his sorrow was so intense that it could have killed him. Clement's friend and colleague Polycarp used the same phrase around the same time in a manner certainly referring to the death of Jesus: "our Lord Jesus Christ, who for our sins suffered even unto death, [but] 'whom

God raised from the dead, having loosed the bands of the grave'" (*To the Philippians* 1:2). Thus, without contextual considerations, an interpretation based solely on language is inconclusive.

Others have interpreted the Greek word, martyrēsas for "testified" or "martyred" in 1 Clement 5:4, 7. However, it appears that those in the Asia Minor church did not use the word in that sense until the middle of the second century. Our first discovery of the word being certainly employed in this manner is in *The Martyrdom of Polycarp* (see Gerhard Kittel and Gerhard Friedrich, eds., *Theological Dictionary of the New Testament*, 10 vols. [Grand Rapids: Eerdmans, 1981], 4:504–8) where the author uses it several times in this sense. A possible earlier exception is found in Revelation 2:13, although we cannot be certain this is what the author had in mind. It is possible that Clement employs it here in the sense of being a martyr. However, it is arguable that Clement used the term to refer to being a witness and not a martyr, since Clement writes around 95 from Rome.

But the context in which Clement uses the term may lead us to conclude that he was referring to the martyrdoms of Peter and Paul. In 1 Clement 6, Clement continues his thoughts from 5:1–2. Clement says that, in addition to Peter, Paul, and possibly all of the apostles, there was a vast number of other believers who became examples for us, because they had been through horrible persecutions. He adds that Christian women suffered horrible torture but that "they reached and achieved the suitable honorable prize." Note 16 (page 35) in *The Apostolic Fathers: Greek Texts and English Translations of Their Writings*, rev. 2d ed., J. B. Lightfoot and J. R. Harmer, eds. and trans.; M. W. Holmes, ed. and rev. (Grand Rapids: Baker, 1999) comments on the women Danaids and Dircae: "In ancient mythology, the daughters of Danaus were given as prizes to the winners of a race; thus it is likely that this is a reference to Christian women being raped prior to being martyred. Dirce was tied to the horns of a bull and then dragged to death." So it seems that Clement is saying that Christian women were martyred, and the language used was euphemistic (i.e., "they safely reached the goal"). Thus, there is good reason to hold that similar words used for Peter and Paul (i.e., "went to his appointed place of glory" and "went to the holy place") meant that they died a martyr's death, especially since this is attested elsewhere and no conflicting accounts exist.

At minimum, Clement refers to the continuous sufferings of Peter and Paul and probably refers to their martyrdoms for two reasons: (1) A euphemism similar to what Clement uses for their deaths, "went to his appointed place" and "went to the holy place," is used in the chapter that follows for other Christians who were certainly martyred: "they safely reached the goal" (6:2). (2) Their martyrdoms are attested by other sources. See discussion of Eusebius, Origen, and Tertullian, pp. 58–59 (see also chapter 3, n54). Either way, Peter and Paul are described as *willing* to suffer both continuously and greatly for their faith, whether or not they were martyred.

47. *To the Philippians* 9:2 (author's translation).

48. *To the Smyrnaeans* 3:2 (author's translation).

49. Ibid., 3:4.

50. Kittel and Friedrich, eds., *Theological Dictionary of the New Testament*, 3:631– 32. Colin Brown, gen. ed., *The New International Dictionary of New Testament Theology*, 4 vols. (Grand Rapids: Zondervan, 1975), 1:461–62. See also Hebrews 12:2.

51. *Scorpiace*, 15, in Roberts, Donaldson, and Coxe, eds. and trans., *The Ante-Nicene Fathers*.

52. It is uncertain whether "the lives of the Caesars" is the title or the subject matter of a book. This book has either been lost, or Tertullian is referring to the work of Tacitus and is only using it in reference to Nero's campaign to kill Christians (*The Twelve Caesars* 15.44).

53. The text reads:

> But all human efforts, all the lavish gifts of the emperor, and the propitiations of the gods, did not banish the sinister belief that the conflagration was the result of an order. Consequently, to get rid of the report, Nero fastened the guilt and inflicted the most exquisite tortures on a class hated for their abominations, called Christians by the populace. Christus, from whom the name had its origin, suffered the extreme penalty during the reign of Tiberius at the hands of one of our procurators, Pontius Pilatus, and a most mischievous superstition, thus checked for the moment, again broke out not only in Judaea, the first source of the evil, but even in Rome, where all things hideous and shameful from every part of the world find their centre and become popular. Accordingly, an arrest was first made of all who pleaded guilty; then, upon their information, an immense multitude was convicted, not so much of the crime of firing the city, as of hatred against mankind. Mockery of every sort was added to their deaths. Covered with the skins of beasts, they were torn by dogs and perished, or were nailed to crosses, or were

doomed to the flames and burnt, to serve as a nightly illumination, when daylight had expired. Nero offered his gardens for the spectacle, and was exhibiting a show in the circus, while he mingled with the people in the dress of a charioteer or stood aloft on a car. Hence, even for criminals who deserved extreme and exemplary punishment, there arose a feeling of compassion; for it was not, as it seemed, for the public good, but to glut one man's cruelty, that they were being destroyed. (Alfred John Church and William Jackson Brodribb translation)

For the entire text of *The Annals*, go to the Web site www.classics.mit.edu/Tacitus/annals.html. This passage is also interesting in that Tacitus wrote that Jesus' execution by Pontius Pilate "checked for the moment" Christianity, but then it "broke out not only in Judaea . . . but even in Rome." This is strikingly consistent with the accounts in the Gospels and Acts of the transformation of the disciples, who were emboldened through seeing the risen Jesus to publicly proclaim him in all Judea and Samaria, and even to the remotest part of the earth" (Acts 1:8).

It should be noted that most scholars accept this passage in Tacitus as authentic, but a very few question it. Some assert that Tacitus cannot be regarded as a source who confirms the existence of Jesus, because he was not born until about twenty-five years after Jesus, so all of his information is secondhand. This type of thinking is seriously flawed. If we conducted historical inquiry that way today, we could know very little about ancient history. For example, much of what we know about Julius Caesar and Caesar Augustus comes from the ancient Roman historians Tacitus and Suetonius. However, Tacitus and Suetonius are even more removed in time from Julius and Augustus than they were from Jesus. If we listened to this reasoning, we could know very little about these two most famous Roman Caesars. In fact, no one today could write a history of the American Civil War, since it would by no means be firsthand knowledge. But we can write an accurate history of the Civil War, since there are letters, documents, and the written testimonies of those who were there. Tacitus and Suetonius were a lot closer to the events they write about than we are to the American Civil War.

In his book, *A Marginal Jew*, volume 1, critical scholar John Meier states, "despite some feeble attempts to show that this text is a Christian interpolation in Tacitus, the passage is obviously genuine. Not only is it witnessed in all the manuscripts of the Annals, the very anti-Christian tone of the text makes

Christian origin almost impossible" (90). Similarly, in *Jesus Outside the New Testament*, Van Voorst writes that only a few words in the text are generally disputed, such as Tacitus's spelling of the word *Crestians* for *Christians*, and his identification of Pilate as "procurator" instead of the more accurate "prefect." He writes that, on the basis of these problems, a few have claimed that the entire passage is the result of a subsequent Christian editor, but he calls this "pure speculation" (42–43, n. 60). The differences are easily reconciled. Moreover, the style of the text definitely belongs to Tacitus. Pagan editors did not express themselves in the Latin that Tacitus uses, a unique style with an economy of words. He was not prone to use redundant phrases within a sentence, but made his words count in other phrases if possible (ibid., 43) and a Christian editor would not have had Tacitus call Christianity a "deadly superstition." Besides all of this, the passage fits well in the context. Tacitus was a Roman governor and could have had knowledge of past events concerning the Roman Empire. Therefore, there is no reason to doubt that Tacitus mentions Jesus as a historical person and his crucifixion by Pilate and the brutal executions of Christians by Nero as historical events.

54. Origen, *Contra Celsum*, 2.56 in Roberts, Donaldson, and Coxe, eds. and trans., *The Ante-Nicene Fathers*.

55. Ibid., 2.77.

56. Origen's commentary on Genesis, volume 3. This work has been lost but is cited by Eusebius in *Ecclesiastical History* 3.1. Crucifying victims upside down or in positions other than upright is mentioned by Seneca (*Dialogue* 6, 20.3) and Josephus (*Jewish War* 5.449–51). A recent study by a critical historian concluded with the likelihood that Peter was executed between 64 and 68 by Nero. See Michael Grant, *Saint Peter: A Biography* (New York: Scribner's, 1994), ch. 13.

57. *Ecclesiastical History* 2.25.8; 3.1. Ben Witherington III sees the manner of Peter's death reported in John's gospel (21:18–19): "In the reference to the stretching out of his hands, which is a common metaphor for crucifixion, it is likely that we are being told not only how Peter would die but how Peter did die, some twenty-five to thirty years before this Gospel was published, at least in its present form" (Ben Witherington III, *John's Wisdom: A Commentary on the Fourth Gospel* [Louisville: Westminster John Knox, 1995], 356).

58. *Ecclesiastical History* 2.23. Some critical skeptics like to portray Eusebius as a liar. On what basis do they make this assertion? In the table of contents of his work, *Preparation of the Gospel* (or *Evangelical Preparation*) under book 12,

chapter 31, he writes, "That it will be necessary sometimes to use falsehood as a remedy for the benefit of those who require such a mode of treatment." Some critics have claimed on the basis of this statement that Eusebius promoted the practice of deceit in order to advance Christianity. A closer look, however, reveals that this is not the case.

Evangelical Preparation contains fifteen books by Eusebius. In books 10–12, Eusebius argues that Greek writers like Plato had borrowed from the older theology and philosophy of Hebrew writers such as Moses (Eusebius, *Preparation for the Gospel*, Edwin Hamilton Gifford, trans. [Grand Rapids: Baker, 1981], part 1, books 1–9). In order to accomplish his goal, Eusebius's format throughout is to cite the Greek writers, often at length, with acknowledgements, and then to cite the Bible on the same topic. In chapter 31, Eusebius begins by quoting Plato: "But even if the case were not such as our argument has now proved it to be, if a lawgiver, who is to be of ever so little use, could have ventured to tell any falsehood at all to the young for their good, is there any falsehood that he could have told more beneficial than this, and better able to make them all do everything that is just, not by compulsion but willingly? 'Truth, O Stranger, is a noble and an enduring thing; it seems, however, not easy to persuade men of it'" (p. 657). The reference is from Plato's "Laws" 663D where he, of course, is establishing principles with which to base civil law in the land. Eusebius then compares Plato's words with the Old Testament: "Now you may find in the Hebrew Scriptures also thousands of such passages concerning God as though He were jealous, or sleeping, or angry, or subject to any other human passions, which passages are adopted for the benefit of those who need this mode of instruction." Chapter 31 is concluded with that statement, and Eusebius moves on to another topic.

It may be helpful to look at the Greek employed. The word used by Plato is *pseudos,* which typically means a lie or imitation. However, Plato's context and the passage may justify a nuance for the following reasons: (1) Plato uses the term, "good lie" *(agatho pseudesthai),* eliminating harmful intent. Whereas elsewhere the term "lie" usually indicates ill will. One translator renders the term as "useful fiction," instead of "falsehood" (*Plato in Twelve Volumes*, 12 vols., R. G. Bury, trans. [Cambridge, Mass.: Harvard University Press, 1914–1935], 10.125). (2) The context may justify a softer translation than "lies" or "deceit." Plato asks who is happier in life: the righteous person or the one who has everything—health, wealth, prestige, but who is arrogant and unjust. Plato then reasons why the righteous person is happiest. He then says that even if his conclusion is false, it is still a beneficial position to motivate one to live a devout and righteous life. Then he reasons why it is expedient to hold his position. Plato then sums up his position: (a) From arguments, we see that the unjust life is not only shameful, but also in all truth not as pleasant as the righteous life and (b) even if his reasoning is wrong, the conclusion that telling people that being righteous brings the greatest amount of happiness is expedient for the common good. Plato's colleague responds that truth is noble, yet to persuade men is not easy to do. Plato answers that it is quite easy and provides an example. Finally, he says we should pass this teaching to the children (that the just life is the happiest). By doing so we shall "not only be saying what is most true," but we will also convince those who may not normally choose to live a just life. Plato has not encouraged a person to lie. He has merely said that he believes he is correct in his belief, but even if he is not, his belief is still expedient. Finally, he claims we should pass his teaching on because it is true and because by using his reasons for living righteously those inclined toward being unjust may choose to be just. With this in mind, let's see how Eusebius employs Plato.

When Eusebius refers to "falsehood," he is not encouraging Christians to lie for the benefit of the kingdom of Christ. (1) In his comparison with the Hebrew Scriptures he states that thousands of passages similar to Plato's can be found. He then lists a few examples of human passions attributed to God that he claims "are adopted for the benefit of those who need this mode of instruction." These are Jewish reasons why one should live the righteous life. The result is that those who are not naturally inclined to live righteously may be encouraged to do so for fear of the consequences. Writers of the Old Testament obviously believed such consequences were real. So in Eusebius's comparison of Plato to the Hebrew Scriptures, he is saying that Plato copied the idea from them that certain devices that do not exactly reflect reality may be used to persuade to live righteously. The Hebrew writers attributed human qualities to God to explain why we should not worship other gods and the reasons behind other laws. Plato copied this principle, says Eusebius, when he wrote that he presented the truth for why men should be moral because a moral life makes one happier than an immoral one. However, Plato continues, even if he is mistaken and evil men comply, the goal of a moral society is obtained. (2) The Hebrew and Christian Scriptures *never* encourage one to lie. In fact quite the opposite is true (Ps. 120:2; Prov. 6:16–19; 12:19, 22; Rom. 3:7, Col. 3:9; 1 John 2:21; Rev. 21:27; 22:15). (3) A similar section is found in Eusebius's sequel, *Proof of the Gospel* (3.5) about lying to bring people into the kingdom of Christ. However, Eusebius is speaking in a very sarcastic tone in context, clearly intending his readers to understand that such is preposterous. Therefore, there is no reason to believe he would encourage just the opposite in this related writing. Further, Eusebius's examples of anthropopatheia indicate that he saw the value in offering reasons why one should be righteous; namely that this may motivate those to be righteous who would not normally be inclined to do so. God may not sleep or experience jealousy as humans do, but these figures of speech ("good lies"?) motivate people to live righteously. Thus, Eusebius has demonstrated how the Greeks have borrowed from the older Hebrew, which is the intent of the passage. The assertion that Eusebius encouraged deceit should be rejected. At the very least, his solitary statement cannot be taken as having proved this to be his meaning.

59. Hippolytus was a disciple of Irenaeus and a leader in the church of the late second and early third century. In a work attributed to him the fates of the apostles are listed. The true dating and authorship of this text is doubtful. The fates given for Peter and Paul are consistent with what others wrote, for example Tertullian, Origen, and Dionysius of Corinth (as quoted by Eusebius). The accounts regarding the remaining apostles are interesting and may contain historical kernels, but they are anecdotal and cannot be accorded too much weight. Following is the list as it appears in the work attributed to Hippolytus:

> On the Twelve Apostles: Where Each of Them Preached and Where He Met His End: 1. Peter preached the Gospel in Pontus, and Galatia, and Cappadocia, and Betania, and Italy, and Asia, and was afterwards crucified by Nero in Rome with his head downward, as he had himself desired to suffer in that manner. 2. Andrew preached to the Scythians and Thracians, and was crucified, suspended on an olive tree, at Patrae, a town of Achaia; and there too he was buried. 3. John, again, in Asia, was banished by Domitian the king to the isle of Patmos, in which also he wrote his Gospel and saw the apocalyptic vision; and in Trajan's time he fell asleep at Ephesus, where his remains were sought for, but could not be found. 4. James, his brother, when preaching in Judea, was cut off with the sword by Herod the tetrarch, and was buried there. 5. Philip preached in Phrygia, and was crucified in Hierapolis with his head downward in the time of Domitian, and was buried there. 6. Bartholomew, again, preached to the Indians, to whom he also gave the Gospel according to Matthew, and was crucified with his head downward, and was

buried in Allanum, a town of the great Armenia. 7. And Matthew wrote the Gospel in the Hebrew tongue, and published it at Jerusalem, and fell asleep at Hierees, a town of Parthia. 8. And Thomas preached to the Parthians, Medes, Persians, Hyrcanians, Bactrians, and Margians, and was thrust through in the four members of his body with a pine spear at Calamene, the city of India, and was buried there. 9. And James the son of Alphaeus, when preaching in Jerusalem, was stoned to death by the Jews, and was buried there beside the temple. 10. Jude, who is also called Lebbaeus, preached to the people of Edessa, and to all Mesopotamia, and fell asleep at Berytus, and was buried there. 11. Simon the Zealot, the son of Clopas, who is also called Jude, became bishop of Jerusalem after James the Just, and fell asleep and was buried there at the age of 120 years. 12. And Matthias, who was one of the seventy, was numbered along with the eleven apostles, and preached in Jerusalem, and fell asleep and was buried there. 13. And Paul entered into the apostleship a year after the assumption of Christ; and beginning at Jerusalem, he advanced as far as Illyricum, and Italy, and Spain, preaching the Gospel for thirty-five years. And in the time of Nero he was beheaded at Rome, and was buried there." (Roberts, Donaldson, and Coxe, eds. and trans., *The Ante-Nicene Fathers*, Fathers of the Third Century: Hippolytus, Cyprian, Novatian, Appendix [ECF 1.5.0.2.3.0])

In addition, *Foxe's Book of Martyrs* is a sixteenth-century book that gives details of the fate of all of the apostles. Foxe claimed to have reputable sources from which he received his data. However, he cites few of them, and those that he apparently used are now lost. Because of its late dating, we cannot assign much weight to his records for the purpose of historical investigation.

60. Acts 7:54–60.
61. Acts 12:1–3.
62. First Clement 5. From Acts 12 on, a theme of the Acts account is the fortitude of Peter, Paul and others in the midst of persecution and suffering.
63. Any recantation by the disciples would have provided much ammunition for Christian opponents like Celsus, who wrote strongly against the church in the third quarter of the second century (around 170). Celsus's work has since been lost, but he is cited frequently and Origen in particular wrote to answer his charges in *Contra Celsum* (200). Likewise, it would also have provided some powerful arguments for Pliny the Younger, Tacitus, Suetonius, Lucian, first-century Jew-

ish scholars and many others who were critical of Christian claims. For details on these writers and their complaints against Christianity, see Habermas, *Historical Jesus*, chapter 9.

64. There are many statements on the Christians' willingness to suffer martyrdom that are made by friends and enemies. A selection of these sources might include *Shepherd of Hermas* (parable 9, section 28; vision 3, section 1, verse 9–2:1; 5:2); Melito of Sardis (cited by Eusebius, *Ecclesiastical History* 4.26.3); Dionysius of Corinth (cited by Eusebius, *Ecclesiastical History* 2.25.8); Hegesippus (cited by Eusebius, *Ecclesiastical History* 3.32.3; 2.23.18; 4.22.4); Eusebius, *Ecclesiastical History* 2.25; 5.2.2–3; Polycrates, Bishop of Ephesus, in his letter to Victor of Rome; Josephus, *Antiquities* 20.200; and the correspondence of Pliny (10.96–97). The New Testament notes the martyrdoms of Stephen (Acts 7:59–60), James the brother of John (12:2), and Antipas (Rev. 2:13).

65. Luke, Clement of Rome, Polycarp, Ignatius, Dionysius of Corinth, Tertullian, and Origen.

66. In addition to the seven, there is also Paul, Josephus, Hegesippus, and Clement of Alexandria. We have saved for the next chapter a discussion of the significant evidence for Paul and James the brother of Jesus regarding the two primary topics in this chapter—their beliefs that they also saw the risen Jesus and their suffering and martyrdom.

67. Rudolf Bultmann, "New Testament and Mythology," in *Kerygma and Myth*, Hans Werner Bartsch, ed.; Reginald H. Fuller, trans. (New York: Harper and Row, 1961), 42; cf. 39.

68. Gerd Lüdemann, *What Really Happened to Jesus? A Historical Approach to the Resurrection*, John Bowden, trans. (Louisville: Westminster John Knox, 1995), 80. Lüdemann holds that visions caused the beliefs.

69. In an interview by Peter Jennings in *The Search for Jesus* (American Broadcasting Corp. [ABC], July 2000).

70. See details in Gary R. Habermas, "Resurrection Research from 1975 to the Present: What Are Critical Scholars Saying?" *Philosophia Christi*, forthcoming.

Chapter 4: A Quintet of Facts (4 + 1): The Last Three

1. First Corinthians 15:9–10.
2. Galatians 1:12–16, 22–23.
3. Philippians 3:6–7.
4. We may ask the question, "How do we know Paul wrote these letters and why

should we trust him?" The bulk of critical scholarship holds that there was a man named Paul who wrote some letters. This fact is attested by early and multiple witnesses (2 Peter 3:15–16; 1 Clem. 47:1–3 [c. 95–96]; Polycarp in *To the Philippians* 3:2; 11:2–3 [c. 110]; Ignatius, *To the Ephesians* 12:2 [c. 110]). Some early witnesses attribute specific letters to Paul. Clement of Rome (95) attributes 1 Corinthians to Paul (1 Clem. 47:1–3). Polycarp (c. 110) attests to Pauline authorship of Philippians and 1 Corinthians (*To the Philippians* 3:2; 11:2–3). Scholars also note a consistency of writing style and unified content throughout at least some letters ascribed to Paul.

We can trust Paul as a witness for at least two reasons: (1) Like the disciples, he was willing to suffer continually and to die for his belief that the risen Jesus had appeared to him. This is strong evidence that he was not intentionally lying. (2) Early leaders of the church acknowledged his place of authority to be like that of the original apostles. Polycarp wrote that Paul "accurately and reliably taught the word of truth" (*To the Philippians* 3:2), and Polycarp lists Paul among the apostles (9:1). Around the same time as Polycarp, Ignatius wrote of his high regard for Paul (*To the Ephesians* 12:2). Ignatius seems to place Peter and Paul at an apostolic level of authority that is above his own (*To the Romans* 4:3).

In addition, Paul's writings are certainly cited twenty-one times by five of the apostolic fathers and perhaps alluded to on several other occasions. Ignatius cites him once: *To Polycarp* 5:1. Polycarp cites him sixteen times: *To the Philippians* 1:3; 2:2; 4:1 (3 times, the second of which may be a dual reference to 2 Cor. 6:2); 5:1, 3; 6:1, 2 (2 times); 9:2; 11:1, 2, 4; 12:1 (2 times). The author of 2 Clement cites him in 19:2. The author of *Martyrdom of Polycarp* cites him in 1:2. Papias cites him twice in *Fragments,* in *Traditions of the Elders* 2 (2 Cor. 12:4) and 5 (1 Cor. 15:25), although this portion of *Fragments* must be considered later, since it is from Irenaeus rather than the apostolic fathers. The epistle *To Diognetus,* which is included among writings of the apostolic fathers, cites Paul (12.5), but this epistle was probably written after 150 and is, therefore, not included among the twenty-one citations.

The following letters of Paul are certainly cited by the apostolic fathers, although not necessarily attributed to him: Romans twice (one of the references could be from Romans or 2 Corinthians, so it has only been counted once); 1 Corinthians three times; 2 Corinthians five times (one of the references could be from Romans or 1 Corinthians so it has been counted once); Galatians once; Ephesians five times; Philippians twice; 1 Thessalonians once; 2 Thessalonians once; 1 Timothy twice.

5. Acts 7:58; 8:1–3; 9:1–19; 22:3–16; 26:9–23. Luke's record of Paul's remarks concerning his pre-Christian actions against the church are found in 22:1–5; 26:4–5, 9–11. In 22:4–5, Paul says that he persecuted the church to the death, arresting men and women, throwing them into prison, and finally bringing them to Jerusalem in order to be punished ("to death" from the Greek *achri thanatou*. This phrase is not found in the LXX. In the New Testament it appears only in Revelation 2:10 and 12:11. Paul's testimony in Acts 26:10 indicates that these persecutions included seeing Christians put to death. Thus, the phrase *achri thanatou,* like *heōs thanatou* (e.g., Matt. 26:38; Mark. 14:34), most likely includes death. In Acts 26:4–5, Paul says that "all the Jews" knew of his prior life in Judaism as a strict Jew and is very similar to what he writes in Galatians 1:22–23. In Acts 26:9–11, he confesses to imprisoning many Christians, voting that they be put to death resulting in their execution, punishing them often (perhaps through torturous beatings), trying to make them blaspheme Christ, and persecuting them even outside of Jerusalem to foreign cities. See note 4 in this chapter for more information on Paul.

6. Galatians 1:22–23.

7. It would be nice to also have a letter by Paul written prior to his conversion, expressing his hatred for the church or a mention of Saul/Paul by a non-Christian source confirming his anti-Christian actions. Unfortunately, if any of these ever existed, they have not survived.

8. Acts 9:1–19; 22:3–21; 26:9–23; 1 Corinthians 9:1; 15:8. Some ask why Paul added his name to the list in the creed in 15:8. Many hold that by adding his name to the list, Paul regards his experience of the risen Jesus to be in some sense on par with the appearances of Jesus to the other apostles. However, the extent of the comparison is debated. Atheist New Testament scholar Gerd Lüdemann believes that this passage indicates that Paul viewed the nature of his experience to be precisely like those experienced by the disciples (Paul Copan and Ronald K. Tacelli, eds., *Jesus' Resurrection: Fact or Figment? A Debate Between William Lane Craig and Gerd Lüdemann* [Downers Grove, Ill.: InterVarsity, 2000], 61). Lüdemann's theory is somewhat aggressive. The highly critical New Testament scholar John Dominic Crossan of the Jesus Seminar writes, "Paul needs in 1 Cor. 15 to equate his own experience with that of the preceding apostles. To equate, that is, its *validity* and *legitimacy,* but not necessarily its mode or manner. . . . Paul's own entranced revelation should not be . . . the model for all the others" (John Dominic Crossan, *Jesus: A Revolutionary Biography* [San Francisco: HarperSanFrancisco, 1994], 169).

9. The fact that Jews would have considered that Jesus was cursed by God (Gal. 3:13; cf. Deut. 21:23) complicates any suggestion that Paul was leaning toward Christianity.

10. Atheist philosopher Michael Martin attempts to downplay this factor in Paul's conversion by stating: "Why should the fact that Paul persecuted Christians and was subsequently converted to Christianity by his religious experience be given special existential significance? Whatever his past record, at the time of his report he was a zealous, religious believer and not a religious skeptic" (Michael Martin, *The Case Against Christianity* [Philadelphia: Temple University Press, 1991], 84). It seems that for Martin, it is not good enough to be anti-Christian in order to be considered a good witness. One must also be anti-religious—as though that carries no biases. But the knife cuts both ways here—some religious skeptics reveal a different sort of religious bias.

Bible critic Roy Hoover makes a similar move: "No New Testament text claims that the risen Jesus appeared to anyone who had not been a follower of Jesus or who did not become a believer" (Copan and Tacelli, *Jesus' Resurrection: Fact or Figment?* 134). This is quite a leap for Hoover to make, simply writing off those who became believers because they thought they saw the risen Christ. Both Martin and Hoover fail to address the question concerning what led them to this belief against their previous wishes to reject this false Messiah and his followers. So how do Martin and Hoover account for Paul's experience? Hoover writes, "The risen Jesus was seen by one Pharisee who was a zealous enemy of the early church—Paul, from Tarsus; but so far as we know, Paul never met the Jesus of history and cannot, therefore, be counted among his enemies" (ibid., 135). If we followed Hoover's logic, no one who fought against the Nazis in World War II could consider Hitler his enemy unless he had personally met him.

In answer to Paul's conversion, Martin cites the conversion of Muhammad, whom he says converted from polytheism to monotheism based on his testimony of a primary source of revelation (i.e., the archangel Gabriel). Muhammad claimed that Gabriel directly gave him revelation from heaven, which eventually became the Qur'an. Martin is saying that if a primary source of revelation is so strong, why accept Paul's testimony while rejecting Muhammad's (Martin, *Case Against Christianity*, 84). Martin overlooks a few important data: First, testimony as a primary source is only one factor in historical considerations. Anyone can claim to have an experience (e.g., Sun Myung Moon, Joseph Smith, Jim Jones). But one must look at the evidence as well. There is evidence against the Qur'an being from God. This evidence involves textual, historical, and source challenges. Second, it is thought by many that Muhammad's dissatisfaction with the paganism and idolatry in his society existed prior to his alleged revelations. If this is true, his embracing of monotheism is not out of the ordinary, and no conversion from polytheism is required. On the other hand, Paul seems to have been quite content with, and extremely sold out to, his cause in Judaism. Indeed, he was on his way to arrest Christians on his own initiative when his experience occurred. His radical conversion must be accounted for. Third, the quality of the testimony concerning Muhammad is not on the same level as that for Paul. We have Paul's own testimony of what happened to him, described in his own writings. The conversion of Muhammad is recorded in the Hadith, containing traditions that developed much later than Muhammad's lifetime and which were recorded by others. Even if reliable, these are secondary sources, as are Luke's accounts of Paul's conversion, although Luke's accounts are much closer to the time of the events they describe. Another example Martin could have provided is Joseph Smith, the founder of Mormonism, who claimed to have received direct revelation through the angel Moroni. However, Smith's credibility as a prophet is highly dubious due to problems with the *Book of Abraham*, as well as the challenges posed by no specific archaeological confirmation for the *Book of Mormon*, not to mention very serious problems with those who are said to have personally seen Smith's golden plates. For more on Smith and these challenges, see Michael Licona, *Behold, I Stand at the Door and Knock* (Virginia Beach, Va.: TruthQuest, 1998), chaps 3–4.

In spite of the problems intrinsic to the unwillingness of Martin and Hoover to see the full value in Paul's testimony, at least one other problem is evident: Do Martin and Hoover consider more valid the testimony of someone who had seen the risen Christ or believed that he had risen, yet still refused to become a Christian? Wouldn't we want to question the credibility of such a witness?

11. The sufferings of Paul appear on numerous occasions in Acts: Paul is stoned, dragged outside the city and left for dead (14:19); Paul and Silas are flogged, thrown into prison, and their feet fastened in stocks (16:19–24); Paul and Silas are hunted by a mob (17:5); the crowds are stirred up against Paul, forcing him to be escorted out of the city (17:13–15); the Jews arrest Paul and bring him before a Roman proconsul (18:12–13); a Jewish crowd seizes Paul, based on false accusations, drags him from the temple, and attempts to kill him, an action stopped by a Roman commander and troops (21:27–36); more than forty men take an oath not to eat or drink until they have killed Paul, an action again stopped

by a Roman commander (23:12–35). This does not include other persecutions of believers recorded in Acts in which the apostles' involvement is not specified. In 2 Corinthians 11:23–28, Paul says that he has been imprisoned on account of the gospel multiple times, beaten so many times that he cannot count them. He has lived often in danger of death, having received thirty-nine lashes five times from the Jews. He has been beaten with rods three times, stoned once, shipwrecked three times, been in danger in every conceivable place, gone sleepless nights, and endured times without food, as well as cold and exposure. For sources on Paul's tribulations and martyrdom outside of his own writings and Acts, see pp. 57–59.

12. See the previous endnote.

13. For example, Muhammad (see n. 10).

14. Gary R. Habermas, "Resurrection Claims in Non-Christian Religions," in *Religious Studies* 25 (1989), 167–77.

15. For details on the find, reasons for accepting its authenticity, and a historical study on James, see Hershel Shanks and Ben Witherington III, *The Brother of Jesus* (San Francisco: HarperSanFrancisco, 2003).

16. Matthew 13:55–56 and Mark 6:3. That Jesus had brothers is well attested, being recorded in all four gospels and some of the earliest writings in the New Testament: Matthew 12:46–50; Mark 3:31–35; Luke 8:19–21; John 2:12; 7:3, 5, 10; Acts 1:13–14; 1 Corinthians 9:5; Galatians 1:19.

17. Josephus, *Antiquities* 20:200. Unlike Josephus's *Testimonium Flavianum* (18:3), this passage is accepted as authentic by the majority of scholars. Among the reasons for accepting the authenticity of this passage by Josephus are: (1) a Christian editor would have used complimentary language to describe James and more laudatory language referring to Jesus (Robert E. Van Voorst, *Jesus Outside the New Testament* [Grand Rapids: Eerdmans, 2000], 83–84). (2) The point of Josephus is that Ananus was deposed because he instigated illegal executions of several enemies, including James. However, James is mentioned simply as an example. If a Christian editor was responsible for the inclusion of James, we would expect more information to be provided. (3) Josephus's account differs from other Christian accounts of the death of James and, therefore, appears to be independent of Christian tradition (see Clement of Alexandria and Hegesippus in Eusebius, *Ecclesiastical History* 2.23).

   Louis Feldman writes, "The passage about James [20.197–200] has generally been accepted as authentic" (Louis H. Feldman and Gohei Hata, eds. *Josephus, the Bible, and History* [Detroit: Wayne State University Press, 1987],

434). Elsewhere Feldman mentions "the authenticity of which has been almost universally acknowledged" in regard to this text (Louis H. Feldman and Gohei Hata, eds., *Josephus, Judaism, and Christianity* [Detroit: Wayne State University Press, 1989], 56). Another Jewish scholar, Zvi Baras, states that this passage "is considered authentic by most scholars" (ibid., 341). Evangelical Christian historian Edwin Yamauchi comments, "Few scholars have questioned the genuineness of this passage" (Edwin M. Yamauchi, "Jesus and the Scriptures," *Fides et Historia* 13 [1980]: 53). New Testament scholar Van Voorst writes, "The overwhelming majority of scholars holds that the words 'the brother of Jesus called Christ' are authentic, as is the entire passage in which it is found" (Van Voorst, *Jesus Outside the New Testament*, 83). For more on Josephus and the disputed *Testimonium Flavianum*, see pp. 250–54, and chapter 3, n42.

18. Galatians 2:12–13.
19. Acts 15:19–20.
20. Hegesippus's works have been lost. However, Eusebius in *Ecclesiastical History* 2.23 devotes a chapter to the martyrdom of James, in which he writes, "But the most accurate account of him is given by Hegesippus, who came in the generation after the apostles. He writes, in Book 5 of his *Memoirs* . . ." (Eusebius, *Eusebius: The Church History*, Paul L. Maier, ed. and trans. [Grand Rapids: Kregel, 1999], 81). Eusebius then provides this information on James's martyrdom from Hegesippus. Ben Witherington III comments, however, that "the Josephus account is probably both earlier and more circumspect and deserves the nod as best reflecting the historical realities of the situation. While Eusebius is a careful historian by ancient standards, he does not always exercise the sort of critical judgment of his sources one might wish" (Hershel Shanks and Ben Witherington III, *The Brother of Jesus* [San Francisco: HarperSanFrancisco, 2003], 192).
21. John 7:5 is interesting. When verses 3–5 are considered, it seems that his brothers had heard of his alleged miracles, did not believe the reports, and were, in a sense, daring their brother to do them in front of crowds. They were calling his bluff.
22. Matthew may also imply that Jesus' brothers were not sympathetic to his mission. In Matthew 13:55–57 (cf. Mark 6:3–4), Jesus' mother, his brothers, and sisters are mentioned by those in his hometown who were offended at him. Jesus responded, "Only in his hometown and *in his own house* is a prophet without honor" (NIV, emphasis added). This may imply that Matthew was aware that some in Jesus' own home did not believe in him and, thus, would agree with Mark and

John that his brothers were unbelievers. This is confirmed by Mark, who distinguishes between Jesus' birth mother and brothers and those considered his brothers in the faith (3:31–35). New Testament critical scholar John Meier adds, "Mark himself makes this scene even more negative in his redactional introduction (3:21), where he depicts the family of Jesus *(hoi par' autou)* setting out to seize him because they think he has gone mad" (John P. Meier, *A Marginal Jew*, vol. 3 [New York: Doubleday, 2001], 69). Further, the comments of the dying Jesus committing Mary to John's care by designating John as Mary's son and Mary as John's mother may indicate that James was not a believer at this point, since Jesus seems to imply that his mother had no other son in a spiritual sense to care for her (ibid.). Meier also points to the principles of multiple attestation and embarrassment in order to demonstrate the historical veracity of those in Jesus' family who did not believe in him. Unbelief on the part of several of Jesus' family members is found in multiple gospels and may have been "embarrassing, if not deeply offensive, to a good part of the early church" (ibid., 70).

23. We can only speculate when the appearance to James occurred. Luke reports that Jesus' brothers were gathered with his disciples and mother for constant prayer a few days before Pentecost (Acts 1:14), indicating that James had become a believer by then. This would place the appearance within fifty days of Jesus' resurrection.

24. Acts 1:14 and 1 Corinthians 9:5 indicate that more than one of Jesus' brothers became believers. Church tradition reports that two letters in the New Testament were by the brothers after whom they were named: James and Jude.

25. Eusebius cites Josephus, Hegesippus, and Clement of Alexandria on the martyrdom of James (Eusebius, *Ecclesiastical History* 2.23). Josephus reports that James was executed as a lawbreaker (i.e., one who broke the Jewish law [Josephus, *Antiquities* 20.200]). In the New Testament, Christians were often considered lawbreakers by the Jewish authorities because of their beliefs (Acts 6:13; 18:13; 21:28). Darrell L. Bock adds, "What Law was it James broke, given his reputation within Christian circles as a Jewish-Christian leader who was careful about keeping the Law? It would seem likely that the Law had to relate to his christological allegiances and a charge of blasphemy. This would fit the fact that he was stoned, which was the penalty for such a crime, and parallels how Stephen was handled as well." See Darrell L. Bock, *Blasphemy and Exaltation in Judaism: The Charge against Jesus in Mark 14:53–65* (Grand Rapids: Baker, 2000), 196 n. 30.

26. Reginald H. Fuller, *The Formation of the Resurrection Narratives* (New York: Macmillan, 1971), 37.

27. It is generally agreed that the evidence for the empty tomb is not as strong as that for the disciples' belief that they had seen the risen Jesus. However, this is a testimony to the strength of the fact concerning the beliefs of the disciples, rather than the weakness of the evidence for the empty tomb, which is indeed strong. Prominent critical scholars who accept the empty tomb include Blank, Blinzler, Bode, von Campenhausen, Delorme, Dhanis, Grundmann, Hengel, Lehmann, Leon-Dufour, Lichtenstein, Manek, Martini, Mussner, Nauck, Rengstorff, Ruckstuhl, Schenke, Schmitt, Schubert, Schwank, Schweizer, Seidensticker, Strobel, Stuhlmacher, Trilling, Vogtle, and Wilckens. These are listed by New Testament critic, Jacob Kremer, whose own name can be added (*Die Osterevangelien—Geschichten um Geschichte* [Stuttgart, Germany: Katholisches Bibelwerk, 1977], 49–50). Craig lists sixteen additional prominent scholars, most of whom are not evangelical: Benoit, Brown, Clark, Dunn, Ellis, Gundry, Hooke, Jeremias, Klappert, Ladd, Lane, Marshall, Moule, Perry, Robinson, and Schnackenburg (Craig, *Assessing the New Testament Evidence for the Historicity of the Resurrection of Jesus*, 374). These forty-five prominent scholars believe that there was an empty tomb, for whatever reason. Gary Habermas's very recent study identified more than one hundred scholars who accept one or more arguments in favor of the empty tomb versus thirty-five who accept one or more arguments against it. This is about a 3:1 ratio.

28. Habermas has counted a total of twenty-three arguments for an empty tomb posited by a number of critical scholars from 1975–2002.

29. Not only is this the testimony of the New Testament (Acts 2), but Tacitus reports that the church started in Judea (*Annals* 15:44).

30. Pentecost came fifty days after Passover. It was not until after receiving the Holy Spirit that they began their public preaching concerning the risen Jesus.

31. This is much the view of New Testament critic Gerd Lüdemann. See Copan and Tacelli, eds., *Jesus' Resurrection: Fact or Figment?* 153.

32. This information was obtained from the Medical Examiner's Office for the Commonwealth of Virginia. The physician in charge said that even in Virginia, which has a climate warm and damp enough to promote quick decomposition, an unprepared corpse undergoing a normal rate of decomposition should still after fifty days have its hair and an identifying stature. The wounds would "definitely" be identifiable. Thus, a corpse in a much worse state than what would be expected for arid Jerusalem would still be identifiable after fifty days.

33. We have argued that theft of the body by the disciples is an extremely implausible explanation for the empty tomb, given the obvious sincerity of

the disciples in their beliefs, as shown in their willingness to suffer death to bear witness to Jesus' resurrection. Also see the discussion on fraud as an explanation, pp. 93–95.

34. Luke 24:12; John 20:3–9.

35. It is interesting to note the context in which this statement appears in the Talmud (Kiddushin 82b):

> Happy is he who sees his parents in a superior craft, and woe to him who sees his parents in a mean craft. The world cannot exist without a perfume-maker and without a tanner—happy is he whose craft is that of a perfume-maker, and woe to him who is a tanner by trade. The world cannot exist without males and without females—happy is he whose children are males, and woe to him whose children are females. R. Meir said: One should always teach his son a clean and easy craft, and earnestly pray to Him to Whom [all] wealth and property belong. . . .

Perfume-makers and tanners (i.e., leather workers) are contrasted. The former is highly regarded, while the latter is not. The analogy of male and female children seems to be an attempt to clarify the point: the former is highly regarded, while the latter is not. This makes sense, especially if contemporary writers confirm that tanners were not considered among those esteemed. In *Contra Celsum*, Origen quotes the second-century critic of Jesus, Celsus, as saying, "We see, indeed, in private houses workers in wool and leather, and fullers, and persons of the most uninstructed and rustic character, not venturing to utter a word in the presence of their elders and wiser masters" (3.55). According to Celsus, workers in wool and leather were considered to be of questionable character. Given that exceptions could be cited, as a general rule, tanners and females were lowly esteemed.

Origen recorded other remarks by Celsus concerning women: "Speaking next of the statements in the Gospels, that after His resurrection He showed the marks of His punishment, and how His hands had been pierced, he asks, 'Who beheld this?' And discrediting the narrative of Mary Magdalene, who is related to have seen him, he replies, 'A half-frantic woman, as you state.' And because she is not the only one who is recorded to have seen the Savior after His resurrection, but others also are mentioned, this Jew of Celsus culminates these statements also in adding, 'And some one else of those engaged in the same system of deception'" (Origen, *Contra Celsum*, 2.59); "Only foolish and low individuals, and persons devoid of perception, and slaves, and women, and children, of whom the teachers of the divine word wish to make converts" (ibid., 3.49); cf. ibid., 3.55.

The principle of embarrassment applied to the women's testimony can be pressed only so far. There are references where a higher view of women are found. Elsewhere in the Talmud it is written, "God has endowed women with a special sense of wisdom which man lacks" (Niddah 45), and where a woman's testimony is accepted (Ketubot 2:6–7). Of course, the Talmud is later than Josephus, whose Judaism was contemporary with that of Jesus' time. While exceptions exist, by and large a prejudice against the testimony of women can be shown in antiquity. What can be stated with certainty is that a woman's testimony concerning an empty tomb and a risen person would not have been preferable to a man's, whether or not it may have been allowable. The more important the testimony, the less likely a woman's word would have been taken at face value.

36. Josephus, *The Life and Works of Flavius Josephus*, William Whiston, ed. and trans. (Peabody, Mass.: Hendrickson, 1987).

37. W. Arndt, F. W. Danker, and W. Bauer, *A Greek-English Lexicon of the New Testament and Other Early Christian Literature*, 3d ed. (Chicago: University of Chicago Press, 2000), s.v. leeros.

38. Gaius Suetonius, *The Twelve Caesars*, Augustus 44, Robert Graves, trans. (New York: Penguin, 1989), 80.

39. Osiek, Carolyn, "The Women at the Tomb: What Are They Doing There?" in *Ex Auditu* 9 (1993): 97–107.

40. That the disciples did not believe when they saw the empty tomb and were recorded as being stubborn doubters was unquestionably embarrassing to them. Thus we have a double use of the principle of embarrassment regarding the empty tomb.

41. Atheist philosopher Keith Parsons argues that the women naturally would be the first to see the risen Christ in an invented story, since it was their responsibility to anoint the body. However, this does not square with the Gospels' testimony that Joseph of Arimathea and/or Nicodemus prepared the body for burial with a substantial amount of spices. This was before the women's visit (Matt. 27:57–61; Mark 15:42–47; Luke 23:50–56; John 19:38–40). Moreover, an invented story of the resurrection could have recorded the appearance to the men while waiting at the tomb for the women to show up or after the women did their part in dressing the corpse. The women need only have played a secondary role.

42. William Wand, *Christianity: A Historical Religion?* (Valley Forge, Pa.: Judson, 1972), 93–94.

43. New Testament critical scholar John Dominic Crossan believes that after Jesus' body was taken off of the cross, it was put in a common grave for criminals and eaten by dogs. However, there is no evidence whatsoever in support of his theory, not even a single competing account to the empty tomb that would imply that Jesus was buried elsewhere. There is only the assumption that Jesus' body was placed with the corpses of other executed criminals, which is in contrast to all of the accounts that we have. Moreover, it appears that the burial account is accurate and that the tomb's location was known (see "Wrong Tomb Theory," pp. 97–99). See Habermas, *Historical Jesus*, 126–29 for nine critiques of this view.

Introduction to Part 3: Is Jesus' Resurrection the Only Explanation?

1. See Gary R. Habermas and J. P. Moreland, *Beyond Death* (Wheaton, Ill.: Crossway, 1998), 125, which notes in part:

> David Strauss delivered the historical deathblow to the swoon theory held by Karl Venturini, Heinrich Paulus, and others. On the other hand, while Strauss popularized the hallucination theory, Friedrich Schleiermacher and Paulus pointed out errors in it. The major decimation of the hallucination theory came later in the century at the hands of Theodor Keim. Liberal scholars had long before dismissed fraud theories, while the legend theories, popular later in the century, were disproved by later critical research. So these scholars demolished each other's theories, thereby burying the major naturalistic attempts to account for Jesus' resurrection by the late 1800s.

2. Pronounced "bart."

3. Karl Barth, *Church Dogmatics: The Doctrine of Reconciliation*, vol. 4, part 1, E.T., G. W. Bromiley and T. F. Torrance, eds. (Edinburgh: T & T Clark, 1956), 340.

4. Raymond Brown, "The Resurrection and Biblical Criticism," *Commonweal* 24 (Nov. 1967): esp. 233. Brown repeated a similar indictment against these theories in Raymond Brown, *An Introduction to New Testament Christology* (New York: Paulist, 1994), 163–65.

5. See Gary R. Habermas, "The Late Twentieth-Century Resurgence of Naturalistic Responses to Jesus' Resurrection" in *Trinity Journal* 22NS (2001), 179–96.

6. Gary Habermas and Antony Flew, *Did Jesus Rise From the Dead?* Terry L. Miethe, ed. (San Francisco: Harper & Row, 1987), 142.

7. This is referred to as *methodological naturalism*, the method of explaining phenomena by looking for natural processes rather than supernatural causes. This is to be distinguished from *metaphysical naturalism*, which is a philosophy rather than a procedure that rules out even the possibility of a supernatural cause before any evidence is considered. Metaphysical naturalism has serious problems intrinsic to it that are discussed in chapter 8. Methodological naturalism is sometimes accepted as a valid method for scientific investigation by Christian philosophers, although other Christian philosophers are opposed to it. Properly used, it should not limit possible causes to the natural sphere. In explaining phenomena, if we never looked further than "God caused it," we would know very little about the world around us. Nevertheless, this does not justify the leap to metaphysical naturalism made by some critics. Certainly we are justified in seeking a natural cause when attempting to account for an event like a resurrection from the dead. However, this search does not justify the conclusion that resurrections *never* occur or are impossible, since the event being afforded consideration may be the very event that would overthrow such a conclusion. Philosopher and mathematician William Dembski warns that extreme methodogical naturalism is indistinguishable from metaphysical naturalism. See William A. Dembski, *Intelligent Design* (Downers Grove, Ill.: InterVarsity, 1999), 119–20; cf. 67–69.

8. See pp. 166–71.

9. It is in such an evaluation that C. Behan McCullagh's criteria are helpful. See C. Behan McCullagh, *Justifying Historical Descriptions* (Cambridge: Cambridge University Press, 1984), ch. 2. Also see Ben F. Meyer, *The Aims of Jesus* (London: SCM, 1979), ch. 4, and N. T. Wright, *The New Testament and the People of God* (Minneapolis: Fortress, 1992), ch. 4, esp. sec. 4.

10. Since we have attempted to write this book in a manner that would be as easy as possible for the layperson, and because one of our objectives is that the readers remember the refutations, we have not included every possible refutation. We have only included those that we believe are the strongest.

Chapter 5: Always Looking for a Way Out

1. Buddhism scholar Kenneth Ch'en observes,

Obviously, since these various accounts of the Buddha's life are separated by such long intervals of time, they must be assigned different values. Chronologically, the fragments found in the Pali canon form the earliest stage, and for this reason must be accorded the highest consideration as far as reliability is concerned. . . . We will find that the former [Pali] recorded just a matter-of-fact description of the master's experience, with no attempt at adornment and embellishment, whereas the later [Sanskrit] included numerous details embroidered with interesting and miraculous episodes. (Kenneth K. S. Ch'en, *Buddhism* [Woodbury, Conn.: Barron's Educational Series, 1965], 16–17)

2. Robert M. Price, "Is There a Place for Historical Criticism?" *Religious Studies,* 27 (1991): 371–88.

3. For information on the textual purity of both the Old and New Testaments, see Michael Licona, *Behold, I Stand at the Door and Knock* (Virginia Beach, Va.: TruthQuest, 1998), ch. 2.

4. It is insufficient to establish that the biblical text we have today is faithful to the original to refute the embellishment form of the legend theory. The reason is that today's critics deny that eyewitnesses wrote the Gospels. Rather they argue that the authors recorded and embellished oral traditions about Jesus that were being spread in the latter part of the first century. A major reason for this charge, though not the only one, is that most critics reject the possibility of supernatural events. This, of course, includes the fulfillment of specific prophecies. If specific prophecy is never supernaturally given, then Jesus could not have accurately predicted the destruction of the Jerusalem temple in A.D. 70 as was claimed (Matt. 24:1–2; Mark 13:1–2; Luke 21:5–6). The Gospels recording this claim must have been written after 70. Therefore, in order to use the biblical records to refute the legend/embellishment theory, one must either establish that the specific Gospel texts are early and/or that the traditions contained in them are early. In our minimal facts approach, the latter approach has been adopted.

5. See discussion of the experiential testimony of the disciples in chapter 3.

6. In fact, simply for the sake of discussion, since we are using a minimal facts approach, one could even grant that some legend may exist in the New Testament and still demand that the critic must show that legend is responsible for the story of Jesus' resurrection. Indeed, we could go still further and say that details such as the angels and guard at the tomb might have been legends that crept into the story or deliberately placed there for literary functions without weakening

our argument for Jesus' resurrection, since the facts we have are strongly established. This move does not compromise a high view of biblical inspiration and inerrancy, since certain points are being granted as possible only because (1) they are not relevant to determining whether Jesus rose from the dead in our minimal facts approach and (2) granting them allows us to focus on the relevant points.

7. See John Dominic Crossan, *Jesus: A Revolutionary Biography* (San Francisco: HarperSanFrancisco, 1994), 160–61. John Dominic Crossan, *The Historical Jesus: The Life of a Mediterranean Peasant* (San Francisco: HarperSanFrancisco, 1991), 404. It is interesting that Crossan himself admits to at least three things concerning his view: (1) Paul is a Pharisee and believes in the general resurrection of the dead. (2) "For Paul . . . bodily resurrection is the only way that Jesus' continued presence can be expressed." (3) "The question is not what it is that Paul means, because that is surely clear enough" (*Jesus: A Revolutionary Biography*, 164–65). Thus, even though Crossan may hold that *we* don't have to understand Jesus' resurrection in a literal sense, he believes that Paul did teach a literal resurrection.

8. For a straightforward example of this reasoning, see Nancy Gibbs, "The Message of Miracles," *Time* Magazine, 10 April 1995, 70:

> Liberals argue that it is not blasphemy to say the Resurrection never happened, because accounts of Christ's rising are meant metaphorically. . . . One robs the Bible of its richness and poetry by insisting it should be read literally. Jesus was resurrected in the lives and dreams of his followers; the body of Christ is the church, not a reconstituted physical body. The Resurrection represents an explosion of power, a promise of salvation that does not depend on a literal belief in physical resurrection.

9. See the evidence presented for the empty tomb in chapter 4. Note that the arguments of the Jerusalem factor and enemy attestation are practically independent of the New Testament.

10. See pp. 120–22.

11. Deuteronomy 21:23; c.f. Galatians 3:13. John P. Meier writes, "No doubt the Christian claim that the crucified Jesus of Nazareth was the promised Jewish Messiah had seemed shocking to Saul the Jew. Becoming a Christian meant for him overcoming and accepting the scandal of the cross" (John P. Meier, *A Marginal Jew: Rethinking the Historical Jesus*, 3 vols., [New York, Doubleday, 1991–2001], 3:324).

12. Hegesippus quoted by Eusebius. See pp. 57–58.
13. Acts 2:22–32; 13:34–37.
14. Also note that in Peter's sermon as portrayed in Acts 10:40–41, he claims that he and others "ate and drank with Him after He arose from the dead." Luke seems to be intending to record historical events when in Luke 1:1–3, he writes,

> Inasmuch as many have undertaken to compile an account of the things accomplished among us, just as they were handed down to us by those who from the beginning were eyewitnesses and servants of the word, it seemed fitting for me as well, having investigated everything carefully from the beginning, to write it out for you in consecutive order, most excellent Theophilus; so that you may know the exact truth about the things you have been taught.

New Testament critical scholar Bart Ehrman comments,

> There may indeed be fictional elements in the account, as we will see; but judging from the preface to volume one [i.e., Luke's gospel], from the subject matter of the narrative (the spread of the Christian church), and from the main characters themselves (who are, after all, historical persons), we can more plausibly conclude that Luke meant to write a history of early Christianity, not a novel. Moreover, all of the ancient Christian authors who refer to the book appear to have understood it in this way." (Bart D. Ehrman, *The New Testament: A Historical Introduction to the Early Christian Writings*, 2d ed. [New York: Oxford University Press, 2000], 124)

See also A. N. Sherwin-White, *Roman Society and Roman Law in the New Testament* (Oxford: Clarendon, 1963), 188–89. "The work of Luke cannot be evaluated properly if we group it with inferior contemporary literature that treats of heroes, thaumaturges and other popular characters. It is genuine history" (G. Kittel, G. W. Bromiley, and G. Friedrich, eds., *Theological Dictionary of the New Testament*, 10 vols. [Grand Rapids: Eerdmans, 1981], 3:395).

Some scholars have noted that the appearance language in the New Testament is the language of sight (Luke 24:34; Acts 10:40–41; 13:30–31; 1 Cor. 15:5–8). The writers did not use metaphorical language, so they at least *thought* that God had acted literally upon them in the appearances of the risen Jesus. For example, see Gerald O'Collins, *Interpreting the Resurrection: Examining the Major Problems in the Stories of Jesus' Resurrection* (New York: Paulist, 1988), 12–19, and Robert H. Gundry, *Sōma in Biblical Theology: With Emphasis on Pauline Anthropology* (Cambridge: Cambridge University Press, 1976), ch. 13.

We can also note with New Testament scholar Craig Blomberg, "A careful reading of the patristic evidence suggests that indeed the vast majority of early Christians did believe that the type of information the Gospel writers communicated was historical fact, even as they recognized the more superficial parallels with the mythology of other worldviews" (Craig Blomberg, "Resurrection Redux," in Paul Copan, ed., *Will the Real Jesus Please Stand Up? A Debate between William Lane Craig and John Dominic Crossan* [Grand Rapids: Baker, 1998] 106). Furthermore, although 2 Peter cannot be part of a "minimal facts" argument because many scholars question its authorship by Peter, it still provides early testimony that at least some Christians within one hundred years after Jesus were interpreting events such as Jesus' transfiguration and resurrection as historical events.

15. The second-century critic Celsus (c. 170), who wrote against Jesus' resurrection, provides arguments against a literal and bodily resurrection. See Origen, *Contra Celsum*, 1.68 where Origen notes Celsus's reasoning says that if miracles or a resurrection were claimed by Christians, Celsus and others would view them as Egyptian trickery. In 2.56, Origen responds to Celsus's assertion that Jesus' resurrection could have been a deception in which Jesus simply left the area for a while and then returned. In 2.59, Origen notes Celsus's accusation that the first witness of the risen Jesus was a half-frantic woman and the others who claimed to have seen Jesus were engaged in a "system of deception." Whatever else may be said of Celsus's arguments, he obviously was answering the Christian claim that Jesus had a literal resurrection. There is no suggestion that there might have been nonhistorical genre of resurrection claims that were meant to honor Jesus by portraying him as risen from the dead or to symbolize the explosion of power in the church. Regarding the latter theory, without a historical resurrection of Jesus, there would have been nothing to account for the church's explosion of power. The leader was dead, and his followers were in hiding. It was not the explosion of power in the church that led to the resurrection accounts. It was Jesus' resurrection that led to the explosion of power.

16. Justin Martyr, *First Apology,* 21.

17. Ibid. In this chapter Justin Martyr scoffs at this Roman desire to deify emperors, "And what of the emperors who die among yourselves, whom you deem worthy

of deification, and in whose behalf you produce some one who swears he has seen the burning Caesar rise to heaven from the funeral pyre?" The account is likewise mentioned by Suetonius (*The Twelve Caesars*, Augustus 100): "An expraetor actually swore that he had seen Augustus' spirit soaring up to Heaven through the flames."

18. Justin Martyr's *First Apology* was written to the Roman emperor entreating him to investigate the false charges of impiety and wickedness made against Christians. In chapter 11, he says Christians are not a threat to Rome because they don't look for a human kingdom. In fact, Jesus taught civil obedience (ch. 17). Jesus taught a higher level of morality than other religions. For example, not only our works but even our thoughts are open to God (ch. 15). Christians are taught to love their enemies and pray for them (chs. 7–8). In chapter 20 he contends that many Christian teachings reflect the teachings of those the emperor honors. Thus, if on some points Christians teach the same things and on other points present an even higher morality, "and if we alone afford proof of what we assert, why are we unjustly hated more than all others?" Justin Martyr's objective is to demonstrate to the emperor that Christianity has a lot in common with other religions that enjoy Rome's approval, so the persecution should cease.

19. Gary R. Habermas, "Resurrection Claims in Non-Christian Religions," *Journal of Religious Studies* 25 (1989): 167–77. The first account in pagan religions appears in writing around A.D. 150, whereas the creed in 1 Corinthians 15:3–5 can be dated as early as the early 30s and no later than 51. This is approximately a century before the pagan account appeared. It is possible that the account from 150 is earlier in its oral tradition. But there is no evidence that this is the case. In another article, Habermas writes, "the tale of Isis and Osiris seems to be the only known case among the mystery religions where there exists both clear and early evidence that a dead god was said to be resuscitated, which is dated prior to the middle or late second century AD. As far as is known, the other 'resurrection' stories actually *postdate* the Christian message" ("Replies to Evan Fales: The Appearances of Jesus," *Philosophia Christi*, Series 2, 3.1 [2001], 79).

20. Günter Wagner, *Pauline Baptism and the Pagan Mysteries* (Edinburgh: Oliver and Boyd, 1967), 197–201.

21. Ibid., 213, 219, 221, 223–24, 229, 251, 265.

22. Ben Witherington III writes, "Why in the world would a group trying to attract Gentiles make up a resurrection story, much less emphasize the material resurrection of Jesus? This notion was not a regular part of the pagan lexicon of the afterlife at all, as even a cursory study of the relevant passages in the Greek and

Latin classics will show. Indeed, as Acts 17 [vv. 31–32] suggests, pagans were more likely than not to ridicule such an idea" (Copan, ed., *Will the Real Jesus Please Stand Up?* 136).

Not only were accounts of the "mystery religions" uncommon in first-century Israel, but miracle workers were uncommon in the period. Graham Twelftree writes, "In the period of two hundred years on each side of the life of the historical Jesus the number of miracle stories attached to any historical figure is astonishingly small" (Graham H. Twelftree, *Jesus: The Miracle Worker* [Downers Grove, Ill.: InterVarsity, 1999], 247). Citing Werner Kahl's research, Twelftree states that "of approximately 150 miracle stories from antiquity that we know of only one other case in the entire miracle story tradition before Philostratus's Life of Apollonius (written after A.D. 217) of an immanent bearer of numinous or preternatural power (and then in only a singular version of his miracle)—Melampous, according to Diodorus of Sicily (writing c. 60–30 B. C.). Other Jewish and pagan miracle workers of the period he categorizes as petitioners or mediators of numinous power" (ibid.). There is no information from the extant literature of the period to indicate that miracle workers like Jesus were common. Other sources on this subject are Werner Kahl, *New Testament Miracle Stories in Their Religious-Historical Setting* (Göttingen, Germany: Vandenhoeck and Ruprecht, 1994), 236, and A. E. Harvey, *Jesus and the Constraints of History* (London: Duckworth, 1982), 103.

This is not to claim that miracle accounts were unknown in ancient historical writings. Some miracle accounts did exist. However, although these historians did not *a priori* dismiss the possibility of miracles on philosophical grounds as most do today (see ch. 8), they viewed such stories with skepticism. In *The Book of Acts in the Setting of Hellenistic History* (Winona Lake, Ind.: Eisenbrauns, 1990), Colin Hemer discusses ancient historiography (ch. 3), then later sums up his findings, "Miracle has some considerable prominence in many of the Hellenistic and Roman historiographers, especially in the form of bizarre prodigies popularly taken to presage disaster." Hemer points out "the fluctuation and ambivalence between skepticism and credulity which characterizes many of these writers. In any case the supernatural is little more or less than an anomalous curiosity with historians in antiquity" (428–29). Elsewhere he comments, "It is clear that ancient writers were not completely naïve or gullible, but accepted or rejected miraculous stories on the basis of their regard for the evidence, albeit differently weighted than modern historians. See for example Herodotus (2.73) on the story of the Phoenix" (441). For examples of historians of the period who did not accept miracle claims uncritically, see also Tacitus, *Annals* 1:28, and Suetonius, *The Twelve Caesars*, e.g., Nero 56, and Vespasian 4.

23. Günter Wagner, *Pauline Baptism and the Pagan Mysteries* (Edinburgh: Oliver & Boyd, 1967), 164–66.

24. Ibid., 180–83, 195, 197–201. Wagner answers most of the alleged parallels of dying and rising gods in this work.

25. Gary R. Habermas. "Replies to Evan Fales: The Appearances of Jesus," *Philosophia Christi,* Series 2, 3.1 (2001), 79. In this article, Habermas provides other differences between the accounts of Osiris and Jesus.

26. This point is not insignificant. Christians, Jews, and Muslims all believe in an afterlife. However, when someone dies and begins to experience that afterlife, he or she is not considered to have risen from the dead. Rather, a transition has occurred. Thus, Osiris did not rise from the dead, since the accounts report that he was assigned a high status in the underworld.

27. There are other marks that distinguish Jesus' death and resurrection from the alleged pagan parallels: (1) In the mystery religions, the gods did not die willingly as Jesus did. As Martin Hengel points out, "Attis and Adonis were killed by a wild boar, Osiris was torn to pieces by Typhon-Seth and Dionysus-Zagreus by the Titans. Heracles alone of the 'Greeks' voluntarily immolated himself [as a sacrifice]. However, not only did all this take place in the darkest and most distant past [so as not to be at all verifiable], but it was narrated in questionable myths" (Martin Hengel, *Crucifixion* [Philadelphia: Fortress, 1977], 5–6). (2) Hengel likewise points out that "crucifixion plays no part in the mysteries" and cites the contribution of A. D. Nock, *Essays on Religion and the Ancient World*, vol. 1, Z. Stewart, ed. (Oxford: Oxford University Press, 1972), 170, as an authoritive refutation of those, specifically Charles Kerényi, who claim that crucified gods are found in the mysteries. (3) In ancient romance literature, the hero was always saved at the last moment prior to being crucified, and there was the obligatory happy ending (Hengel, *Crucifixion*, 81–82, 88).

  Some critics appeal to the 1875 comparison of Christianity and other religions by Kersey Graves, *The World's Sixteen Crucified Saviors*. However, this book suffers from the problems mentioned above and in this section. Even one of the Internet's main Web sites for skeptics, infidels.org, notes their concern regarding the conclusions and overall scholarship of the book, although they offer it online: "Note: the scholarship of Kersey Graves has been questioned by numerous freethinkers; the inclusion of *The World's Sixteen Crucified Saviors* in the Secular Web's Historical Library does not constitute endorsement by Internet Infidels,

Inc. This document was included for historical purposes; readers should be extremely cautious in trusting anything in this book" (www.infidels.org/library/historical/kersey_graves/16/index.shtml. Accessed 20 December 2003.

No archaeological remains exist to tell precisely what pagan cults existed within first-century Palestine. According to Bruce Metzger of Princeton University, the earliest extant artifact is an early second-century invocation to Isis containing a list of sixty-seven places in Egypt and fifty-five sites outside Egypt where Isis was worshiped. One of those places was in Palestine (Bruce M. Metzger, *Historical and Literary Studies: Pagan, Jewish, and Christian* [Grand Rapids: Eerdmans, 1968], 18–22). Thus, it appears that the cult had little if any known influence in the geographical region of Christianity's beginning.

28. Emory University's Islamic scholar, Gordon Newby, claims that the first account of Muhammad's phenomenal birth appeared between seventy-five and one hundred years after his death. He adds that there is no way to know if an oral tradition with an earlier date is responsible for the written account. He adds that the account is not historically reliable for several reasons: There is no Qur'anic base, the line of transmission is weak, and the tradition is not well substantiated by accounts known to be trustworthy (from a conversation with Gordon Newby, 21 October 1997). Another scholar writes the "oldest collections of historical traditions available to us date from about 125 years after the Prophet's lifetime" (Maxime Rodinson, *Muhammad*, Anne Carter, trans. [New York: Pantheon, 1980], 44). For this and other accounts, see Michael R. Licona, *Cross Examined* (Virginia Beach: TruthQuest, 1999), 153–55.

29. For discussion of Augustus's birth, see p. 170.

30. Colin Hemer, *The Book of Acts in the Setting of Hellenistic History* (Winona Lake, Ind.: Eisenbrauns, 1990), 94. Hemer cites two sources in support of this conclusion: D. L. Tiede, *The Charismatic Figure as Miracle Worker* (Missoula, Mont.: SBL, 1972); C. H. Holladay, *"Theos Aner" in Hellenistic Judaism* (Missoula, Mont.: Scholars Press, 1977). Gary Habermas offers a number of serious problems with several ancient parallels, especially Apollonius's narrative in Gary R. Habermas, "Did Jesus Perform Miracles?" Michael J. Wilkins and J. P. Moreland, eds., *Jesus Under Fire* (Grand Rapids: Zondervan, 1995), 119–24.

31. See pp. 86–89.

32. In fact, many of the accounts of Jesus' miracles possess attributes that solicit historical confidence in the event. See note 12 in chapter 8. For in-depth analysis of Jesus' miracles and their historical credibility, see Twelftree, *Jesus: The Miracle Worker*, esp. 249–359.

33. Matthew 24:23–25; Mark 13:22.

34. Further refutations may be found on p. 143.

35. Matthew 28:11–15.

36. Justin Martyr, *Dialogue With Trypho,* ch. 108: "You have sent chosen and ordained men throughout all the world to proclaim that a godless and lawless heresy had sprung from one Jesus, a Galilaean deceiver, whom we crucified, but his disciples stole him by night from the tomb, where he was laid when unfastened from the cross, and now deceive men by asserting that he has risen from the dead and ascended to heaven" (cf. ch. 17) in A. Roberts, J. Donaldson, and A. C. Coxe, eds. and trans., *The Ante-Nicene Fathers: Translations of the Writings of the Fathers Down to* A.D. *325* (Oak Harbor, Ore.: Logos Research Systems, 1997).

37. Charles Colson, "An Unholy Hoax? The Authenticity of Christ," *BreakPoint* syndicated column 020329, (29 March 2002).

38. Another difference between Jesus' disciples and those who suffer and die for their religious faith today is that the latter do it because they have believed the testimony of someone else. It is a matter of faith. The former suffered and died for what they believed were appearances of the risen Jesus to them. Those who suffer and die for their faith today die for what they *believe* is true. The disciples died for what they *knew* was either true or false. For example, being sure we saw someone on several occasions is generally a more sure belief than is accepting a religious ideology by faith. See the sections on the beliefs of the disciples (pp. 49–62) and Paul (pp. 64–66).

39. Arguably the most recent well-known critical scholar was Hermann Samuel Reimarus (1694–1768) whose works were published posthumously in 1778 by Gotthold Ephraim Lessing (1729–1781).

40. Luke 24:9–11; John 20:8.

41. John 20:2, 13–15.

42. John 20:3–9. In Luke 24:10–12, we also are told the disciples rejected the women's story of the empty tomb.

43. John 20:24–25. The only disciple who seemed to believe was John. See John 20:8, which reports that John "saw [that the body was not in the tomb] and believed."

44. Matthew 28:17; Luke 24:34–53; John 20:15–20, 24–28.

45. See pp. 48–49.

46. Ignatius speaks of an apparent death theory that was circulating in about 110 (Ignatius, *To the Smyrnaeans* 1:1). He probably was referring to some form of Gnostic teaching.

47. William D. Edwards, Wesley J. Gabel, and Floyd E. Hosmer, "On the Physical Death of Jesus Christ," *Journal of the American Medical Association*, 255.11, (21 March 1986): 1457.

48. Ibid., 1460.

49. Alex Metherell, in an interview with Lee Strobel in *The Case for Christ* (Grand Rapids: Zondervan, 1998), 197. Dr. Metherell is an engineer and medical researcher who specializes in bio-muscular physics, the study of what happens to muscles when they are under stress.

50. Edwards, Gabel, and Hosmer, "On the Physical Death," 1461.

51. With this in mind, the intent of breaking the legs of crucifixion victims in John's gospel is clear; to bring death on more quickly by making it impossible to breathe. See John 19:31–33.

52. Edwards, Gabel, and Hosmer, "On the Physical Death," 1463. Also of interest is Josephus' autobiography, *The Life of Flavius Josephus*, in which he reports of seeing three friends on crosses during the siege of Jerusalem in A.D. 70. He went to Titus who had them removed from the crosses and provided with the best medical care. Of the three, two died and one survived:

> And when I was sent by Titus Caesar with Cerealius, and a thousand horsemen, to a certain village called Thecoa, in order to know whether it were a place fit for a camp, as I came back, I saw many captives crucified; and remembered three of them as my former acquaintance. I was very sorry at this, and went with tears in my eyes to Titus, and told him of them; so he immediately commanded them to be taken down, and to have the greatest care taken of them, in order to their recovery; yet two of them died under the physician's hands, while the third recovered. (Josephus, *The Life of Flavius Josephus*, in *The New Complete Works of Flavius Josephus*, William Whiston, trans. [Grand Rapids: Kregel, 1999], 420–21)

The fact that one of Josephus's friends survived crucifixion does not negate the modern medical opinion just stated. Taken from the cross, the victims could breathe normally. Further, the Gospels report that Jesus was brutally beaten and scourged prior to his crucifixion, whereas the Roman soldiers could not give such individual attention to the "many captives" crucified simultaneously as reported by Josephus. Even under the best of medical care of the day, two of the three still succumbed to their wounds. If historical, the spear thrust also confirms the death of Jesus. The medical implications of the spear wound are described in Edwards, Gabel, and Hosmer, "On the Physical Death," 1462–63.

53. Quintilian, *Declarationes maiores* 6:9.

54. David Strauss, *A New Life of Jesus*, 2 vols. (Edinburgh: Williams and Norgate, 1879), 1:412.

55. In *The Case for Christ,* Lee Strobel quotes from his interview with Dr. Alex Metherell:

> After suffering that horrible abuse, with all the catastrophic blood loss and trauma, he would have looked so pitiful that the disciples would never have hailed him as a victorious conqueror of death; they would have felt sorry for him and tried to nurse him back to health. So it's preposterous to think that if he had appeared to them in that awful state, his followers would have been prompted to start a worldwide movement based on the hope that someday they too would have a resurrection body like his. (Lee Strobel, *The Case for Christ* [Grand Rapids: Zondervan, 1998], 202)

56. The acquaintance, Tom Dark, is a journalist.

57. Acts 9. Paul reflects on the implications of a physical resurrection in Philippians 3:21, a text that would be meaningless if Paul did not believe Jesus had been raised to a physical "glorious" body.

58. According to Raymond Brown, "Except for the romantic few who think that Jesus did not die on the cross but woke up in the tomb and ran off to India with Mary Magdalene, most scholars accept the uniform testimony of the Gospels that Jesus died" (Raymond E. Brown, *The Death of the Messiah*, 2 vols. [New York: Doubleday, 1994], 2:1373).

Chapter 6: Mind Games

1. The technical definition of a delusion is a "false belief based on incorrect inference about reality that is firmly sustained despite what almost everyone else believes and incontrovertible evidence to the contrary" (C. D. Campbell, "Delusion," in *Baker Encyclopedia of Psychology and Counseling*, David G. Benner and Peter C. Hill, eds., 2d ed. [Grand Rapids: Baker], 1999).

2. There are no properties outside of the mind having a direct correlation to reality in a hallucination. A technical definition of a hallucination is a "sensory experi-

ence such as seeing persons or objects, hearing voices, and smelling odors in the absence of environmental stimuli" (I. Al-Issa, "Hallucination," in Benner and Hill, eds., Baker Encyclopedia of Psychology and Counseling).

3. A technical definition of an illusion is a "distorted perception that misrepresents external stimuli" (M. P. Cosgrove, "Illusion," in Benner and Hill, eds., Baker Encyclopedia of Psychology and Counseling).

4. Clinical psychologist Gary R. Collins in a personal conversation recorded in Gary R. Habermas and J. P. Moreland, Beyond Death (Wheaton, Ill.: Crossway, 1998), 119–20: "Hallucinations are individual occurrences. By their very nature only one person can see any given hallucination at a time. They certainly are not something which can be seen by a group of people. Neither is it possible that one person could somehow induce a hallucination in somebody else. Since a hallucination exists only in this subjective, personal sense, it is obvious that others cannot witness it."

5. In the early 1990s, Michael Licona, one of the authors, interviewed twenty-five or thirty United States Navy SEALs. The SEAL acronym stands for "Sea, Air, and Land," indicating the versatility expected of SEAL teams. Licona asked about hallucinations during their most intensive week of training, called "Hell Week." More than 75 percent of those interviewed claimed that they had experienced hallucinations and shared that most other SEAL candidates they knew had reported similar experiences to them.

6. See pp. 52–53.

7. A good question is why the creed mentions "the twelve" when Judas had killed himself, leaving eleven. We cannot know the answer to that question for certain. However, most scholars believe that "the Twelve" was a designation given to the disciples as a whole, which had continued to be used by the early church. In college sports, teams in the Midwest are still referred to as belonging to the "Big Ten," even though there are now eleven teams. This seems to be supported by the fact that Matthias was selected to replace Judas. The initial qualification to be considered for this position was that the replacement had to have accompanied Jesus during his entire ministry (i.e., from baptism by John to the Ascension, Acts 1:21–22). Specifically, the one filling Judas's position was to be "a witness with us of his resurrection" (v. 22). Verse 23 indicates that there was at least one other among them besides Matthias who met the criteria, but only one man was added to bring the number back to twelve. The Twelve were, therefore, a special group within all of Jesus' followers, and still existed as such, with Matthias having replaced Judas. Bullinger writes that we have here a figure of

speech referred to as *ampliatio*, used "when an old name is retained after the reason for it is passed away" (E. W. Bullinger, *Figures of Speech Used in the Bible*, New York: Young & Co., 1898), 689–90.

8. Luke 24:33–36. Notice that the appearance to Simon Peter (i.e., Cephas) is mentioned here. See 1 Corinthians 15:5. The other Gospels also record group appearances: Matthew 28:9, 16–20; Mark 16:7; John 20:19–30; 21:1–22.

9. Acts 1:3–9.

10. Galatians 1:13–14; Philippians 3:4–8.

11. See pp. 64–66.

12. See p. 285, n21–22.

13. Deuteronomy 21:23; Galatians 3:13.

14. Gary R. Habermas, "Explaining Away Jesus' Resurrection: The Recent Revival of Hallucination Theories," *Christian Research Journal* 23.4 (2001): 26–31, 47–49.

15. Delusions usually fall into the following categories: persecutory ("I am being followed"), jealous ("My spouse is unfaithful."), referential ("That group is secretly talking about me"), grandiose ("I am very important and have special powers"), erotomanic ("She loves me and will not admit it"), and somatic ("Something is wrong with my body"). Philip C. Kendall and Constance Hammen, *Abnormal Psychology* (Boston: Houghton Mifflin, 1995), 296.

16. Gary Habermas has named this latter thesis "the illumination theory" in "The Late Twentieth-Century Resurgence of Naturalistic Responses to Jesus' Resurrection," *Trinity Journal* 22NS, 2 (Fall, 2001):188–90.

17. Acts 7:58–8:3; 9:1–2; Philippians 3:6.

18. Perhaps the skeptic might posit that during the period in which Paul persecuted Christians, he began to feel sorry for them or for some other reason wanted to stop persecuting them and was self-deluded into believing that he saw the risen Jesus. The writings of Paul and very early testimony about him in Acts are incompatible with this theory. Therefore, unless the skeptic can provide good evidence that these were indeed the thoughts of Paul, this theory can be rejected.

19. Prominent atheist philosopher Antony Flew held this position in his first debate with Habermas. For a transcript of the debate with follow-up notes, see Gary Habermas and Antony Flew, *Did Jesus Rise from the Dead?* Terry Miethe, ed., (San Francisco: Harper & Row, 1987).

20. Acts 7:55–56.

21. Besides Stephen's, examples of objective visions in the New Testament might include the experiences of Cornelius and Peter in Acts 10:1–16, and that of John

recorded in the Revelation. Of course a skeptic might claim these visions were subjective. There is no way to prove one view over another. Our point here is merely to define the difference between objective and subjective visions.

22. There is no extramental correlate to a subjective vision. See Paul Copan and Ronald K. Tacelli, eds., *Jesus' Resurrection: Fact or Figment? A Debate between William Lane Craig and Gerd Lüdemann* (Downers Grove, Ill.: InterVarsity, 2000), 197. If the biblical record is correct, Joseph's dream (Matt. 1:20–24) would be objective in nature, since an extramental cause was responsible for it. If a mother dreamed that she opened a door, and her son was standing there, although her son was really hundreds of miles away, one would assume that the mother did not actually see the son. She might insist that she "really" saw the son in her dream, but the son was not "really" there, nor was anyone else. When the son actually goes to her home for a visit and knocks on the door and she opens it, then there is reality to what is seen.

23. Another way of stating this inadequacy of the objective vision theory is that it shifts the question to the nature of Jesus' resurrection body rather than addressing the question of whether he rose from the dead.

24. Copan and Tacelli, eds., *Jesus' Resurrection: Fact or Figment?* 61.

25. The reader will also benefit from reading chapter 9: Heavenly Vision or Bodily Appearance?

26. One may rightly ask how we might define Paul's experience, since it appears to be different than those of the disciples. It certainly does not appear to have been a subjective vision. Yet it does not appear to have been an objective vision either, since the experience was perceived fully by Paul's natural senses and partially by those of his traveling companions.

27. The technical definition of conversion disorder is "the presence of symptoms or deficits affecting voluntary motor or sensory function that appear to have a neurological or other medical origin and are not intentionally produced" (A. J. Weaver, "Conversion Disorder," in Benner and Hill, eds., *Baker Encyclopedia of Psychology and Counseling*).

28. *Diagnostic and Statistical Manual of Mental Disorders: DSM-IV* (Washington, D. C.: American Psychiatric Association, 1994).

29. Not only does Paul fall outside of the typical profile of those who experience conversion disorder, but we have no evidence that he experienced any of the most common symptoms in males who suffer from conversion disorder, which are "non-headache pain, paresis [i.e., slight or partial paralysis], anesthesia [i.e., partial to total loss of sensation], headache, and mock heart attack" (Kendall

and Hammen, *Abnormal Psychology*, 207). One might suggest that Paul's frame of mind while he severely persecuted the church might have been equivalent to that of a soldier in combat. However, even if Paul could be made to fit a single profile for a conversion disorder, this would only suggest that the bright light he claimed to have seen might have been a visual hallucination. A visual hallucination would still not account for the accompanying auditory hallucination of Jesus' voice, nor would it answer the fact that he does not seem to have suffered from any of the most common symptoms experienced by males with the disorder.

30. Flew based his argument for conversion disorder on Jack A. Kent's book, *The Psychological Origins of the Resurrection Myth* (London: Open Gate, 1999), 21, 28, 33, 47, 85–86, 89. This is a new opposing theory to account for the conversion of Paul. Flew claimed that hallucinations on the part of the disciples and conversion psychosis on the part of Paul accounted for the postmortem appearances of Jesus. Flew explained that during the past fifteen years since his first debate with Habermas, he had learned about these and now held that they were the best explanation to account for the data (recorded in Gary Habermas and Antony Flew, "Did Jesus Rise from the Dead?" [3 video tapes], *The John Ankerberg Show*, 2000). For the ideas of another scholar proposing conversion disorder, see the writings of Michael Goulder, for example, "The Baseless Fabric of a Vision" in *Resurrection Reconsidered*, Gavin D'Costa, ed. (Oxford: Oneworld, 1996), 48–61.

31. Evan Fales, "Successful Defense? A Review of *In Defense of Miracles*," *Philosophia Christi*, Series 2, 3.1 (2001): 32.

32. See Gary R. Habermas, "Replies to Evan Fales: The Appearances of Jesus," in ibid., 81–83.

33. Galatians 2:1–10.

34. Matthew 4:16; 5:14; Mark 4:22; Luke 2:32; 16:8; John 1:4–9; 3:19–21; 5:35; 9:5; 12:35–36, 46; Romans 2:19; 13:12; 1 Corinthians 4:5; 2 Corinthians 4:4, 6; 11:14; Ephesians 5:8–9, 13; Colossians 1:12; 1 Thessalonians 5:5; 2 Timothy 1:10; 1 John 1:5, 7; 2:8–10; Revelation 18:23.

35. John 8:12; 9:5.

36. See Tobit 10:5; 14:10; Wisdom 7:10, 26, 29 (where wisdom is said to be brighter than the sun); 18:4; Ecclesiasticus 22:11; 24:27, 32; 50:29; Baruch 3:14; 4:2. Among numerous occurrences in Philo are *On the Creation* 31, 33, 55; *Allegorical Interpretation I* 17, 18; *Allegorical Interpretation III* 45, 167; *On the Cherubim* 62; *On the Unchangeableness of God* 3, 135; *On Husbandry* 162.

37. Acts 9:7; 22:9; 26:13–14.

38. If a critic desired to pursue this further by suggesting that the disciples and James also experienced epiphanies and that the genre of the accounts of the appearances to them allows this, we might respond that (1) The sermon summaries in Acts (embedded in Acts 1–5, 10, 13, 17), which predate its writing, strongly suggest a literal interpretation of Jesus' resurrection. (2) Paul and all the witnesses speak of a bodily resurrection. The Jews did not expect a resurrection of the body until the last day. Assumption into heaven, as Christians believe happens at the moment of a believer's death, would have most likely been the claim. (3) This is essentially similar to the objections regarding nonhistorical genre, which we addressed in detail on pp. 86–89, and delusions that we addressed on pp. 109–110. As such there are *many* serious difficulties to be overcome. (4) The empty tomb refutes this entire scenario.

39. See chapter 5, note 15.

40. If the critic claims that even though Acts is written after Paul's letters, Luke received his information from Paul and, therefore, it is earlier than what Luke reported concerning the claims of the disciples, we might reply: (1) Luke also reports Paul's sermon in Acts 13, the content of which strongly implies a bodily resurrection of Jesus (vv. 35–36). (2) Since Luke was written prior to his sequel Acts where we find Paul's words pertaining to Jesus' appearance to him, how can the critic know that Paul's testimony recorded in Acts is earlier than the reports of the disciples recorded in Luke's earlier gospel?

Chapter 7: Stopping at Nothing

1. Probabilities here are subjective estimations assigned by the person who is considering the force of the argument, but some may find it helpful to use probability to quantify one's confidence in the historical truth of a fact or theory. The obvious observation is that in a combination theory each component theory must be true or the conbination is invalid. Therefore, even if one assigned an 80 percent probability to each of the five opposing theories posited in our example (which would be charitable to say the least), the probability that the combination of all of these theories is true would be much less than 80 percent. It would be 80 percent of 80 percent of 80 percent of 80 percent of 80 percent (.8 x .8 x .8 x .8 x .8 = .328 or 33 percent). If something has a one in three chance of being true, it has a two in three chance of being false (67 percent). This is different than calculating the probability that a theory is true using data that do not all have to be totally accurate for the theory to explain what really occurred.

Statisticians speak of a "Probability Via Non-Occurrence" equation for analyzing the probability of theories. This process begins as the researcher decides the level of probability that something occurred. Let's say you are 65 percent (.65) certain that the disciples saw something that was not a hallucination, delusion, or some other sort of psychosis. That leaves a 35 percent chance (.35) that they did suffer from a delusion or psychological phenomena of some sort. Moreover, we assign an 80 percent (.8) probability that Paul saw something that cannot be explained in terms of natural causes. That makes a 20 percent (.2) chance that it can be explained naturally. We assign a 50 percent probability (.5) that James's experience cannot be interpreted naturally, leaving a 50 percent chance (.5) that it can be. Second, the researcher uses the numbers of what seems to be the improbability that something occurred in a certain way. Third, the researcher multiplies the numbers indicating *improbability*—in our example, .35 x .2 x .5 = .035. Fourth, subtract the resulting indication of improbability from total probability or 100 percent (1) In the example, 1 – .035 = .965. This gives us a 96.5 percent chance (based upon our subjective analysis) that the disciples Paul and James experienced a supernatural occurrence. For a fuller explanation, see the article by Gary R. Habermas, "Probability Calculus, Proof and Christian Apologetics" in *The Simon Greenleaf Review of Law and Religion* 8 (1989): 57–88. Again, the reason this is different than the first procedure is that all of the data need not be true. If someone did not accept the experience of James, the evidence of the disciples and Paul still must be answered (1 – [.35 x .2] = .93 or 93 percent probability that Jesus' resurrection is true). Using a more sophisticated method called Bayes' Theorem, philosopher Richard Swinburne of Oxford University has attempted to demonstrate that the probability of Jesus' resurrection is 97 percent (Emily Eakin. "So God's Really in the Details?" in the May 11, 2002 issue of the *New York Times*. Available to subscribers at www.nytimes.com/2002/05/11/arts/11GOD.html [Jan. 6, 2004]). Swinburne's argument has been published in Richard Swinburne, *The Resurrection of God Incarnate* (New York: Oxford University Press, 2003).

2. It would not suffice to claim that, if we consider the group of the many opposing theories, the probability of at least one of them being true is greater than that the Resurrection occurred. For one thing, several of these theories are mutually exclusive. One cannot claim that the disciples were hallucinating when they really thought they saw the risen Jesus, and also claim that the disciples were lying in their claim that they had seen the risen Jesus. Nor can one claim that the original disciples were deluded into believing that they saw the risen Jesus, and

also claim that the disciples never claimed that the risen Jesus appeared to them and that the account was the result of legendary influences in the years that followed. Additionally, a number of weak and highly improbable arguments do not add up to one good argument.

3. "The view held by some Bible students that admission of one error in a book makes all the rest of it equally suspect presupposes a method which no reputable historian would adopt." Craig Blomberg, *The Historical Reliability of the Gospels* (Downers Grove, Ill.: InterVarsity, 1987), 236. This book is a summary of Blomberg, *Gospel Perspectives*, 6 vols. (Sheffield: JSOT, 1980–86).

4. Paul Maier, *In the Fulness of Time: A Historian Looks at Christmas, Easter, and the Early Church* (San Francisco: HarperCollins, 1991), 180. Although the details about the fire in ancient accounts cannot be harmonized, the conclusion of historians that the fire itself occurred is what is referred to as a "basic layer of historical truth." We may not have a great deal of historical confidence in details about Rome's fire, but the basic layer of history we can accept is that the fire occurred. Historians believe they can identify this basic layer in the worst of thirdhand sources. See A. N. Sherwin-White, *Roman Society and Roman Law in the New Testament* (New York: Oxford University Press, 1963), 186.

5. New Testament scholar N. T. Wright puts it this way: "If I read about the Prime Minister in the *Telegraph*, the *Times*, the *Mail* and the *Guardian*, there are four different views, but that doesn't mean I don't have [a pretty good idea] of what the Prime Minister did." David Van Biema, "The Gospel Truth," *Time* Magazine, 8 April 1996, 58.

6. "Apparent discrepancies are just that—apparent and not genuine—and that they do not call into question the reliability of the Gospel witness. If anything, the minor variations that do occur, when coupled with the much greater amount of close agreement in detail, actually strengthen confidence in the evangelists' trustworthiness. Verbatim parallelism, on the other hand, where it occurs, only proves that one writer has copied from another and offers no independent corroboration of his testimony" (Blomberg, *Historical Reliability*, 114).

7. On the Resurrection, see John Wenham, *Easter Enigma: Are the Resurrection Accounts in Conflict?* (Grand Rapids: Zondervan, 1984). Regarding discrepancies in general, see Norm Geisler and Thomas Howe, *When Critics Ask: A Popular Handbook on Bible Difficulties* (Wheaton, Ill.: Victor, 1992) and Gleason Archer, *Encyclopedia of Biblical Difficulties* (Grand Rapids: Zondervan, 1982).

8. A. N. Sherwin-White writes, "But it can be maintained that those who had a passionate interest in the story of Christ, even if their interest in events was

parabolical and didactic rather than historical, would not be led by that very fact to pervert and utterly destroy the historical kernel of their material" (White, *Roman Society and Roman Law*, 191).

9. Blomberg makes his comment in *Real Answers: Jesus, the Search Continues* (produced for Inspiration Network), tape 1. A transcript of this video series is available at www.insp.com/jesus/transcripts.htm.

10. Cornelius Tacitus, *Annals* 1:1.

11. Colin Hemer, *The Book of Acts in the Setting of Hellenistic History* (Winona Lake, Ind.: Eisenbrauns, 1990), 89.

12. Ibid., 89–90.

13. N. T. Wright, *The New Testament and the People of God* (Minneapolis: Fortress, 1992), 89.

14. *Gospel Perspectives.*

15. Blomberg, *Historical Reliability*, 197. See Gary R. Habermas, *The Historical Jesus* (Joplin, Mo.: College Press, 1996), 64–67.

16. We are indebted to Paul Maier, Distinguished Professor of Ancient History at Western Michigan University, for the information on Nicholas of Damascus and Livy.

17. Papias, *Expositions of the Sayings of the Lord.* For a detailed discussion of Papias see Robert H. Gundry, *Mark: A Commentary on His Apology for the Cross* (Grand Rapids: Eerdmans, 1993), 1026–45.

18. See the *Fragments of Papias* for direct quotes and information contained in these books. Papias's five books are mentioned in fragments 3, 5, 6, 7, 14, 15, 16, 18, 19.

19. *Ecclesiastical History* 3:37; 4:3.

20. Clement of Rome's letter to the church in Corinth; 2 Clement whose author is unknown; the seven letters of Ignatius; Polycarp's letter to the Philippians; The Martyrdom of Polycarp; Didache; the letter of Barnabas; The Shepherd of Hermas; Fragments of Papias; the letter of Diognetus; the Apocalypse of Peter (not to be confused with the Nag Hammadi text of similar name); the Gospel of Peter; the Epistula Apostolorum; and the works of Justin Martyr, Aristides, Athenagoras, Theophilus of Antioch, Quadratus, Aristo of Pella, and Melito of Sardis. It is possible that Diognetus and the Gospel of Peter were written at about our 150-year boundary. In either case, it is impossible to arrive at a precise date. It is also difficult to categorize the Gospel of Peter because of its brevity and because it may contain some Gnostic ideas.

21. These include at least the Gnostic *Gospel of Thomas, Gospel of Truth,*

Apocryphon of John, and *Treatise on Resurrection* (which may have been written slightly later than 150 years after Jesus' death). See Habermas, *Historical Jesus*, 208–15.

22. See Habermas, *Historical Jesus*, ch. 9.

23. Appian is early second century and may have written more than 150 years after Caesar's death in 44 B.C. The passages of all five sources have been translated and appear in James Sabben-Clare, trans., *Caesar and Roman Politics 60–50 BC: Source Material in Translation* (London: Bristol Classical, 1995), 51–68.

24. Once again we thank Paul Maier for this information. We are only considering extant sources here. Cassius Dio likewise mentions Tiberius. But as an early third-century source, he is roughly 170 years or more removed from Tiberius. If we were to extend our 150-year period by just twenty years in order to include Cassius Dio for Tiberius, we would add Dionysius of Corinth, Irenaeus, Tertullian, and perhaps Clement of Alexandria to those testifying of Jesus.

25. Tiberius's number reduces from ten to nine since Luke is a Christian source.

26. See ch. 10.

27. See ch. 8, note 12.

28. See pp. 174–81.

29. We owe this answer to Dr. Chris Clayton.

30. For some examples, see the chapter "Big Bang Model Refined by Fire" by Hugh Ross in William A. Dembski, ed., *Mere Creation: Science, Faith and Intelligent Design* (Downers Grove, Ill.: InterVarsity, 1998), 363–84; See also the chapter by Hugh Ross, "Astronomical Evidences for a Personal, Transcendent God" in J. P. Moreland, ed., *The Creation Hypothesis: Scientific Evidence for an Intelligent Designer* (Downers Grove, Ill.: InterVarsity, 1994), 169–70.

31. See "Arguments for the Existence of God," pp. 174–81.

32. For good presentations of the argument for an intelligent Designer, see Moreland, ed., *The Creation Hypothesis;* Dembski, ed., *Mere Creation;* and Michael J. Behe, *Darwin's Black Box* (New York: Free Press, 1996).

33. For some general treatments, see W. David Beck, "God's Existence" in R. Douglas Geivett and Gary R. Habermas, eds., *In Defense of Miracles* (Downers Grove, Ill.: InterVarsity, 1997), 150–55; J. P. Moreland, *Scaling the Secular City: A Defense of Christianity* (Grand Rapids: Baker, 1987), 15–42; William Lane Craig, *Reasonable Faith* (Wheaton, Ill.: Crossway, 1994), 79–83, 91–122; Norman L. Geisler, *Baker Encyclopedia of Christian Apologetics* (Grand Rapids: Baker, 1999), 276–77, 399–401; Peter Kreeft and Ronald K. Tacelli, *Handbook of Christian Apologetics* (Downers Grove, Ill.: InterVarsity, 1994), 58–62.

34. For details, see Gary R. Habermas, *The Resurrection of Jesus* (Lanham, Md.: University Press of America, 1984), esp. chapters 1–5. See also Gary R. Habermas, *The Risen Jesus and Future Hope* (Lanham: Rowman & Littlefield, 2003).

Chapter 8: Naturally Speaking

1. This view is not new. Cicero (106–43 B.C.), the Roman orator, politician, and philosopher, wrote, "naturalemque rationem omnium" (i.e., "all things have a natural explanation"). He also wrote that if something happens, it does so because there is a natural cause and that there are no departures from this rule (*De div* 2.28.61 and 2.22.49. See Harold Remus, *Pagan-Christian Conflict Over Miracle in the Second Century* [Cambridge, Mass.: Philadelphia Patristic Foundation, 1983]) 35. Cicero's philosophical bias is easily recognized. How would he know this unless he knew the cause of all events? His position also requires him to expand the laws of nature to encompass all events. If Cicero had known of Jesus' resurrection, would he have abandoned his naturalistic philosophy, expanded the laws of nature calling the resurrection a "natural event," or perhaps even devised a naturalistic theory like those we have discussed?

2. This chapter cannot give an exhaustive treatment to each of these objections. The standard is to limit refutations to no more than four apiece. Also, we avoid repeating refutations, although some responses fit multiple objections.

3. In like manner, Willard Van Orman Quine's philosophical principle of *indeterminacy* in quantum physics takes into account experimental results that are not always either predictable or precisely repeatable, except in terms of probability.

4. Other examples exist: "I don't speak a word of English" (uttered in English); "You cannot know anything for certain." (How does the person making the statement know that?)

5. The skeptic may retort: "Fine. I don't think that science is the only way to learn something. But I still think that science rules out miracles." Then we need to point out two other items. (1) This was not the original objection, but we still appreciate the agreement that science is not the only way to know something. (2) Further, since we agree that there *are* other ways to learn, it may just be that miracles are known by one of these other options.

6. Historical investigation is well recognized as a.worthy pursuit, even by some philosophers who hold that experience through the senses of sight, hearing, smell,

taste, and touch is the only (or at least the best) means to obtain knowledge. Well-known skeptics such as David Hume, Bertrand Russell, A. J. Ayer, and Antony Flew all have acknowledged that history is an appropriate avenue for obtaining knowledge. See Hume, "Skeptical Solution of those Doubts" in *An Inquiry Concerning Human Understanding* (1748); V, Part 1; Ayer, *Language, Truth, and Logic* (New York: Dover, 1936), 19; and Russell, "Truth and Falsehood" in *The Problems of Philosophy* (Oxford: Clarendon, 1912), 284; Flew accepted all of Gary's twelve historical facts in "Did Jesus Rise From the Dead?" [3 video tapes], *The John Ankerberg Show*, 2000. If it can be concluded with a reasonable certainty that in the past some persons witnessed the presence of a person who had previously died, that event would be a part of human experience. Since the evidence that we have for Jesus' resurrection is exceptional, especially when using accepted standards of historical research, it cannot be ruled out without an investigation. If the skeptic refuses to acknowledge that history can yield knowable conclusions, then ask how someone will know that the Holocaust occurred after the last eyewitness has died. Or how do we really know that Julius Caesar crossed the Rubicon River or that George Washington was the first president of the United States? If he responds that we have written accounts from people who were there, then point out that this is also what we have with Jesus' appearances. In fact, we have similar evidence to what the skeptic might have, with the exception of photographs—and if the Shroud of Turin is real, we may just have that, too! The shroud of Turin is a cloth that bears a negative imprint of a man who appears to have been crucified. He has wounds all over his body, but especially in his wrists, feet, and head. Pollen from the area of Palestine has also been found on the cloth, and it is likely that a coin minted by Pontius Pilate was placed over at least one eye. For centuries many have held that this is the burial cloth of Jesus. This position, of course, is not without problems. However, many of the more recent test results that others have cited to claim that the shroud is a forgery are also not without problems. In our minimal facts approach we will not consider the shroud, since it is not accepted as genuine by the vast majority of all scholars who study the subject. However, interested readers may want to refer to the following: Kenneth E. Stevenson and Gary R. Habermas, *Verdict on the Shroud* (Banbury, Conn.: Dell, 1982); Kenneth E. Stevenson and Gary R. Habermas, *The Shroud and the Controversy: Science, Skepticism, and the Search for Authenticity* (Nashville: Thomas Nelson, 1990); John Heller, *Report on the Shroud* (Boston: Houghton Mifflin, 1983); Ian Wilson, *The Shroud of Turin* (Garden City, N.J.: Doubleday, 1978); Mary and Alan

Whanger, *The Shroud of Turin: An Adventure of Discovery* (Franklin, Tenn.: Providence House, 1998); Mark Antonacci, *The Resurrection of the Shroud* (New York: M. Evans, 2000).

7. Philosopher and mathematician William A. Dembski comments that, for the scientist, the contrast should not be in determining whether the cause was *natural* or *supernatural*. The contrast should be whether the cause was *undirected* (natural) or *directed* (intelligent). See William A. Dembski, ed., "Introduction" in *Mere Creation* (Downers Grove, Ill.: InterVarsity, 1998), 15.

8. Gary R. Habermas, *The Historical Jesus* (Joplin, Mo.: College Press, 1996), 60–61 and Appendix 1: "Historiography."

9. Perhaps someone will ask: "What is more probable, that Jesus rose from the dead or that he did not?" We may answer accurately by stating that the chances of Jesus rising from the dead by natural causes are about zero. However, if the God of traditional Christian theism exists and desired to raise Jesus from the dead under circumstances like the ones we have hinted at here, these natural chances do not affect Jesus' rising from the dead.

10. For example, see Acts 2:24, 32; 3:15, 26; 4:10; 10:40; 13:30, 37; Romans 10:9; Galatians 1:1; 1 Thessalonians 1:10, Hebrews 13:20; 1 Peter 1:21.

11. See ch. 10.

12. That Jesus performed deeds that appeared miraculous in nature is not only attested by the New Testament authors, but also by non-Christian sources. The Jewish historian Josephus calls Jesus a "doer of marvelous works" (*Antiquities* 18:3). Robert Van Voorst writes that Josephus' reference to Jesus as a worker of amazing deeds may be a positive statement about Jesus, "but the wording is not likely to come from a Christian. The phrase 'amazing deeds' itself is ambiguous; it can also be translated 'startling/controversial deeds,' and the whole sentence can be read to mean simply that Jesus had a reputation as a wonder-worker" (Robert E. Van Voorst, *Jesus Outside the New Testament* [Grand Rapids: Eerdmans, 2000], 89). Elsewhere Van Voorst writes that Luke may imply the same in 5:26 where the same Greek word, paradoxos, is employed. However, Van Voorst adds, "This phrase is not attested elsewhere [in the New Testament or early Christian writings other than 1 Clement 25:1], and its careful neutrality certainly does not express the typical New Testament attitude to the miracles of Jesus" (Ibid., 102). Graham Twelftree notes that Josephus uses the word to mean "miraculous" in *Antiquities* 3:38; 9:58, "surprising" in *Antiquities* 2:223, 285, 295, 345, 347; 3:1, 30, 38; 5:28; 9:58, 60; 10:214, 235, as well as "strange" in *Antiquities* 2:91; 5:125; 6:171, 290; 9:14, 182; 10:21, 266; 15:379; *Against Apion* 2:114. See

Graham H. Twelftree, *Jesus: The Miracle Worker* (Downers Grove, Ill.: InterVarsity, 1999), 254, 411.

The tradition that Jesus was a miracle-worker continued past the first century. In the Talmud (Sanh. 43a), Jesus is accused of being one who "practiced sorcery." This charge was associated with one who performed deeds that appeared miraculous or magical in nature. Celsus, the second-century critic of Christianity, in similar manner wrote that Jesus, "having been brought up as an illegitimate child, and having served for hire in Egypt, and then coming to the knowledge of certain miraculous powers, returned from thence to his own country, and by means of those powers proclaimed himself a God" (Origen, *Contra Celsum* 1:38; cf. 1:160). Jesus' name was continually appealed to by healers. The rabbis prohibited healing in Jesus' name [t. Hul. 2:22–23; y./abb. 14:4:14d; y. ʿAbod. Zar. 2:2; b. ʿAbod. Zar. 27b]). Arnobius, a Christian apologist who died around 330, writes that Jesus' name was used in exorcisms in his day [*Disputationes Adversus Gentes* 1:43].

Because they are late, neither the Talmud, Celsus, nor Arnobius can be said to provide testimony about Jesus that is certainly independent of Christian accounts. What they tell us is that during the second and later centuries, Jesus was known as a miracle-worker. The negative reactions of these non-Christian sources at minimal tell us that Jesus was being proclaimed by Christians as a miracle-worker during that period. Twelftree concludes, "The relevant material from outside the New Testament is small but significant in giving us evidence that Jesus was known as or had a reputation as a successful miracle worker" (Twelftree, *Jesus: The Miracle Worker*, 255).

13. See Mark 8:31; 9:31; 10:33–34; Matthew 12:38–40; 16:1–4; John 2:18–21. We say "possibly" only because many critical scholars today hold that Jesus' predictions concerning his resurrection were invented later and, thus, cannot be included in our "minimal facts" approach. However, a surprising number of other scholars think that Jesus did make predictions regarding his death and/or his resurrection. See "Did Jesus Predict His Resurrection," pp. 29–30.

14. As stated above, this objection is an extension of the previous scientific response. As such, it is additionally burdened by many of those objections, as well as a few that we now list.

15. This chapter is only entertaining *a priori* objections.

16. Paula Fredriksen of Boston University writes on method and history:

> The methods of other fields refresh and challenge our work in our own, and I think this is all to the good. But we need to be sensitive to the

utility of the method: and we can never let the method control the evidence. We—the historians—must control both. If we relinquish control, or fail to exercise it, or so enjoy where the method is taking us that we fail to direct our own way, we risk wandering in a past exclusively of our own imagining, distant not only from our own time, but also from the reality of those ancient persons whose lives and worlds we seek to understand. (Paula Fredriksen, "What You See is What You Get: Context and Content in Current Research on the Historical Jesus," at www.bu.edu/religion/faculty/fredriksen/context.htm (Jan. 6, 2004), section 97.

17. Michael J. Behe, *Darwin's Black Box* (New York: Free Press, 1996), 192.
18. For example, the empty tomb, the conversion of the church persecutor Paul based on the risen Jesus appearing to him, the conversion of the skeptic James based also on the risen Jesus appearing to him, the religio-historical context of Jesus' claims to divinity, his miracles, and his predictions concerning his resurrection.
19. Richard Swinburne, "Violation of a Law of Nature," in *Miracles*, Richard Swinburne, ed. (New York: Macmillan, 1989), 75–84. See also R.F. Holland, "The Miraculous," in ibid., 53–69.
20. See Gary R. Habermas, "Resurrection Claims in Non-Christian Religions" in *Journal of Religious Studies* 25 (1989): 167–77.
21. Interestingly, this is even admitted more than once by atheistic philosopher Antony Flew. See Gary R. Habermas and Antony Flew, *Did Jesus Rise From The Dead?* Terry L. Miethe, ed. (San Francisco: Harper & Row, 1987), 3, 39, 49–50). For a theist who develops this idea, see Norman L. Geisler, *Miracles and the Modern Mind: A Defense of Biblical Miracles* (Grand Rapids: Baker, 1992).
22. See note 12.
23. Second Kings 5.
24. Also see chapters 5–7.
25. See Edwin Yamauchi, *Jesus, Zoroaster, Buddha, Socrates, Mohammad*, Revised Edition (Downers Grove, Ill.: InterVarsity, 1972), esp. 4–7, 18, 38–41.
26. See pp. 187–88.
27. In chapter 12 we will look at a close relative of this species of the objection of naturalism.
28. Although David Owen is a critic who supports this objection, he still acknowledges that the existence of God would alter the miracles issue. See David Owen,

"Hume Versus Price on Miracles and Prior Probabilities," in Swinburne, ed., *Miracles*, 132.

29. This critique is more forceful here than with other objections in this chapter, since this challenge often explicitly states that *no* evidence could *ever* qualify an event as a miracle.

30. Jesus' resurrection provides one such example. Our next point will cast our net even further, in the direction of contemporary miracle-claims.

31. Perhaps scientific testing can begin to look into the supernatural. An interesting study conducted by a physician, the beneficial effects of prayer on sick patients, have been documented. Using strict scientific guidelines in a double-blind study, 393 patients in a coronary care unit were the subjects. About half were prayed for over a ten-month period. In twenty-one of the twenty-six categories monitored, patients receiving prayer fared better than those who did not receive prayer. The results were published in Randolph C. Byrd, "Positive Therapeutic Effects of Intercessory Prayer in a Coronary Care Unit Population," *Southern Medical Journal* 81.7 (July 1988): 826–29.

32. For details, see the two audio tape lecture set by Gary R. Habermas, "Ten Ways God Interacts with Us," available from Impact by calling 704-846-1226 or at impactapologetics.com.

33. For more information along with many detailed accounts, see Gary R. Habermas and J. P. Moreland, *Beyond Death* (Wheaton, Ill.: Crossway, 1998), chapters 7–9. For some articles published in medical journals, see Ian Stevenson and Bruce Greyson, "Near-Death Experiences: Relevance to the Question of Survival After Death," *Journal of the American Medical Association* 242 (1979): 265–67; Bruce Greyson and Ian Stevenson, "The Phenomenology of Near-Death Experiences," *American Journal of Psychiatry* 137 (1980): 1193–96; Melvin Morse, "Near Death Experiences and Death-Related Visions in Children: Implications for the Clinician," *Current Problems in Pediatrics* 24 (1994): 55–83.

34. From conversations between Habermas and Morse, 15 November 1994 and 2 November 1994. See Melvin Morse with Paul Perry, *Closer to the Light: Learning from Children's Near-Death Experiences* (New York: Random House, 1990), 3–9.

35. Cited in David Winter, *Hereafter: What Happens After Death?* (Wheaton, Ill.: Harold Shaw, 1972), 33–34.

36. A. J. Ayer, "What I Saw When I Was Dead: Intimations of Immortality," *National Review*, 14 October 1988, 39.

37. Ibid., 40.

38. From personal correspondence of Gary Habermas with Flew, 9 September 2000.

39. There is a difference in that NDEs only argue for what Habermas terms "minimalistic" life after death (Habermas and Moreland, *Beyond Death*, 193–97). For an argument from NDEs to an afterlife, see ibid., esp. 184–97.

40. The Qur'an is clear in its rejection of Jesus' resurrection, since it rejects Jesus' death: "That they said (in boast), 'We killed Christ Jesus the son of Mary, the Messenger of Allah';—but they killed him not, nor crucified him, but so it was made to appear to them, and those who differ therein are full of doubts, with no (certain) knowledge, but only conjecture to follow, for of a surety they killed him not:—Nay, Allah raised him up unto Himself; and Allah is Exalted in Power, Wise" (Surah 4:157–158). Another Muslim source is the *Gospel of Barnabas*, although even most Muslim scholars reject this document as a forgery (see pp. 184–85).

41. Habermas and Flew, *Did Jesus Rise?* 142.

Chapter 9: Heavenly Vision or Bodily Appearance?

1. Also see "Vision Theory," pp. 184–85.

2. See pp. 184–85.

3. Paul writes that "the dead will be raised imperishable, and we will be changed." The term, "changed," may imply that it is not an elimination of our body, but a metamorphosis (1 Corinthians 15:52). There is a connection between the mortal and the immortal body. There is continuity. Paul goes on in the next verse to describe this change by writing, "For this perishable must put on the imperishable, and this mortal must put on immortality."

4. We are aware that a little more than half of all critical scholars today doubt the Pauline authorship of Colossians (e.g., Raymond E. Brown, *An Introduction to the New Testament* [New York: Doubleday, 1997], 610). But there are good reasons for holding that Paul wrote Colossians. Even most critics hold that Pauline thought heavily influenced the letter. Even by critical standards, then, we have a first-century document, written in the same period as the Gospels that attests to the belief of the early church in the bodily resurrection of Jesus.

5. Psalm 16:10.

6. Matthew 28:9; Luke 24:36–43; John 20:24–28.

7. Acts 9:3–8; 22:6–11; 26:12–18.

8. Acts 9:7; 22:9.

9. It may be objected that in Acts, Paul describes the appearance of the risen Jesus

to him in terms that lead us to believe it was a subjective experience. He uses the term *optasia* for "vision"(Acts 26:19). The objection continues that throughout Acts, Luke usually uses the Greek word, *horama,* to describe nonphysical events that did not occur in space-time, such as the sheet and living creatures Peter saw while in a trance (11:5) and in doing so attempts to contrast "vision" with "physical reality" (12:9). However, this objection fails. Words that can be translated "vision" appear in the writings of Luke (Gospel of Luke and Acts) a total of thirteen times (Luke 1:22 [optasia]; 24:23 [optasia]; Acts 9:10, 12 [horama]; 10:3, 17, 19 [horama]; 11:5 [horama]; 12:9 [horama]; 16:9, 10 [horama]; 18:9 [horama]; 26:19 [optasia]).We must consider how these words are used not only by Luke, but by other authors of the New Testament writings. *Optasia* appears only five times in the New Testament (Luke 1:22; 24:23; Acts 1:3; 26:19; and 2 Corinthians 12:1) and only once in the LXX. Luke employs *optasia* to describe Zechariah's experience of the angel (Luke 1:22), the women seeing the angels at the empty tomb (Luke 24:23), the risen Jesus presenting himself alive to his disciples, appearing to them for forty days (Acts 1:3), and Paul's description of his experience of the risen Jesus (Acts 26:19). In 2 Corinthians 12:1, Paul also uses *optasia* to describe his experience of being caught up into heaven. He adds that he doesn't know whether he experienced this event in his body. Some scholars have argued that in some occurrences, such as the angels at the empty tomb, *optasia* was used within a literary device that conveyed a truth (e.g., Jesus' resurrection from the dead) by drama (e.g., using angels and guards), so it was not describing historical reality. However, even if this interpretation turned out true, it is physical sight that is used as a metaphor for the reality of Jesus' resurrection and, thus, it is difficult to define the term as referring to a vision. Moreover, since we are using a minimal facts approach, we will settle for concluding that Luke's use of *optasia* for physical sight is inconclusive. See Raymond E. Brown, *The Death of the Messiah,* 2 vols. (New York: Doubleday, 1994), 2.1303–13.

Horama is used more frequently, appearing twelve times in the New Testament (Matt. 17:9; Acts 7:31; 9:10, 12; 10:3, 17, 19; 11:5; 12:9; 16:9; 18:9) and forty-eight times in the LXX. The closely related *horasis* is found on four occasions in the New Testament (Acts 2:17; Rev. 4:3 [2x]; 9:17) and 133 times in the LXX. In Acts, Luke who describes Paul's experience, employs *horama* to describe a nonphysical experience outside of space-time by Peter while in a trance (Acts 10:9–17; 11:5). This type of vision was not unreal or subjective. For Peter, who had experienced visions from God, it was difficult to distinguish between a vision and an event in space-time. At least once he confused these events (12:9).

Used by Paul, at least Luke's depiction of his conversion experience, *horama* cannot mean a subjective vision, since his traveling companions likewise saw the light and heard the words. The word certainly can mean something that is seen. As examples, see Genesis 1:9 (LXX) which speaks of the dry land appearing and Sirach (Ecclesiasticus) 43:2 which speaks of the sun appearing. Thus, both *optasia* and *horama* denote language of sight. That is not to say that this sight is required from our mortal eyes. However, it did not appear that these terms were used in a metaphorical sense of "to understand" something, as in "I see what you are saying."

Unfortunately, word studies alone are inconclusive in determining whether Luke meant for us to believe that Paul's experience of the risen Jesus was a physical event in space-time. Both terms are used by Luke to describe an experience that may or may not have occurred in space-time. But if the Greek words employed to describe Paul's experience are inconclusive regarding the nature of the experience, and are sometimes used to describe physical sight, they cannot be used to defend the argument that they must mean a nonphysical appearance.

10. Although Luke writes Acts, portions of this sermon assigned to Peter are considered by many critical scholars to be of earlier, perhaps even genuine, apostolic origin. The Greek syntax of verses 36–38 is awkward and contains Semitisms, suggesting that it may be a translation of a Semitic source. "We may conclude, therefore, that the awkwardness of the syntax in the account of this sermon probably stems from Peter himself as he spoke before his Gentile audience in somewhat 'broken' Greek. Had it been Luke's own composition, it would have been much clearer" (Richard N. Longenecker, *Commentary on Acts*, in The Expositor's Bible Commentary on CD-ROM, Frank Gaebelein, ed., updated (Grand Rapids: Zondervan, 1998), comments on Acts 10:36).

11. The Greek *ēgerthē* is in the passive in Mark 16:6, denoting the body itself was raised. R. T. France comments,

> But the [neaniskos or young man/angel] goes on to make it clear that he is talking not merely about survival beyond death, but about a physical event: the place where Jesus' body had been laid (. . . not merely the tomb in general but the specific shelf or 'tunnel' within it which had been used for Jesus' body) is now empty. The body has gone, and from the promise made in the following verse it is plain that it has gone not by passive removal but in the form of a living, traveling Jesus. However philosophy and theology may find it possible to come to terms with the

event, it is clear that Mark is describing a bodily resurrection leading to continuing life and activity on earth. (R. T. France, "The Gospel of Mark." *The New International Greek Testament Commentary*, I. Howard Marshall, Donald A. Hagner, eds. [Grand Rapids: Eerdmans, 2002], 680).

12. Elsewhere Paul states, "flesh and blood cannot inherit the kingdom of God" (1 Corinthians 15:50). "Flesh and blood" here is a Jewish idiom that indicates the mortal, corruptible, natural body, which will be "changed" (15:51, 52) to the incorruptible, immortal, spiritual body. See the comments below on 1 Corinthians 15:37–50.

13. Elsewhere John writes of himself and others hearing, seeing, gazing upon, and touching Christ with their hands in 1 John 1:1–3, a reference that possibly includes the risen Jesus.

14. John 20:27.

15. "In a number of languages 'doubt' is expressed by means of idioms, for example, 'to have two thoughts' or 'to think only perhaps' or 'to believe only a little' or 'to question one's heart about'" (J. P. Louw and E. A. Nida, *Greek-English Lexicon of the New Testament: Based on Semantic Domains*, 2d ed.[CD ROM version, New York: United Bible Societies, 1996], 31:37.

16. Leon Morris, *The Gospel According to Matthew* (Grand Rapids: Eerdmans, 1992), 774–75; Craig L. Blomberg, *Matthew*, The New American Commentary, vol. 22 (Nashville: Broadman & Holman, 1992), 430; R. T. France, *Matthew: Evangelist and Teacher* (Grand Rapids: Zondervan, 1989), 314, n. 83; Daniel J. Harrington, *The Gospel of Matthew*, Sacra Pagina Series, vol. 1, Daniel J. Harrington, ed. (Collegeville: Liturgical, 1991), 414.

17. Morris, *The Gospel According to Matthew*, 745; M. D. Goulder, *Midrash and Lection in Matthew* (London: SPCK, 1974), 344; A. T. Robertson, *Word Pictures in the New Testament on CD-ROM* (Oak Harbor. Ore.: Logos Research Systems, 1997), Matthew 28:17; D. A. Carson, *Matthew*; Frank Gaebelein, ed. *The Expositor's Bible Commentary on CD-ROM* (Grand Rapids: Zondervan, 1998), Matthew 28:17.

18. Blomberg, *Matthew*, 430; Robert H. Gundry, *Matthew: A Commentary on His Handbook for a Mixed Church Under Persecution*, 2d ed. (Grand Rapids: Eerdmans, 1994), 594; William Hendriksen, *The Gospel of Matthew* (Edinburgh: Banner of Truth Trust, 1974), 997; D. A. Hagner, *Matthew 14–28*, vol. 33B, Word Biblical Commentary (Dallas: Word, 1995).

19. Luke 24:16; 37, 41; John 21:4. Hendriksen suggests that the simplest solution is that "at first this mysterious person appears to them from a considerable distance. He then steps closer, and the doubt disappeared, though this is not recorded in so many words. What we read [v. 18] 'Then Jesus came nearer and spoke to them, saying. . . . Jesus steps forward, so that they may be able to see and hear him better" (Hendriksen, *Gospel of Matthew*, 997).

20. Blomberg suggests that the hesitation may not have had to do with belief but rather the act of worship ("they worshiped him, but some hesitated," Matt. 28:17). See Blomberg, *Matthew*, 430. However, this does not appear to be a problem for the disciples elsewhere (e.g., Matt. 14:25–33; 28:8–10).

21. This comment is by Norm Geisler in Lee Strobel, *The Case for Faith* (Grand Rapids: Zondervan, 2000), p. 138.

22. See 1 Corinthians 15:12–13; 20–23.

23. *Psychikos* comes from the root *psychē*, which generally means "soul" or "life." Paul uses the term four times in his writings, all in 1 Corinthians (2:14; 15:44 (2x); and 15:46). Four times is not a large sampling, and the word does not occur at all in the ancient Greek translation of the Old Testament call the Septuagint (LXX). But observe how other New Testament writers and intertestamental writings employ *psychikos*. James 3:15 uses psychikos to contrast a proper spiritual state of the heart with one that is not from God (described as earthly, natural [*psychikos*], or even demonic). In Jude 1:19, the word is used of the lost who live by "natural instinct" (*psychikos*), not having the Holy Spirit. In the Greek version of the Old Testament apocrypha, *psychikos* is used of a bodily appetite (4 Macc. 1:32). The writer of Maccabees uses it as an adverb to mean "heartily" in reference to feelings of grief and warmth (2 Macc. 4:37; 14:24). Therefore, *psychikos* refers to the carnal nature as opposed to the spiritual. Neither Paul nor any other New Testament author nor any writer of intertestamental books ever uses psychikos in the sense of something that is material. See also Gerhard Kittel, Gerhard Friedrich, eds., *Theological Dictionary of the New Testament*, 10 vols. (Grand Rapids: Eerdmans, 1981), 9.662–63.

24. *Pneumatikos* comes from the root *pneuma*, which generally means "spirit." Elsewhere in 1 Corinthians, Paul uses *pneumatikos* in the sense of the spiritually mature in this world (2:15; 3:1; 14:37; cf. Gal. 6:1) or of something that has to do with or has as its origin the Holy Spirit (2:13 [2x]–14; 9:11; 10:3–4 [2x]; 12:1; 14:1). Other occurrences in Paul include Romans 1:11; 7:14; 15:27; Galatians 6:1; Ephesians 1:3; 5:19; 6:12; Colossians 1:9; 3:16. With the *possible* exception of Ephesians 6:12, the term is never used in the Pauline letters to refer to or describe

anything as immaterial. The word also appears in 1 Peter 2:5 (2 x) and Revelation 11:8. In Revelation 11, the word may possibly be translated "figuratively" (NIV). *Pneumatikos* does not appear in the LXX or in the intertestamental books. See also Kittel and Friedrich, eds., *Theological Dictionary,* 6.421.

25. See 1 Corinthians 2:13.

26. Ben Witherington III writes, "The truth is, upon close inspection, 1 Corinthians 15 shows that Paul wished to affirm both continuity and discontinuity between the two states. In both situations it is the same person who has life in an embodied state" (Paul Copan, ed., *Will The Real Jesus Please Stand Up? A Debate between William Lane Craig and John Dominic Crossan* [Grand Rapids: Baker, 1998]) 134.

27. See p. 156.

28. *Sarkikos,* from the root word *sarx,* means "fleshly" or "substantive." Besides 1 Corinthians 9:11, *sarkikos* is used seven times in the New Testament: Romans 15:27; 1 Corinthians 3:3 (2x); 9:11; 2 Corinthians 1:12; 10:4; 1 Peter 2:11. All of these except 1 Peter 2:11 are in the writings of Paul. Only in 1 Corinthians 3:3 is the term used in a more negative sense than *psychikos.* There Paul uses it to describe Christians who are living sinfully. We have observed that Paul never uses *pneumatikos* to refer to or describe a being as immaterial. Instead, he employed the term *aorotos* to mean "invisible" or "formless" (Rom. 1:20; Col. 1:16; 1 Tim. 1:17). In the New Testament, *aorotos* also occurs in Hebrews 11:27. In the LXX it occurs in the Old Testament texts of Genesis 1:2 and Isaiah 45:3, as well as in 2 Maccabees 9:5.

29. The expression occurs in the New Testament in Matthew 16:17; 1 Corinthians 15:50; Galatians 1:16; Ephesians 6:12; and Hebrews 2:14. Its use in the LXX Apocrypha text of Ecclesiasticus is interesting: "As the green leaf on a thick tree, some fall, and some grow: so is the generation of flesh and blood, one cometh to an end, and another is born" (Ecclus. 14:18); "What is brighter than the sun? Yet the light thereof faileth: and flesh and blood will imagine evil (17:31)." Ecclesiasticus quotations are from Lancelot C. L. Brenton, translator, *The Septuagint with Apocrypha: Greek and English* (London: Samuel Bagster and Sons, 1851).

30. See comments on Matthew 16:17 in Carson, *Matthew.*

31. Paul Copan and Ronald K. Tacelli, eds., *Jesus' Resurrection: Fact or Figment? A Debate Between William Lane Craig and Gerd Lüdemann* (Downers Grove, Ill.: InterVarsity, 2000), 151.

32. John Dominic Crossan, *Jesus: A Revolutionary Biography* (San Francisco: Harper San Francisco, 1994), 165.

Chapter 10: Who Did Jesus Think He Was?

1. Acts 7:56; Revelation 1:13; 14:14.

2. In Ignatius of Antioch's, *To the Ephesians* 19 the term applies to Jesus' human- ity; Ignatius also quotes Jesus' use of the term in *To the Trallians* 9, and the anonymous Epistle of Barnabas 12 applies the term to Jesus' humanity. Ignatius died around 110, and the Epistle of Barnabas was written in the late first to early second century. It definitely is not by the Barnabas of the New Testament.

3. For an indepth reading of Jesus' use of this title and its authenticity, see Darrell L. Bock, *Blasphemy and Exaltation in Judaism: The Charge against Jesus in Mark 14:52–65* (Grand Rapids: Baker, 2000), 209–33, and Bruce Chilton, "(The) Son of (The) Man, and Jesus" in *Authenticating the Words of Jesus,* Bruce Chilton and Craig A. Evans, eds. (Boston: Brill, 2002), 259–87.

4. Two other passages that are helpful in understanding the Jewish significance of the title and that date to around the first century A.D. are 4 Ezra 13 and 1 Enoch 37–71. See *The New Testament Background: Selected Documents,* C. K. Barrett, ed. (New York: Harper and Brothers, 1961), 235–37, 250–55.

5. Raymond E. Brown, *An Introduction to New Testament Christology* (New York: Paulist, 1994), 92–96.

6. Cf. Matthew 26:63–64; Luke 22:67–70.

7. Moreover, the act of riding the clouds is something that God does in the Old Testament. See especially Psalm 104:3 and Isaiah 19:1 (cf. Exod. 14:20; 34:5; Num. 10:34). See John Collins, *Daniel: A Commentary on the Book of Daniel* (Minneapolis: Fortress, 1993), 290.

8. Mark 14:63–65; Matthew 26:65–68.

9. Besides Jesus' direct affirmative response, the reference to "coming with the clouds," and the use of both titles, there is some strong scholarly agreement that Jesus' central claim here was being able to co-occupy God's throne. Craig Evans asserts that, for the high priest, such a claim was "scandalous" and "un- thinkable." Craig Evans, "In What Sense 'Blasphemy'? Jesus Before Caiaphas in Mark 14:61–64," *Society of Biblical Literature Seminar Papers,* 30 (1991): 221–22; Cf. the agreement in N. T. Wright, "Looking Again for Jesus," *Stimu- lus,* 4.4 (November 1996): 34–35; Brown, *Introduction to New Testament Christology,* 92–100; Peter Stuhlmacher, *Jesus of Nazareth—Christ of Faith,* Siegfried S. Schatzmann, trans. (Peabody, Mass.: Hendrickson, 1993), 26–28; Ben Witherington III, *The Christology of Jesus* (Minneapolis: Fortress, 1990), 258–62.

10. It will not do to respond that the Legend/Embellishment Theory has already been refuted and does not need to be considered. We have established that Legend/Embellishment is not responsible for *the disciples' claims* that they experienced postmortem appearances of the risen Jesus. The claims of Jesus must be considered as a separate question.

11. John Hick, "A Pluralist View" in *More Than One Way?* Dennis L. Okholm and Timothy R. Phillips, eds. (Grand Rapids: Zondervan, 1995), 35. See 2 Samuel 7:14 and Psalm 2:7.

12. Job 38:7 and possibly Genesis 6:2.

13. Hosea 11:1.

14. John Dominic Crossan, "Opening Addresses" in Paul Copan, ed., *Will The Real Jesus Please Stand Up? A Debate between William Lane Craig and John Dominic Crossan* (Grand Rapids: Baker, 1998), 38. The story of Augustus' birth is found in Suetonius, *The Twelve Caesars*, E.T., Robert Graves, trans. (London: Penguin, 1989), 2.94.

15. See John 1:1, 20:28; Philippians 2:6; Colossians 2:9 for a few of the strongest proclamations of Jesus' deity. We are not claiming, however, that these were the result of theological evolution, especially since the Philippians passage has an early date, both as Paul's letter and as a probable early hymn that Paul was quoting.

16. New Testament scholar R. T. France comments: "It is ironic that a saying which has such far-reaching christological implications has in fact become more familiar in theological discussion as a christological embarrassment. The assertion of Jesus' ignorance on a subject of such importance as the time of his own parousia seems to many, imcompatible with His status as Son of God. If this title implies that He is Himself divine, and God is omniscient, how can the Son of God be ignorant?" (R. T. France. *The Gospel of Mark*, New International Greek Testament Commentary, I. Howard Marshall and Donald A. Hagner, eds.(Grand Rapids: Eerdmans, 2002), 543–44.

17. See Witherington, *Christology of Jesus*, 228–33; Brown, *Introduction to New Testament Christology*, 89. It will not suffice to claim that Mark does not include claims to divinity and that these were only included in later Gospels, since Mark, the earliest gospel, elsewhere contains statements indicating a high Christology. See Mark 1:11; 9:7; 14:61–64.

18. France, *Gospel of Mark*, 543.

19. It is unknown if "Q" really existed and, if it did, if it was a document or an oral tradition. Critics hold that oral traditions were used by the authors of the Gospels.

When textual content is found in Matthew, Mark, and Luke, it is considered to be from the tradition of Mark. When it is found only in Mark, it is considered Markan. When a tradition is found only in Matthew, it is considered "M" for Matthean. When a tradition is found only in Luke, it is considered "L" for Lukan. When a tradition is found in Matthew and Luke but not in Mark, it is considered to be from "Q."

20. Witherington, *Christology of Jesus*, 221–28; Brown, *Introduction to New Testament Christology*, 88–89.

21. Joachim Jeremias, *The Central Message of the New Testament* (Philadelphia: Fortress, 1965), 30. Also see France, *Gospel of Mark*, 543.

22. Peter Stuhlmacher concludes, "Precisely by means of this new kind of address to God as *Father*, Jesus proves to be the Son of God." Quoted in *Ibid.*, 16; cf. esp. 28.

23. See Georg Wissowa, ed., *Paulys Real-Encyclopädie Der Classischen Altertumswissenschaft* (Stuttgart: A. Druckenmuller, 1893). Thanks to Edwin Yamauchi of the Miami University of Ohio who referred us to this source.

24. Raymond E. Brown, *The Birth of the Messiah* (New York: Doubleday, 1993), 34. Brown states "it is generally agreed among scholars that Matthew and Luke wrote independently of each other, without knowing the other's work." However, because of the quantity of agreement between the two accounts, Brown opts for the position that Matthew and Luke received their information from a common infancy narrative.

25. Luke 1:1–4. This verse seems to refer to the original disciples, who would have known Mary.

26. No manuscript ever found for either Matthew or Luke omits the phenomenal birth passages. It is also noteworthy that the apostolic father Ignatius in about AD 110 mentions the Virgin Birth of Jesus on two occasions (*To the Ephesians* 19:1; *To the Smyrnaeans* 1:1). In the second reference he writes that Jesus "is truly of the family of David with respect to human descent, Son of God with respect to the divine will and power, truly born of a virgin, baptized by John in order that all righteousness might be fulfilled by him, truly nailed in the flesh for us under Pontius Pilate and Herod the tetrarch ... truly suffered just as he truly raised himself—not, as certain unbelievers say, that he suffered in appearance only ..." (*Apostolic Fathers: Greek Texts and English Translations of their Writings, The*, rev. 2d ed. J. B. Lightfoot and J. R. Harmer, eds. and trans.; M. W. Holmes, ed. and rev. [Grand Rapids: Baker, 1999], 1:1–2:1).

As pointed out earlier, Ignatius either personally knew the apostles or was closely related to their associates, so his writings likely reflect what the apostles taught. He tells the Smyrnaeans that Jesus was truly from the line of David, truly born of a virgin, truly nailed in his flesh to the cross, and that his sufferings were as true as his resurrection. For Ignatius, the Virgin Birth was a real event.

27. For more on the inadequacy of parallel phenomenal birth accounts in pagan religions, Judaism, and Rome to account for the biblical accounts, see Brown, *Birth of the Messiah,* 517–31, 697–708; and J. Gresham Machen, *The Virgin Birth of Christ* (repr., Grand Rapids: Baker, 1967). Also see Craig Blomberg's contribution in Copan, ed., *Will The Real Jesus Please Stand Up?,* 106. From these sources, we can conclude: (1) "There is no clear example of *virginal* conception in world or pagan religions that plausibly could have given first-century Jewish Christians the idea of the virginal conception of Jesus" (Brown, *Birth of the Messiah,* 523); (2) "although the limited NT evidence is not conclusively probative, to posit historical fact as an explanation of Matthew's and Luke's agreement on the v.c. [i.e., virginal conception] is more conformable to the evidence than to posit fictional creation" (ibid., 704); (3) "A careful reading of the patristic evidence suggests that indeed the vast majority of early Christians did believe that the type of information the Gospel writers communicated was historical fact, even as they recognized the more superficial parallels with the mythology of other worldviews" (Blomberg, 106).

Chapter 11: What Does God Have to Do with This?

1. William Lane Craig and Frank R. Zindler, "Atheism Vs. Christianity Debate: Where Does The Evidence Point?" Debate in 1992, available on audio cassette through Seeds Tape Ministry, South Barrington, Illinois.

2. An objection like this one appears to have been first offered by the Greek philosopher Epicurus (341–270 B.C.).

3. This "Free Will Defense" has been most associated with philosopher Alvin Plantiga. See Alvin Plantinga, *God, Freedom and Evil* (Grand Rapids: Eerdmans, 1978).

4. Chris Rice, "Smell The Color 9," © 2000, Clumsy Fly Music.

5. "Reasonable possibility" does not mean "any possibility that might be stated." Otherwise, anyone could propose any absurd idea to account for something, without rational reasoning.

6. For example, see Brian Hebblethwaite, *Evil, Suffering and Religion* (New York: Hawthorn, 1976); John Hick, *Evil and the God of Love* (New York: Harper and Row, 1966).

7. In a debate with Christian philosopher William Lane Craig, agnostic Professor Eric Dayton admitted that the existence of suffering and evil do not contradict the Christian worldview. William Lane Craig and Eric Dayton, "Do Suffering and Evil Disprove the Existence of God?" audio cassette recording, 1997. Available by calling 800-729-4351 or online at www.leaderu.com/offices/billcraig/menus/resources.html.

8. Theists believe that a personal God exists. Christians, Muslims, and Jews who believe the historic tenets of their faiths are theists. There are variations of these arguments. Those presented here are well-accepted representative versions.

9. Gary Habermas and Antony Flew, *Did Jesus Rise From The Dead?* Terry L. Miethe, ed. (San Francisco: Harper & Row, 1987), 39.

10. William A. Dembski, *Intelligent Design* (Downers Grove, Ill.: InterVarsity, 1999), esp. chapters 4–6. For a summary, see William A. Dembski, ed., "Introduction," *Mere Creation: Science, Faith and Intelligent Design* (Downers Grove, Ill.: InterVarsity, 1998).

11. Some scientists who come from a theistic worldview and some scientists who are not theists have called into question the "Big Bang." For a Christian presentation of an alternate theory, see D. Russell Humphreys, *Starlight and Time* (Green Forest: Master, 1994). For a nontheistic alternate theory, see Stephen W. Hawking, *A Brief History of Time* (New York: Bantam, 1988). Hawking admits, "Only if we could picture the universe in terms of imaginary time would there be no singularities. . . . When one goes back to the real time in which we live, however, there will still appear to be singularities" (138–39), quoted in William Lane Craig, *Reasonable Faith* (Wheaton, Ill.: Crossway, 1994), 112.

12. Neither is this the place to have a discussion on issues relating to the creation/evolution debate. An interesting presentation containing critical discussions on the major views may be found in J. P. Moreland and John Mark Reynolds, eds., *Three Views on Creation and Evolution* (Grand Rapids: Zondervan, 1999).

13. L. Stafford Betty and Bruce Cordell, "God and Modern Science: New Life for the Teleological Argument," *International Philosophical Quarterly* 27 (1987): 416. This statistic was cited by William Lane Craig in his debate with Michael Tooley, "A Classic Debate on the Existence of God," November 1994, University of Colorado at Boulder. A transcript is available at www.leaderu.com/offices/billcraig/menus/resources.html.

14. Roy Abraham Varghese, ed., *The Intellectuals Speak Out About God* (Chicago: Regnery Gateway, 1984), 22.

15. Paul Davies, *God and the New Physics* (New York: Simon & Schuster, 1983) viii, 3–42, 142–143.

16. Paul Davies, *Superforce: The Search for a Grand Unified Theory of Nature* (New York: Simon & Schuster, 1984), 243.

17. Paul Davies, *The Cosmic Blueprint: New Discoveries in Nature's Creative Ability to Order the Universe* (New York: Simon & Schuster, 1988), 203. See Hugh Ross, "Astronomical Evidences for a Personal, Transcendent God" in *The Creation Hypothesis*, J. P. Moreland, ed. (Downers Grove, Ill.: InterVarsity, 1994), 164.

18. Hugh Ross, "Big Bang Model Refined by Fire" in Dembski, ed., *Mere Creation*, 372–80.

19. Hugh Ross, "Fine-Tuning for Life in the Universe," www.reasons.org/resources/apologetics/design_evidences/20020502_universe_design.shtml?main (Jan. 8, 2004).

20. Hugh Ross, "Fine-Tuning of Physical Life Support Body," www.reasons.org/resources/apologetics/design_evidences/20020502_solar_system_design.shtml?main.

21. Quoted by Walter Bradley in Dembski, ed., *Mere Creation*, 40. While Bradley's original source, D. L. Brock, *Our Universe: Accident or Design?* (Wits, South Africa: Star Watch, 1992), was not available, Penzias was contacted by e-mail (24 July 2002) and affirmed that the quote accurately reflects his thoughts.

22. Lisa Dyson, Matthew Kleban, and Leonard Susskind, "Disturbing Implications of a Cosmological Constant," at www.arxiv.org/abs/hep-th/0208013v2 (Aug. 15, 2002), 21.

23. For a detailed explanation on how we can recognize design, see Dembski, *Intelligent Design*, esp. chapters 4–6.

24. For extensive treatment, see Michael J. Behe, *Darwin's Black Box* (New York: Free Press, 1996); Michael J. Denton, *Nature's Destiny: How the Laws of Biology Reveal Purpose in the Universe* (New York: Free Press, 1998); Nancy R. Pearcey and Charles B. Thaxton, *The Soul of Science: Christian Faith and Natural Philosophy* (Wheaton, Ill.: Crossway, 1994), esp. ch. 10; Dembski, ed, *Mere Creation,* esp. chapters 1, 6, 7, 16, 18; and Moreland, ed., *Creation Hypothesis*, esp. ch. 5.

25. Antony Flew, "God and the Big Bang," (forthcoming).

26. Francis Crick, *What Mad Pursuit* (New York: Norton, 1986), 1.

27. Francis Crick, *Life Itself: Its Origin and Nature* (New York: Simon & Schuster, 1981), 88.

28. Fred Hoyle, *Astronomy and Cosmology* (San Francisco: W.H. Freeman, 1975), 658, cited in Craig, *Reasonable Faith*, 102.

29. John Barrow and Frank Tipler, *The Anthropic Cosmological Principle* (Oxford: Oxford University Press, 1986), 442.

30. If the cause of the universe is not timeless, then it either came into being out of nothing, or it was itself caused. Since an infinite number of causes is impossible, there must be a final cause that is itself uncaused.

31. The ancient Latin expression states, "ex nihilo, nihil fit" or "out of nothing, nothing comes."

32. William Lane Craig and Quentin Smith. *Theism, Atheism and Big Bang Cosmology* (Oxford: Clarendon, 1993), 135. Also see John Barrow and Frank Tipler, *The Anthropic Cosmological Principle* (Oxford: Oxford University Press, 1986), 442. Fred Hoyle, *Astronomy and Cosmology*, 658 quoted in Craig, *Reasonable Faith*, 102.

33. Some astronomers once proposed an oscillating universe that continuously bangs-contracts, bangs-contracts, and so on. However, this theory has been disproved. For example, an Associated Press article (1/9/98) reported findings from the previous day's meeting of the American Astronomical Association. The results from five studies by groups of astronomers employing different research methods agreed in their conclusion: The Big Bang was a singular event. The universe has not and will not implode in a "Big Crunch." The teams of astronomers represented Princeton and Yale universities, the Lawrence Berkeley National Laboratory, and the Harvard-Smithsonian Astrophysics Institute.

34. This is the Kalaam cosmolgical argument, as stated in Craig, *Reasonable Faith*, 91–122. Some skeptics respond, "Well, this argument also requires God to have a beginning too." Not at all, because this argument only applies to what begins to exist. We know the universe began to exist. However, there are no good arguments that require God to have had a beginning. Indeed, precisely the opposite can be argued: There must be a final and uncaused Cause that is eternal.

35. See Norman L. Geisler, "Why I Believe the God of the Bible is the One True God," in *Why I Am a Christian: Leading Thinkers Explain Why They Believe*, Norman L. Geisler and Paul K Hoffman, eds. (Grand Rapids: Baker, 2001).

36. Habermas and Flew, *Did Jesus Rise From The Dead?* 39. Also see chapter 8 of this volume regarding naturalistic objections to miracles.

Chapter 12: Some Final Issues

1. Matthew 12:38–42; 16: 4; John 2:18–21; cf. 10:18.

2. Acts 2:24, 32; 3:15, 26; 4:10; 10:40; 13:30–31; 17: 31; 1 Corinthians 6:14; 15:15.

3. Gary R. Habermas, *The Historical Jesus*, 60–61 and Appendix 1: "Historiography."

4. For an examination of this comment, see Habermas, "Resurrection Claims in Non-Christian Religions," *Journal of Religious Studies* 25 (1989): 167–77.

5. For details of this argument, see Gary R. Habermas, *The Risen Jesus and Future Hope*, esp. chapters 1–6.

6. Qurʾan, Surah 4:157–58.

7. *Gospel of Barnabas* 217.

8. Qurʾan, Surah 4:157–58.

9. According to Norman L. Geisler and Abdul Saleeb, there is a reference to the *Gospel of Barnabas* in a work at the end of the fifth century (The Gelasian Decree, by Pope Gelasius, 492–95). However, given the medieval anachronisms in the *Gospel of Barnabas* we have today, they add that this reference is probably to a different document by that name. They further point out that only its name is mentioned and that it was regarded in that decree as a spurious book rejected by the church. See Norman L. Geisler and Abdul Saleeb, *Answering Islam* (Grand Rapids: Baker, 1995), 296.

10. In the opening sentence of the *Gospel of Barnabas* we read, "Barnabas, apostle of Jesus the Nazarene, called Christ." In the very next sentence we read, "Dearly beloved the great and wonderful God hath during these past days visited us by his prophet Jesus Christ in great mercy of teaching and miracles . . ." (cf. *Gospel of Barnabas,* ch. 6). Compare this with Jesus' clear denial in *Gospel of Barnabas* that he is the Messiah (chs. 42, 70, 82, 96, 97, 198, 206).

11. *Gospel of Barnabas* 83.

12. See Geisler and Saleeb, *Answering Islam*, appendix 3.

13. *Gospel of Barnabas* 122.

14. Ibid., 121.

15. Ibid., 152.

16. See *Testimony of the Prophet Joseph Smith, Testimony of Three Witnesses,* and *Testimony of Eleven Witnesses*, published as introduction to the *Book of Mormon.*

17. For more on the problems with Mormonism, see Michael R. Licona, *Behold, I Stand at the Door and Knock* (Virginia Beach, Va.: TruthQuest, 1998). See also ch. 1 note 14 in this volume.

18. See pp. 99–103.

19. See ch. 10.

20. See ch. 8 note 12.

21. See pp. 174–81.

22. See Hugh Ross, Kenneth Samples, and Mark Clark, *Lights in the Sky and Little*

Green Men (Colorado Springs, Colo.: NavPress, 2002), 69–71. Those who see UFOs report the absense of sonic booms when the craft seem to be exceeding the speed of sound. Others report that the craft make impossibly sharp turns and sudden stops and rapid accelerations to speeds approaching fifteen thousand miles an hour. Samples and Clark also record a report that UFOs "change momentum without yielding an opposite change of momentum in matter or in an energy field either coupled to the object or in the vicinity of the object" (70). Also see the excellent articles: Mark Albrecht and Brooks Alexander, "UFOs: Is Science Fiction Coming True?" in *Spiritual Counterfeits Project Journal* 1.2 (1977): 12–23 and "A Sum of Shipwrecked Stars: UFOs and the Logic of Discernment" in ibid.: 25–30.

23. Many of the arguments on pp. 143–46 will also be helpful in addressing this similar objection. We include it here as well because the objection is frequently framed in this manner by skeptics.

Chapter 13: People Skills

1. Terry L. Miethe and Gary R. Habermas, *Why Believe? God Exists!* (Joplin, Mo.: College Press, 1993), 323.

2. Author Michael Licona believes that many of these problems can be explained by first bifurcating between judicial versus personal action. In the New Testament this can be seen in Jesus' words in Matthew 5:38–39: "You have heard that it was said, 'An eye for an eye, and a tooth for a tooth.' But I say to you, do not resist an evil person; but whoever slaps you on your right cheek, turn the other to him also." Most commentators agree that Jesus is not nullifying the Mosaic law. Rather, the principle had been meant for use by judges as a limitation of punishment, yet it was being misinterpreted as a justification for personal revenge, something like, "You dented my chariot so I'm going to dent yours." Jesus forbids such an action. Similarly, God commanded individuals, "You shall not kill," as a prohibition of murder, yet He authorized taking of life under certain limited judicial circumstances, such as capital punishment and just war. What about those times when God commanded the killing of everyone in a community, including women, children, and animals? First, this was the exception and not the norm. Second, there may have been morally justifiable reasons for doing so. A discussion of these reasons can be found in a number of apologetic books, such as Walter C. Kaiser Jr., et al., *Hard Sayings of the Bible* (Downers Grove, Ill.: InterVarsity, 1996), 206–7. A brief summary of the points in *Hard Sayings*

is that (1) Total destruction was not the norm. (2) God dedicated things or persons to destruction because they violently and steadfastly impeded or opposed his work over a long period. (3) These people were cut off to prevent the corruption of Israel and the rest of the world, since they were burning children as a gift to the gods and practicing other loathsome vices. (4) While some who might be deemed "innocent" died, it is understood that individuals share in the life of their families and nations and, therefore, in their rewards and punishments. If the children had been spared, a fresh crop of adults would soon emerge to continue the evil work of their predecessors. (5) In one instance when God commanded the complete destruction of the Amalekites, it was because Amalekite raiding parties were brutally murdering the weak, sick, and elderly who fell behind as the Israelites traveled through the wilderness (Deut. 25:17–18).

3. Luke 16:31.
4. The actual saying is "Never wrestle with a pig in the mud. You both get dirty, and the pig likes it."
5. Matthew 7:6.
6. The four minimal facts are: (1) Jesus' death by crucifixion; (2) the beliefs of the apostles that the risen Jesus had appeared to them; (3) the conversion of the church persecutor Paul; and (4) the conversion of the skeptic James. Our fifth fact, though not a "minimal fact," is the empty tomb, which is well-supported and granted by an impressive majority of scholars.
7. See pp. 51–56.

Conclusion

1. The friend who provided this example is Andrew Webster.
2. See pp. 49–63.
3. In the New Testament, the terms *disciple* and *apostle* are sometimes used interchangeably for the twelve main followers of Jesus. As the early church began, however, the term *apostle* came to include Paul, James, and probably a few others.
4. In more technical usage, nonbiblical sources are called "extrabiblical," but such technical language should be avoided.
5. See ch. 1 note 24.
6. Romans 3:23: "For all have sinned; all fall short of God's glorious standard" (NLT). See Mark 1:14–15 where Jesus teaches this.
7. Romans 6:23a: "For the wages of sin is death"; cf. 2 Thessalonians 1:9; 20:15; also see Mark 9:42–48 where Jesus teaches this.

8. Romans 5:8: "But God showed his great love for us by sending Christ to die for us while we were still sinners" (NLT); cf. Philippians 2:7; Romans 3:25; 1 John 4:10. Also see Mark 10:45 and Luke 19:10 where Jesus teaches this.

9. Romans 10:9: "For if you confess with your mouth that Jesus is Lord and believe in your heart that God raised him from the dead, you will be saved" (NLT). Also see John 11:25–26 where Jesus teaches this.

10. Ephesians 2:8–9: "God saved you by his special favor when you believed. And you can't take credit for this; it is a gift from God. Salvation is not a reward for the good things we have done, so none of us can boast about it" (NLT); cf. Titus 3:5. Jesus teaches this in Mark 10:26–27.

11. See pp. 194–97.

Bibliography

Antonacci, Mark. *The Resurrection of the Shroud.* New York: M. Evans, 2000.

Arndt, W.; F. W. Danker; and W. Bauer. *A Greek-English Lexicon of the New Testament and Other Early Christian Literature,* 3d ed. Ed. Kurt Aland and Barbara Aland. Chicago: University of Chicago Press, 2000.

Ayer, A. J. *Language, Truth, and Logic.* New York: Dover, 1936.

___. "'What I Saw When I Was Dead': Intimations of Immortality." *National Review,* 14 October 1988: 38–40.

Barnett, Paul. *Is the New Testament Reliable? A Look at the Historical Evidence.* Downers Grove, Ill.: InterVarsity, 1993.

Barrett, C. K., ed. *The New Testament Background: Selected Documents.* New York: Harper & Brothers, 1961.

Barth, Karl. *The Doctrine of Reconciliation.* Vol. 4, pt. 1 of *Church Dogmatics.* Ed. G. Bromiley and T. Torrance. Edinburgh: T & T Clark, 1956.

Beckwith, Francis J.; Carl Mosser; and Paul Owen, eds., *The New Mormon Challenge.* Grand Rapids: Zondervan, 2002.

Behe, Michael J. *Darwin's Black Box.* New York: Free Press, 1996.

Benner, David G., and Peter C. Hill, eds. *Baker Encyclopedia of Psychology and Counseling,* 2d ed. Grand Rapids: Baker, 1999.

Blomberg, Craig L. *Matthew.* New American Commentary, vol. 22. Nashville: Broadman & Holman, 1992.

___. *The Historical Reliability of the Gospels.* Downers Grove, Ill.: InterVarsity, 1987.

Bock, Darrell L. *Blasphemy and Exaltation in Judaism: The Charge against Jesus in Mark 14:52–65.* Grand Rapids: Baker, 2000.

Brenton, Lancelot C. L., trans. *The Septuagint with Apocrypha: Greek and English.* London: Bagster & Sons, 1851.

Brown, Colin, ed. *The New International Dictionary of New Testament Theology,* 4 vols. Grand Rapids: Zondervan, 1975.

Brown, Raymond E. *An Introduction to New Testament Christology.* New York: Paulist, 1994.

___. *An Introduction to the New Testament.* New York: Doubleday, 1997.

___. *The Birth of the Messiah.* New York: Doubleday, 1993.

___. *The Death of the Messiah,* 2 vols. New York: Doubleday, 1994.

___. "The Resurrection and Biblical Criticism," *Commonweal,* 87 (24 November 1967): 232–36.

Bruce, F. F. *Jesus and Christian Origins Outside the New Testament.* Grand Rapids: Eerdmans, 1974.

___. *The New Testament Documents: Are They Reliable?* Downers Grove, Ill.: InterVarsity, 1984.

Bullinger, E. W. *Figures of Speech Used in the Bible.* New York: E. & J. B. Young, 1898.

Bultmann, Rudolf. "New Testament and Mythology." In *Kerygma and Myth.* Ed. Hans Werner Bartsch; trans. Reginald H. Fuller. New York: Harper & Row, 1961.

Byrd, Randolph C. "Positive Therapeutic Effects of Intercessory Prayer in a Coronary Care Unit Population." *Southern Medical Journal,* 81.7 (July 1988): 826–29.

Carson, D. A. *Matthew.* Expositor's Bible Commentary on CD-ROM. Ed. Frank Gaebelein. Grand Rapids: Zondervan, 1998.

Ch'en, Kenneth K. S. *Buddhism.* Woodbury, Conn.: Baron's Educational Series, 1965.

Chilton, Bruce, and Craig A. Evans, eds. *Authenticating the Words of Jesus.* Boston: Brill, 2002.

___. *Studying the Historical Jesus: Evaluations of the State of Current Research.* Leiden: Brill, 1994.

Collings, John. *Daniel: A Commentary on the Book of Daniel.* Minneapolis: Fortress, 1993.

Copan, Paul, ed. *Will The Real Jesus Please Stand Up? A Debate between William Lane Craig and John Dominic Crossan.* Grand Rapids: Baker, 1998.

Copan, Paul, and Ronald K. Tacelli, eds. *Jesus' Resurrection: Fact or Figment? A Debate Between William Lane Craig and Gerd Lüdemann.* Downers Grove, Ill.: InterVarsity, 2000.

Cornelius Tacitus. *The Annals by Tacitus.* Trans. Alfred John Church and William Jackson Brodribb. www.classics.mit.edu/Tacitus/annals.html.

Covey, Stephen R.; A. Roger Merrill; and Rebecca R. Merrill. *First Things First.* New York: Simon & Schuster, 1994.

Cowan, Steven B., ed. *Five Views on Apologetics.* Grand Rapids: Zondervan, 2000.

Craig, William Lane. *Assessing the New Testament Evidence for the Historicity of the Resurrection of Jesus.* Lewiston, N.Y.: Edwin Mellen, 1989.

___. *Reasonable Faith.* Wheaton, Ill.: Crossway, 1994.

Craig, William Lane, and Eric Dayton. *Do Suffering and Evil Disprove the Existence of God?* Debate in 1997, available at www.leaderu.com/offices/billcraig/menus/resources.html.

Craig, William Lane, and Frank R. Zindler. "Atheism vs. Christianity Debate, Where Does The Evidence Point?" Debate in 1992, available on audio cassette recording through Seeds Tape Ministry, South Barrington, Illinois.

Craig, William Lane, and Michael Tooley. "A Classic Debate on the Existence of God." Debate in November 1994 on the campus of the University of Colorado (Boulder). Transcript available at www.leaderu.com/offices/billcraig/menus/resources.html.

Craig, William Lane, and Quentin Smith. *Theism, Atheism and Big Bang Cosmology.* Oxford: Clarendon, 1993.

Crick, Francis. *Life Itself: Its Origin and Nature.* New York: Simon & Schuster, 1981.

___. *What Mad Pursuit.* New York: Norton, 1986.

Crossan, John Dominic. *Jesus: A Revolutionary Biography.* San Francisco: HarperSanFrancisco, 1994.

___. *The Historical Jesus: The Life of a Mediterranean Peasant.* San Francisco: HarperSanFrancisco, 1991.

D'Costa, Gavin, ed., *Resurrection Reconsidered.* Oxford: Oneworld, 1996.

Davies, Paul. *The Cosmic Blueprint: New Discoveries in Nature's Creative Ability to Order the Universe.* New York: Simon & Schuster, 1988.

___. *God and the New Physics.* New York: Simon & Schuster, 1983.

___. *Superforce: The Search for a Grand Unified Theory of Nature.* New York: Simon & Schuster, 1984.

Deedat, Ahmed. "What was the Sign of Jonah?" www.islamworld.net/ jonah.html. Accessed 16 September 2003.

Dembski, William A. *Intelligent Design.* Downers Grove, Ill.: InterVarsity, 1999.

Dembski, William A., ed. *Mere Creation: Science, Faith and Intelligent Design.* Downers Grove, Ill.: InterVarsity, 1998. See esp., introduction.

Denton, Michael J. *Nature's Destiny: How the Laws of Biology Reveal Purpose in the Universe.* New York: Free Press, 1998.

Diagnostic and Statistical Manual of Mental Disorders: DSM-IV. Washington, D.C.: American Psychiatric Association, 1994.

Dodd, C. H. *The Apostolic Preaching and its Developments.* Reprint, Grand Rapids: Baker, 1980.

Dyson, Lisa; Matthew Kleban; and Leonard Susskind, "Disturbing Implications of a Cosmological Constant." At www.arxiv.org/abs/hep-th/ 0208013v2. Accessed 15 August 2002.

Eakin, Emily. "So God's Really in the Details?" *New York Times,* 11 May 2002. Available at www.nytimes.com/2002/05/11/arts/11GOD.html. Accessed 6 January 2004.

Edwards, William D.; Wesley J. Gabel; and Floyd E. Hosmer, "On the Physical Death of Jesus Christ." *Journal of the American Medical Association,* 255.11, 21 March 1986, 1455–63.

Ehrman, Bart D. *The New Testament: A Historical Introduction to the Early Christian Writings,* 2d ed. New York: Oxford University Press, 2000.

Epstein, I., ed. and trans. *Babylonian Talmud.* London: Soncino, 1935–1952.

Eusebius. *Eusebius: The Church History.* Ed. and trans. by Paul L. Maier. Grand Rapids: Kregel, 1999.

___. *Preparation for the Gospel.* Trans. Edwin Hamilton Gifford. Grand Rapids: Baker, 1981.

___. *Proof of the Gospel.* Ed. and trans. W. J. Ferrar. Grand Rapids: Baker, 1981.

Evans, Craig. "In What Sense 'Blasphemy'? Jesus Before Caiphas in Mark 14:61– 64." *Society of Biblical Literature Seminar Papers* 30 (1991).

Fales, Evan, "Successful Defense? A Review of *In Defense of Miracles.*" *Philosophia Christi* NS3.1 (2001).

Feldman, Louis H. *Josephus and Modern Scholarship: 1937–1980.* New York: de Gruyter, 1984.

Feldman, Louis H., and Gohei Hata, eds. *Josephus, Judaism, and Christianity.* Detroit: Wayne State University Press, 1989.

___. *Josephus, the Bible, and History.* Detroit: Wayne State University Press, 1989.

France, R. T. *Matthew: Evangelist and Teacher.* Grand Rapids: Zondervan, 1989.

___. "The Gospel of Mark." In New International Greek Testament Commentary. Ed. I. Howard Marshall and Donald A. Hagner. Grand Rapids: Eerdmans, 2002.

Fredriksen, Paula. "What You See is What You Get: Context and Content in Current Research on the Historical Jesus." At www.bu.edu/religion/faculty/fredriksen/context.htm. Accessed 6 January 2004).

Gaius Suetonius. *The Twelve Caesars.* Trans. Robert Graves. New York: Penguin, 1989.

Geisler, Norman L. *Baker Encyclopedia of Christian Apologetics.* Grand Rapids: Baker, 1999.

___. *Miracles and the Modern Mind: A Defense of Biblical Miracles.* Grand Rapids: Baker, 1992.

Geisler, Norman L. and Abdul Saleeb. *Answering Islam.* Grand Rapids: Baker, 1995.

Geisler, Norman L., and Paul K. Hoffman, eds. *Why I Am a Christian: Leading Thinkers Explain Why They Believe.* Grand Rapids: Baker, 2001.

Geivett, R. Douglas, and Gary R. Habermas, eds. *In Defense of Miracles.* Downers Grove, Ill.: InterVarsity, 1997.

Gibbs, Nancy. "The Message of Miracles." *Time* Magazine, 10 April 1995, 70.

Goodacre, Mark. *The Case Against Q.* Harrisburg, Pa.: Trinity, 2002.

Gordon-Reed, Annette. *Thomas Jefferson and Sally Hemings: An American Controversy.* Charlottesville, Va.: University Press of Virginia, 1997.

Goulder, Michael. *Midrash and Lection in Matthew.* London: SPCK, 1974.

___. "The Baseless Fabric of a Vision," in *Resurrection Reconsidered.* Ed. Gavin D'Costa. Oxford: Oneworld, 1996.

Greyson, Bruce, and Ian Stevenson, "The Phenomenology of Near-Death Experiences." *American Journal of Psychiatry,* 137 (1980).

Gundry, Robert H. *Mark: A Commentary on His Apology for the Cross.* Grand Rapids: Eerdmans, 1993.

___. *Matthew: A Commentary on His Handbook for a Mixed Church Under Persecution,* Second Edition. Grand Rapids: Eerdmans, 1994.

Habermas, Gary R. "Evidential Apologetics," in *Five Views on Apologetics.* Ed. Steven B. Cowan. (Grand Rapids: Zondervan, 2000).

___. "Explaining Away Jesus' Resurrection: The Recent Revival of Hallucination Theories." *Christian Research Journal* 23.4 (2001): 26–31, 47–49.

___. *The Historical Jesus.* Joplin, Mo.: College Press, 1996.

___. "The Late Twentieth-Century Resurgence of Naturalistic Responses to Jesus' Resurrection." *Trinity Journal* 22NS, 2 (fall 2001): 179–96.

___. "The Personal Testimony of the Holy Spirit to the Believer and Christian Apologetics." *Journal of Christian Apologetics* 1.1 (1997): 49–64.

___. "Probability Calculus, Proof and Christian Apologetics." *The Simon Greenleaf Review of Law and Religion* 8 (1988–1989): 57–88.

___. "Replies to Evan Fales: The Appearances of Jesus." *Philosophia Christi* NS3.1 (2001), 76–87.

___. "Resurrection Claims in Non-Christian Religions." *Journal of Religious Studies* 25 (1989): 167–77.

___. *The Resurrection of Jesus.* Lanham, Md.: University Press of America, 1984.

___. *Risen Jesus and Future Hope, The.* Lanham, Md.: Rowman & Littlefield, 2003.

___. "Ten Ways God Interacts with Us." Audio cassette recordings from Impact, at either (704) 846–1226 or www.impactapologetics.com.

Habermas, Gary R., and J. P. Moreland. *Beyond Death.* Wheaton, Ill.: Crossway, 1998.

Habermas, Gary R., and Antony Flew. "Did Jesus Rise From the Dead?" *The John Ankerberg Show,* 2000. Available through www.johnankerberg.org/TV/ankjasrd.html.

___. *Did Jesus Rise From The Dead?* Ed. Terry L. Miethe. San Francisco: Harper & Row, 1987.

Hagner, D. A. *Matthew 14–28.* Word Biblical Commentary, vol. 33B. Dallas: Word, 1995.

Harrington, Daniel J. *The Gospel of Matthew.* Sacra Pagina Series, vol. 1. Ed. Daniel J. Jarrington. Collegeville, Minn.: Liturgical, 1991.

Hebblethwaite, Brian. *Evil, Suffering and Religion.* New York: Hawthorn, 1976.

Heller, John. *Report on the Shroud.* Boston: Houghton Mifflin, 1983.

Hemer, Colin. *The Book of Acts in the Setting of Hellenistic History.* Winona Lake, Ind.: Eisenbrauns, 1990.

Hendriksen, William. *The Gospel of Matthew.* Edinburgh: Banner of Truth Trust, 1974.

Hengel, Martin. *Crucifixion.* Philadelphia: Fortress, 1977.

Hick, John. *Evil and the God of Love.* New York: Harper and Row, 1966.

Hume, David. "Skeptical Solution of Those Doubts." Sec. 5 of *An Inquiry Concerning Human Understanding,* Section 5. 1748.

Humphreys, D. Russell. *Starlight and Time.* Green Forest: Master, 1994.

Jeremias, Joachim. *The Central Message of the New Testament.* Philadelphia: Fortress, 1965.

Jesus: The Search Continues. Produced by The Ankerberg Theological Research Institute, Chattanooga, Tenn., 2001, videocassettes.

Josephus. *Josephus in Ten Volumes: Jewish Antiquities.* Trans. Louis H. Feldman. Loeb Classical Library, vol. 9. Cambridge: Harvard University Press, 1981.

———. *Josephus: The Essential Works.* Ed. and trans. Paul L. Maier. Grand Rapids: Kregel, 1994.

———. *The New Complete Works of Flavius Josephus.* Trans. William Whiston. Grand Rapids: Kregel, 1999.

Kaiser, Walter C. Jr.; Peter H. Davids; F. F. Bruce; and Manfred T. Brauch. *Hard Sayings of the Bible.* Downers Grove, Ill.: InterVarsity, 1996.

Kendall, Philip C., and Constance Hammen. *Abnormal Psychology.* Boston: Houghton Mifflin, 1995.

Kennedy, D. James, with Jerry Newcombe, *Who Is This Jesus: Is He Risen?* Fort Lauderdale, Fla.: Coral Ridge Ministries, 2002.

Kent, Jack A. *The Psychological Origins of the Resurrection Myth.* London: Open Gate, 1999.

Kittel, Gerhard, and Gerhard Friedrich, eds. *Theological Dictionary of the New Testament.* 10 vols. Grand Rapids: Eerdmans, 1981.

Kloppenborg, John. "An Analysis of the Pre-Pauline Formula 1 Cor 15:3–5b In Light of Some Recent Literature." *The Catholic Biblical Quarterly,* 40 (1978), 351–67.

Kreeft, Peter, and Ronald K. Tacelli. *Handbook of Christian Apologetics.* Downers Grove, Ill.: InterVarsity, 1994.

Licona, Michael R. *Behold, I Stand at the Door and Knock.* Virginia Beach, Va.: TruthQuest, 1998.

———. *Cross Examined.* Virginia Beach, Va.: TruthQuest, 1999.

Lightfoot, J. B., and J. R. Harmer, eds. and trans. *The Apostolic Fathers: Greek Texts and English Translations of their Writings.* 2d rev. ed. by M. W. Holmes. Grand Rapids: Baker, 1999.

Longenecker, Richard N. *Acts.* The Expositor's Bible Commentary on CD-ROM. Ed. Frank Gaebelein. Grand Rapids: Zondervan, 1998.

Louw, J. P., and E. A. Nida. *Greek-English Lexicon of the New Testament: Based on Semantic Domains,* 2d ed. New York: United Bible Societies, c1989.

Lüdemann, Gerd. *What Really Happened to Jesus? A Historical Approach to the Resurrection.* Trans. John Bowden. Louisville: Westminster John Knox, 1995.

Machen, J. Gresham. *The Virgin Birth of Christ.* Grand Rapids: Baker, 1967.

Maier, Paul L. *In the Fullness of Time: A Historian Looks at Christmas, Easter, and the Early Church.* San Francisco: HarperSanFrancisco, 1991.

Martin, Michael. *The Case Against Christianity.* Philadelphia: Temple University Press, 1991.

McCullagh, C. Behan. *Justifying Historical Descriptions.* Cambridge: Cambridge University Press, 1984.

McCullough, David. *John Adams.* New York: Simon & Schuster, 2001.

Meier, John P. *A Marginal Jew: Rethinking the Historical Jesus.* 3 vols. New York: Doubleday, 1991–2001.

Metzger, Bruce M. *A Textual Commentary on the Greek New Testament.* Stuttgart: United Bible Societies, 1975.

___. *Historical and Literary Studies: Pagan, Jewish, and Christian.* New Testament Tools and Studies Series, vol. 8. Grand Rapids: Eerdmans, 1968.

Meyer, Ben F. *The Aims of Jesus.* London: SCM, 1979.

Meyer, Heinrich August Wilhelm. *Meyer's Commentary on the New Testament,* vol. 1. Peabody: Hendrickson, 1985.

Miethe, Terry L., and Gary R. Habermas. *Why Believe? God Exists!* Joplin, Mo.: College Press, 1993.

Moreland, J. P. *Scaling the Secular City: A Defense of Christianity.* Grand Rapids: Baker, 1987.

Moreland, J. P., ed. *The Creation Hypothesis.* Downers Grove, Ill.: InterVarsity, 1994.

Moreland, J. P., and John Mark Reynolds, eds. *Three Views on Creation and Evolution.* Grand Rapids: Zondervan, 1999.

Morris, Leon. *The Gospel According to Matthew.* Grand Rapids: Eerdmans, 1992.

Morse, Melvin. "Near Death Experiences and Death-Related Visions in Children: Implications for the Clinician," *Current Problems in Pediatrics* 24 (1994): 55–83.

Morse, Melvin, with Paul Perry. *Closer to the Light: Learning from Children's Near-Death Experiences.* New York: Random, 1990.

Newcombe, Jerry. *Coming Again.* Colorado Springs: Chariot Victor, 1999.

O'Collins, Gerald. *Interpreting Jesus.* London: Geoffrey Chapman, 1983.

___. *Interpreting the Resurrection: Examining the Major Problems in the Stories of Jesus' Resurrection*. New York: Paulist, 1988.

Okholm, Dennis L., and Timothy R. Phillips, eds. *More Than One Way?* Grand Rapids: Zondervan, 1995.

Ostling, Richard N. "Who Was Jesus?" *Time* Magazine, 15 August 1988.

Pearcey, Nancy R., and Charles B. Thaxton. *The Soul of Science: Christian Faith and Natural Philosophy*. Wheaton, Ill.: Crossway, 1994.

Perrin, Norman. *The Resurrection According to Matthew, Mark, and Luke*. Philadelphia: Fortress, 1977.

Philostratus, Flavius. *The Life of Apollonius*. 2 vols. Trans. F. C. Conybeare. Cambridge, Mass.: Harvard University Press, 1912.

Plantinga, Alvin. *God, Freedom and Evil*. Grand Rapids: Eerdmans, 1978.

Plato. *Plato in Twelve Volumes*. Trans. R. G. Bury. Cambridge, Mass.: Harvard University Press, 1914–1935.

Price, Robert M. "Is There a Place for Historical Criticism?" *Religious Studies* 27 (1991).

Remus, Harold. *Pagan-Christian Conflict Over Miracle in the Second Century*. Cambridge, Mass.: The Philadelphia Patristic Foundation, 1983.

Roberts, A.; J. Donaldson; and A. C. Coxe, eds. and trans. *The Ante-Nicene Fathers: Translations of the Writings of the Fathers Down to* A.D. *325*. Oak Harbor. Ore.: Logos Research Systems, 1997.

Robertson, A. T. *Word Pictures in the New Testament on CD-ROM*. Oak Harbor. Ore.: Logos Research Systems, 1997).

Rodinson, Maxime. *Muhammad*. Trans. Anne Carter. New York: Pantheon, 1980.

Ross, Hugh. "Astronomical Evidences for a Personal, Transcendent God." In *The Creation Hypothesis*. Ed. J. P. Moreland. Downers Grove, Ill.: InterVarsity, 1994.

Russell, Bertrand. *The Problems of Philosophy*. Oxford: Clarendon, 1912.

Sabben-Clare, James, ed. and trans. *Caesar and Roman Politics 60–50 BC: Source Material in Translation*. London: Bristol Classical, 1995.

Shanks, Hershel, and Ben Witherington III. *The Brother of Jesus*. San Francisco: HarperSanFrancisco, 2003.

Sherwin-White, A. N. *Roman Society and Roman Law in the New Testament*. New York: Oxford University Press, 1963.

Sloyan, Gerard S. *The Crucifixion of Jesus: History, Myth, Faith*. Minneapolis: Fortress, 1995.

Snyder, Tom. An interview with John Shelby Spong on CNBC, 8 March 1994. Livingston: Burrelle's Information Services, 1994.

Stevenson, Ian, and Bruce Greyson. "Near-Death Experiences: Relevance to the Question of Survival After Death." *Journal of the American Medical Association* 242 (1979): 265–67.

Stevenson, Kenneth E., and Gary R. Habermas. *The Shroud and the Controversy: Science, Skepticism, and the Search for Authenticity.* Nashville: Thomas Nelson, 1990.

___. *Verdict on the Shroud.* Banbury, Conn.: Dell, 1982.

Strauss, David. *A New Life of Jesus.* 2 vols. Edinburgh: Williams & Norgate, 1879.

Strobel, Lee. *The Case for Christ.* Grand Rapids: Zondervan, 1998.

___. *The Case for Faith.* Grand Rapids: Zondervan, 2000.

Stuhlmacher, Peter. *Jesus of Nazareth—Christ of Faith.* Trans. Siegfried S. Schatzmann. Peabody, Mass.: Hendrickson, 1993.

Swinburne, Richard. "Violation of a Law of Nature," in *Miracles.* Ed. Richard Swinburne. New York: Macmillan, 1989.

Syrett, Harold C., ed., *Papers of Alexander Hamilton* 25. New York: Columbia University Press, 1974.

Theissen, Gerd, and Annette Merz. *The Historical Jesus.* Minneapolis: Fortress, 1996.

Twelftree, Graham H. *Jesus: The Miracle Worker.* Downers Grove, Ill.: InterVarsity, 1999.

Van Biema, David. "The Gospel Truth." *Time* Magazine, 8 April 1996 (online archives).

Van Daalen, D. H. *The Real Resurrection.* London: Collins, 1972.

Van Voorst, Robert E. *Jesus Outside the New Testament.* Grand Rapids: Eerdmans, 2000.

Varghese, Roy Abraham, ed. *The Intellectuals Speak Out about God.* Chicago: Regnery Gateway, 1984.

Wagner, Günter. *Pauline Baptism and The Pagan Mysteries.* Edinburgh: Oliver & Boyd, 1967.

Wand, William. *Christianity: A Historical Religion?* Valley Forge, Pa.: Judson, 1972.

Whanger, Mary, and Alan Whanger. *The Shroud of Turin: An Adventure of Discovery.* Franklin, Tenn.: Providence House, 1998.

Wilkins, Michael J., and J. P. Moreland, eds. *Jesus Under Fire.* Grand Rapids: Zondervan, 1995.

Wilson, Ian. *The Shroud of Turin.* Garden City: Doubleday, 1978.

Winter, David. *Hereafter: What Happens After Death?.* Wheaton, Ill.: Harold Shaw, 1972.

Wissowa, Georg, ed. *Paulys Real-Encyclopädie Der Classischen Altertumswissenschaft.* Stuttgart: A. Druckenmuller, 1893.

Witherington, Ben, III. *John's Wisdom: A Commentary on the Fourth Gospel.* Louisville: Westminster John Knox Press, 1995.

___. *The Christology of Jesus.* Minneapolis: Fortress, 1990.

___. *The Jesus Quest: The Third Search for the Jew of Nazareth.* Downers Grove, Ill.: InterVarsity, 1995.

Wright, N. T. "Looking Again for Jesus," *Stimulus,* 4.4 (November 1996).

___. *The New Testament and the People of God.* Minneapolis: Fortress, 1992.

___. *What Saint Paul Really Said: Was Paul of Tarsus the Real Founder of Christianity?* Grand Rapids: Eerdmans, 1997.

Yamauchi, Edwin. *Jesus, Zoroaster, Buddha, Socrates, Mohammad,* Revised Edition. Downers Grove, Ill.: InterVarsity, 1972).

___. "Josephus and the Scriptures." *Fides et Historia* 13 (1980): section 42.

Index